Neural Network Methods for Natural Language Processing

Synthesis Lectures on Human Language Technologies

Editor

Graeme Hirst, *University of Toronto*

Synthesis Lectures on Human Language Technologies is edited by Graeme Hirst of the University of Toronto. The series consists of 50- to 150-page monographs on topics relating to natural language processing, computational linguistics, information retrieval, and spoken language understanding. Emphasis is on important new techniques, on new applications, and on topics that combine two or more HLT subfields.

Neural Network Methods for Natural Language Processing
Yoav Goldberg
2017

Syntax-based Statistical Machine Translation
Philip Williams, Rico Sennrich, Matt Post, and Philipp Koehn
2016

Domain-Sensitive Temporal Tagging
Jannik Strötgen and Michael Gertz
2016

Linked Lexical Knowledge Bases: Foundations and Applications
Iryna Gurevych, Judith Eckle-Kohler, and Michael Matuschek
2016

Bayesian Analysis in Natural Language Processing
Shay Cohen
2016

Metaphor: A Computational Perspective
Tony Veale, Ekaterina Shutova, and Beata Beigman Klebanov
2016

Grammatical Inference for Computational Linguistics
Jeffrey Heinz, Colin de la Higuera, and Menno van Zaanen
2015

iv

Neural Network Methods for Natural Language Processing

Yoav Goldberg

www.morganclaypool.com

ISBN: 9781627052986   paperback
ISBN: 9781627052955   ebook

DOI 10.2200/S00762ED1V01Y201703HLT037

A Publication in the Morgan & Claypool Publishers series
SYNTHESIS LECTURES ON HUMAN LANGUAGE TECHNOLOGIES

Lecture #37
Series Editor: Graeme Hirst, *University of Toronto*
Series ISSN
Print 1947-4040   Electronic 1947-4059

Neural Network Methods for Natural Language Processing

Yoav Goldberg
Bar Ilan University

SYNTHESIS LECTURES ON HUMAN LANGUAGE TECHNOLOGIES #37

MORGAN & CLAYPOOL PUBLISHERS

ABSTRACT

Neural networks are a family of powerful machine learning models. This book focuses on the application of neural network models to natural language data. The first half of the book (Parts I and II) covers the basics of supervised machine learning and feed-forward neural networks, the basics of working with machine learning over language data, and the use of vector-based rather than symbolic representations for words. It also covers the computation-graph abstraction, which allows to easily define and train arbitrary neural networks, and is the basis behind the design of contemporary neural network software libraries.

The second part of the book (Parts III and IV) introduces more specialized neural network architectures, including 1D convolutional neural networks, recurrent neural networks, conditioned-generation models, and attention-based models. These architectures and techniques are the driving force behind state-of-the-art algorithms for machine translation, syntactic parsing, and many other applications. Finally, we also discuss tree-shaped networks, structured prediction, and the prospects of multi-task learning.

KEYWORDS

natural language processing, machine learning, supervised learning, deep learning, neural networks, word embeddings, recurrent neural networks, sequence to sequence models

Contents

Preface

Natural language processing (NLP) is a collective term referring to automatic computational processing of human languages. This includes both algorithms that take human-produced text as input, and algorithms that produce natural looking text as outputs. The need for such algorithms is ever increasing: human produce ever increasing amounts of text each year, and expect computer interfaces to communicate with them in their own language. Natural language processing is also very challenging, as human language is inherently ambiguous, ever changing, and not well defined.

Natural language is symbolic in nature, and the first attempts at processing language were symbolic: based on logic, rules, and ontologies. However, natural language is also highly ambiguous and highly variable, calling for a more statistical algorithmic approach. Indeed, the current-day dominant approaches to language processing are all based on *statistical machine learning*. For over a decade, core NLP techniques were dominated by linear modeling approaches to supervised learning, centered around algorithms such as Perceptrons, linear Support Vector Machines, and Logistic Regression, trained over very high dimensional yet very sparse feature vectors.

Around 2014, the field has started to see some success in switching from such linear models over sparse inputs to *nonlinear neural network models* over dense inputs. Some of the neural-network techniques are simple generalizations of the linear models and can be used as almost drop-in replacements for the linear classifiers. Others are more advanced, require a change of mindset, and provide new modeling opportunities. In particular, a family of approaches based on *recurrent neural networks* (RNNs) alleviates the reliance on the Markov Assumption that was prevalent in sequence models, allowing to condition on arbitrarily long sequences and produce effective feature extractors. These advances led to breakthroughs in language modeling, automatic machine translation, and various other applications.

While powerful, the neural network methods exhibit a rather strong barrier of entry, for various reasons. In this book, I attempt to provide NLP practitioners as well as newcomers with the basic background, jargon, tools, and methodologies that will allow them to understand the principles behind neural network models for language, and apply them in their own work. I also hope to provide machine learning and neural network practitioners with the background, jargon, tools, and mindset that will allow them to effectively work with language data.

Finally, I hope this book can also serve a relatively gentle (if somewhat incomplete) introduction to both NLP and machine learning for people who are newcomers to both fields.

INTENDED READERSHIP

This book is aimed at readers with a technical background in computer science or a related field, who want to get up to speed with neural network techniques for natural language processing. While the primary audience of the book is graduate students in language processing and machine learning, I made an effort to make it useful also to established researchers in either NLP or machine learning (by including some advanced material), and to people without prior exposure to either machine learning or NLP (by covering the basics from the grounds up). This last group of people will, obviously, need to work harder.

While the book is self contained, I do assume knowledge of mathematics, in particular undergraduate level of probability, algebra, and calculus, as well as basic knowledge of algorithms and data structures. Prior exposure to machine learning is very helpful, but not required.

This book evolved out of a survey paper [Goldberg, 2016], which was greatly expanded and somewhat re-organized to provide a more comprehensive exposition, and more in-depth coverage of some topics that were left out of the survey for various reasons. This book also contains many more concrete examples of applications of neural networks to language data that do not exist in the survey. While this book is intended to be useful also for people without NLP or machine learning backgrounds, the survey paper assumes knowledge in the field. Indeed, readers who are familiar with natural language processing as practiced between roughly 2006 and 2014, with heavy reliance on machine learning and linear models, may find the journal version quicker to read and better organized for their needs. However, such readers may also appreciate reading the chapters on word embeddings (10 and 11), the chapter on conditioned generation with RNNs (17), and the chapters on structured prediction and multi-task learning (MTL) (19 and 20).

FOCUS OF THIS BOOK

This book is intended to be self-contained, while presenting the different approaches under a unified notation and framework. However, the main purpose of the book is in introducing the neural-networks (deep-learning) machinery and its application to language data, and not in providing an in-depth coverage of the basics of machine learning theory and natural language technology. I refer the reader to external sources when these are needed.

Likewise, the book is not intended as a comprehensive resource for those who will go on and develop the next advances in neural network machinery (although it may serve as a good entry point). Rather, it is aimed at those readers who are interested in taking the existing, useful technology and applying it in useful and creative ways to their favorite language-processing problems.

Further reading For in-depth, general discussion of neural networks, the theory behind them, advanced optimization methods, and other advanced topics, the reader is referred to other existing resources. In particular, the book by Bengio et al. [2016] is highly recommended.

For a friendly yet rigorous introduction to practical machine learning, the freely available book of Daumé III [2015] is highly recommended. For more theoretical treatment of machine learning, see the freely available textbook of Shalev-Shwartz and Ben-David [2014] and the textbook of Mohri et al. [2012].

For a strong introduction to NLP, see the book of Jurafsky and Martin [2008]. The information retrieval book by Manning et al. [2008] also contains relevant information for working with language data.

Finally, for getting up-to-speed with linguistic background, the book of Bender [2013] in this series provides a concise but comprehensive coverage, directed at computationally minded readers. The first chapters of the introductory grammar book by Sag et al. [2003] are also worth reading.

As of this writing, the progress of research in neural networks and Deep Learning is very fast paced. The state-of-the-art is a moving target, and I cannot hope to stay up-to-date with the latest-and-greatest. The focus is thus with covering the more established and robust techniques, that were proven to work well in several occasions, as well as selected techniques that are not yet fully functional but that I find to be established and/or promising enough for inclusion.

Yoav Goldberg
March 2017

Acknowledgments

This book grew out of a survey paper I've written on the topic [Goldberg, 2016], which in turn grew out of my frustration with the lack organized and clear material on the intersection of deep learning and natural language processing, as I was trying to learn it and teach it to my students and collaborators. I am thus indebted to the numerous people who commented on the survey paper (in its various forms, from initial drafts to post-publication comments), as well as to the people who commented on various stages of the book's draft. Some commented in person, some over email, and some in random conversations on Twitter. The book was also influenced by people who did not comment on it per-se (indeed, some never read it) but discussed topics related to it. Some are deep learning experts, some are NLP experts, some are both, and others were trying to learn both topics. Some (few) contributed through very detailed comments, others by discussing small details, others in between. But each of them influenced the final form of the book. They are, in alphabetical order: Yoav Artzi, Yonatan Aumann, Jason Baldridge, Miguel Ballesteros, Mohit Bansal, Marco Baroni, Tal Baumel, Sam Bowman, Jordan Boyd-Graber, Chris Brockett, Ming-Wei Chang, David Chiang, Kyunghyun Cho, Grzegorz Chrupala, Alexander Clark, Raphael Cohen, Ryan Cotterell, Hal Daumé III, Nicholas Dronen, Chris Dyer, Jacob Eisenstein, Jason Eisner, Michael Elhadad, Yad Faeq, Manaal Faruqui, Amir Globerson, Fréderic Godin, Edward Grefenstette, Matthew Honnibal, Dirk Hovy, Moshe Koppel, Angeliki Lazaridou, Tal Linzen, Thang Luong, Chris Manning, Stephen Merity, Paul Michel, Margaret Mitchell, Piero Molino, Graham Neubig, Joakim Nivre, Brendan O'Connor, Nikos Pappas, Fernando Pereira, Barbara Plank, Ana-Maria Popescu, Delip Rao, Tim Rocktäschel, Dan Roth, Alexander Rush, Naomi Saphra, Djamé Seddah, Erel Segal-Halevi, Avi Shmidman, Shaltiel Shmidman, Noah Smith, Anders Søgaard, Abe Stanway, Emma Strubell, Sandeep Subramanian, Liling Tan, Reut Tsarfaty, Peter Turney, Tim Vieira, Oriol Vinyals, Andreas Vlachos, Wenpeng Yin, and Torsten Zesch.

The list excludes, of course, the very many researchers I've communicated with through their academic writings on the topic.

The book also benefited a lot from—and was shaped by—my interaction with the Natural Language Processing Group at Bar-Ilan University (and its soft extensions): Yossi Adi, Roee Aharoni, Oded Avraham, Ido Dagan, Jessica Ficler, Jacob Goldberger, Hila Gonen, Joseph Keshet, Eliyahu Kiperwasser, Ron Konigsberg, Omer Levy, Oren Melamud, Gabriel Stanovsky, Ori Shapira, Micah Shlain, Vered Shwartz, Hillel Taub-Tabib, and Rachel Wities. Most of them belong in both lists, but I tried to keep things short.

The anonymous reviewers of the book and the survey paper—while unnamed (and sometimes annoying)—provided a solid set of comments, suggestions, and corrections, which I can safely say dramatically improved many aspects of the final product. Thanks, whoever you are!

And thanks also to Graeme Hirst, Michael Morgan, Samantha Draper, and C.L. Tondo for orchestrating the effort.

As usual, all mistakes are of course my own. Do let me know if you find any, though, and be listed in the next edition if one is ever made.

Finally, I would like to thank my wife, Noa, who was patient and supportive when I disappeared into writing sprees, my parents Esther and Avner and brother Nadav who were in many cases more excited about the idea of me writing a book than I was, and the staff at The Streets Cafe (King George branch) and Shne'or Cafe who kept me well fed and served me drinks throughout the writing process, with only very minimal distractions.

Yoav Goldberg
March 2017

CHAPTER 1

Introduction

1.1 THE CHALLENGES OF NATURAL LANGUAGE PROCESSING

Natural language processing (NLP) is the field of designing methods and algorithms that take as input or produce as output unstructured, natural language data. Human language is highly ambiguous (consider the sentence *I ate pizza with friends*, and compare it to *I ate pizza with olives*), and also highly variable (the core message of *I ate pizza with friends* can also be expressed as *friends and I shared some pizza*). It is also ever changing and evolving. People are great at producing language and understanding language, and are capable of expressing, perceiving, and interpreting very elaborate and nuanced meanings. At the same time, while we humans are great *users* of language, we are also very poor at formally understanding and describing the rules that *govern* language.

Understanding and producing language using computers is thus highly challenging. Indeed, the best known set of methods for dealing with language data are using *supervised machine learning* algorithms, that attempt to infer usage patterns and regularities from a set of pre-annotated input and output pairs. Consider, for example, the task of classifying a document into one of four categories: SPORTS, POLITICS, GOSSIP, and ECONOMY. Obviously, the words in the documents provide very strong hints, but which words provide what hints? Writing up rules for this task is rather challenging. However, readers can easily categorize a document into its topic, and then, based on a few hundred human-categorized examples in each category, let a supervised machine learning algorithm come up with the patterns of word usage that help categorize the documents. Machine learning methods excel at problem domains where a good set of rules is very hard to define but annotating the expected output for a given input is relatively simple.

Besides the challenges of dealing with ambiguous and variable inputs in a system with ill-defined and unspecified set of rules, natural language exhibits an additional set of properties that make it even more challenging for computational approaches, including machine learning: it is *discrete*, *compositional*, and *sparse*.

Language is symbolic and discrete. The basic elements of written language are characters. Characters form words that in turn denote objects, concepts, events, actions, and ideas. Both characters and words are discrete symbols: words such as "hamburger" or "pizza" each evoke in us a certain mental representations, but they are also distinct symbols, whose meaning is external to them and left to be interpreted in our heads. There is no inherent relation between "hamburger" and "pizza" that can be inferred from the symbols themselves, or from the individual letters they are made of. Compare that to concepts such as color, prevalent in machine vision, or acoustic signals: these concepts are continuous, allowing, for example, to move from a colorful image to a gray-scale one using a simple mathematical operation, or to compare two different colors based on inherent properties such as hue and intensity. This cannot be easily done with words—there is no simple operation that will allow us to move from the word "red" to the word "pink" without using a large lookup table or a dictionary.

Language is also compositional: letters form words, and words form phrases and sentences. The meaning of a phrase can be larger than the meaning of the individual words that comprise it, and follows a set of intricate rules. In order to interpret a text, we thus need to work beyond the level of letters and words, and look at long sequences of words such as sentences, or even complete documents.

The combination of the above properties leads to *data sparseness*. The way in which words (discrete symbols) can be combined to form meanings is practically infinite. The number of possible valid sentences is tremendous: we could never hope to enumerate all of them. Open a random book, and the vast majority of sentences within it you have not seen or heard before. Moreover, it is likely that many sequences of four-words that appear in the book are also novel to you. If you were to look at a newspaper from just 10 years ago, or imagine one 10 years in the future, many of the words, in particular names of persons, brands, and corporations, but also slang words and technical terms, will be novel as well. There is no clear way of generalizing from one sentence to another, or defining the similarity between sentences, that does not depend on their meaning— which is unobserved to us. This is very challenging when we come to learn from examples: even with a huge example set we are very likely to observe events that never occurred in the example set, and that are very different than all the examples that did occur in it.

1.2   NEURAL NETWORKS AND DEEP LEARNING

Deep learning is a branch of machine learning. It is a re-branded name for neural networks—a family of learning techniques that was historically inspired by the way computation works in the brain, and which can be characterized as learning of parameterized differentiable mathematical functions.[1] The name deep-learning stems from the fact that many layers of these differentiable function are often chained together.

While all of machine learning can be characterized as learning to make predictions based on past observations, deep learning approaches work by learning to not only predict but also to *correctly represent* the data, such that it is suitable for prediction. Given a large set of desired input-output mapping, deep learning approaches work by feeding the data into a network that produces successive transformations of the input data until a final transformation predicts the output. The transformations produced by the network are learned from the given input-output mappings, such that each transformation makes it easier to relate the data to the desired label.

---

[1]In this book we take the mathematical view rather than the brain-inspired view.

While the human designer is in charge of designing the network architecture and training regime, providing the network with a proper set of input-output examples, and encoding the input data in a suitable way, a lot of the heavy-lifting of learning the correct representation is performed automatically by the network, supported by the network's architecture.

1.3   DEEP LEARNING IN NLP

Neural networks provide a powerful learning machinery that is very appealing for use in natural language problems. A major component in neural networks for language is the use of an *embedding layer*, a mapping of discrete symbols to continuous vectors in a relatively low dimensional space. When embedding words, they transform from being isolated distinct symbols into mathematical objects that can be operated on. In particular, distance between vectors can be equated to distance between words, making it easier to generalize the behavior from one word to another. This representation of words as vectors is learned by the network as part of the training process. Going up the hierarchy, the network also learns to combine word vectors in a way that is useful for prediction. This capability alleviates to some extent the discreteness and data-sparsity problems.

There are two major kinds of neural network architectures, that can be combined in various ways: feed-forward networks and recurrent/recursive networks.

Feed-forward networks, in particular multi-layer perceptrons (MLPs), allow to work with fixed sized inputs, or with variable length inputs in which we can disregard the order of the elements. When feeding the network with a set of input components, it learns to combine them in a meaningful way. MLPs can be used whenever a linear model was previously used. The nonlinearity of the network, as well as the ability to easily integrate pre-trained word embeddings, often lead to superior classification accuracy.

Convolutional feed-forward networks are specialized architectures that excel at extracting local patterns in the data: they are fed arbitrarily sized inputs, and are capable of extracting meaningful local patterns that are sensitive to word order, regardless of where they appear in the input. These work very well for identifying indicative phrases or idioms of up to a fixed length in long sentences or documents.

Recurrent neural networks (RNNs) are specialized models for sequential data. These are network components that take as input a sequence of items, and produce a fixed size vector that summarizes that sequence. As "summarizing a sequence" means different things for different tasks (i.e., the information needed to answer a question about the sentiment of a sentence is different from the information needed to answer a question about its grammaticality), recurrent networks are rarely used as standalone component, and their power is in being trainable components that can be fed into other network components, and trained to work in tandem with them. For example, the output of a recurrent network can be fed into a feed-forward network that will try to predict some value. The recurrent network is used as an input-transformer that is trained to produce informative representations for the feed-forward network that will operate on top of it. Recurrent networks are very impressive models for sequences, and are arguably the most exciting offer of neural networks for language processing. They allow abandoning the *markov assumption* that was prevalent in NLP for decades, and designing models that can condition on entire sentences, while taking word order into account when it is needed, and not suffering much from statistical estimation problems stemming from data sparsity. This capability leads to impressive gains in *language-modeling*, the task of predicting the probability of the next word in a sequence (or, equivalently, the probability of a sequence), which is a cornerstone of many NLP applications. Recursive networks extend recurrent networks from sequences to trees.

Many of the problems in natural language are *structured*, requiring the production of complex output structures such as sequences or trees, and neural network models can accommodate that need as well, either by adapting known structured-prediction algorithms for linear models, or by using novel architectures such as sequence-to-sequence (encoder-decoder) models, which we refer to in this book as conditioned-generation models. Such models are at the heart of state-of-the-art machine translation.

Finally, many language prediction tasks are related to each other, in the sense that knowing to perform one of them will help in learning to perform the others. In addition, while we may have a shortage of *supervised* (labeled) training data, we have ample supply of raw text (unlabeled data). Can we learn from related tasks and un-annotated data? Neural network approaches provide exciting opportunities for both MTL (learning from related problems) and semi-supervised learning (learning from external, unannotated data).

1.3.1   SUCCESS STORIES

Fully connected feed-forward neural networks (MLPs) can, for the most part, be used as a drop-in replacement wherever a linear learner is used. This includes binary and multi-class classification problems, as well as more complex structured prediction problems. The nonlinearity of the network, as well as the ability to easily integrate pre-trained word embeddings, often lead to superior classification accuracy. A series of works[2] managed to obtain improved syntactic parsing results by simply replacing the linear model of a parser with a fully connected feed-forward network. Straightforward applications of a feed-forward network as a classifier replacement (usually coupled with the use of pre-trained word vectors) provide benefits for many language tasks, including the very well basic task of language modeling[3] CCG supertagging,[4] dialog state tracking,[5] and pre-ordering for statistical machine translation.[6] Iyyer et al. [2015] demonstrate that multi-layer feed-forward networks can provide competitive results on sentiment classification and factoid question answering. Zhou et al. [2015] and Andor et al. [2016] integrate them in a beam-search structured-prediction system, achieving stellar accuracies on syntactic parsing, sequence tagging and other tasks.

---

[2][Chen and Manning, 2014, Durrett and Klein, 2015, Pei et al., 2015, Weiss et al., 2015]
[3]See **Chapter 9**, as well as Bengio et al. [2003], Vaswani et al. [2013].
[4][Lewis and Steedman, 2014]
[5][Henderson et al., 2013]
[6][de Gispert et al., 2015]

Networks with convolutional and pooling layers are useful for classification tasks in which we expect to find strong local clues regarding class membership, but these clues can appear in different places in the input. For example, in a document classification task, a single key phrase (or an ngram) can help in determining the topic of the document [Johnson and Zhang, 2015]. We would like to learn that certain sequences of words are good indicators of the topic, and do not necessarily care where they appear in the document. Convolutional and pooling layers allow the model to learn to find such local indicators, regardless of their position. Convolutional and pooling architecture show promising results on many tasks, including document classification,[7] short-text categorization,[8] sentiment classification,[9] relation-type classification between entities,[10] event detection,[11] paraphrase identification,[12] semantic role labeling,[13] question answering,[14] predicting box-office revenues of movies based on critic reviews,[15] modeling text interestingness,[16] and modeling the relation between character-sequences and part-of-speech tags.[17]

In natural language we often work with structured data of arbitrary sizes, such as sequences and trees. We would like to be able to capture regularities in such structures, or to model similarities between such structures. Recurrent and recursive architectures allow working with sequences and trees while preserving a lot of the structural information. Recurrent networks [Elman, 1990] are designed to model sequences, while recursive networks [Goller and Küchler, 1996] are generalizations of recurrent networks that can handle trees. Recurrent models have been shown to produce very strong results for language modeling,[18] as well as for sequence tagging,[19] machine translation,[20] parsing,[21] and many other tasks including noisy text normalization,[22] dialog state tracking,[23] response generation,[24] and modeling the relation between character sequences and part-of-speech tags.[25]

---

[7][Johnson and Zhang, 2015]
[8][Wang et al., 2015a]
[9][Kalchbrenner et al., 2014, Kim, 2014]
[10][dos Santos et al., 2015, Zeng et al., 2014]
[11][Chen et al., 2015, Nguyen and Grishman, 2015]
[12][Yin and Schütze, 2015]
[13][Collobert et al., 2011]
[14][Dong et al., 2015]
[15][Bitvai and Cohn, 2015]
[16][Gao et al., 2014]
[17][dos Santos and Zadrozny, 2014]
[18]Some notable works are Adel et al. [2013], Auli and Gao [2014], Auli et al. [2013], Duh et al. [2013], Jozefowicz et al. [2016], Mikolov [2012], Mikolov et al. [2010, 2011].
[19][Irsoy and Cardie, 2014, Ling et al., 2015b, Xu et al., 2015]
[20][Cho et al., 2014b, Sundermeyer et al., 2014, Sutskever et al., 2014, Tamura et al., 2014]
[21][Dyer et al., 2015, Kiperwasser and Goldberg, 2016b, Watanabe and Sumita, 2015]
[22][Chrupala, 2014]
[23][Mrkšić et al., 2015]
[24][Kannan et al., 2016, Sordoni et al., 2015]
[25][Ling et al., 2015b]

Recursive models were shown to produce state-of-the-art or near state-of-the-art results for constituency[26] and dependency[27] parse re-ranking, discourse parsing,[28] semantic relation classification,[29] political ideology detection based on parse trees,[30] sentiment classification,[31] target-dependent sentiment classification,[32] and question answering.[33]

1.4   COVERAGE AND ORGANIZATION

The book consists of four parts. Part I introduces the basic learning machinery we'll be using throughout the book: supervised learning, MLPs, gradient-based training, and the computation-graph abstraction for implementing and training neural networks. Part II connects the machinery introduced in the first part with language data. It introduces the main sources of information that are available when working with language data, and explains how to integrate them with the neural networks machinery. It also discusses word-embedding algorithms and the distributional hypothesis, and feed-forward approaches to language modeling. Part III deals with specialized architectures and their applications to language data: 1D convolutional networks for working with ngrams, and RNNs for modeling sequences and stacks. RNNs are the main innovation of the application of neural networks to language data, and most of Part III is devoted to them, including the powerful conditioned-generation framework they facilitate, and attention-based models. Part IV is a collection of various advanced topics: recursive networks for modeling trees, structured prediction models, and multi-task learning.

Part I, covering the basics of neural networks, consists of four chapters. Chapter 2 introduces the basic concepts of supervised machine learning, parameterized functions, linear and log-linear models, regularization and loss functions, training as optimization, and gradient-based training methods. It starts from the ground up, and provides the needed material for the following chapters. Readers familiar with basic learning theory and gradient-based learning may consider skipping this chapter. Chapter 3 spells out the major limitation of linear models, motivates the need for nonlinear models, and lays the ground and motivation for multi-layer neural networks. Chapter 4 introduces feed-forward neural networks and the MLPs. It discusses the definition of multi-layer networks, their theoretical power, and common subcomponents such as nonlinearities and loss functions. Chapter 5 deals with neural network training. It introduces the computation-graph abstraction that allows for automatic gradient computations for arbitrary networks (the back-propagation algorithm), and provides several important tips and tricks for effective network training.

---

[26][Socher et al., 2013a]
[27][Le and Zuidema, 2014, Zhu et al., 2015a]
[28][Li et al., 2014]
[29][Hashimoto et al., 2013, Liu et al., 2015]
[30][Iyyer et al., 2014b]
[31][Hermann and Blunsom, 2013, Socher et al., 2013b]
[32][Dong et al., 2014]
[33][Iyyer et al., 2014a]

Part II introducing language data, consists of seven chapters. Chapter 6 presents a typology of common language-processing problems, and discusses the available sources of information (features) available for us when using language data. Chapter 7 provides concrete case studies, showing how the features described in the previous chapter are used for various natural language tasks. Readers familiar with language processing can skip these two chapters. Chapter 8 connects the material of Chapters 6 and 7 with neural networks, and discusses the various ways of encoding language-based features as inputs for neural networks. Chapter 9 introduces the language modeling task, and the feed-forward neural language model architecture. This also paves the way for discussing pre-trained word embeddings in the following chapters. Chapter 10 discusses distributed and distributional approaches to word-meaning representations. It introduces the word-context matrix approach to distributional semantics, as well as neural language-modeling inspired word-embedding algorithms, such as GLOVE and WORD2VEC, and discusses the connection between them and the distributional methods. Chapter 11 deals with using word embeddings outside of the context of neural networks. Finally, Chapter 12 presents a case study of a task-specific feed-forward network that is tailored for the Natural Language Inference task.

Part III introducing the specialized convolutional and recurrent architectures, consists of five chapters. Chapter 13 deals with convolutional networks, that are specialized at learning informative ngram patterns. The alternative hash-kernel technique is also discussed. The rest of this part, Chapters 14–17, is devoted to RNNs. Chapter 14 describes the RNN abstraction for modeling sequences and stacks. Chapter 15 describes concrete instantiations of RNNs, including the Simple RNN (also known as Elman RNNs) and gated architectures such as the Long Short-term Memory (LSTM) and the Gated Recurrent Unit (GRU). Chapter 16 provides examples of modeling with the RNN abstraction, showing their use within concrete applications. Finally, Chapter 17 introduces the conditioned-generation framework, which is the main modeling technique behind state-of-the-art machine translation, as well as unsupervised sentence modeling and many other innovative applications.

Part IV is a mix of advanced and non-core topics, and consists of three chapters. Chapter 18 introduces tree-structured recursive networks for modeling trees. While very appealing, this family of models is still in research stage, and is yet to show a convincing success story. Nonetheless, it is an important family of models to know for researchers who aim to push modeling techniques beyond the state-of-the-art. Readers who are mostly interested in mature and robust techniques can safely skip this chapter. Chapter 19 deals with structured prediction. It is a rather technical chapter. Readers who are particularly interested in structured prediction, or who are already familiar with structured prediction techniques for linear models or for language processing, will likely appreciate the material. Others may rather safely skip it. Finally, Chapter 20 presents multitask and semi-supervised learning. Neural networks provide ample opportunities for multi-task and semi-supervised learning. These are important techniques, that are still at the research stage. However, the existing techniques are relatively easy to implement, and do provide real gains. The chapter is not technically challenging, and is recommended to all readers.

Dependencies   For the most part, chapters, depend on the chapters that precede them. An exception are the first two chapters of Part II, which do not depend on material in previous chapters and can be read in any order. Some chapters and sections can be skipped without impacting the understanding of other concepts or material. These include Section 10.4 and Chapter 11 that deal with the details of word embedding algorithms and the use of word embeddings outside of neural networks; Chapter 12, describing a specific architecture for attacking the Stanford Natural Language Inference (SNLI) dataset; and Chapter 13 describing convolutional networks. Within the sequence on recurrent networks, Chapter 15, dealing with the details of specific architectures, can also be relatively safely skipped. The chapters in Part IV are for the most part independent of each other, and can be either skipped or read in any order.

1.5   WHAT'S NOT COVERED

The focus is on applications of neural networks to language processing tasks. However, some subareas of language processing with neural networks were deliberately left out of scope of this book. Specifically, I focus on processing written language, and do not cover working with speech data or acoustic signals. Within written language, I remain relatively close to the lower level, relatively well-defined tasks, and do not cover areas such as dialog systems, document summarization, or question answering, which I consider to be vastly open problems. While the described techniques can be used to achieve progress on these tasks, I do not provide examples or explicitly discuss these tasks directly. Semantic parsing is similarly out of scope. Multi-modal applications, connecting language data with other modalities such as vision or databases are only very briefly mentioned. Finally, the discussion is mostly English-centric, and languages with richer morphological systems and fewer computational resources are only very briefly discussed.

Some important basics   are also not discussed. Specifically, two crucial aspects of good work in language processing are *proper evaluation* and *data annotation*. Both of these topics are left outside the scope of this book, but the reader should be aware of their existence.

Proper evaluation includes the choice of the right metrics for evaluating performance on a given task, best practices, fair comparison with other work, performing error analysis, and assessing statistical significance.

Data annotation is the bread-and-butter of NLP systems. Without data, we cannot train supervised models. As researchers, we very often just use "standard" annotated data produced by someone else. It is still important to know the source of the data, and consider the implications resulting from its creation process. Data annotation is a very vast topic, including proper formulation of the annotation task; developing the annotation guidelines; deciding on the source of annotated data, its coverage and class proportions, good train-test splits; and working with annotators, consolidating decisions, validating quality of annotators and annotation, and various similar topics.

1.6   A NOTE ON TERMINOLOGY

The word "feature" is used to refer to a concrete, linguistic input such as a word, a suffix, or a part-of-speech tag. For example, in a first-order part-of-speech tagger, the features might be "current word, previous word, next word, previous part of speech." The term "input vector" is used to refer to the actual input that is fed to the neural network classifier. Similarly, "input vector entry" refers to a specific value of the input. This is in contrast to a lot of the neural networks literature in which the word "feature" is overloaded between the two uses, and is used primarily to refer to an input-vector entry.

1.7   MATHEMATICAL NOTATION

We use bold uppercase letters to represent matrices (X, Y, Z), and bold lowercase letters to represent vectors (b). When there are series of related matrices and vectors (for example, where each matrix corresponds to a different layer in the network), superscript indices are used (W^1, W^2). For the rare cases in which we want indicate the power of a matrix or a vector, a pair of brackets is added around the item to be exponentiated: $(W)^2, (W^3)^2$. We use [] as the index operator of vectors and matrices: $b_{[i]}$ is the ith element of vector b, and $W_{[i,j]}$ is the element in the ith column and jth row of matrix W. When unambiguous, we sometimes adopt the more standard mathematical notation and use b_i to indicate the ith element of vector b, and similarly $w_{i,j}$ for elements of a matrix W. We use $\cdot$ to denote the dot-product operator: $w \cdot v = \sum_i w_i v_i = \sum_i w_{[i]} v_{[i]}$. We use $x_{1:n}$ to indicate a sequence of vectors $x_1, \ldots, x_n$, and similarly $x_{1:n}$ is the sequence of items $x_1, \ldots, x_n$. We use $x_{n:1}$ to indicate the reverse sequence. $x_{1:n}[i] = x_i$, $x_{n:1}[i] = x_{n-i+1}$. We use $[v_1; v_2]$ to denote vector concatenation.

   While somewhat unorthodox, **unless otherwise stated, vectors are assumed to be row vectors.** The choice to use row vectors, which are right multiplied by matrices $(xW + b)$, is somewhat non standard—a lot of the neural networks literature use column vectors that are left multiplied by matrices $(Wx + b)$. We trust the reader to be able to adapt to the column vectors notation when reading the literature.[34]

---

[34]The choice to use the row vectors notation was inspired by the following benefits: it matches the way input vectors and network diagrams are often drawn in the literature; it makes the hierarchical/layered structure of the network more transparent and puts the input as the left-most variable rather than being nested; it results in fully connected layer dimensions being $d_{in} \times d_{out}$ rather than $d_{out} \times d_{in}$; and it maps better to the way networks are implemented in code using matrix libraries such as numpy.

PART I

Supervised Classification and Feed-forward Neural Networks

CHAPTER 2

Learning Basics and Linear Models

Neural networks, the topic of this book, are a class of supervised machine learning algorithms.

This chapter provides a quick introduction to supervised machine learning terminology and practices, and introduces linear and log-linear models for binary and multi-class classification.

The chapter also sets the stage and notation for later chapters. Readers who are familiar with linear models can skip ahead to the next chapters, but may also benefit from reading Sections 2.4 and 2.5.

Supervised machine learning theory and linear models are very large topics, and this chapter is far from being comprehensive. For a more complete treatment the reader is referred to texts such as Daumé III [2015], Shalev-Shwartz and Ben-David [2014], and Mohri et al. [2012].

2.1 SUPERVISED LEARNING AND PARAMETERIZED FUNCTIONS

The essence of supervised machine learning is the creation of mechanisms that can look at examples and produce generalizations. More concretely, rather than designing an algorithm to perform a task ("distinguish spam from non-spam email"), we design an algorithm whose input is a set of labeled examples ("This pile of emails are spam. This other pile of emails are not spam."), and its output is a function (or a program) that receives an instance (an email) and produces the desired label (spam or not-spam). It is expected that the resulting function will produce correct label predictions also for instances it has not seen during training.

As searching over the set of all possible programs (or all possible functions) is a very hard (and rather ill-defined) problem, we often restrict ourselves to search over specific families of functions, e.g., the space of all linear functions with d_{in} inputs and d_{out} outputs, or the space of all decision trees over d_{in} variables. Such families of functions are called *hypothesis classes*. By restricting ourselves to a specific hypothesis class, we are injecting the learner with *inductive bias*—a set of assumptions about the form of the desired solution, as well as facilitating efficient procedures for searching for the solution. For a broad and readable overview of the main families of learning algorithms and the assumptions behind them, see the book by Domingos [2015].

The hypothesis class also determines what can and cannot be represented by the learner. One common hypothesis class is that of high-dimensional linear function, i.e., functions of the form:[1]

$$f(x) = x \cdot W + b \tag{2.1}$$

$$x \in \mathbb{R}^{d_{in}} \quad W \in \mathbb{R}^{d_{in} \times d_{out}} \quad b \in \mathbb{R}^{d_{out}}.$$

Here, the vector x is the *input* to the function, while the matrix W and the vector b are the *parameters*. The goal of the learner is to set the values of the parameters W and b such that the function behaves as intended on a collection of input values $x_{1:k} = x_1, \ldots, x_k$ and the corresponding desired outputs $y_{1:k} = y_i, \ldots, y_k$. The task of searching over the space of functions is thus reduced to one of searching over the space of parameters. It is common to refer to parameters of the function as Θ. For the linear model case, $\Theta = W, b$. In some cases we want the notation to make the parameterization explicit, in which case we include the parameters in the function's definition: $f(x; W, b) = x \cdot W + b$.

As we will see in the coming chapters, the hypothesis class of linear functions is rather restricted, and there are many functions that it cannot represent (indeed, it is limited to *linear* relations). In contrast, *feed-forward neural networks with hidden layers*, to be discussed in Chapter 4, are also parameterized functions, but constitute a very strong hypothesis class—they are *universal approximators*, capable of representing any Borel-measurable function.[2] However, while restricted, linear models have several desired properties: they are easy and efficient to train, they often result in convex optimization objectives, the trained models are somewhat interpretable, and they are often very effective in practice. Linear and log-linear models were the dominant approaches in statistical NLP for over a decade. Moreover, they serve as the basic building blocks for the more powerful nonlinear feed-forward networks which will be discussed in later chapters.

2.2   TRAIN, TEST, AND VALIDATION SETS

Before delving into the details of linear models, let's reconsider the general setup of the machine learning problem. We are faced with a dataset of k input examples $x_{1:k}$ and their corresponding gold labels $y_{1:k}$, and our goal is to produce a function $f(x)$ that correctly maps inputs x to outputs $\hat{y}$, as evidenced by the training set. How do we know that the produced function $f()$ is indeed a good one? One could run the training examples $x_{1:k}$ through $f()$, record the answers $\hat{y}_{1:k}$, compare them to the expected labels $y_{1:k}$, and measure the accuracy. However, this process will not be very informative—our main concern is the ability of $f()$ to generalize well to unseen examples. A function $f()$ that is implemented as a lookup table, that is, looking for the input x in its memory and returning the corresponding value y for instances is has seen and a random value otherwise, will get a perfect score on this test, yet is clearly not a good classification function as it has zero generalization ability. We rather have a function $f()$ that gets some of the training examples wrong, providing that it will get unseen examples correctly.

---

[1]As discussed in Section 1.7. This book takes a somewhat un-orthodox approach and assumes vectors are *row vectors* rather than column vectors.
[2]See further discussion in Section 4.3.

Leave-one out   We must assess the trained function's accuracy on instances it has not seen during training. One solution is to perform *leave-one-out cross-validation*: train k functions $f_{1:k}$, each time leaving out a different input example x_i, and evaluating the resulting function $f_i()$ on its ability to predict x_i. Then train another function $f()$ on the entire trainings set $x_{1:k}$. Assuming that the training set is a representative sample of the population, this percentage of functions $f_i()$ that produced correct prediction on the left-out samples is a good approximation of the accuracy of $f()$ on new inputs. However, this process is very costly in terms of computation time, and is used only in cases where the number of annotated examples k is very small (less than a hundred or so). In language processing tasks, we very often encounter training sets with well over 10^5 examples.

Held-out set   A more efficient solution in terms of computation time is to split the training set into two subsets, say in a 80%/20% split, train a model on the larger subset (the *training set*), and test its accuracy on the smaller subset (the *held-out set*). This will give us a reasonable estimate on the accuracy of the trained function, or at least allow us to compare the quality of different trained models. However, it is somewhat wasteful in terms training samples. One could then re-train a model on the entire set. However, as the model is trained on substantially more data, the error estimates of the model trained on less data may not be accurate. This is generally a good problem to have, as more training data is likely to result in better rather than worse predictors.[3]

Some care must be taken when performing the split—in general it is better to shuffle the examples prior to splitting them, to ensure a balanced distribution of examples between the training and held-out sets (for example, you want the proportion of gold labels in the two sets to be similar). However, sometimes a random split is not a good option: consider the case where your input are news articles collected over several months, and your model is expected to provide predictions for new stories. Here, a random split will over-estimate the model's quality: the training and held-out examples will be from the same time period, and hence on more similar stories, which will not be the case in practice. In such cases, you want to ensure that the training set has older news stories and the held-out set newer ones—to be as similar as possible to how the trained model will be used in practice.

A three-way split   The split into train and held-out sets works well if you train a single model and wants to assess its quality. However, in practice you often train several models, compare their quality, and select the best one. Here, the two-way split approach is insufficient—selecting the best model according to the held-out set's accuracy will result in an overly optimistic estimate of the model's quality. You don't know if the chosen settings of the final classifier are good in general, or are just good for the particular examples in the held-out sets. The problem will be even worse if you perform error analysis based on the held-out set, and change the features or the architecture of the model based on the observed errors. You don't know if your improvements based on the held-

---

[3]Note, however, that some setting in the training procedure, in particular the learning rate and regularization weight may be sensitive to the training set size, and tuning them based on some data and then re-training a model with the same settings on larger data may produce sub-optimal results.

out sets will carry over to new instances. The accepted methodology is to use a three-way split of the data into train, validation (also called *development*), and test sets. This gives you two held-out sets: a *validation set* (also called *development set*), and a *test set*. All the experiments, tweaks, error analysis, and model selection should be performed based on the validation set. Then, a single run of the final model over the test set will give a good estimate of its expected quality on unseen examples. It is important to keep the test set as pristine as possible, running as few experiments as possible on it. Some even advocate that you should not even look at the examples in the test set, so as to not bias the way you design your model.

2.3   LINEAR MODELS

Now that we have established some methodology, we return to describe linear models for binary and multi-class classification.

2.3.1   BINARY CLASSIFICATION

In binary classification problems we have a single output, and thus use a restricted version of Equation (2.1) in which $d_{out} = 1$, making w a vector and b a scalar.

$$f(x) = x \cdot w + b. \tag{2.2}$$

The range of the linear function in Equation (2.2) is $[-\infty, +\infty]$. In order to use it for binary classification, it is common to pass the output of $f(x)$ through the $sign$ function, mapping negative values to -1 (the negative class) and non-negative values to $+1$ (the positive class).

Consider the task of predicting which of two neighborhoods an apartment is located at, based on the apartment's price and size. Figure 2.1 shows a 2D plot of some apartments, where the x-axis denotes the monthly rent price in USD, while the y-axis is the size in square feet. The blue circles are for Dupont Circle, DC and the green crosses are in Fairfax, VA. It is evident from the plot that we can separate the two neighborhoods using a straight line—apartments in Dupont Circle tend to be more expensive than apartments in Fairfax of the same size.[4] The dataset is *linearly separable*: the two classes can be separated by a straight line.

Each data-point (an apartment) can be represented as a 2-dimensional (2D) vector x where $x_{[0]}$ is the apartment's size and $x_{[1]}$ is its price. We then get the following linear model:

$$\hat{y} = \text{sign}(f(x)) = \text{sign}(x \cdot w + b)$$

$$= \text{sign}(\text{size} \times w_1 + \text{price} \times w_2 + b),$$

where $\cdot$ is the dot-product operation, b and $w = [w_1, w_2]$ are free parameters, and we predict Fairfax if $\hat{y} \geq 0$ and Dupont Circle otherwise. The goal of learning is setting the values of w_1,

---

[4]Note that looking at either size or price alone would not allow us to cleanly separate the two groups.

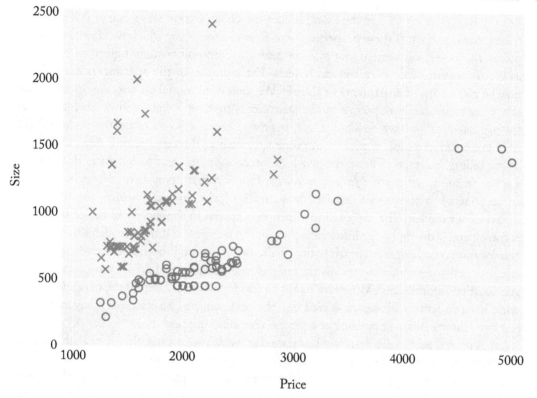

Figure 2.1: Housing data: rent price in USD vs. size in square ft. Data source: Craigslist ads, collected from June 7–15, 2015.

w_2, and b such that the predictions are correct for all data-points we observe.[5] We will discuss learning in Section 2.7 but for now consider that we expect the learning procedure to set a high value to w_1 and a low value to w_2. Once the model is trained, we can classify new data-points by feeding them into this equation.

It is sometimes not possible to separate the data-points using a straight line (or, in higher dimensions, a linear hyperplane)—such datasets are said to be *nonlinearly separable*, and are beyond the hypothesis class of linear classifiers. The solution would be to either move to a higher dimension (add more features), move to a richer hypothesis class, or allow for some mis-classification.[6]

---

[5]Geometrically, for a given $\boldsymbol{w}$ the points $\boldsymbol{x} \cdot \boldsymbol{w} + b = 0$ define a *hyperplane* (which in two dimensions corresponds to a line) that separates the space into two regions. The goal of learning is then finding a hyperplane such that the classification induced by it is correct.

[6]Misclassifying some of the examples is sometimes a good idea. For example, if we have reason to believe some of the data-points are *outliers*—examples that belong to one class, but are labeled by mistake as belonging to the other class.

Feature Representations   In the example above, each data-point was a pair of size and price measurements. Each of these properties is considered a *feature* by which we classify the data-point. This is very convenient, but in most cases the data-points are not given to us directly as lists of features, but as real-world objects. For example, in the apartments example we may be given a list of apartments to classify. We then need to make a concious decision and select the measurable properties of the apartments that we believe will be useful features for the classification task at hand. Here, it proved effective to focus on the price and the size. We could also look at additional properties, such as the number of rooms, the height of the ceiling, the type of floor, the geo-location coordinates, and so on. After deciding on a set of features, we create a *feature extraction* function that maps a real world object (i.e., an apartment) to a vector of measurable quantities (price and size) which can be used as inputs to our models. The choice of the features is crucial to the success of the classification accuracy, and is driven by the informativeness of the features, and their availability to us (the geo-location coordinates are much better predictors of the neighborhood than the price and size, but perhaps we only observe listings of past transactions, and do not have access to the geo-location information). When we have two features, it is easy to plot the data and see the underlying structures. However, as we see in the next example, we often use many more than just two features, making plotting and precise reasoning impractical.

A central part in the design of linear models, which we mostly gloss over in this text, is the design of the feature function (so called *feature engineering*). One of the promises of deep learning is that it vastly simplifies the feature-engineering process by allowing the model designer to specify a small set of core, basic, or "natural" features, and letting the trainable neural network architecture combine them into more meaningful higher-level features, or *representations*. However, one still needs to specify a suitable set of core features, and tie them to a suitable architecture. We discuss common features for textual data in Chapters 6 and 7.

We usually have many more than two features. Moving to a language setup, consider the task of distinguishing documents written in English from documents written in German. It turns out that letter frequencies make for quite good predictors (features) for this task. Even more informative are counts of letter *bigrams*, i.e., pairs of consecutive letters.[7] Assuming we have an alphabet of 28 letters (a–z, space, and a special symbol for all other characters including digits, punctuations, etc.) we represent a document as a 28×28 dimensional vector $x \in \mathbb{R}^{784}$, where each entry $x_{[i]}$ represents a count of a particular letter combination in the document, normalized by the document's length. For example, denoting by x_{ab} the entry of x corresponding to the

---

[7]While one may think that *words* will also be good predictors, letters, or letter-bigrams are far more robust: we are likely to encounter a new document without any of the words we observed in the training set, while a document without any of the distinctive letter-bigrams is significantly less likely.

letter-bigram ab:

$$x_{ab} = \frac{\#_{ab}}{|D|},\qquad(2.3)$$

where $\#_{ab}$ is the number of times the bigram ab appears in the document, and $|D|$ is the total number of bigrams in the document (the document's length).

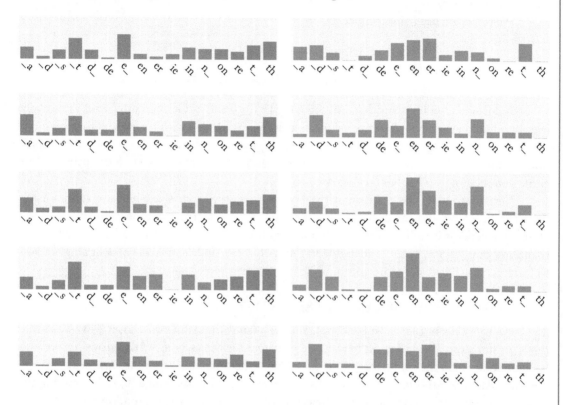

Figure 2.2: Character-bigram histograms for documents in English (left, blue) and German (right, green). Underscores denote spaces.

Figure 2.2 shows such bigram histograms for several German and English texts. For readability, we only show the top frequent character-bigrams and not the entire feature vectors. On the left, we see the bigrams of the English texts, and on the right of the German ones. There are clear patterns in the data, and, given a new item, such as:

you could probably tell that it is more similar to the German group than to the English one. Note, however, that you couldn't use a single definite rule such as "if it has th its English" or "if it has ie its German": while German texts have considerably less th than English, the th may and does occur in German texts, and similarly the ie combination does occur in English. The decision requires weighting different factors relative to each other. Let's formalize the problem in a machine-learning setup.

We can again use a linear model:

$$\hat{y} = \text{sign}(f(\boldsymbol{x})) = \text{sign}(\boldsymbol{x} \cdot \boldsymbol{w} + b)$$
$$= \text{sign}(x_{aa} \times w_{aa} + x_{ab} \times w_{ab} + x_{ac} \times w_{ac} \ldots + b). \tag{2.4}$$

A document will be considered English if $f(\boldsymbol{x}) \geq 0$ and as German otherwise. Intuitively, learning should assign large positive values to $\boldsymbol{w}$ entries associated with letter pairs that are much more common in English than in German (i.e., th) negative values to letter pairs that are much more common in German than in English (ie, en), and values around zero to letter pairs that are either common or rare in both languages.

Note that unlike the 2D case of the housing data (price vs. size), here we cannot easily visualize the points and the decision boundary, and the geometric intuition is likely much less clear. In general, it is difficult for most humans to think of the geometries of spaces with more than three dimensions, and it is advisable to think of linear models in terms of assigning weights to features, which is easier to imagine and reason about.

2.3.2 LOG-LINEAR BINARY CLASSIFICATION

The output $f(\boldsymbol{x})$ is in the range $[-\infty, \infty]$, and we map it to one of two classes $\{-1, +1\}$ using the *sign* function. This is a good fit if all we care about is the assigned class. However, we may be interested also in the confidence of the decision, or the probability that the classifier assigns to the class. An alternative that facilitates this is to map instead to the range $[0, 1]$, by pushing the output through a squashing function such as the sigmoid $\sigma(x) = \frac{1}{1+e^{-x}}$, resulting in:

$$\hat{y} = \sigma(f(\boldsymbol{x})) = \frac{1}{1 + e^{-(\boldsymbol{x} \cdot \boldsymbol{w} + b)}}. \tag{2.5}$$

Figure 2.3 shows a plot of the sigmoid function. It is monotonically increasing, and maps values to the range $[0, 1]$, with 0 being mapped to $\frac{1}{2}$. When used with a suitable *loss function* (discussed in Section 2.7.1) the binary predictions made through the log-linear model can be interpreted as class membership probability estimates $\sigma(f(\boldsymbol{x})) = P(\hat{y} = 1 \mid \boldsymbol{x})$ of $\boldsymbol{x}$ belonging to the positive class. We also get $P(\hat{y} = 0 \mid \boldsymbol{x}) = 1 - P(\hat{y} = 1 \mid \boldsymbol{x}) = 1 - \sigma(f(\boldsymbol{x}))$. The closer the value is to 0 or 1 the more certain the model is in its class membership prediction, with the value of 0.5 indicating model uncertainty.

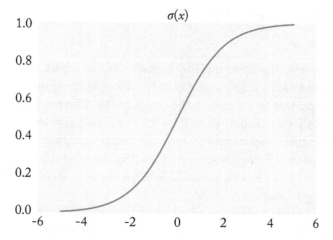

Figure 2.3: The sigmoid function $\sigma(x)$.

2.3.3   MULTI-CLASS CLASSIFICATION

The previous examples were of *binary classification*, where we had two possible classes. Binary-classification cases exist, but most classification problems are of a *multi-class* nature, in which we should assign an example to one of k different classes. For example, we are given a document and asked to classify it into one of six possible languages: *English, French, German, Italian, Spanish, Other*. A possible solution is to consider six weight vectors $\boldsymbol{w}^{EN}$, $\boldsymbol{w}^{FR}$, ... and biases, one for each language, and predict the language resulting in the highest score:[8]

$$\hat{y} = f(\boldsymbol{x}) = \underset{L\in\{E_N,F_R,G_R,I_T,S_P,O\}}{\mathrm{argmax}} \boldsymbol{x} \cdot \boldsymbol{w}^L + b^L. \qquad (2.6)$$

The six sets of parameters $\boldsymbol{w}^L \in \mathbb{R}^{784}$, b^L can be arranged as a matrix $\boldsymbol{W} \in \mathbb{R}^{784\times6}$ and vector $\boldsymbol{b} \in \mathbb{R}^6$, and the equation re-written as:

$$\hat{y} = f(\boldsymbol{x}) = \boldsymbol{x} \cdot \boldsymbol{W} + \boldsymbol{b}$$
$$\mathrm{prediction} = \hat{y} = \underset{i}{\mathrm{argmax}}\, \hat{y}_{[i]}. \qquad (2.7)$$

Here $\hat{y} \in \mathbb{R}^6$ is a vector of the scores assigned by the model to each language, and we again determine the predicted language by taking the argmax over the entries of $\hat{y}$.

---

[8]There are many ways to model multi-class classification, including binary-to-multi-class reductions. These are beyond the scope of this book, but a good overview can be found in Allwein et al. [2000].

2.4   REPRESENTATIONS

Consider the vector $\hat{y}$ resulting from applying Equation 2.7 of a trained model to a document. The vector can be considered as a *representation* of the document, capturing the properties of the document that are important to us, namely the scores of the different languages. The representation $\hat{y}$ contains strictly more information than the prediction $\hat{y} = \text{argmax}_i \, \hat{y}_{[i]}$: for example, $\hat{y}$ can be used to distinguish documents in which the main language in German, but which also contain a sizeable amount of French words. By clustering documents based on their vector representations as assigned by the model, we could perhaps discover documents written in regional dialects, or by multilingual authors.

The vectors x containing the normalized letter-bigram counts for the documents are also representations of the documents, arguably containing a similar kind of information to the vectors $\hat{y}$. However, the representations in $\hat{y}$ is more compact (6 entries instead of 784) and more specialized for the language prediction objective (clustering by the vectors x would likely reveal document similarities that are not due to a particular mix of languages, but perhaps due to the document's topic or writing styles).

The trained matrix $W \in \mathbb{R}^{784 \times 6}$ can also be considered as containing learned representations. As demonstrated in Figure 2.4, we can consider two views of W, as rows or as columns. Each of the 6 columns of W correspond to a particular language, and can be taken to be a 784-dimensional vector representation of this language in terms of its characteristic letter-bigram patterns. We can then cluster the 6 language vectors according to their similarity. Similarly, each of the 784 rows of W correspond to a particular letter-bigram, and provide a 6-dimensional vector representation of that bigram in terms of the languages it prompts.

Representations are central to deep learning. In fact, one could argue that the main power of deep-learning is the ability to learn good representations. In the linear case, the representations are interpretable, in the sense that we can assign a meaningful interpretation to each dimension in the representation vector (e.g., each dimension corresponds to a particular language or letter-bigram). This is in general not the case—deep learning models often learn a cascade of representations of the input that build on top of each other, in order to best model the problem at hand, and these representations are often not interpretable—we do not know which properties of the input they capture. However, they are still very useful for making predictions. Moreover, at the boundaries of the model, i.e., at the input and the output, we get representations that correspond to particular aspects of the input (i.e., a vector representation for each letter-bigram) or the output (i.e., a vector representation of each of the output classes). We will get back to this in Section 8.3 after discussing neural networks and encoding categorical features as dense vectors. It is recommended that you return to this discussion once more after reading that section.

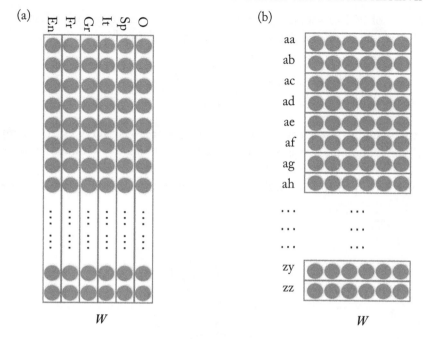

Figure 2.4: Two views of the W matrix. (a) Each column corresponds to a language. (b) Each row corresponds to a letter bigram.

2.5   ONE-HOT AND DENSE VECTOR REPRESENTATIONS

The input vector x in our language classification example contains the normalized bigram counts in the document D. This vector can be decomposed into an average of $|D|$ vectors, each corresponding to a particular document position i:

$$x = \frac{1}{|D|} \sum_{i=1}^{|D|} x^{D_{[i]}};$$

(2.8)

here, $D_{[i]}$ is the bigram at document position i, and each vector $x^{D_{[i]}} \in \mathbb{R}^{784}$ is a *one-hot* vector, in which all entries are zero except the single entry corresponding to the letter bigram $D_{[i]}$, which is 1.

The resulting vector x is commonly referred to as an *averaged bag of bigrams* (more generally *averaged bag of words*, or just *bag of words*). Bag-of-words (BOW) representations contain information about the identities of all the "words" (here, bigrams) of the document, without considering their order. A one-hot representation can be considered as a bag-of-a-single-word.

The view of the rows of the matrix W as representations of the letter bigrams suggests an alternative way of computing the document representation vector $\hat{y}$ in Equation (2.7). Denoting by $W^{D_{[i]}}$ the row of W corresponding to the bigram $D_{[i]}$, we can take the representation y of a document D to be the average of the representations of the letter-bigrams in the document:

$$\hat{y} = \frac{1}{|D|} \sum_{i=1}^{|D|} W^{D_{[i]}}.$$

(2.9)

This representation is often called a *continuous bag of words* (CBOW), as it is composed of a sum of word representations, where each "word" representation is a low-dimensional, continuous vector.

We note that Equation (2.9) and the term $x \cdot W$ in Equation (2.7) are equivalent. To see why, consider:

$$y = x \cdot W$$

$$= \left(\frac{1}{|D|} \sum_{i=1}^{|D|} x^{D_{[i]}} \right) \cdot W$$

$$= \frac{1}{|D|} \sum_{i=1}^{|D|} (x^{D_{[i]}} \cdot W)$$

(2.10)

$$= \frac{1}{|D|} \sum_{i=1}^{|D|} W^{D_{[i]}}.$$

In other words, the continuous-bag-of-words (CBOW) representation can be obtained either by summing word-representation vectors or by multiplying a bag-of-words vector by a matrix in which each row corresponds to a dense word representation (such matrices are also called *embedding matrices*). We will return to this point in Chapter 8 (in particular Section 8.3) when discussing feature representations in deep learning models for text.

2.6   LOG-LINEAR MULTI-CLASS CLASSIFICATION

In the binary case, we transformed the linear prediction into a probability estimate by passing it through the sigmoid function, resulting in a log-linear model. The analog for the multi-class case is passing the score vector through the *softmax* function:

$$\text{softmax}(x)_{[i]} = \frac{e^{x_{[i]}}}{\sum_j e^{x_{[j]}}}.$$

(2.11)

Resulting in:

$$\hat{y} = \mathrm{softmax}(xW + b)$$

$$\hat{y}_{[i]} = \frac{e^{(xW+b)_{[i]}}}{\sum_j e^{(xW+b)_{[j]}}}. \qquad (2.12)$$

The *softmax* transformation forces the values in $\hat{y}$ to be positive and sum to 1, making them interpretable as a probability distribution.

2.7   TRAINING AS OPTIMIZATION

Recall that the input to a supervised learning algorithm is a *training set* of n training examples $x_{1:n} = x_1, x_2, \ldots, x_n$ together with corresponding labels $y_{1:n} = y_1, y_2, \ldots, y_n$. Without loss of generality, we assume that the desired inputs and outputs are vectors: $x_{1:n}, y_{1:n}$.[9]

The goal of the algorithm is to return a function $f()$ that accurately maps input examples to their desired labels, i.e., a function $f()$ such that the predictions $\hat{y} = f(x)$ over the training set are accurate. To make this more precise, we introduce the notion of a *loss function*, quantifying the loss suffered when predicting $\hat{y}$ while the true label is y. Formally, a loss function $L(\hat{y}, y)$ assigns a numerical score (a scalar) to a predicted output $\hat{y}$ given the true expected output y. The loss function should be bounded from below, with the minimum attained only for cases where the prediction is correct.

The parameters of the learned function (the matrix W and the biases vector b) are then set in order to minimize the loss L over the training examples (usually, it is the sum of the losses over the different training examples that is being minimized).

Concretely, given a labeled training set $(x_{1:n}, y_{1:n})$, a per-instance loss function L and a parameterized function $f(x; \Theta)$ we define the corpus-wide loss with respect to the parameters Θ as the average loss over all training examples:

$$\mathcal{L}(\Theta) = \frac{1}{n} \sum_{i=1}^{n} L(f(x_i; \Theta), y_i). \qquad (2.13)$$

In this view, the training examples are fixed, and the values of the parameters determine the loss. The goal of the training algorithm is then to set the values of the parameters Θ such that the value of $\mathcal{L}$ is minimized:

$$\hat{\Theta} = \operatorname*{argmin}_{\Theta} \mathcal{L}(\Theta) = \operatorname*{argmin}_{\Theta} \frac{1}{n} \sum_{i=1}^{n} L(f(x_i; \Theta), y_i). \qquad (2.14)$$

Equation (2.14) attempts to minimize the loss at all costs, which may result in *overfitting* the training data. To counter that, we often pose soft restrictions on the form of the solution. This

---

[9]In many cases it is natural to think of the expected output as a scalar (class assignment) rather than a vector. In such cases, y is simply the corresponding one-hot vector, and $\operatorname{argmax}_i y_{[i]}$ is the corresponding class assignment.

is done using a function $R(\Theta)$ taking as input the parameters and returning a scalar that reflect their "complexity," which we want to keep low. By adding R to the objective, the optimization problem needs to balance between low loss and low complexity:

$$\hat{\Theta} = \underset{\Theta}{\operatorname{argmin}} \left(\overbrace{\frac{1}{n} \sum_{i=1}^{n} L(f(\boldsymbol{x}_i; \Theta), \boldsymbol{y}_i)}^{loss} + \overbrace{\lambda R(\Theta)}^{regularization} \right). \tag{2.15}$$

The function R is called a *regularization term*. Different combinations of loss functions and regularization criteria result in different learning algorithms, with different inductive biases.

We now turn to discuss common loss functions (Section 2.7.1), followed by a discussion of regularization and regularizers (Section 2.7.2). Then, in Section 2.8 we present an algorithm for solving the minimization problem (Equation (2.15)).

2.7.1   LOSS FUNCTIONS

The loss can be an arbitrary function mapping two vectors to a scalar. For practical purposes of optimization, we restrict ourselves to functions for which we can easily compute gradients (or sub-gradients).[10] In most cases, it is sufficient and advisable to rely on a common loss function rather than defining your own. For a detailed discussion and theoretical treatment of loss functions for binary classification, see Zhang [2004]. We now discuss some loss functions that are commonly used with linear models and with neural networks in NLP.

Hinge (binary)   For binary classification problems, the classifier's output is a single scalar $\tilde{y}$ and the intended output y is in $\{+1, -1\}$. The classification rule is $\hat{y} = \operatorname{sign}(\tilde{y})$, and a classification is considered correct if $y \cdot \tilde{y} > 0$, meaning that y and $\tilde{y}$ share the same sign. The hinge loss, also known as margin loss or SVM loss, is defined as:

$$L_{\text{hinge(binary)}}(\tilde{y}, y) = \max(0, 1 - y \cdot \tilde{y}). \tag{2.16}$$

The loss is 0 when y and $\tilde{y}$ share the same sign and $|\tilde{y}| \geq 1$. Otherwise, the loss is linear. In other words, the binary hinge loss attempts to achieve a correct classification, with a *margin* of at least 1.

Hinge (multi-class)   The hinge loss was extended to the multi-class setting by Crammer and Singer [2002]. Let $\hat{y} = \hat{y}_{[1]}, \ldots, \hat{y}_{[n]}$ be the classifier's output vector, and $\boldsymbol{y}$ be the one-hot vector for the correct output class.

The classification rule is defined as selecting the class with the highest score:

$$\text{prediction} = \underset{i}{\operatorname{argmax}} \, \hat{y}_{[i]}. \tag{2.17}$$

---

[10]A gradient of a function with k variables is a collection of k partial derivatives, one according to each of the variables. Gradients are discussed further in Section 2.8.

Denote by $t = \text{argmax}_i \, y_{[i]}$ the correct class, and by $k = \text{argmax}_{i \neq t} \, \hat{y}_{[i]}$ the highest scoring class such that $k \neq t$. The multi-class hinge loss is defined as:

$$L_{\text{hinge(multi-class)}}(\hat{y}, y) = \max(0, 1 - (\hat{y}_{[t]} - \hat{y}_{[k]})).$$ (2.18)

The multi-class hinge loss attempts to score the correct class above all other classes with a margin of at least 1.

Both the binary and multi-class hinge losses are intended to be used with linear outputs. The hinge losses are useful whenever we require a hard decision rule, and do not attempt to model class membership probability.

Log loss   The log loss is a common variation of the hinge loss, which can be seen as a "soft" version of the hinge loss with an infinite margin [LeCun et al., 2006]:

$$L_{log}(\hat{y}, y) = \log(1 + exp(-(\hat{y}_{[t]} - \hat{y}_{[k]}))).$$ (2.19)

Binary cross entropy   The binary cross-entropy loss, also referred to as *logistic loss* is used in binary classification with conditional probability outputs. We assume a set of two target classes labeled 0 and 1, with a correct label $y \in \{0, 1\}$. The classifier's output $\tilde{y}$ is transformed using the sigmoid (also called the logistic) function $\sigma(x) = 1/(1 + e^{-x})$ to the range $[0, 1]$, and is interpreted as the conditional probability $\hat{y} = \sigma(\tilde{y}) = P(y = 1|x)$. The prediction rule is:

$$\text{prediction} = \begin{cases} 0 & \hat{y} < 0.5 \\ 1 & \hat{y} \geq 0.5. \end{cases}$$

The network is trained to maximize the log conditional probability $\log P(y = 1|x)$ for each training example (x, y). The logistic loss is defined as:

$$L_{\text{logistic}}(\hat{y}, y) = -y \log \hat{y} - (1 - y) \log(1 - \hat{y}).$$ (2.20)

The logistic loss is useful when we want the network to produce class conditional probability for a binary classification problem. When using the logistic loss, it is assumed that the output layer is transformed using the sigmoid function.

Categorical cross-entropy loss   The categorical cross-entropy loss (also referred to as *negative log likelihood*) is used when a probabilistic interpretation of the scores is desired.

Let $y = y_{[1]}, \ldots, y_{[n]}$ be a vector representing the true multinomial distribution over the labels $1, \ldots, n,$[11] and let $\hat{y} = \hat{y}_{[1]}, \ldots, \hat{y}_{[n]}$ be the linear classifier's output, which was transformed by the softmax function (Section 2.6), and represent the class membership conditional distribution $\hat{y}_{[i]} = P(y = i|x)$. The categorical cross entropy loss measures the dissimilarity between the true label distribution y and the predicted label distribution $\hat{y}$, and is defined as cross entropy:

$$L_{\text{cross-entropy}}(\hat{y}, y) = -\sum_i y_{[i]} \log(\hat{y}_{[i]}).$$ (2.21)

---

[11]This formulation assumes an instance can belong to several classes with some degree of certainty.

For hard-classification problems in which each training example has a single correct class assignment, y is a one-hot vector representing the true class. In such cases, the cross entropy can be simplified to:

$$L_{\text{cross-entropy(hard classification)}}(\hat{y}, y) = -\log(\hat{y}_{[t]}), \quad (2.22)$$

where t is the correct class assignment. This attempts to set the probability mass assigned to the correct class t to 1. Because the scores $\hat{y}$ have been transformed using the softmax function to be non-negative and sum to one, increasing the mass assigned to the correct class means decreasing the mass assigned to all the other classes.

The cross-entropy loss is very common in the log-linear models and the neural networks literature, and produces a multi-class classifier which does not only predict the one-best class label but also predicts a distribution over the possible labels. When using the cross-entropy loss, it is assumed that the classifier's output is transformed using the softmax transformation.

Ranking losses   In some settings, we are not given supervision in term of labels, but rather as pairs of correct and incorrect items x and x', and our goal is to score correct items above incorrect ones. Such training situations arise when we have only positive examples, and generate negative examples by corrupting a positive example. A useful loss in such scenarios is the margin-based ranking loss, defined for a pair of correct and incorrect examples:

$$L_{\text{ranking(margin)}}(x, x') = \max(0, 1 - (f(x) - f(x'))), \quad (2.23)$$

where $f(x)$ is the score assigned by the classifier for input vector x. The objective is to score (rank) correct inputs over incorrect ones with a margin of at least 1.

A common variation is to use the log version of the ranking loss:

$$L_{\text{ranking(log)}}(x, x') = \log(1 + \exp(-(f(x) - f(x')))). \quad (2.24)$$

Examples using the ranking hinge loss in language tasks include training with the auxiliary tasks used for deriving pre-trained word embeddings (see Section 10.4.2), in which we are given a correct word sequence and a corrupted word sequence, and our goal is to score the correct sequence above the corrupt one [Collobert and Weston, 2008]. Similarly, Van de Cruys [2014] used the ranking loss in a selectional-preferences task, in which the network was trained to rank correct verb-object pairs above incorrect, automatically derived ones, and Weston et al. [2013] trained a model to score correct (head, relation, tail) triplets above corrupted ones in an information-extraction setting. An example of using the ranking log loss can be found in Gao et al. [2014]. A variation of the ranking log loss allowing for a different margin for the negative and positive class is given in dos Santos et al. [2015].

2.7.2   REGULARIZATION

Consider the optimization problem in Equation (2.14). It may admit multiple solutions, and, especially in higher dimensions, it can also over-fit. Consider our language identification example, and a setting in which one of the documents in the training set (call it x_o) is an outlier: it is actually in German, but is labeled as French. In order to drive the loss down, the learner can identify features (letter bigrams) in x_o that occur in only few other documents, and give them very strong weights toward the (incorrect) French class. Then, for other German documents in which these features occur, which may now be mistakenly classified as French, the learner will find other German letter bigrams and will raise their weights in order for the documents to be classified as German again. This is a bad solution to the learning problem, as it learns something incorrect, and can cause test German documents which share many words with x_o to be mistakenly classified as French. Intuitively, we would like to control for such cases by driving the learner away from such misguided solutions and toward more natural ones, in which it is OK to mis-classify a few examples if they don't fit well with the rest.

This is achieved by adding a *regularization term* R to the optimization objective, whose job is to control the complexity of the parameter value, and avoid cases of overfitting:

$$
\hat{\Theta} = \underset{\Theta}{\operatorname{argmin}} \mathcal{L}(\Theta) + \lambda R(\Theta)
$$

$$
= \underset{\Theta}{\operatorname{argmin}} \frac{1}{n} \sum_{i=1}^{n} L(f(x_i; \Theta), y_i) + \lambda R(\Theta). \tag{2.25}
$$

The regularization term considers the parameter values, and scores their complexity. We then look for parameter values that have both a low loss and low complexity. A hyperparameter[12] λ is used to control the amount of regularization: do we favor simple model over low loss ones, or vice versa. The value of λ has to be set manually, based on the classification performance on a development set. While Equation (2.25) has a single regularization function and λ value for all the parameters, it is of course possible to have a different regularizer for each item in Θ.

In practice, the regularizers R equate complexity with large weights, and work to keep the parameter values low. In particular, the regularizers R measure the norms of the parameter matrices, and drive the learner toward solutions with low norms. Common choices for R are the L_2 norm, the L_1 norm, and the elastic-net.

L_2 regularization   In L_2 regularization, R takes the form of the squared L_2 norm of the parameters, trying to keep the sum of the squares of the parameter values low:

$$
R_{L_2}(W) = \|W\|_2^2 = \sum_{i,j}(W_{[i,j]})^2. \tag{2.26}
$$

---

[12]A *hyperparameter* is a parameter of the model which is not learned as part of the optimization process, but needs to be set by hand.

The L_2 regularizer is also called a *gaussian prior* or *weight decay*.

Note that L_2 regularized models are severely punished for high parameter weights, but once the value is close enough to zero, their effect becomes negligible. The model will prefer to decrease the value of one parameter with high weight by 1 than to decrease the value of ten parameters that already have relatively low weights by 0.1 each.

L_1 regularization   In L_1 regularization, R takes the form of the L_1 norm of the parameters, trying to keep the sum of the absolute values of the parameters low:

$$R_{L_1}(W) = ||W||_1 = \sum_{i,j} |W_{[i,j]}|. \tag{2.27}$$

In contrast to L_2, the L_1 regularizer is punished uniformly for low and high values, and has an incentive to decrease all the non-zero parameter values toward zero. It thus encourages a sparse solutions—models with many parameters with a zero value. The L_1 regularizer is also called a *sparse prior* or *lasso* [Tibshirani, 1994].

Elastic-Net   The elastic-net regularization [Zou and Hastie, 2005] combines both L_1 and L_2 regularization:

$$R_{\text{elastic-net}}(W) = \lambda_1 R_{L_1}(W) + \lambda_2 R_{L_2}(W). \tag{2.28}$$

Dropout   Another form of regularization which is very effective in neural networks is *Dropout*, which we discuss in Section 4.6.

2.8 GRADIENT-BASED OPTIMIZATION

In order to train the model, we need to solve the optimization problem in Equation (2.25). A common solution is to use a gradient-based method. Roughly speaking, gradient-based methods work by repeatedly computing an estimate of the loss $\mathcal{L}$ over the training set, computing the gradients of the parameters Θ with respect to the loss estimate, and moving the parameters in the opposite directions of the gradient. The different optimization methods differ in how the error estimate is computed, and how "moving in the opposite direction of the gradient" is defined. We describe the basic algorithm, *stochastic gradient descent* (SGD), and then briefly mention the other approaches with pointers for further reading.

Motivating Gradient-based Optimization   Consider the task of finding the scalar value x that minimizes a function $y = f(x)$. The canonical approach is computing the second derivative $f''(x)$ of the function, and solving for $f''(x) = 0$ to get the extrema points. For the sake of example, assume this approach cannot be used (indeed, it is challenging to use this approach in function of multiple variables). An alternative approach is a numeric one: compute the first derivative $f'(x)$. Then, start with an initial guess value x_i. Evaluating $u = f'(x_i)$

will give the direction of change. If $u = 0$, then x_i is an optimum point. Otherwise, move in the opposite direction of u by setting $x_{i+1} \leftarrow x_i - \eta u$, where η is a *rate parameter*. With a small enough value of η, $f(x_{i+1})$ will be smaller than $f(x_i)$. Repeating this process (with properly decreasing values of η) will find an optimum point x_i. If the function $f()$ is convex, the optimum will be a global one. Otherwise, the process is only guaranteed to find a local optimum.

Gradient-based optimization simply generalizes this idea for functions with multiple variables. A gradient of a function with k variables is the collections of k partial derivatives, one according to each of the variables. Moving the inputs in the direction of the gradient will increase the value of the function, while moving them in the opposite direction will decrease it. When optimizing the loss $\mathcal{L}(\Theta; x_{1:n}, y_{1:n})$, the parameters Θ are considered as inputs to the function, while the training examples are treated as constants.

Convexity   In gradient-based optimization, it is common to distinguish between *convex* (or *concave*) functions and *non-convex* (*non-concave*) functions. A *convex function* is a function whose second-derivative is always non-negative. As a consequence, convex functions have a single minimum point. Similarly, *concave functions* are functions whose second-derivatives are always negative or zero, and as a consequence have a single maximum point. Convex (concave) functions have the property that they are easy to minimize (maximize) using gradient-based optimization—simply follow the gradient until an extremum point is reached, and once it is reached we know we obtained the global extremum point. In contrast, for functions that are neither convex nor concave, a gradient-based optimization procedure may converge to a local extremum point, missing the global optimum.

2.8.1   STOCHASTIC GRADIENT DESCENT

An effective method for training linear models is using the SGD algorithm [Bottou, 2012, LeCun et al., 1998a] or a variant of it. SGD is a general optimization algorithm. It receives a function f parameterized by Θ, a loss function L, and desired input and output pairs $x_{1:n}, y_{1:n}$. It then attempts to set the parameters Θ such that the cumulative loss of f on the training examples is small. The algorithm works, as shown in Algorithm 2.1.

The goal of the algorithm is to set the parameters Θ so as to minimize the total loss $\mathcal{L}(\Theta) = \sum_{i=1}^{n} L(f(x_i; \theta), y_i)$ over the training set. It works by repeatedly sampling a training example and computing the gradient of the error on the example with respect to the parameters Θ (line 4)—the input and expected output are assumed to be fixed, and the loss is treated as a function of the parameters Θ. The parameters Θ are then updated in the opposite direction of the gradient, scaled by a learning rate η_t (line 5). The learning rate can either be fixed throughout the

---

Algorithm 2.1 Online stochastic gradient descent training.

Input:
- Function $f(x; \Theta)$ parameterized with parameters Θ.
- Training set of inputs $x_1, \ldots, x_n$ and desired outputs $y_1, \ldots, y_n$.
- Loss function L.

1: **while** stopping criteria not met **do**
2:      Sample a training example x_i, y_i
3:      Compute the loss $L(f(x_i; \Theta), y_i)$
4:      $\hat{g} \leftarrow$ gradients of $L(f(x_i; \Theta), y_i)$ w.r.t Θ
5:      $\Theta \leftarrow \Theta - \eta_t \hat{g}$
6: **return** Θ

---

training process, or decay as a function of the time step t.[13] For further discussion on setting the learning rate, see Section 5.2.

Note that the error calculated in line 3 is based on a single training example, and is thus just a rough estimate of the corpus-wide loss $\mathcal{L}$ that we are aiming to minimize. The noise in the loss computation may result in inaccurate gradients. A common way of reducing this noise is to estimate the error and the gradients based on a sample of m examples. This gives rise to the *minibatch SGD* algorithm (Algorithm 2.2).

In lines 3–6, the algorithm estimates the gradient of the corpus loss based on the minibatch. After the loop, $\hat{g}$ contains the gradient estimate, and the parameters Θ are updated toward $\hat{g}$. The minibatch size can vary in size from $m = 1$ to $m = n$. Higher values provide better estimates of the corpus-wide gradients, while smaller values allow more updates and in turn faster convergence. Besides the improved accuracy of the gradients estimation, the minibatch algorithm provides opportunities for improved training efficiency. For modest sizes of m, some computing architectures (i.e., GPUs) allow an efficient parallel implementation of the computation in lines 3–6. With a properly decreasing learning rate, SGD is guaranteed to converge to a global optimum if the function is convex, which is the case for linear and log-linear models coupled with the loss functions and regularizers discussed in this chapter. However, it can also be used to optimize non-convex functions such as multi-layer neural network. While there are no longer guarantees of finding a global optimum, the algorithm proved to be robust and performs well in practice.[14]

---

[13]Learning rate decay is required in order to prove convergence of SGD.

[14]Recent work from the neural networks literature argue that the non-convexity of the networks is manifested in a proliferation of saddle points rather than local minima [Dauphin et al., 2014]. This may explain some of the success in training neural networks despite using local search techniques.

Algorithm 2.2 Minibatch stochastic gradient descent training.

Input:
- Function $f(x; \Theta)$ parameterized with parameters Θ.
- Training set of inputs $x_1, \ldots, x_n$ and desired outputs $y_1, \ldots, y_n$.
- Loss function L.

1: **while** stopping criteria not met **do**
2:      Sample a minibatch of m examples $\{(x_1, y_1), \ldots, (x_m, y_m)\}$
3:      $\hat{g} \leftarrow 0$
4:      **for** $i = 1$ to m **do**
5:          Compute the loss $L(f(x_i; \Theta), y_i)$
6:          $\hat{g} \leftarrow \hat{g} +$ gradients of $\frac{1}{m} L(f(x_i; \Theta), y_i)$ w.r.t Θ
7:      $\Theta \leftarrow \Theta - \eta_t \hat{g}$
8: **return** Θ

2.8.2   WORKED-OUT EXAMPLE

As an example, consider a multi-class linear classifier with hinge loss:

$$\hat{y} = \underset{i}{\operatorname{argmax}} \; \hat{y}_{[i]}$$

$$\hat{y} = f(x) = xW + b$$

$$L(\hat{y}, y) = \max(0, 1 - (\hat{y}_{[t]} - \hat{y}_{[k]}))$$
$$= \max(0, 1 - ((xW + b)_{[t]} - (xW + b)_{[k]}))$$

$$t = \underset{i}{\operatorname{argmax}} \; y_{[i]}$$

$$k = \underset{i}{\operatorname{argmax}} \; \hat{y}_{[i]} \quad i \neq t.$$

We want to set the parameters W and b such that the loss is minimized. We need to compute the gradients of the loss with respect to the values W and b. The gradient is the collection of the partial derivatives according to each of the variables:

$$\frac{\partial L(\hat{y}, y)}{\partial W} = \begin{pmatrix} \frac{\partial L(\hat{y}, y)}{\partial W_{[1,1]}} & \frac{\partial L(\hat{y}, y)}{\partial W_{[1,2]}} & \cdots & \frac{\partial L(\hat{y}, y)}{\partial W_{[1,n]}} \\ \frac{\partial L(\hat{y}, y)}{\partial W_{[2,1]}} & \frac{\partial L(\hat{y}, y)}{\partial W_{[2,2]}} & \cdots & \frac{\partial L(\hat{y}, y)}{\partial W_{[2,n]}} \\ \vdots & \vdots & \ddots & \vdots \\ \frac{\partial L(\hat{y}, y)}{\partial W_{[m,1]}} & \frac{\partial L(\hat{y}, y)}{\partial W_{[m,2]}} & \cdots & \frac{\partial L(\hat{y}, y)}{\partial W_{[m,n]}} \end{pmatrix}$$

$$\frac{\partial L(\hat{y}, y)}{\partial b} = \begin{pmatrix} \frac{\partial L(\hat{y}, y)}{\partial b_{[1]}} & \frac{\partial L(\hat{y}, y)}{\partial b_{[2]}} & \cdots & \frac{\partial L(\hat{y}, y)}{\partial b_{[n]}} \end{pmatrix}.$$

More concretely, we will compute the derivate of the loss w.r.t each of the values $W_{[i,j]}$ and $b_{[j]}$. We begin by expanding the terms in the loss calculation:[15]

$$L(\hat{y}, y) = \max(0, 1 - (\hat{y}_{[t]} - \hat{y}_{[k]}))$$
$$= \max(0, 1 - ((xW + b)_{[t]} - (xW + b)_{[k]}))$$
$$= \max\left(0, 1 - \left(\left(\sum_i x_{[i]} \cdot W_{[i,t]} + b_{[t]}\right) - \left(\sum_i x_{[i]} \cdot W_{[i,k]} + b_{[k]}\right)\right)\right)$$
$$= \max\left(0, 1 - \sum_i x_{[i]} \cdot W_{[i,t]} - b_{[t]} + \sum_i x_{[i]} \cdot W_{[i,k]} + b_{[k]}\right)$$

$$t = \operatorname*{argmax}_i y_{[i]}$$

$$k = \operatorname*{argmax}_i \hat{y}_{[i]} \quad i \neq t.$$

The first observation is that if $1 - (\hat{y}_{[t]} - \hat{y}_{[k]}) \leq 0$ then the loss is 0 and so is the gradient (the derivative of the max operation is the derivative of the maximal value). Otherwise, consider the derivative of $\frac{\partial L}{\partial b_{[i]}}$. For the partial derivative, $b_{[i]}$ is treated as a variable, and all others are considered as constants. For $i \neq k, t$, the term $b_{[i]}$ does not contribute to the loss, and its derivative it is 0. For $i = k$ and $i = t$ we trivially get:

$$\frac{\partial L}{\partial b_{[i]}} = \begin{cases} -1 & i = t \\ 1 & i = k \\ 0 & \text{otherwise.} \end{cases}$$

---

[15]More advanced derivation techniques allow working with matrices and vectors directly. Here, we stick to high-school level techniques.

Similarly, for $W_{[i,j]}$, only $j = k$ and $j = t$ contribute to the loss. We get:

$$\frac{\partial L}{\partial W_{[i,j]}} = \begin{cases} \frac{\partial(-x_{[i]} \cdot W_{[i,t]})}{\partial W_{[i,t]}} = -x_{[i]} & j = t \\ \frac{\partial(x_{[i]} \cdot W_{[i,k]})}{\partial W_{[i,k]}} = x_{[i]} & j = k \\ 0 & \text{otherwise.} \end{cases}$$

This concludes the gradient calculation.

As a simple exercise, the reader should try and compute the gradients of a multi-class linear model with hinge loss and L_2 regularization, and the gradients of multi-class classification with softmax output transformation and cross-entropy loss.

2.8.3 BEYOND SGD

While the SGD algorithm can and often does produce good results, more advanced algorithms are also available. The *SGD+Momentum* [Polyak, 1964] and *Nesterov Momentum* [Nesterov, 1983, 2004, Sutskever et al., 2013] algorithms are variants of SGD in which previous gradients are accumulated and affect the current update. Adaptive learning rate algorithms including AdaGrad [Duchi et al., 2011], AdaDelta [Zeiler, 2012], RMSProp [Tieleman and Hinton, 2012], and Adam [Kingma and Ba, 2014] are designed to select the learning rate for each minibatch, sometimes on a per-coordinate basis, potentially alleviating the need of fiddling with learning rate scheduling. For details of these algorithms, see the original papers or [Bengio et al., 2016, Sections 8.3, 8.4].

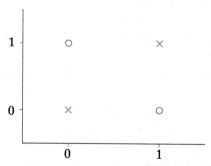

CHAPTER 3

From Linear Models to Multi-layer Perceptrons

3.1 LIMITATIONS OF LINEAR MODELS: THE XOR PROBLEM

The hypothesis class of linear (and log-linear) models is severely restricted. For example, it cannot represent the XOR function, defined as:

$$\text{xor}(0,0) = 0$$
$$\text{xor}(1,0) = 1$$
$$\text{xor}(0,1) = 1$$
$$\text{xor}(1,1) = 0.$$

That is, there is no parameterization $\boldsymbol{w} \in \mathbb{R}^2, b \in \mathbb{R}$ such that:

$$(0,0) \cdot \boldsymbol{w} + b < 0$$
$$(0,1) \cdot \boldsymbol{w} + b \geq 0$$
$$(1,0) \cdot \boldsymbol{w} + b \geq 0$$
$$(1,1) \cdot \boldsymbol{w} + b < 0.$$

To see why, consider the following plot of the XOR function, where blue Os denote the positive class and green Xs the negative class.

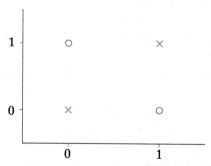

It is clear that no straight line can separate the two classes.

3.2   NONLINEAR INPUT TRANSFORMATIONS

However, if we transform the points by feeding each of them through the nonlinear function $\phi(x_1, x_2) = [x_1 \times x_2, x_1 + x_2]$, the XOR problem becomes linearly separable.

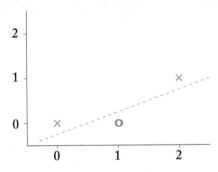

The function ϕ mapped the data into a representation that is suitable for linear classification. Having ϕ at our disposal, we can now easily train a linear classifier to solve the XOR problem.

$$\hat{y} = f(x) = \phi(x)W + b.$$

In general, one can successfully train a linear classifier over a dataset which is not linearly separable by defining a function that will map the data to a representation in which it is linearly separable, and then train a linear classifier on the resulting representation. In the XOR example the transformed data has the same dimensions as the original one, but often in order to make the data linearly separable one needs to map it to a space with a much higher dimension.

This solution has one glaring problem, however: we need to manually define the function ϕ, a process which is dependent on the particular dataset, and requires a lot of human intuition.

3.3   KERNEL METHODS

Kernelized Support Vectors Machines (SVMs) [Boser and et al., 1992], and Kernel Methods in general [Shawe-Taylor and Cristianini, 2004], approach this problem by defining a set of generic mappings, each of them mapping the data into very high dimensional—and sometimes even infinite—spaces, and then performing linear classification in the transformed space. Working in very high dimensional spaces significantly increase the probability of finding a suitable linear separator.

One example mapping is the *polynomial mapping*, $\phi(x) = (x)^d$. For $d = 2$, we get $\phi(x_1, x_2) = (x_1 x_1, x_1 x_2, x_2 x_1, x_2 x_2)$. This gives us all combinations of the two variables, allowing to solve the XOR problem using a linear classifier, with a polynomial increase in the number of parameters. In the XOR problem the mapping increased the dimensionality of the input (and hence the number of parameters) from 2–4. For the language identification example, the input dimensionality would have increased from 784 to $784^2 = 614,656$ dimensions.

Working in very high dimensional spaces can become computationally prohibitive, and the ingenuity in kernel methods is the use of the *kernel trick* [Aizerman et al., 1964, Schölkopf, 2001] that allows one to work in the transformed space without ever computing the transformed representation. The generic mappings are designed to work on many common cases, and the user needs to select the suitable one for its task, often by trial and error. A downside of the approach is that the application of the kernel trick makes the classification procedure for SVMs dependent linearly on the size of the training set, making it prohibitive for use in setups with reasonably large training sets. Another downside of high dimensional spaces is that they increase the risk of overfitting.

3.4   TRAINABLE MAPPING FUNCTIONS

A different approach is to define a *trainable* nonlinear mapping function, and train it in conjunction with the linear classifier. That is, finding the suitable representation becomes the responsibility of the training algorithm. For example, the mapping function can take the form of a parameterized linear model, followed by a nonlinear activation function g that is applied to each of the output dimensions:

$$\hat{y} = \phi(x)W + b$$
$$\phi(x) = g(xW' + b').$$

$$(3.1)$$

By taking $g(x) = \max(0, x)$ and $W' = \left(\begin{smallmatrix} 1 & 1 \\ 1 & 1 \end{smallmatrix} \right)$, $b' = (-1 \ 0)$ we get an equivalent mapping to $(x_1 \times x_2, x_1 + x_2)$ for the our points of interest (0,0), (0,1), (1,0), and (1,1), successfully solving the XOR problem. The entire expression $g(xW' + b')W + b$ is differentiable (although not convex), making it possible to apply gradient-based techniques to the model training, learning both the representation function and the linear classifier on top of it at the same time. This is the main idea behind deep learning and neural networks. In fact, Equation (3.1) describes a very common neural network architecture called a *multi-layer perceptron* (MLP). Having established the motivation, we now turn to describe multi-layer neural networks in more detail.

CHAPTER 4

Feed-forward Neural Networks

4.1 A BRAIN-INSPIRED METAPHOR

As the name suggests, neural networks were inspired by the brain's computation mechanism, which consists of computation units called neurons. While the connections between artificial neural networks and the brain are in fact rather slim, we repeat the metaphor here for completeness. In the metaphor, a neuron is a computational unit that has scalar inputs and outputs. Each input has an associated weight. The neuron multiplies each input by its weight, and then sums[1] them, applies a nonlinear function to the result, and passes it to its output. Figure 4.1 shows such a neuron.

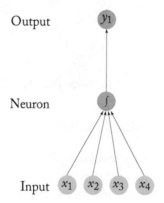

Figure 4.1: A single neuron with four inputs.

The neurons are connected to each other, forming a network: the output of a neuron may feed into the inputs of one or more neurons. Such networks were shown to be very capable computational devices. If the weights are set correctly, a neural network with enough neurons and a nonlinear activation function can approximate a very wide range of mathematical functions (we will be more precise about this later).

A typical feed-forward neural network may be drawn as in Figure 4.2. Each circle is a neuron, with incoming arrows being the neuron's inputs and outgoing arrows being the neuron's outputs. Each arrow carries a weight, reflecting its importance (not shown). Neurons are arranged in layers, reflecting the flow of information. The bottom layer has no incoming arrows, and is

---

[1]While summing is the most common operation, other functions, such as a max, are also possible.

the input to the network. The top-most layer has no outgoing arrows, and is the output of the network. The other layers are considered "hidden." The sigmoid shape inside the neurons in the middle layers represent a nonlinear function (i.e., the logistic function $1/(1 + e^{-x})$) that is applied to the neuron's value before passing it to the output. In the figure, each neuron is connected to all of the neurons in the next layer—this is called a *fully connected layer* or an *affine layer*.

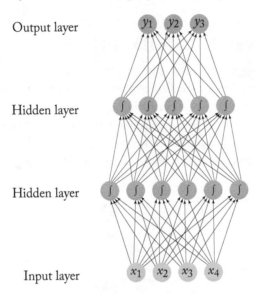

Figure 4.2: Feed-forward neural network with two hidden layers.

While the brain metaphor is sexy and intriguing, it is also distracting and cumbersome to manipulate mathematically. We therefore switch back to using more concise mathematical notation. As will soon become apparent, a feed-forward network as the one in Figure 4.2 is simply a stack of linear models separated by nonlinear functions.

The values of each row of neurons in the network can be thought of as a vector. In Figure 4.2 the input layer is a 4-dimensional vector (x), and the layer above it is a 6-dimensional vector (h^1). The fully connected layer can be thought of as a linear transformation from 4 dimensions to 6 dimensions. A fully connected layer implements a vector-matrix multiplication, $h = xW$ where the weight of the connection from the ith neuron in the input row to the jth neuron in the output row is $W_{[i,j]}$.[2] The values of h are then transformed by a nonlinear function g that is applied to each value before being passed on as input to the next layer. The whole computation from input to output can be written as: $(g(xW^1))W^2$ where W^1 are the weights of the first layer and W^2 are the weights of the second one. Taking this view, the single neuron in Figure 4.1 is equivalent to a logistic (log-linear) binary classifier $\sigma(xw)$ without a bias term .

---

[2]To see why this is the case, denote the weight of the ith input of the jth neuron in h as $W_{[i,j]}$. The value of $h_{[j]}$ is then $h_{[j]} = \sum_{i=1}^{4} x_{[i]} \cdot W_{[i,j]}$.

4.2   IN MATHEMATICAL NOTATION

From this point on, we will abandon the brain metaphor and describe networks exclusively in terms of vector-matrix operations.

The simplest neural network is called *a perceptron*. It is simply a linear model:

$$\text{NN}_{\text{Perceptron}}(x) = xW + b \tag{4.1}$$

$$x \in \mathbb{R}^{d_{in}}, \quad W \in \mathbb{R}^{d_{in} \times d_{out}}, \quad b \in \mathbb{R}^{d_{out}},$$

where W is the weight matrix and b is a bias term.[3] In order to go beyond linear functions, we introduce a nonlinear hidden layer (the network in Figure 4.2 has two such layers), resulting in the Multi Layer Perceptron with one hidden-layer (MLP1). A feed-forward neural network with one hidden-layer has the form:

$$\text{NN}_{\text{MLP1}}(x) = g(xW^1 + b^1)W^2 + b^2 \tag{4.2}$$

$$x \in \mathbb{R}^{d_{in}}, \quad W^1 \in \mathbb{R}^{d_{in} \times d_1}, \quad b^1 \in \mathbb{R}^{d_1}, \quad W^2 \in \mathbb{R}^{d_1 \times d_2}, \quad b^2 \in \mathbb{R}^{d_2}.$$

Here W^1 and b^1 are a matrix and a bias term for the first linear transformation of the input, g is a nonlinear function that is applied element-wise (also called a *nonlinearity* or an *activation function*), and W^2 and b^2 are the matrix and bias term for a second linear transform.

Breaking it down, $xW^1 + b^1$ is a linear transformation of the input x from d_{in} dimensions to d_1 dimensions. g is then applied to each of the d_1 dimensions, and the matrix W^2 together with bias vector b^2 are then used to transform the result into the d_2 dimensional output vector. The nonlinear activation function g has a crucial role in the network's ability to represent complex functions. Without the nonlinearity in g, the neural network can only represent linear transformations of the input.[4] Taking the view in Chapter 3, the first layer transforms the data into a good representation, while the second layer applies a linear classifier to that representation.

We can add additional linear-transformations and nonlinearities, resulting in an MLP with two hidden-layers (the network in Figure 4.2 is of this form):

$$\text{NN}_{\text{MLP2}}(x) = (g^2(g^1(xW^1 + b^1)W^2 + b^2))W^3. \tag{4.3}$$

It is perhaps clearer to write deeper networks like this using intermediary variables:

$$\begin{aligned} \text{NN}_{\text{MLP2}}(x) &= y \\ h^1 &= g^1(xW^1 + b^1) \\ h^2 &= g^2(h^1W^2 + b^2) \\ y &= h^2W^3. \end{aligned} \tag{4.4}$$

---

[3]The network in Figure 4.2 does not include bias terms. A bias term can be added to a layer by adding to it an additional neuron that does not have any incoming connections, whose value is always 1.

[4]To see why, consider that a sequence of linear transformations is still a linear transformation.

The vector resulting from each linear transform is referred to as a *layer*. The outer-most linear transform results in the *output layer* and the other linear transforms result in *hidden layers*. Each hidden layer is followed by a nonlinear activation. In some cases, such as in the last layer of our example, the bias vectors are forced to 0 ("dropped").

Layers resulting from linear transformations are often referred to as *fully connected*, or *affine*. Other types of architectures exist. In particular, image recognition problems benefit from *convolutional* and *pooling* layers. Such layers have uses also in language processing, and will be discussed in Chapter 13. Networks with several hidden layers are said to be *deep* networks, hence the name *deep learning*.

When describing a neural network, one should specify the *dimensions* of the layers and the input. A layer will expect a d_{in} dimensional vector as its input, and transform it into a d_{out} dimensional vector. The dimensionality of the layer is taken to be the dimensionality of its output. For a fully connected layer $l(x) = xW + b$ with input dimensionality d_{in} and output dimensionality d_{out}, the dimensions of x is $1 \times d_{in}$, of W is $d_{in} \times d_{out}$ and of b is $1 \times d_{out}$.

Like the case with linear models, the output of a neural network is a d_{out} dimensional vector. In case $d_{out} = 1$, the network's output is a scalar. Such networks can be used for regression (or scoring) by considering the value of the output, or for binary classification by consulting the sign of the output. Networks with $d_{out} = k > 1$ can be used for k-class classification, by associating each dimension with a class, and looking for the dimension with maximal value. Similarly, if the output vector entries are positive and sum to one, the output can be interpreted as a distribution over class assignments (such output normalization is typically achieved by applying a softmax transformation on the output layer, see Section 2.6).

The matrices and the bias terms that define the linear transformations are the *parameters* of the network. Like in linear models, it is common to refer to the collection of all parameters as Θ. Together with the input, the parameters determine the network's output. The training algorithm is responsible for setting their values such that the network's predictions are correct. Unlike linear models, the loss function of multi-layer neural networks with respect to their parameters is not convex,[5] making search for the optimal parameter values intractable. Still, the gradient-based optimization methods discussed in Section 2.8 can be applied, and perform very well in practice. Training neural networks is discussed in detail in Chapter 5.

4.3   REPRESENTATION POWER

In terms of representation power, it was shown by Hornik et al. [1989] and Cybenko [1989] that MLP1 is a universal approximator—it can approximate with any desired non-zero amount of error a family of functions that includes all continuous functions on a closed and bounded subset of $\mathbb{R}^n$, and any function mapping from any finite dimensional discrete space to another.[6] This

---

[5]Strictly convex functions have a single optimal solution, making them easy to optimize using gradient-based methods.
[6]Specifically, a feed-forward network with linear output layer and at least one hidden layer with a "squashing" activation function can approximate any Borel measurable function from one finite dimensional space to another. The proof was later extended by Leshno et al. [1993] to a wider range of activation functions, including the ReLU function $g(x) = \max(0, x)$.

may suggest there is no reason to go beyond MLP1 to more complex architectures. However, the theoretical result does not discuss the learnability of the neural network (it states that a representation exists, but does not say how easy or hard it is to set the parameters based on training data and a specific learning algorithm). It also does not guarantee that a training algorithm will find the *correct* function generating our training data. Finally, it does not state how large the hidden layer should be. Indeed, Telgarsky [2016] show that there exist neural networks with many layers of bounded size that cannot be approximated by networks with fewer layers unless these layers are exponentially large.

In practice, we train neural networks on relatively small amounts of data using local search methods such as variants of stochastic gradient descent, and use hidden layers of relatively modest sizes (up to several thousands). As the universal approximation theorem does not give any guarantees under these non-ideal, real-world conditions, there is definitely benefit to be had in trying out more complex architectures than MLP1. In many cases, however, MLP1 does indeed provide strong results. For further discussion on the representation power of feed-forward neural networks, see Bengio et al. [2016, Section 6.5].

4.4   COMMON NONLINEARITIES

The nonlinearity g can take many forms. There is currently no good theory as to which nonlinearity to apply in which conditions, and choosing the correct nonlinearity for a given task is for the most part an empirical question. I will now go over the common nonlinearities from the literature: the sigmoid, tanh, hard tanh and the rectified linear unit (ReLU). Some NLP researchers also experimented with other forms of nonlinearities such as cube and tanh-cube.

Sigmoid   The sigmoid activation function $\sigma(x) = 1/(1 + e^{-x})$, also called the logistic function, is an S-shaped function, transforming each value x into the range $[0, 1]$. The sigmoid was the canonical nonlinearity for neural networks since their inception, but is currently considered to be deprecated for use in internal layers of neural networks, as the choices listed below prove to work much better empirically.

Hyperbolic tangent (tanh)   The hyperbolic tangent $\tanh(x) = \frac{e^{2x}-1}{e^{2x}+1}$ activation function is an S-shaped function, transforming the values x into the range $[-1, 1]$.

Hard tanh   The hard-tanh activation function is an approximation of the tanh function which is faster to compute and to find derivatives thereof:

$$\text{hardtanh}(x) = \begin{cases} -1 & x < -1 \\ 1 & x > 1 \\ x & \text{otherwise.} \end{cases} \quad (4.5)$$

Rectifier (ReLU)   The rectifier activation function [Glorot et al., 2011], also known as the rectified linear unit is a very simple activation function that is easy to work with and was shown many times to produce excellent results.[7] The ReLU unit clips each value $x < 0$ at 0. Despite its simplicity, it performs well for many tasks, especially when combined with the dropout regularization technique (see Section 4.6):

$$\text{ReLU}(x) = \max(0, x) = \begin{cases} 0 & x < 0 \\ x & \text{otherwise.} \end{cases} \quad (4.6)$$

As a rule of thumb, both ReLU and tanh units work well, and significantly outperform the sigmoid. You may want to experiment with both tanh and ReLU activations, as each one may perform better in different settings.

Figure 4.3 shows the shapes of the different activations functions, together with the shapes of their derivatives.

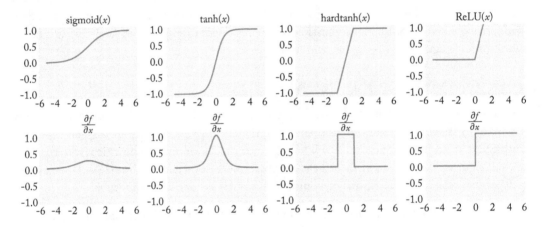

Figure 4.3: Activation functions (top) and their derivatives (bottom).

4.5   LOSS FUNCTIONS

When training a neural network (more on training in Chapter 5), much like when training a linear classifier, one defines a loss function $L(\hat{y}, y)$, stating the loss of predicting $\hat{y}$ when the true output is y. The training objective is then to minimize the loss across the different training examples. The loss $L(\hat{y}, y)$ assigns a numerical score (a scalar) to the network's output $\hat{y}$ given the true expected output y. The loss functions discussed for linear models in Section 2.7.1 are relevant and widely used also for neural networks. For further discussion on loss functions in the

---

[7]The technical advantages of the ReLU over the sigmoid and tanh activation functions is that it does not involve expensive-to-compute functions, and more importantly that it does not saturate. The sigmoid and tanh activation are capped at 1, and the gradients at this region of the functions are near zero, driving the entire gradient near zero. The ReLU activation does not have this problem, making it especially suitable for networks with multiple layers, which are susceptible to the vanishing gradients problem when trained with the saturating units.

context of neural networks, see LeCun and Huang [2005], LeCun et al. [2006] and Bengio et al. [2016].

4.6   REGULARIZATION AND DROPOUT

Multi-layer networks can be large and have many parameters, making them especially prone to overfitting. Model regularization is just as important in deep neural networks as it is in linear models, and perhaps even more so. The regularizers discussed in Section 2.7.2, namely L_2, L_1 and the elastic-net, are also relevant for neural networks. In particular, L_2 regularization, also called *weight decay* is effective for achieving good generalization performance in many cases, and tuning the regularization strength λ is advisable.

Another effective technique for preventing neural networks from overfitting the training data is *dropout training* [Hinton et al., 2012, Srivastava et al., 2014]. The dropout method is designed to prevent the network from learning to rely on specific weights. It works by randomly dropping (setting to 0) half of the neurons in the network (or in a specific layer) in each training example in the stochastic-gradient training. For example, consider the multi-layer perceptron with two hidden layers (MLP2):

$$\text{NN}_{\text{MLP2}}(\boldsymbol{x}) = \boldsymbol{y}$$
$$\boldsymbol{h^1} = g^1(\boldsymbol{x}\boldsymbol{W^1} + \boldsymbol{b^1})$$
$$\boldsymbol{h^2} = g^2(\boldsymbol{h^1}\boldsymbol{W^2} + \boldsymbol{b^2})$$
$$\boldsymbol{y} = \boldsymbol{h^2}\boldsymbol{W^3}.$$

When applying dropout training to MLP2, we randomly set some of the values of $\boldsymbol{h^1}$ and $\boldsymbol{h^2}$ to 0 at each training round:

$$\text{NN}_{\text{MLP2}}(\boldsymbol{x}) = \boldsymbol{y}$$
$$\boldsymbol{h^1} = g^1(\boldsymbol{x}\boldsymbol{W^1} + \boldsymbol{b^1})$$
$$\boldsymbol{m^1} \sim \text{Bernouli}(r^1)$$
$$\tilde{\boldsymbol{h}}^1 = \boldsymbol{m^1} \odot \boldsymbol{h^1}$$
$$\boldsymbol{h^2} = g^2(\tilde{\boldsymbol{h}}^1\boldsymbol{W^2} + \boldsymbol{b^2}) \qquad (4.7)$$
$$\boldsymbol{m^2} \sim \text{Bernouli}(r^2)$$
$$\tilde{\boldsymbol{h}}^2 = \boldsymbol{m^2} \odot \boldsymbol{h^2}$$
$$\boldsymbol{y} = \tilde{\boldsymbol{h}}^2\boldsymbol{W^3}.$$

Here, $\boldsymbol{m^1}$ and $\boldsymbol{m^2}$ are random *masking vectors* with the dimensions of $\boldsymbol{h^1}$ and $\boldsymbol{h^2}$, respectively, and $\odot$ is the element-wise multiplication operation. The values of the elements in the masking vectors are either 0 or 1, and are drawn from a Bernouli distribution with parameter r (usually $r = 0.5$). The values corresponding to zeros in the masking vectors are then zeroed out, replacing the hidden layers h with $\tilde{h}$ before passing them on to the next layer.

Work by Wager et al. [2013] establishes a strong connection between the dropout method and L_2 regularization. Another view links dropout to model averaging and ensemble techniques [Srivastava et al., 2014].

The dropout technique is one of the key factors contributing to very strong results of neural-network methods on image classification tasks [Krizhevsky et al., 2012], especially when combined with ReLU activation units [Dahl et al., 2013]. The dropout technique is effective also in NLP applications of neural networks.

4.7   SIMILARITY AND DISTANCE LAYERS

We sometimes wish to calculate a scalar value based on two vectors, such that the value reflects the *similarity, compatibility* or *distance* between the two vectors. For example, vectors $v_1 \in \mathbb{R}^d$ and $v_2 \in \mathbb{R}^d$ may be the output layers of two MLPs, and we would like to train the network to produce similar vectors for some training examples, and dissimilar vectors for others.

In what follows we describe common functions that take two vectors $u \in \mathbb{R}^d$ and $v \in \mathbb{R}^d$, and return a scalar. These functions can (and often are) integrated in feed-forward neural networks.

Dot Product   A very common options is to use the dot-product:

$$\text{sim}_{\text{dot}}(u, v) = u \cdot v = \sum_{i=1}^{d} u_{[i]} v_{[i]} \qquad (4.8)$$

Euclidean Distance   Another popular options is the Euclidean Distance:

$$\text{dist}_{\text{euclidean}}(u, v) = \sqrt{\sum_{i=1}^{d} (u_{[i]} - v_{[i]})^2} = \sqrt{(u - v) \cdot (u - v)} = ||u - v||_2 \qquad (4.9)$$

Note that this is a distance metric and not a similarity: here, small (near zero) values indicate similar vectors and large values dissimilar ones. The square-root is often omitted.

Trainable Forms   The dot-product and the euclidean distance above are fixed functions. We sometimes want to use a parameterized function, that can be trained to produce desired similarity (or dissimilarity) values by focusing on specific dimensions of the vectors. A common trainable similarity function is the *bilinear form*:

$$\text{sim}_{\text{bilinear}}(\boldsymbol{u}, \boldsymbol{v}) = \boldsymbol{u} \boldsymbol{M} \boldsymbol{v} \qquad (4.10)$$

$$\boldsymbol{M} \in \mathbb{R}^{d \times d}$$

where the matrix $\boldsymbol{M}$ is a parameter that needs to be trained.

Similarly, for a trainable distance function we can use:

$$\text{dist}(\boldsymbol{u}, \boldsymbol{v}) = (\boldsymbol{u} - \boldsymbol{v}) \boldsymbol{M} (\boldsymbol{u} - \boldsymbol{v}) \qquad (4.11)$$

Finally, a multi-layer perceptron with a single output neuron can also be used for producing a scalar from two vectors, by feeding it the concatenation of the two vectors.

4.8   EMBEDDING LAYERS

As will be further discussed in Chapter 8, when the input to the neural network contains symbolic categorical features (e.g., features that take one of k distinct symbols, such as words from a closed vocabulary), it is common to associate each possible feature value (i.e., each word in the vocabulary) with a d-dimensional vector for some d. These vectors are then considered parameters of the model, and are trained jointly with the other parameters. The mapping from a symbolic feature values such as "word number 1249" to d-dimensional vectors is performed by an *embedding layer* (also called a *lookup layer*). The parameters in an embedding layer are simply a matrix $\boldsymbol{E} \in \mathbb{R}^{|\text{vocab}| \times d}$ where each row corresponds to a different word in the vocabulary. The lookup operation is then simply indexing: $v_{1249} = \boldsymbol{E}_{[1249,:]}$. If the symbolic feature is encoded as a one-hot vector $\boldsymbol{x}$, the lookup operation can be implemented as the multiplication $\boldsymbol{x} \boldsymbol{E}$.

The word vectors are often concatenated to each other before being passed on to the next layer. Embeddings are discussed in more depth in Chapter 8 when discussing dense representations of categorical features, and in Chapter 10 when discussing pre-trained word representations.

CHAPTER 5

Neural Network Training

Similar to linear models, neural network are differentiable parameterized functions, and are trained using gradient-based optimization (see Section 2.8). The objective function for nonlinear neural networks is not convex, and gradient-based methods may get stuck in a local minima. Still, gradient-based methods produce good results in practice.

Gradient calculation is central to the approach. The mathematics of gradient computation for neural networks are the same as those of linear models, simply following the chain-rule of differentiation. However, for complex networks this process can be laborious and error-prone. Fortunately, gradients can be efficiently and automatically computed using the *backpropagation algorithm* [LeCun et al., 1998b, Rumelhart et al., 1986]. The backpropagation algorithm is a fancy name for methodically computing the derivatives of a complex expression using the chain-rule, while caching intermediary results. More generally, the backpropagation algorithm is a special case of the reverse-mode automatic differentiation algorithm [Neidinger, 2010, Section 7], [Baydin et al., 2015, Bengio, 2012]. The following section describes reverse mode automatic differentiation in the context of the *computation graph* abstraction. The rest of the chapter is devoted to practical tips for training neural networks in practice.

5.1 THE COMPUTATION GRAPH ABSTRACTION

While one can compute the gradients of the various parameters of a network by hand and implement them in code, this procedure is cumbersome and error prone. For most purposes, it is preferable to use automatic tools for gradient computation [Bengio, 2012]. The computation-graph abstraction allows us to easily construct arbitrary networks, evaluate their predictions for given inputs (forward pass), and compute gradients for their parameters with respect to arbitrary scalar losses (backward pass).

A computation graph is a representation of an arbitrary mathematical computation as a graph. It is a directed acyclic graph (DAG) in which nodes correspond to mathematical operations or (bound) variables and edges correspond to the flow of intermediary values between the nodes. The graph structure defines the order of the computation in terms of the dependencies between the different components. The graph is a DAG and not a tree, as the result of one operation can be the input of several continuations. Consider for example a graph for the computation of $(a * b + 1) * (a * b + 2)$:

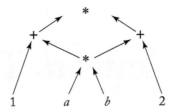

The computation of $a * b$ is shared. We restrict ourselves to the case where the computation graph is connected (in a disconnected graph, each connected component is an independent function that can be evaluated and differentiated independently of the other connected components).

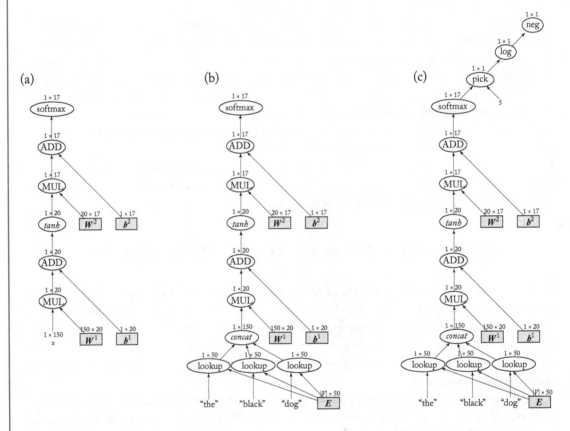

Figure 5.1: (a) Graph with unbound input. (b) Graph with concrete input. (c) Graph with concrete input, expected output, and a final loss node.

Since a neural network is essentially a mathematical expression, it can be represented as a computation graph. For example, Figure 5.1a presents the computation graph for an MLP with one hidden-layer and a softmax output transformation. In our notation, oval nodes represent mathematical operations or functions, and shaded rectangle nodes represent parameters (bound variables). Network inputs are treated as constants, and drawn without a surrounding node. Input and parameter nodes have no incoming arcs, and output nodes have no outgoing arcs. The output of each node is a matrix, the dimensionality of which is indicated above the node.

This graph is incomplete: without specifying the inputs, we cannot compute an output. Figure 5.1b shows a complete graph for an MLP that takes three words as inputs, and predicts the distribution over part-of-speech tags for the third word. This graph can be used for prediction, but not for training, as the output is a vector (not a scalar) and the graph does not take into account the correct answer or the loss term. Finally, the graph in Figure 5.1c shows the computation graph for a specific training example, in which the inputs are the (embeddings of) the words "the," "black," "dog," and the expected output is "NOUN" (whose index is 5). The *pick* node implements an indexing operation, receiving a vector and an index (in this case, 5) and returning the corresponding entry in the vector.

Once the graph is built, it is straightforward to run either a forward computation (compute the result of the computation) or a backward computation (computing the gradients), as we show below. Constructing the graphs may look daunting, but is actually very easy using dedicated software libraries and APIs.

5.1.1   FORWARD COMPUTATION

The forward pass computes the outputs of the nodes in the graph. Since each node's output depends only on itself and on its incoming edges, it is trivial to compute the outputs of all nodes by traversing the nodes in a topological order and computing the output of each node given the already computed outputs of its predecessors.

More formally, in a graph of N nodes, we associate each node with an index i according to their topological ordering. Let f_i be the function computed by node i (e.g., *multiplication. addition*, etc.). Let $\pi(i)$ be the parent nodes of node i, and $\pi^{-1}(i) = \{j \mid i \in \pi(j)\}$ the children nodes of node i (these are the arguments of f_i). Denote by $v(i)$ the output of node i, that is, the application of f_i to the output values of its arguments $\pi^{-1}(i)$. For variable and input nodes, f_i is a constant function and $\pi^{-1}(i)$ is empty. The computation-graph forward pass computes the values $v(i)$ for all $i \in [1, N]$.

Algorithm 5.3 Computation graph forward pass.

===

1: **for** i = 1 to N **do**
2:     Let $a_1, \ldots, a_m = \pi^{-1}(i)$
3:     $v(i) \leftarrow f_i(v(a_1), \ldots, v(a_m))$

===

5.1.2   BACKWARD COMPUTATION (DERIVATIVES, BACKPROP)

The backward pass begins by designating a node N with scalar (1×1) output as a loss-node, and running forward computation up to that node. The backward computation computes the gradients of the parameters with respect to that node's value. Denote by $d(i)$ the quantity $\frac{\partial N}{\partial i}$. The backpropagation algorithm is used to compute the values $d(i)$ for all nodes i.
The backward pass fills a table of values $d(1), \ldots, d(N)$ as in Algorithm 5.4.

Algorithm 5.4 Computation graph backward pass (backpropagation).

1: $d(N) \leftarrow 1$ $\qquad\qquad\qquad\qquad\qquad\qquad\qquad\qquad\qquad\quad \triangleright \frac{\partial N}{\partial N} = 1$

2: **for** i = N-1 to 1 **do**

3: $\qquad d(i) \leftarrow \sum_{j \in \pi(i)} d(j) \cdot \frac{\partial f_j}{\partial i}$ $\qquad\qquad\quad \triangleright \frac{\partial N}{\partial i} = \sum_{j \in \pi(i)} \frac{\partial N}{\partial j} \frac{\partial j}{\partial i}$

The backpropagation algorithm (Algorithm 5.4) is essentially following the chain-rule of differentiation. The quantity $\frac{\partial f_j}{\partial i}$ is the partial derivative of $f_j(\pi^{-1}(j))$ w.r.t the argument $i \in \pi^{-1}(j)$. This value depends on the function f_j and the values $v(a_1), \ldots, v(a_m)$ (where $a_1, \ldots, a_m = \pi^{-1}(j)$) of its arguments, which were computed in the forward pass.

Thus, in order to define a new kind of node, one needs to define two methods: one for calculating the forward value $v(i)$ based on the node's inputs, and the another for calculating $\frac{\partial f_i}{\partial x}$ for each $x \in \pi^{-1}(i)$.

Derivatives of "non-mathematical" functions   While defining $\frac{\partial f_i}{\partial x}$ for mathematical functions such is as log or $+$ is straightforward, some find it challenging to think about the derivative of operations as as $pick(x, 5)$ that selects the fifth element of a vector. The answer is to think in terms of the contribution to the computation. After picking the ith element of a vector, only that element participates in the remainder of the computation. Thus, the gradient of $pick(x, 5)$ is a vector g with the dimensionality of x where $g_{[5]} = 1$ and $g_{[i \neq 5]} = 0$. Similarly, for the function $\max(0, x)$ the value of the gradient is 1 for $x > 0$ and 0 otherwise.

For further information on automatic differentiation, see Neidinger [2010, Section 7] and Baydin et al. [2015]. For more in depth discussion of the backpropagation algorithm and computation graphs (also called flow graphs), see Bengio et al. [2016, Section 6.5] and Bengio [2012], LeCun et al. [1998b]. For a popular yet technical presentation, see Chris Olah's description at http://colah.github.io/posts/2015-08-Backprop/.

5.1.3   SOFTWARE

Several software packages implement the computation-graph model, including Theano,[1] [Bergstra et al., 2010], TensorFlow[2] [Abadi et al., 2015], Chainer,[3] and DyNet[4] [Neubig et al., 2017]. All these packages support all the essential components (node types) for defining a wide range of neural network architectures, covering the structures described in this book and more. Graph creation is made almost transparent by use of operator overloading. The framework defines a type for representing graph nodes (commonly called *expression*s), methods for constructing nodes for inputs and parameters, and a set of functions and mathematical operations that take expressions as input and result in more complex expressions. For example, the python code for creating the computation graph from Figure 5.1c using the DyNet framework is:

```python
import dynet as dy
# model initialization.
model = dy.Model()
mW1 = model.add_parameters((20,150))
mb1 = model.add_parameters(20)
mW2 = model.add_parameters((17,20))
mb2 = model.add_parameters(17)
lookup = model.add_lookup_parameters((100, 50))
trainer = dy.SimpleSGDTrainer(model)

def get_index(x):
    pass # Logic omitted.
Maps words to numeric IDs.

# The following builds and executes the computation graph,
# and updates model parameters.
# Only one data point is shown, in practice the following
# should run in a data-feeding loop.

# Building the computation graph:
dy.renew_cg() # create a new graph.
# Wrap the model parameters as graph-nodes.
W1 = dy.parameter(mW1)
b1 = dy.parameter(mb1)
W2 = dy.parameter(mW2)
b2 = dy.parameter(mb2)
# Generate the embeddings layer.
vthe   = dy.lookup[get_index("the")]
vblack = dy.lookup[get_index("black")]
vdog   = dy.lookup[get_index("dog")]

# Connect the leaf nodes into a complete graph.
x = dy.concatenate([vthe, vblack, vdog])
output = dy.softmax(W2*(dy.tanh(W1*x+b1))+b2)
loss = -dy.log(dy.pick(output, 5))
```

---

[1]http://deeplearning.net/software/theano/
[2]https://www.tensorflow.org/
[3]http://chainer.org
[4]https://github.com/clab/dynet

```
loss_value = loss.forward()
loss.backward() # the gradient is computed
                # and stored in the corresponding
                # parameters.
trainer.update() # update the parameters according to the gradients.
```

Most of the code involves various initializations: the first block defines model parameters that are be shared between different computation graphs (recall that each graph corresponds to a specific training example). The second block turns the model parameters into the graph-node (Expression) types. The third block retrieves the Expressions for the embeddings of the input words. Finally, the fourth block is where the graph is created. Note how transparent the graph creation is— there is an almost a one-to-one correspondence between creating the graph and describing it mathematically. The last block shows a forward and backward pass. The equivalent code in the TensorFlow package is:[5]

```
import tensorflow as tf

W1 = tf.get_variable("W1", [20, 150])
b1 = tf.get_variable("b1", [20])
W2 = tf.get_variable("W2", [17, 20])
b2 = tf.get_variable("b2", [17])
lookup = tf.get_variable("W", [100, 50])

def get_index(x):
    pass # Logic omitted

p1 = tf.placeholder(tf.int32, [])
p2 = tf.placeholder(tf.int32, [])
p3 = tf.placeholder(tf.int32, [])
target = tf.placeholder(tf.int32, [])

v_w1 = tf.nn.embedding_lookup(lookup, p1)
v_w2 = tf.nn.embedding_lookup(lookup, p2)
v_w3 = tf.nn.embedding_lookup(lookup, p3)

x = tf.concat([v_w1, v_w2, v_w3], 0)
output = tf.nn.softmax(
    tf.einsum("ij,j->i", W2, tf.tanh(
        tf.einsum("ij,j->i", W1, x) + b1)) + b2)
loss = -tf.log(output[target])
trainer = tf.train.GradientDescentOptimizer(0.1).minimize(loss)

# Graph definition done, compile it and feed concrete data.
# Only one data-point is shown, in practice we will use
# a data-feeding loop.
with tf.Session() as sess:
    sess.run(tf.global_variables_initializer())
    feed_dict = {
        p1: get_index("the"),
        p2: get_index("black"),
        p3: get_index("dog"),
```

---

[5]TensorFlow code provided by Tim Rocktäschel. Thanks Tim!

```
        target: 5
}
loss_value = sess.run(loss, feed_dict)
# update, no call of backward necessary
sess.run(trainer, feed_dict)
```

The main difference between DyNet (and Chainer) to TensorFlow (and Theano) is that the formers use *dynamic graph construction* while the latters use *static graph construction*. In dynamic graph construction, a different computation graph is created from scratch for each training sample, using code in the host language. Forward and backward propagation are then applied to this graph. In contrast, in the static graph construction approach, the shape of the computation graph is defined once in the beginning of the computation, using an API for specifying graph shapes, with place-holder variables indicating input and output values. Then, an optimizing graph compiler produces an optimized computation graph, and each training example is fed into the (same) optimized graph. The graph compilation step in the static toolkits (TensorFlow and Theano) is both a blessing and a curse. On the one hand, once compiled, large graphs can be run efficiently on either the CPU or a GPU, making it ideal for large graphs with a fixed structure, where only the inputs change between instances. However, the compilation step itself can be costly, and it makes the interface more cumbersome to work with. In contrast, the dynamic packages focus on building large and dynamic computation graphs and executing them "on the fly" without a compilation step. While the execution speed may suffer compared to the static toolkits, in practice the computation speeds of the dynamic toolkits are very competitive. The dynamic packages are especially convenient when working with the recurrent and recursive networks described in Chapters 14 and 18 as well as in structured prediction settings as described in Chapter 19, in which the graphs of different data-points have different shapes. See Neubig et al. [2017] for further discussion on the dynamic-vs.-static approaches, and speed benchmarks for the different toolkits. Finally, packages such as Keras[6] provide a higher level interface on top of packages such as Theano and TensorFlow, allowing the definition and training of complex neural networks with even fewer lines of code, provided that the architectures are well established, and hence supported in the higher-level interface.

5.1.4   IMPLEMENTATION RECIPE

Using the computation graph abstraction and dynamic graph construction, the pseudo-code for a network training algorithm is given in Algorithm 5.5.

Here, build_computation_graph is a user-defined function that builds the computation graph for the given input, output, and network structure, returning a single loss node. update_parameters is an optimizer specific update rule. The recipe specifies that a new graph is created for each training example. This accommodates cases in which the network structure varies between training examples, such as recurrent and recursive neural networks, to be discussed in

---

[6]https://keras.io

Algorithm 5.5 Neural network training with computation graph abstraction (using minibatches of size 1).

1: Define network parameters.
2: **for** iteration = 1 to T **do**
3:     **for** Training example x_i, y_i in dataset **do**
4:         loss_node ← build_computation_graph(x_i, y_i, parameters)
5:         loss_node.forward()
6:         gradients ← loss_node().backward()
7:         parameters ← update_parameters(parameters, gradients)
8: **return** parameters.

Chapters 14–18. For networks with fixed structures, such as an MLPs, it may be more efficient to create one base computation graph and vary only the inputs and expected outputs between examples.

5.1.5   NETWORK COMPOSITION

As long as the network's output is a vector ($1 \times k$ matrix), it is trivial to compose networks by making the output of one network the input of another, creating arbitrary networks. The computation graph abstractions makes this ability explicit: a node in the computation graph can itself be a computation graph with a designated output node. One can then design arbitrarily deep and complex networks, and be able to easily evaluate and train them thanks to automatic forward and gradient computation. This makes it easy to define and train elaborate recurrent and recursive networks, as discussed in Chapters 14–16 and 18, as well as networks for structured outputs and multi-objective training, as we discuss in Chapters 19 and 20.

5.2   PRACTICALITIES

Once the gradient computation is taken care of, the network is trained using SGD or another gradient-based optimization algorithm. The function being optimized is not convex, and for a long time training of neural networks was considered a "black art" which can only be done by selected few. Indeed, many parameters affect the optimization process, and care has to be taken to tune these parameters. While this book is not intended as a comprehensive guide to successfully training neural networks, we do list here a few of the prominent issues. For further discussion on optimization techniques and algorithms for neural networks, refer to Bengio et al. [2016, Chapter 8]. For some theoretical discussion and analysis, refer to Glorot and Bengio [2010]. For various practical tips and recommendations, see Bottou [2012], LeCun et al. [1998a].

5.2.1   CHOICE OF OPTIMIZATION ALGORITHM

While the SGD algorithm works well, it may be slow to converge. Section 2.8.3 lists some alternative, more advanced stochastic-gradient algorithms. As most neural network software frameworks provide implementations of these algorithms, it is easy and often worthwhile to try out different variants. In my research group, we found that when training larger networks, using the Adam algorithm [Kingma and Ba, 2014] is very effective and relatively robust to the choice of the learning rate.

5.2.2   INITIALIZATION

The non-convexity of the objective function means the optimization procedure may get stuck in a local minimum or a saddle point, and that starting from different initial points (e.g., different random values for the parameters) may result in different results. Thus, it is advised to run several restarts of the training starting at different random initializations, and choosing the best one based on a development set.[7] The amount of variance in the results due to different random seed selections is different for different network formulations and datasets, and cannot be predicted in advance.

The magnitude of the random values has a very important effect on the success of training. An effective scheme due to Glorot and Bengio [2010], called *xavier initialization* after Glorot's first name, suggests initializing a weight matrix $W \in \mathbb{R}^{d_{in} \times d_{out}}$ as:

$$W \sim U \left[-\frac{\sqrt{6}}{\sqrt{d_{in} + d_{out}}}, +\frac{\sqrt{6}}{\sqrt{d_{in} + d_{out}}} \right], \tag{5.1}$$

where $U[a, b]$ is a uniformly sampled random value in the range $[a, b]$. The suggestion is based on properties of the tanh activation function, works well in many situations, and is the preferred default initialization method by many.

Analysis by He et al. [2015] suggests that when using ReLU nonlinearities, the weights should be initialized by sampling from a zero-mean Gaussian distribution whose standard deviation is $\sqrt{\frac{2}{d_{in}}}$. This initialization was found by He et al. [2015] to work better than xavier initialization in an image classification task, especially when deep networks were involved.

5.2.3   RESTARTS AND ENSEMBLES

When training complex networks, different random initializations are likely to end up with different final solutions, exhibiting different accuracies. Thus, if your computational resources allow, it is advisable to run the training process several times, each with a different random initialization, and choose the best one on the development set. This technique is called *random restarts*. The average model accuracy across random seeds is also interesting, as it gives a hint as to the stability of the process.

---

[7]When debugging, and for reproducibility of results, it is advised to used a fixed random seed.

While the need to "tune" the random seed used to initialize models can be annoying, it also provides a simple way to get different models for performing the same task, facilitating the use *model ensembles*. Once several models are available, one can base the prediction on the ensemble of models rather than on a single one (for example by taking the majority vote across the different models, or by averaging their output vectors and considering the result as the output vector of the ensembled model). Using ensembles often increases the prediction accuracy, at the cost of having to run the prediction step several times (once for each model).

5.2.4   VANISHING AND EXPLODING GRADIENTS

In deep networks, it is common for the error gradients to either vanish (become exceedingly close to 0) or explode (become exceedingly high) as they propagate back through the computation graph. The problem becomes more severe in deeper networks, and especially so in recursive and recurrent networks [Pascanu et al., 2012]. Dealing with the vanishing gradients problem is still an open research question. Solutions include making the networks shallower, step-wise training (first train the first layers based on some auxiliary output signal, then fix them and train the upper layers of the complete network based on the real task signal), performing batch-normalization [Ioffe and Szegedy, 2015] (for every minibatch, normalizing the inputs to each of the network layers to have zero mean and unit variance) or using specialized architectures that are designed to assist in gradient flow (e.g., the LSTM and GRU architectures for recurrent networks, discussed in Chapter 15). Dealing with the exploding gradients has a simple but very effective solution: clipping the gradients if their norm exceeds a given threshold. Let $\hat{g}$ be the gradients of all parameters in the network, and $\|\hat{g}\|$ be their L_2 norm. Pascanu et al. [2012] suggest to set: $\hat{g} \leftarrow \frac{\text{threshold}}{\|\hat{g}\|} \hat{g}$ if $\|\hat{g}\| > \text{threshold}$.

5.2.5   SATURATION AND DEAD NEURONS

Layers with tanh and sigmoid activations can become saturated—resulting in output values for that layer that are all close to one, the upper-limit of the activation function. Saturated neurons have very small gradients, and should be avoided. Layers with the ReLU activation cannot be saturated, but can "die"—most or all values are negative and thus clipped at zero for all inputs, resulting in a gradient of zero for that layer. If your network does not train well, it is advisable to monitor the network for layers with many saturated or dead neurons. Saturated neurons are caused by too large values entering the layer. This may be controlled for by changing the initialization, scaling the range of the input values, or changing the learning rate. Dead neurons are caused by all signals entering the layer being negative (for example this can happen after a large gradient update). Reducing the learning rate will help in this situation. For saturated layers, another option is to normalize the values in the saturated layer after the activation, i.e., instead of $g(h) = \tanh(h)$ using $g(h) = \frac{\tanh(h)}{\|\tanh(h)\|}$. Layer normalization is an effective measure for countering saturation, but is also expensive in terms of gradient computation. A related technique is *batch normalization*, due to Ioffe and Szegedy [2015], in which the activations at each layer are normalized so that they have mean 0 and variance 1 across each mini-batch. The batch-normalization techniques became a key component for effective training of deep networks in computer vision. As of this writing, it is less popular in natural language applications.

5.2.6 SHUFFLING

The order in which the training examples are presented to the network is important. The SGD formulation above specifies selecting a random example in each turn. In practice, most implementations go over the training example in random order, essentially performing random sampling without replacement. It is advised to shuffle the training examples before each pass through the data.

5.2.7 LEARNING RATE

Selection of the learning rate is important. Too large learning rates will prevent the network from converging on an effective solution. Too small learning rates will take a very long time to converge. As a rule of thumb, one should experiment with a range of initial learning rates in range $[0, 1]$, e.g., $0.001, 0.01, 0.1, 1$. Monitor the network's loss over time, and decrease the learning rate once the loss stops improving on a held-out development set. *Learning rate scheduling* decreases the rate as a function of the number of observed minibatches. A common schedule is dividing the initial learning rate by the iteration number. Léon Bottou [2012] recommends using a learning rate of the form $\eta_t = \eta_0(1 + \eta_0\lambda t)^{-1}$ where η_0 is the initial learning rate, η_t is the learning rate to use on the tth training example, and λ is an additional hyperparameter. He further recommends determining a good value of η_0 based on a small sample of the data prior to running on the entire dataset.

5.2.8 MINIBATCHES

Parameter updates occur either every training example (minibatches of size 1) or every k training examples. Some problems benefit from training with larger minibatch sizes. In terms of the computation graph abstraction, one can create a computation graph for each of the k training examples, and then connecting the k loss nodes under an averaging node, whose output will be the loss of the minibatch. Large minibatched training can also be beneficial in terms of computation efficiency on specialized computing architectures such as GPUs, and replacing vector-matrix operations by matrix-matrix operations. This is beyond the scope of this book.

PART II

Working with Natural Language Data

CHAPTER 6

Features for Textual Data

In the previous chapters we discussed the general learning problem, and saw some machine learning models and algorithms for training them. All of these models take as input vectors x and produce predictions. Up until now we assumed the vectors x are given. In language processing, the vectors x are derived from textual data, in order to reflect various linguistic properties of the text. The mapping from textual data to real valued vectors is called *feature extraction* or *feature representation*, and is done by a *feature function*. Deciding on the right features is an integral part of a successful machine learning project. While deep neural networks alleviate a lot of the need in feature engineering, a good set of core features still needs to be defined. This is especially true for language data, which comes in the form of a sequence of discrete symbols. This sequence needs to be converted somehow to a numerical vector, in a non-obvious way.

We now diverge from the training machinery in order to discuss the feature functions that are used for language data, which will be the topic of the next few chapters.

This chapter provides an overview of the common kinds of information sources that are available for use as features when dealing with textual language data. Chapter 7 discusses feature choices for some concrete NLP problems. Chapter 8 deals with encoding the features as input vectors that can be fed to a neural network.

6.1 TYPOLOGY OF NLP CLASSIFICATION PROBLEMS

Generally speaking, classification problems in natural language can be categorized into several broad categories, depending on the item being classified (some problems in natural language processing do not fall neatly into the classification framework. For example, problems in which we are required to produce sentences or longer texts—i.e., in document summarization and machine translation. These will be discussed in Chapter 17).

Word In these problems, we are faced with a word, such as "dog," "magnificent," "magnificant," or "parlez" and need to say something about it: Does it denote a living thing? What language is it in? How common is it? What other words are similar to it? Is it a mis-spelling of another word? And so on. These kind of problems are actually quite rare, as words seldom appear in isolation, and for many words their interpretation depends on the context in which they are used.

Texts In these problems we are faced with a piece of text, be it a phrase, a sentence, a paragraph or a document, and need to say something about it. Is it spam or not? Is it about politics or sports? Is it sarcastic? Is it positive, negative or neutral (toward some issue)? Who wrote it? Is it reliable? Which of a fixed set of intents does this text reflect (or none)? Will this text be liked by 16–18 years old males? And so on. These types of problems are very common, and we'll refer to them collectively as *document classification* problems.

Paired Texts In these problems we are given a pair of words or longer texts, and need to say something about the pair. Are words A and B synonyms? Is word A a valid translation for word B? Are documents A and B written by the same author? Can the meaning of sentence A be inferred from sentence B?

Word in Context Here, we are given a piece of text, and a particular word (or phrase, or letter, etc.) within it, and we need to classify the word in the context of the text. For example, is the word *book* in *I want to book a flight* a noun, a verb or an adjective? Is the word *apple* in a given context referring to a company or a fruit? Is *on* the right preposition to use in *I read a book on London*? Does a given period denote a sentence boundary or an abbreviation? Is the given word part of a name of a person, location, or organization? And so on. These types of questions often arise in the context of larger goals, such as annotating a sentence for parts-of-speech, splitting a document into sentences, finding all the named entities in a text, finding all documents mentioning a given entity, and so on.

Relation between two words Here we are given two words or phrases within the context of a larger document, and need to say something about the relations between them. Is word A the subject of verb B in a given sentence? Does the "purchase" relation hold between words A and B in a given text? And so on.

Many of these classification cases can be extended to *structured problems* in which we are interested in performing several related classification decisions, such that the answer to one decision can influence others. These are discussed in Chapter 19.

What is a word?   We are using the term *word* rather loosely. The question "what is a word?" is a matter of debate among linguists, and the answer is not always clear.

One definition (which is the one being loosely followed in this book) is that words are sequences of letters that are separated by whitespace. This definition is very simplistic. First, punctuation in English is not separated by whitespace, so according to our definition dog, dog?, dog. and dog) are all different words. Our corrected definition is then words separated by whitespace or punctuation. A process called *tokenization* is in charge of splitting text into tokens (what we call here words) based on whitespace and punctuation. In English, the job of the tokenizer is quite simple, although it does need to consider cases such as abbreviations (I.B.M) and titles (Mr.) that needn't be split. In other languages, things can become much tricker: in Hebrew and Arabic some words attach to the next one without whitespace, and in Chinese there are no whitespaces at all. These are just a few examples.

When working in English or a similar language (as this book assumes), tokenizing on whitespace and punctuation (while handling a few corner cases) can provide a good approximation of words. However, our definition of word is still quite technical: it is derived from the way things are written. Another common (and better) definition take a word to be "the smallest unit of meaning." By following this definition, we see that our whitespace-based definition is problematic. After splitting by whitespace and punctuation, we still remain with sequences such as don't, that are actually two words, do not, that got merged into one symbol. It is common for English tokenizers to handle these cases as well. The symbols cat and Cat have the same meaning, but are they the same word? More interestingly, take something like New York, is it two words, or one? What about ice cream? Is it the same as ice-cream or icecream? And what about idioms such as kick the bucket?

In general, we distinguish between *words* and *tokens*. We refer to the output of a tokenizer as a *token*, and to the meaning-bearing units as *words*. A token may be composed of multiple words, multiple tokens can be a single word, and sometimes different tokens denote the same underlying word.

Having said that, in this book, we use the term *word* very loosely, and take it to be interchangeable with *token*. It is important to keep in mind, however, that the story is more complex than that.

6.2 FEATURES FOR NLP PROBLEMS

In what follows, we describe the common features that are used for the above problems. As words and letters are discrete items, our features often take the form of indicators or counts. An *indicator feature* takes a value of 0 or 1, depending on the existence of a condition (e.g., a feature taking the value of 1 if the word *dog* appeared at least once in the document, and 0 otherwise). A *count* takes a value depending on the number of times some event occurred, e.g., a feature indicating the number of times the word *dog* appears in the text.

6.2.1 DIRECTLY OBSERVABLE PROPERTIES

Features for Single Words   When our focus entity is a word outside of a context, our main source of information is the *letters* comprising the word and their order, as well as properties derived from these such as the length of the word, the orthographic shape of the word (Is the first letter capitalized? Are all letters capitalized? Does the word include a hyphen? Does it include a digit? And so on), and prefixes and suffixes of the word (Does it start with *un*? Does it end with *ing*?).

We may also look at the word with relation to external sources of information: How many times does the word appear in a large collection of text? Does the word appear in a list of common person names in the U.S.? And so on.

Lemmas and Stems We often look at the *lemma* (the dictionary entry) of the word, mapping forms such as *booking*, *booked*, *books* to their common lemma *book*. This mapping is usually performed using lemma lexicons or morphological analyzers, that are available for many languages. The lemma of a word can be ambiguous, and lemmatizing is more accurate when the word is given in context. Lemmatization is a linguistically defined process, and may not work well for forms that are not in the lemmatization lexicon, or for mis-spelling. A coarser process than lemmatization, that can work on any sequence of letters, is called *stemming*. A stemmer maps sequences of words to shorter sequences, based on some language-specific heuristics, such that different inflections will map to the same sequence. Note that the result of stemming need not be a valid word: picture and pictures and pictured will all be stemmed to pictur. Various stemmers exist, with different levels of aggressiveness.

Lexical Resources An additional source of information about word forms are *lexical resources*. These are essentially dictionaries that are meant to be accessed programmatically by machines rather than read by humans. A lexical resource will typically contain information about words, linking them to other words and/or providing additional information.

For example, for many languages there are lexicons that map inflected word forms to their possible morphological analyses (i.e., telling you that a certain word may be either a plural feminine noun or a past-perfect verb). Such lexicons will typically also include lemma information.

A very well-known lexical resource in English is *WordNet* [Fellbaum, 1998]. WordNet is a very large manually curated dataset attempting to capture conceptual semantic knowledge about words. Each word belongs to one or several *synsets*, where each synsets describes a cognitive concept. For example, the word *star* as a noun belongs to the synsets *astronomical celestial body*, *someone who is dazzlingly skilled*, *any celestial body visible from earth* and *an actor who plays a principle role*, among others. The second synset of star contains also the words *ace, adept, champion, sensation, maven, virtuoso*, among others. Synsets are linked to each other by means of semantic relations such as hypernymy and hyponymy (more specific or less specific words). For example, for the first synset of star these would include *sun* and *nova* (hyponyms) and *celestial body* (hypernym). Other semantic relations in WordNet contain antonyms (opposite words) and holonyms and meronyms (part-whole and whole-part relations). WordNet contains information about nouns, verbs, adjectives, and adverbs.

FrameNet [Fillmore et al., 2004] and VerbNet [Kipper et al., 2000] are manually curated lexical resources that focus around verbs, listing for many verbs the kinds of argument they take (i.e., that *giving* involves the core arguments DONOR, RECIPIENT, and THEME (the thing that is being given), and may have non-core arguments such as TIME, PURPOSE, PLACE, and MANNER, among others.

The Paraphrase Database (PPDB) [Ganitkevitch et al., 2013, Pavlick et al., 2015] is a large, automatically created dataset of paraphrases. It lists words and phrases, and for each one provides a list of words and phrases that can be used to mean roughly the same thing.

Lexical resources such as these contain a lot of information, and can serve a good source of features. However, the means of using such symbolic information effectively is task dependent, and often requires non-trivial engineering efforts and/or ingenuity. They are currently not often used in neural network models, but this may change.

Distributional Information Another important source of information about words is *distributional*—which other words behave similar to it in the text? These deserve their own separate treatment, and are discussed in Section 6.2.5 below. In Section 11.8, we discuss how lexical resources can be used to inject knowledge into distributional word vectors that are derived from neural network algorithms.

Features for Text   When we consider a sentence, a paragraph, or a document, the observable features are the counts and the order of the *letters* and the *words* within the text.

Bag of words A very common feature extraction procedures for sentences and documents is the bag-of-words approach (BOW). In this approach, we look at the histogram of the words within the text, i.e., considering each word count as a feature. By generalizing from words to "basic elements," the bag-of-letter-bigrams we used in the language identification example in Section 2.3.1 is an example of the bag-of-words approach.

We can also compute quantities that are directly derived from the words and the letters, such as the *length* of the sentence in terms of number of letters or number of words. When considering individual words, we may of course use the word-based features from above, counting for example the number of words in the document that have a specific prefix or suffix, or compute the ratio of short words (with length below a given length) to long words in a document.

Weighting As before, we can also integrate statistics based on external information, focusing for example on words that appear many times in the given document, yet appear relatively few times in an external set of documents (this will distinguish words that have high counts in the documents because they are generally common, like *a* and *for* from words that have a high count because they relate to the document's topic). When using the bag-of-words approach, it is common to use TF-IDF weighting [Manning et al., 2008, Chapter 6]. Consider a document d which is part of a larger corpus D. Rather than representing each word w in d by its normalized count in the document $\frac{\#_d(w)}{\sum_{w' \in d} \#_d(w')}$ (the **T**erm **F**requency), TF-IDF weighting represent it instead by $\frac{\#_d(w)}{\sum_{w' \in d} \#_d(w')} \times \log \frac{|D|}{|\{d \in D : w \in d\}|}$. The second term is the **I**nverse **D**ocument **F**requency: the inverse of the number of distinct documents in the corpus in which this word occurred. This highlights words that are distinctive of the current text.

Besides words, one may also look at consecutive pairs or triplets of words. These are called *ngrams*. Ngram features are discussed in depth in Section 6.2.4.

Features of Words in Context   When considering a word *within* a sentence or a document, the directly observable features of the word are its position within the sentence, as well as the words or letters surrounding it. Words that are closer to the target word are often more informative about it than words that are further apart.[1]

---

[1]However, note that this is a gross generalization, and in many cases language exhibit a long-range dependencies between words: a word at the end of a text may well be influenced by a word at the beginning.

Windows For this reason, it is often common to focus on the immediate context of a word by considering a *window* surrounding it (i.e., k words to each side, with typical values of k being 2, 5, and 10), and take the features to be the identities of the words within the window (e.g., a feature will be "word X appeared within a window of five words surrounding the target word"). For example, consider the sentence *the brown fox jumped over the lazy dog*, with the target word *jumped*. A window of 2 words to each side will produce the set of features { word=brown, word=fox, word=over, word=the }. The window approach is a version of the bag-of-words approach, but restricted to items within the small window.

The fixed size of the window gives the opportunity to relax the bag-of-word assumption that order does not matter, and take the relative positions of the words in the window into account. This results in *relative-positional features* such as "word X appeared two words to the left of the target word." For example, in the example above the positional window approach will result in the set of features { word-2=brown, word-1=fox, word+1=over, word+2=the }.

Encoding of window-based features as vectors is discussed in Section 8.2.1. In Chapters 14 and 16 we will introduce the biRNN architecture, that generalizes window features by providing a flexible, adjustable, and trainable window.

Position Besides the context of the word, we may be interested in its absolute position within a sentence. We could have features such as "the target word is the 5th word in the sentence," or a binned version indicating more coarse grained categories: does it appear within the first 10 words, between word 10 and 20, and so on.

Features for Word Relations   When considering two words in context, besides the position of each one and the words surrounding them, we can also look at the *distance* between the words and the *identities* of the words that appear between them.

6.2.2   INFERRED LINGUISTIC PROPERTIES

Sentences in natural language have structures beyond the linear order of their words. The structure follows an intricate set of rules that are not directly observable to us. These rules are collectively referred to as syntax, and the study of the nature of these rules and regularities in natural language is the study-object of linguistics.[2] While the exact structure of language is still a mystery, and rules governing many of the more intricate patterns are either unexplored or still open for debate among linguists, a subset of phenomena governing language are well documented and well understood. These include concepts such as word classes (part-of-speech tags), morphology, syntax, and even parts of semantics.

While the linguistic properties of a text are not observable directly from the surface forms of words in sentences and their order, they can be inferred from the sentence string with vary-

---

[2]This last sentence, is, of course, a gross simplification. Linguistics has much wider breadth than syntax, and there are other systems that regulate the human linguistic behavior besides the syntactic one. But for the purpose of this introductory book, this simplistic view will be sufficient. For a more in depth overview, see the further reading recommendations at the end of this section.

ing degrees of accuracy. Specialized systems exist for the prediction of parts of speech, syntactic trees, semantic roles, discourse relations, and other linguistic properties with various degrees of accuracy,[3] and these predictions often serve as good features for further classification problems.

Linguistic Annotation Let's explore some forms of linguistic annotations. Consider the sentence *the boy with the black shirt opened the door with a key*. One level of annotation assigns to each word its *part of speech*:

the	boy	with	the	black	shirt	opened	the	door	with	a	key
DET	NOUN	PREP	DET	ADJ	NOUN	VERB	DET	NOUN	PREP	DET	NOUN

Going further up the chain, we mark *syntactic chunk* boundaries, indicating the *the boy* is a noun phrase.

[$_{NP}$ the boy] [$_{PP}$ with] [$_{NP}$ the black shirt] [$_{VP}$ opened] [$_{NP}$ the door] [$_{PP}$ with] [$_{NP}$ a key]

Note that the word *opened* is marked as a verbal-chunk (VP). This may not seem very useful because we already know its a verb. However, VP chunks may contain more elements, covering also cases such as *will opened* and *did not open*.

The chunking information is local. A more global syntactic structure is a *constituency tree*, also called a *phrase-structure tree*:

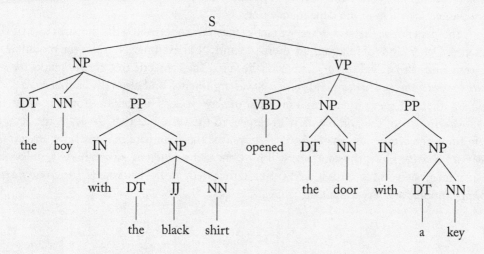

Constituency trees are nested, labeled bracketing over the sentence, indicating the hierarchy of syntactic units: the noun phrase *the boy with the black shirt* is made of the noun

---

[3]Indeed, for many researchers, improving the prediction of these linguistic properties *is* the natural language processing problem they are trying to solve.

phrase *the boy* and the preposition phrase (PP) *with the black shirt*. The latter itself contains the noun phrase *the black shirt*. Having *with a key* nested under the VP and not under the NP *the door* signals that *with a key* modifies the verb *opened* (*opened with a key*) rather than the NP (*a door with a key*).

A different kind of syntactic annotation is a *dependency tree*. Under dependency syntax, each word in the sentence is a modifier of another word, which is called its head. Each word in the sentence is headed by another sentence word, except for the main word, usually a verb, which is the root of the sentence and is headed by a special "root" node.

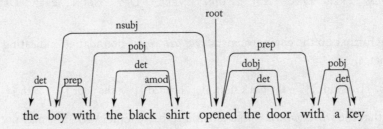

While constituency trees make explicit the grouping of words into phrases, dependency trees make explicit the *modification relations* and *connections* between words. Words that are far apart in the surface form of the sentence may be close in its dependency tree. For example, *boy* and *opened* have four words between them in the surface form, but have a direct *nsubj* edge connecting them in the dependency tree.

The dependency relations are syntactic: they are concerned with the structure of the sentence. Other kinds of relations are more semantic. For example, consider the modifiers of the verb *open*, also called the *arguments* of the verb. The syntactic tree clearly marks *the boy (with the black shirt)*, *the door*, and *with a key* as arguments, and also tells us that *with a key* is an argument of *open* rather than a modifier of *door*. It does not tell us, however, what are the *semantic-roles* of the arguments with respect to the verb, i.e., that *the boy* is the AGENT performing the action, and that *a key* is an INSTRUMENT (compare that to *the boy opened the door with a smile*. Here, the sentence will have the same syntactic structure, but, unless we are in a magical-world, *a smile* is a MANNER rather than an INSTRUMENT. The *semantic role labeling* annotations reveal these structures:

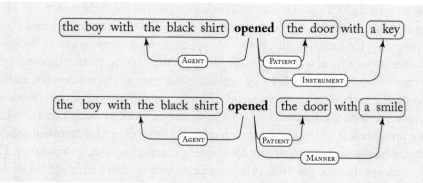

Besides the observable properties (letters, words, counts, lengths, linear distances, frequencies, etc.), we can also look such inferred linguistic properties of words, sentences, and documents. For example, we could look at the *part-of-speech tag* (POS) of a word within a document (Is it a noun, a verb, adjective, or a determiner?), the *syntactic role* of a word (Does it serve as a subject or an object of a verb? Is it the main verb of the sentence? Is it used as an adverbial modifier?), or the *semantic role* of it (e.g., in "the key opened the door," *key* acts as an INSTRUMENT, while in "the boy opened the door" *boy* is an AGENT). When given two words in a sentence, we can consider the *syntactic dependency tree* of the sentence, and the subtree or paths that connect the two words within the this tree, as well as properties of that path. Words that are far apart in the sentence in terms of the number of words separating them can be close to each other in the syntactic structure.

When moving beyond the sentence, we may want to look at the *discourse relations* that connect sentences together, such as ELABORATION, CONTRADICTION, CAUSEEFFECT, and so on. These relations are often expressed by discourse-connective words such as *moreover, however,* and *and*, but are also expressed with less direct cues.

Another important phenomena is that of *anaphora*—consider the sentence sequence *the boy opened the door with a key. It₁ wasn't locked and he₁ entered the room. He₂ saw a man. He₃ was smiling.* Anaphora resolution (also called *coreference resolution*) will tell us that It₁ refers to the door (and not the key or the boy), he₂ refers to the boy and he₃ is likely to refer to the man.

Part of speech tags, syntactic roles, discourse relations, anaphora, and so on are concepts that are based on linguistic theories that were developed by linguists over a long period of time, with the aim of capturing the rules and regularities in the very messy system of the human language. While many aspects of the rules governing language are still open for debate, and others may seem overly rigid or simplistic, the concepts explored here (and others) do indeed capture a wide and important array of generalizations and regularities in language.

Are linguistic concepts needed? Some proponents of deep-learning argue that such inferred, manually designed, linguistic properties are not needed, and that the neural network will learn these intermediate representations (or equivalent, or better ones) on its own. The jury is still out on this. My current personal belief is that many of these linguistic concepts can indeed be inferred by the network on its own if given enough data and perhaps a push in the right direction.[4] However, for many other cases we do not have enough training data available for the task we care about, and in these cases providing the network with the more explicit general concepts can be very valuable. Even if we do have enough data, we may want to focus the network on certain aspects of the text and hint to it that it should ignore others, by providing the generalized concepts in addition to, or even instead of, the surface forms of the words. Finally, even if we do not use these linguistic properties as input features, we may want to help guide the network by using them as additional supervision in a multi-task learning setup (see Chapter 20) or by designing network architecture or training paradigms that are more suitable for learning certain linguistic phenomena. Overall, we see enough evidence that the use of linguistic concepts help improve language understanding and production systems.

Further Reading   When dealing with natural language text, it is well advised to be aware of the linguistic concepts beyond letters and words, as well as of the current computational tools and resources that are available. This book barely scratches the surface on this topic. The book of Bender [2013] provides a good and concise overview of linguistic concepts directed at computational-minded people. For a discussion on current NLP methods, tools, and resources see the book by Jurafsky and Martin [2008] as well as the various specialized titles in this series.[5]

6.2.3   CORE FEATURES VS. COMBINATION FEATURES

In many cases, we are interested in a conjunction of features occurring together. For example, knowing that the two indicators "the word *book* appeared in a window" and "the part-of-speech VERB appeared in a window" is strictly less informative than knowing "the word *book* with the assigned part of speech VERB appeared in a window." Similarly, if we assign a distinct parameter weight for each indicator feature (as is the case in linear models), then knowing that the two distinct features "word in position -1 is *like*," "word in position -2 is *not*" occur is almost useless compared to the very indicative combined indicator "word in position -1 is *like* and word in position -2 is *not*." Similarly, knowing that a document contains the word *Paris* is an indication toward the document being in the TRAVEL category, and the same holds for the word *Hilton*. However, if the document contains both words, it is an indication away from the TRAVEL category and toward the CELEBRITY or GOSSIP categories.

Linear models cannot assign a score to a conjunction of events (X occurred and Y occurred and ...) that is not a sum of their individual scores, unless the conjunction itself is modeled as its own feature. Thus, when designing features for a linear model, we must define not only the *core features* but also many *combination features*.[6] The set of possible combination is very large, and

---

[4]See, for example, the experiment in Section 16.1.2 in which a neural networks learns the concept of subject-verb agreement in English, inferring the concepts of nouns, verbs, grammatical number and some hierarchical linguistics structures.

[5]Syntactic dependency structures are discussed in Kübler et al. [2008] and semantic roles in Palmer et al. [2010].

[6]This is a direct manifestation of the XOR problem discussed in Chapter 3, and the manually defined combination-features are the mapping function ϕ that maps the nonlinearly separable vectors of core-features to a higher dimensional space in which the data is more likely to be separable by a linear model.

human expertise, coupled with trial and error, is needed in order to construct a set of combinations that is both informative and relatively compact. Indeed, a lot of effort has gone into design decisions such as "include features of the form word at position -1 is X and at position +1 is Y but do not include features of the form word at position -3 is X and at position -1 is Y."

Neural networks provide nonlinear models, and do not suffer from this problem. When using a neural network such as a multi-layer perceptron (Chapter 4), the model designer can specify only the set of core features, and rely on the network training procedure to pick up on the important combinations on its own. This greatly simplifies the work of the model designer. In practice, neural networks indeed manage to learn good classifiers based on core features only, sometimes surpassing the best linear classifier with human-designed feature combinations. However, in many other cases a linear classifier with a good hand-crafted feature-set is hard to beat, with the neural network models with core features getting close to but not surpassing the linear models.

6.2.4   NGRAM FEATURES

A special case of feature combinations is that of *ngrams*—consecutive word sequences of a given length. We already saw letter-bigram features in the language classification case (Chapter 2). Word-bigrams, as well as *trigrams* (sequences of three items) of letters or words are also common. Beyond that, 4-grams and 5-grams are sometimes used for letters, but rarely for words due to sparsity issues. It should be intuitively clear why word-bigrams are more informative than individual words: it captures structures such as *New York*, *not good*, and *Paris Hilton*. Indeed, a bag-of-bigrams representation is much more powerful than bag-of-words, and in many cases proves very hard to beat. Of course, not all bigrams are equally informative, bigrams such as *of the*, *on a*, *the boy*, etc. are very common and, for most tasks, not more informative than their individual components. However, it is very hard to know a-priori which ngrams will be useful for a given task. The common solution is to include all ngrams up to a given length, and let the model regularization discard of the less interesting ones by assigning them very low weights.

Note that vanilla neural network architectures such as the MLP *cannot* infer ngram features from a document on their own in the general case: a multi-layer perceptron fed with a bag-of-words feature vector of a document could learn combinations such as "word X appear in the document and word Y appears in the document" but not "the bigram X Y appears in the document." Thus, ngram features are useful also in the context of nonlinear classification.

Multi-layer perceptrons *can* infer ngrams when applied to a fixed size windows with positional information—the combination of "word at position -1 is X" and "word at position -2 is Y" is in effect the bigram XY. More specialized neural network architectures such as convolutional networks (Chapter 13) are designed to find informative ngram features for a given task based on a sequence of words of varying lengths. Bidirectional RNNs (Chapters 14 and 16) generalize the ngram concept even further, and can be sensitive to informative ngrams of varying lengths, as well as ngrams with gaps in them.

6.2.5   DISTRIBUTIONAL FEATURES

Up until now our treatment of words was as discrete and unrelated symbols: the words *pizza*, *burger*, and *chair* are all equally similar (and equally dis-similar) to each other as far as the algorithm is concerned.

We did achieve some form of generalization across word types by mapping them to coarser-grained categories such as parts-of-speech or syntactic roles ("*the, a, an, some* are all determiners"); generalizing from inflected words forms to their lemmas ("*book, booking, booked* all share the lemma *book*"); looking at membership in lists or dictionaries ("*John, Jack,* and *Ralph* appear in a list of common U.S. first names"); or looking at their relation to other words using lexical resources such as WordNet. However, these solutions are quite limited: they either provide very coarse grained distinctions, or otherwise rely on specific, manually compiled dictionaries. Unless we have a specialized list of foods we will not learn that *pizza* is more similar to *burger* than it is to *chair*, and it will be even harder to learn that *pizza* is more similar to *burger* than it is to *icecream*.

The *distributional hypothesis* of language, set forth by Firth [1957] and Harris [1954], states that the meaning of a word can be inferred from the contexts in which it is used. By observing co-occurrence patterns of words across a large body of text, we can discover that the contexts in which *burger* occur are quite similar to those in which *pizza* occurs, less similar to those in which *icecream* occurs, and very different from those in which *chair* occurs. Many algorithms were derived over the years to make use of this property, and learn generalizations of words based on the contexts in which they occur. These can be broadly categorized into *clustering-based methods*, which assign similar words to the same cluster and represent each word by its cluster membership [Brown et al., 1992, Miller et al., 2004], and to *embedding-based methods* which represent each word as a vector such that similar words (words having a similar distribution) have similar vectors [Collobert and Weston, 2008, Mikolov et al., 2013b]. Turian et al. [2010] discuss and compare these approaches.

These algorithms uncover many facets of similarity between words, and can be used to derive good word features: for example, one could replace words by their cluster ID (e.g., replacing both the words *June* and *aug* by cluster732), replace rare or unseen words with the common word most similar to them, or just use the word vector itself as the representation of the word.

However, care must be taken when using such word similarity information, as it can have unintended consequences. For example, in some applications it is very useful to treat London and Berlin as similar, while for others (for example when booking a flight or translating a document) the distinction is crucial.

We will discuss word embeddings methods and the use of word vectors in more detail in Chapters 10 and 11.

CHAPTER 7

Case Studies of NLP Features

After discussing the different sources of information available for us for deriving features from natural language text, we will now explore examples of concrete NLP classification tasks, and suitable features for them. While the promise of neural networks is to alleviate the need for manual feature engineering, we still need to take these sources of information into consideration when designing our models: we want to make sure that the network we design can make effective use of the available signals, either by giving it direct access to them by use of feature-engineering; by designing the network architecture to expose the needed signals; or by adding them as an additional loss signals when training the models.[1]

7.1 DOCUMENT CLASSIFICATION: LANGUAGE IDENTIFICATION

In the language identification task, we are given a document or a sentence, and want to classify it into one of a fixed set of languages. As we saw in Chapter 2, a *bag of letter-bigrams* is a very strong feature representation for this task. Concretely, each possible letter-bigram (or each letter bigram appearing at least k times in at least one language) is a core feature, and the value of a core feature for a given document is the count of that feature in the document.

A similar task is the one of *encoding detection*. Here, a good feature representation is a bag-of byte-bigrams.

7.2 DOCUMENT CLASSIFICATION: TOPIC CLASSIFICATION

In the Topic Classification task, we are given a document and need to classify it into one of a predefined set of topics (e.g., Economy, Politics, Sports, Leisure, Gossip, Lifestyle, Other).

Here, the letter level is not very informative, and our basic units will be words. Word order is not very informative for this task (except maybe for consecutive word pairs such as bigrams). Thus, a good set of features will be the *bag-of-words* in the document, perhaps accompanied by a *bag-of-word-bigrams* (each word and each word-bigram is a core feature).

---

[1]Additionally, linear or log-linear models with manually designed features are still very effective for many tasks. They can be very competitive in terms of accuracy, as well as being very easy to train and deploy at scale, and easier to reason about and debug than neural networks. If nothing else, such models should be considered as strong baselines for whatever networks you are designing.

If we do not have many training examples, we may benefit from pre-processing the document by replacing each word with its lemma. We may also replace or supplement words by distributional features such as word clusters or word-embedding vectors.

When using a linear classifier, we may want to also consider word pairs, i.e., consider each pair of words (not necessarily consecutive) that appear in the same document as a core feature. This will result in a huge number of potential core features, and the number will need to be trimmed down by designing some heuristic, such as considering only word pairs which appear in a specified number of documents. Nonlinear classifiers alleviate this need.

When using a bag-of-words, it is sometimes useful to weight each word with proportion to its informativeness, for example using TF-IDF weighting (Section 6.2.1). However, the learning algorithm is often capable of coming up with the weighting on its own. Another option is to use word indicators rather than word counts: each word in the document (or each word above a given count) will be represented once, regardless of its number of occurrences in the document.

7.3   DOCUMENT CLASSIFICATION: AUTHORSHIP ATTRIBUTION

In the authorship attribution task [Koppel et al., 2009] we are given a text and need to infer the identify of its author (from a fixed set of possible authors), or other characteristics of the author of the text, such as their gender, their age or their native language.

The kind of information used to solve this task is very different than that of topic classification—the clues are subtle, and involve stylistic properties of the text rather than content words.

Thus, our choice of features should shy away from content words and focus on more stylistic properties.[2] A good set for such tasks focus on *parts of speech (POS) tags* and *function words*. These are words like *on, of, the, and, before* and so on that do not carry much content on their own but rather serve to connect to content-bearing words and assign meanings to their compositions, as well as pronouns (*he, she, I, they*, etc.) A good approximation of function words is the list of top-300 or so most frequent words in a large corpus. By focusing on such features, we can learn to capture subtle stylistic variations in writing, that are unique to an author and very hard to fake.

A good feature set for authorship attribution task include a bag-of-function-words-and-pronouns, bag-of-POS-tags, and bags of POS bigrams, trigrams, and 4grams. Additionally, we may want to consider the *density* of function words (i.e., the ratio between the number of function words and content words in a window of text), a bag of bigrams of function words after removing the content words, and the distributions of the distances between consecutive function words.

---

[2]One could argue that for age or gender identification, we may as well observe also the content-words, as there are strong correlation between age and gender of a person and the topics they write about and the language register they use. This is generally true, but if we are interested in a forensic or adversarial setting in which the author has an incentive to hide their age or gender, we better not rely on content-based features, as these are rather easy to fake, compared to the more subtle stylistic cues.

7.4   WORD-IN-CONTEXT: PART OF SPEECH TAGGING

In the parts-of-speech tagging task, we are given a sentence, and need to assign the correct part-of-speech to each word in the sentence. The parts-of-speech come from a pre-defined set, for this example assume we will be using the tagset of the *Universal Treebank Project* [McDonald et al., 2013, Nivre et al., 2015], containing 17 tags.[3]

Part-of-speech tagging is usually modeled as a structured task—the tag of the first word may depend on the tag of the third one—but it can be approximated quite well by classifying each word in isolation into a POS-tag based on a window of two words to each side of the word. If we tag the words in a fixed order, for example from left to right, we can also condition each tagging prediction on tag predictions made on previous tags. Our feature function when classifying a word w_i has access to all the words in the sentence (and their letters) as well as all the previous tagging decisions (i.e., the assigned tags for words $w_1, \ldots, w_{i-1}$). Here, we discuss features as if they are used in an isolated classification task. In Chapter 19 we discuss the structured learning case—using the same set of features.

The sources of information for the POS-tagging task can be divided into intrinsic cues (based on the word itself) and extrinsic cues (based on its context). Intrinsic cues include the identify of the word (some words are more likely than others to be nouns, for example), prefixes, suffixes, and orthographic shape of the word (in English, words ending in -ed are likely past-tense verbs, words starting with un- are likely to be adjectives, and words starting with a capital letter are likely to be proper names), and the frequency of the word in a large corpus (for example, rare words are more likely to be nouns). Extrinsic cues include the word identities, prefixes, and suffixes of words surrounding the current word, as well as the part-of-speech prediction for the previous words.

Overlapping features   If we have the word form as a feature, why do we need the prefixes and suffixes? After all they are deterministic functions of the word. The reason is that if we encounter a word that we have not seen in training (*out of vocabulary* or *OOV* word) or a word we've seen only a handful of times in training (*a rare word*), we may not have robust enough information to base a decision on. In such cases, it is good to back-off to the prefixes and suffixes, which can provide useful hints. By including the prefix and suffix features also for words that are observed many times in training, we allow the learning algorithms to better adjust their weights, and hopefully use them properly when encountering OOV words.

---

[3] adjective, adposition, adverb, auxiliary verb, coordinating conjunction, determiner, interjection, noun, numeral, particle, pronoun, proper noun, punctuation, subordinating conjunction, symbol, verb, other.

An example of a good set of core features for POS tagging is:

- word=X

- 2-letter-suffix=X

- 3-letter-suffix=X

- 2-letter-prefix=X

- 3-letter-prefix=X

- word-is-capitalized

- word-contains-hyphen

- word-contains-digit

- for P in $[-2, -1, +1, +2]$:

    - Word at position P=X
    - 2-letter-suffix of word at position P=X
    - 3-letter-suffix of word at position P=X
    - 2-letter-prefix of word at position P=X
    - 3-letter-prefix of word at position P=X
    - word at position P=X is capitalized
    - word at position P=X contains hyphen
    - word at position P=X contains digit

- Predicted POS of word at position -1=X

- Predicted POS of word at position -2=X

In addition to these, distributional information such as word clusters or word-embedding vectors of the word and of surrounding words can also be useful, especially for words not seen in the training corpus, as words with similar POS-tags tend to occur in more similar contexts to each other than words of different POS-tags.

7.5   WORD-IN-CONTEXT: NAMED ENTITY RECOGNITION

In the named-entity recognition (NER) task we are given a document and need to find named entities such as *Milan*, *John Smith*, *McCormik Industries*, and *Paris*, as well as to categorize them into a pre-defined set of categories such as LOCATION, ORGANIZATION, PERSON, or OTHER. Note that this task is context dependent, as Milan can be a location (the city) or an organization (a sports team, "Milan played against Barsa Wednesday evening"), and Paris can be the name of a city or a person.

A typical input to the problem would be a sentence such as:

John Smith , president of McCormik Industries visited his niece Paris in Milan , reporters say .

and the expected output would be:

[PER John Smith] , president of [ORG McCormik Industries] visited his niece [PER Paris] in [LOC Milan], reporters say .

While NER is a *sequence segmentation task*—it assigns labeled brackets over non-overlapping sentence spans—it is often modeled as a sequence tagging task, like POS-tagging. The use of tagging to solve segmentation tasks is performed using *BIO encoded tags*.[4] Each word is assigned one of the following tags, as seen in Table 7.1:

Table 7.1: BIO tags for named entity recognition

Tag	Meaning
O	Not part of a named entity
B-PER	First word of a person name
I-PER	Continuation of a person name
B-LOC	First word of a location name
I-LOC	Continuation of a location name
B-ORG	First word of an organization name
I-ORG	Continuation of an organization name
B-MISC	First word of another kind of named entity
I-MISC	Continuation of another kind of named entity

---

[4]Variants on the BIO tagging scheme are explored in the literature, and some perform somewhat better than it. See Lample et al. [2016], Ratinov and Roth [2009].

The sentence above would be tagged as:

John/B-PER Smith/I-PER ,/O president/O of/O McCormik/B-ORG Industries/I-ORG visited/O his/O niece/O Paris/B-PER in/O Milan/B-LOC ,/O reporters/O say/O ./O

The translation from non-overlapping segments to BIO tags and back is straightforward.

Like POS-tagging, the NER task is a structured one, as tagging decisions for different words interact with each other (it is more likely to remain within the same entity type than to switch, it is more likely to tag "John Smith Inc." as B-ORG I-ORG I-ORG than as B-PER I-PER B-ORG). However, we again assume it can be approximated reasonably well using independent classification decisions.

The core feature set for the NER task is similar to that of the POS-tagging task, and relies on words within a 2-words window to each side of the focus word. In addition to the features of the POS-tagging task which are useful for NER as well (e.g., -ville is a suffix indicating a location, Mc- is a prefix indicating a person), we may want to consider also the identities of the words that surround *other* occurrences of the same word in the text, as well as indicator functions that check if the word occurs in pre-compiled lists of persons, locations and organizations. Distributional features such word clusters or word vectors are also extremely useful for the NER task. For a comprehensive discussion on features for NER, see Ratinov and Roth [2009].

7.6   WORD IN CONTEXT, LINGUISTIC FEATURES: PREPOSITION SENSE DISAMBIGUATION

Prepositions, words like *on*, *in*, *with*, and *for*, serve for connecting predicates with their arguments and nouns with their prepositional modifiers. Preposions are very common, and also very ambiguous. Consider, for example, the word *for* in the following sentences.

(1)   a.   We went there *for* lunch.
      b.   He paid *for* me.
      c.   We ate *for* two hours.
      d.   He would have left *for* home, but it started raining.

The word *for* plays a different role in each of them: in (a) it indicates a PURPOSE in (b) a BENEFICIARY, in (c) a DURATION and in (d) a LOCATION.

In order to fully understand the meaning of a sentence, one should arguablly know the correct senses of the prepositions within it. The *preposition-sense disambiguation* task deals with assigning the correct sense to a preposition in context, from a finite inventory of senses. Schneider et al. [2015, 2016] discuss the task, present a unified sense inventory that covers many prepositions, and provide a small annotated corpus of sentences from online reviews, covering 4,250 preposition mentions, each annotated with its sense.[5]

Which are a good set of features for the preposition sense disambiguation task? We follow here the feature set inspired by the work of Hovy et al. [2010].

Obviously, the preposition itself is a useful feature (the distribution of possible senses for *in* is very different from the distribution of senses for *with* or *about*, for example). Besides that, we will look in the context in which the word occurs. A fixed window around the preposition may not be ideal in terms of information content, thought. Consider, for example, the following sentences.

(2)   a.   He liked the round object *from* the very first time he saw it.
       b.   He saved the round object *from* him the very first time they saw it.

The two instances of *from* have different senses, but most of the words in a window around the word are either not informative or even misleading. We need a better mechanism for selecting informative contexts. One option would be to use a heuristic, such as "the first verb on the left" and "the first noun on the right." These will capture the triplets (liked,from,time) and (saved,from,him), which indeed contain the essence of the preposition sense. In linguistic terms, we say that this heuristic helps us capture the *governor* and the and *object* of the preposition. By knowing the identify of the preposition, as well as its governor and objects, humans can in many cases infer the sense of the preposition, using reasoning processes about the fine-grained semantics of the words. The heuristic for extracting the object and governor requires the use of a POS-tagger in order to identify the nouns and verbs. It is also somewhat brittle—it is not hard to imagine cases in which it fails. We could refine the heuristic with more rules, but a more robust approach would be to use a dependency parser: the governor and object information is easily readable from the syntactic tree, reducing the need for complex heuristics:

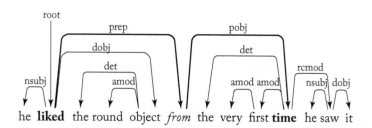

Of course, the parser used for producing the tree may be wrong too. For robustness, we may look at both the governor and object extracted from the parser *and* the governor and object extracted using the heuristic, and use all four as sources for features (i.e., parse_gov=X, parse_obj=Y,

---

[5]Earlier sense inventories and annotated corpora for the task are also available. See, for example, Litkowski and Hargraves [2005, 2007], Srikumar and Roth [2013a].

heur_gov=Z, heur_obj=W), letting the learning process decide which of the sources is more reliable and how to balance between them.

After extracting the governor and the object (and perhaps also words adjacent to the governor and the object), we can use them as the basis for further feature extraction. For each of the items, we could extract the following pieces of information:

- the actual *surface form* of the word;

- the *lemma* of the word;

- the *part-of-speech* of the word;

- *prefixes* and *suffixes* of the word (indicating adjectives of degree, number, order, etc such as *ultra-*, *poly-*, *post-*, as well as some distinctions between agentive and non-agentive verbs); and

- *word cluster* or *distributional vector* of the word.

If we allow the use of external lexical resources and don't mind greatly enlarging the feature space, Hovy et al. [2010] found the use of *WordNet-based features* to be helpful as well. For each of the governor and the object, we could extract many WordNet indicators, such as:

- does the word have a WordNet entry?;

- hypernyms of the first synset of the word;

- hypernyms of all synsets of the word;

- synonyms for first synset of the word;

- synonyms for all synsets of the word;

- all terms in the definition of the word;

- the super-sense of the word (super-senses, also called lexicographer-files in the WordNet jargon, are relatively high levels in the WordNet hierarchy, indicating concepts such as being an animal, being a body part, being an emotion, being food, etc.); and

- various other indicators.

This process may result in tens or over a hundred of core features for each preposition instance, i.e., hyper_1st_syn_gov=a, hyper_all_syn_gov=a, hyper_all_syn_gov=b, hyper_all_syn_gov=c, ..., hyper_1st_syn_obj=x, hyper_all_syn_obj=y, ..., term_in_def_gov=q, term_in_def_gov=w, etc.
See the work of Hovy et al. [2010] for the finer details.

The preposition-sense disambiguation task is an example of a high-level semantic classification problem, for which we need a set of features that cannot be readily inferred from the surface forms, and can benefit from linguistic pre-processing (i.e., POS-tagging and syntactic parsing) as well as from selected pieces of information from manually curated semantic lexicons.

7.7 RELATION BETWEEN WORDS IN CONTEXT: ARC-FACTORED PARSING

In the *dependency parsing* task, we are given a sentence and need to return a *syntactic dependency tree* over it, such as the tree in Figure 7.1. Each word is assigned a parent word, except for the main word of the sentence whose parent is a special *ROOT* symbol.

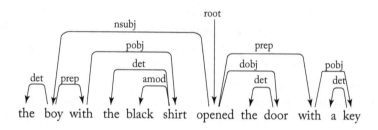

Figure 7.1: Dependency tree.

For more information on the dependency parsing task, its linguistic foundations and approaches to its solution, see the book by Kübler et al. [2008].

One approach to modeling the task is the arc-factored approach [McDonald et al., 2005], where each of the possible n^2 word-word relations (arcs) is assigned a score independent of the others, and then we search for the valid tree with the maximal overall score. The score assignment is made by a trained scoring function ARCSCORE($h, m, sent$), receiving a sentence as well as the indices h and m of two words within it that are considered as candidates for attachment (h is the index of the candidate head-word and m is the index of the candidate modifier). Training the scoring function such that it works well with the search procedure will be discussed in Chapter 19. Here, we focus on the features used in the scoring function.

Assume a sentence of n words $w_{1:n}$ and their corresponding parts-of-speech $p_{1:n}$, $sent = (w_1, w_2, \ldots, w_n, p_1, p_2, \ldots, p_n)$ When looking at an arc between words w_h and w_m, we can make use of the following pieces of information.

We begin with the usual suspects:

- The word form (and POS-tag) of the *head word.*

- The word form (and POS-tag) of the *modifier word.* (Some words are less likely to be heads or modifiers, regardless to who they are connected to. For example, determiners ("the," "a") are often modifiers, and are never heads.)

- Words (POS-tags) in a window of two words to each side of the head word, including the relative positions.

- Words (POS-tags) in a window of two words to each side of the modifier word, including the relative positions. (The window information is needed to give some context to the word. Words behave differently in different contexts.)

We use the parts-of-speech as well as the word forms themselves. Word-forms give us very specific information (for example, that *cake* is a good candidate object for *ate*), while the parts-of-speech provide lower level syntactic information that is more generalizable (for example, that determiners and adjectives are good modifiers for nouns, and that nouns are good modifiers for verbs). As the training corpora for dependency-trees are usually rather limited in size, it could be a good idea to supplement or replace the words using distributional information, in the form of word clusters or pre-trained word embeddings, that will capture generalizations across similar words, also for words that may not have a good coverage in the training data.

We do not look at prefixes and suffixes of words, because these are not directly relevant to the parsing task. While the affixes of words indeed carry important syntactic information (is the word likely to be a noun? a past verb?), this information is already available to us in through the POS-tags. If we were parsing without access to POS-tag features (for example, if the parser was in charge for both parsing and POS-tag assignments), it would be wise to include the suffix information as well.

Of course, if we use a linear classifier, we need to take care also of *feature combinations,* with features such as "head candidate word is X and modifier word candidate is Y and head part-of-speech is Z and the word before the modifier word is W." Indeed, it is common for dependency parsers based on linear models to have hundreds of such feature combinations.

In addition to these usual suspects, it is also informative to consider the following.

- The *distance* between words w_h and w_m in the sentence, $dist = |h - m|$. Some distances are more likely to stand in a dependency relation than others.

- The *direction* between the words. In English, assume w_m is a determiner ("the") and w_h is a noun ("boy"), it is quite likely that there will be an arc between them if $m < h$ and very unlikely if $m > h$.

- All the words (POS-tags) of words that appear *between* the head and the modifier words in the sentence. This information is useful as it hints at possible competing attachments.

For example, a determiner at w_m is likely to modify a noun at $w_{h>m}$, but not if a word w_k ($m < k < h$) between them is also a determiner. Note that the number of words between the head and the modifier is potentially unbounded (and also changes from instance to instance) and so we need a way to encode a variable number of features, hinting at a bag-of-words approach.

CHAPTER 8

From Textual Features to Inputs

In Chapters 2 and 4 we discussed classifiers that accept feature vectors as input, without getting into much details about the contents of these vectors. In Chapters 6 and 7 we discussed the sources of information which can serve as the core features for various natural language tasks. In this chapter, we discuss the details of going from a list of core-features to a feature-vector that can serve as an input to a classifier.

To recall, in Chapters 2 and 4 we presented machine-trainable models (either linear, log-linear, or multi-layer perceptron). The models are parameterized functions $f(x)$ that take as input a d_{in} dimensional vector x and produce a d_{out} dimensional output vector. The function is often used as a *classifier*, assigning the input x a degree of membership in one or more of d_{out} classes. The function can be either simple (for a linear model) or more complex (for arbitrary neural networks). In this chapter we focus on the input, x.

8.1 ENCODING CATEGORICAL FEATURES

When dealing with natural language, most of the features represent discrete, categorical features such as words, letters, and part-of-speech tags. How do we encode such categorical data in a way which is amenable for use by a statistical classifier? We discuss two options, *one-hot encodings* and *dense embedding vectors*, as well as the trade-offs and the relations between them.

8.1.1 ONE-HOT ENCODINGS

In linear and log-linear models of the form $f(x) = xW + b$, it is common to think in term of indicator functions, and assign a unique dimension for each possible feature. For example, when considering a bag-of-words representation over a vocabulary of 40,000 items, x will be a 40,000-dimensional vector, where dimension number 23,227 (say) corresponds to the word *dog*, and dimension number 12,425 corresponds to the word *cat*. A document of 20 words will be represented by a very sparse 40,000-dimensional vector in which at most 20 dimensions have non-zero values. Correspondingly, the matrix W will have 40,000 rows, each corresponding to a particular vocabulary word. When the core features are the words in a 5 words window surrounding and including a target word (2 words to each side) with positional information, and a vocabulary of 40,000 words (that is, features of the form word-2=dog or word0=sofa), x will be a 200,000-dimensional vector with 5 non-zero entries, with dimension number 19,234 corresponding to (say) word-2=dog and dimension number 143,167 corresponding to word0=sofa. This is called a *one-hot* encoding, as each dimension corresponds to a unique feature, and the resulting feature vector can be thought of as a combination of high-dimensional indicator vectors in which a single dimension has a value of 1 and all others have a value of 0.

8.1.2   DENSE ENCODINGS (FEATURE EMBEDDINGS)

Perhaps the biggest conceptual jump when moving from sparse-input linear models to deeper nonlinear models is to stop representing each feature as a unique dimension in a one-hot representation, and representing them instead as dense vectors. That is, each core feature is *embedded* into a d dimensional space, and represented as a vector in that space.[1] The dimension d is usually much smaller than the number of features, i.e., each item in a vocabulary of 40,000 items (encoded as 40,000-dimensional one-hot vectors) can be represented as 100 or 200 dimensional vector. The embeddings (the vector representation of each core feature) are treated as parameters of the network, and are trained like the other parameters of the function f. Figure 8.1 shows the two approaches to feature representation.

The general structure for an NLP classification system based on a feed-forward neural network is thus.

1. Extract a set of core linguistic features $f_1, \ldots, f_k$ that are relevant for predicting the output class.

2. For each feature f_i of interest, retrieve the corresponding vector $v(f_i)$.

3. Combine the vectors (either by concatenation, summation, or a combination of both) into an input vector x.

4. Feed x into a nonlinear classifier (feed-forward neural network).

The biggest change in the input when moving from linear to deeper classifier is, then, the move from sparse representations in which each feature is its own dimension, to a dense representation in which each feature is mapped to a vector. Another difference is that we mostly need to extract only *core features* and not feature combinations. We will elaborate on both these changes briefly.

8.1.3   DENSE VECTORS VS. ONE-HOT REPRESENTATIONS

What are the benefits of representing our features as vectors instead of as unique IDs? Should we always represent features as dense vectors? Let's consider the two kinds of representations.

---

[1]Different feature types may be embedded into different spaces. For example, one may represent word features using 100 dimensions, and part-of-speech features using 20 dimensions.

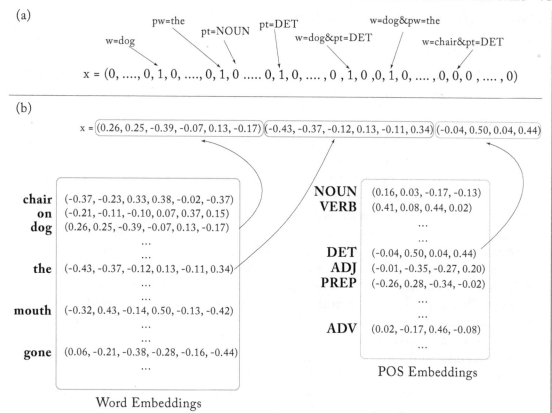

Figure 8.1: **Sparse vs. dense feature representations**. Two encodings of the information: *current word is "dog;" previous word is "the;" previous pos-tag is "DET."* (a) Sparse feature vector. Each dimension represents a feature. Feature combinations receive their own dimensions. Feature values are binary. Dimensionality is very high. (b) Dense, embeddings-based feature vector. Each core feature is represented as a vector. Each feature corresponds to several input vector entries. No explicit encoding of feature combinations. Dimensionality is low. The feature-to-vector mappings come from an embedding table.

One Hot Each feature is its own dimension.

- Dimensionality of one-hot vector is same as number of distinct features.
- Features are completely independent from one another. The feature "word is 'dog' " is as dissimilar to "word is 'thinking' " than it is to "word is 'cat' ".

Dense Each feature is a d-dimensional vector.

- Dimensionality of vector is d.

- Model training will cause similar features to have similar vectors—information is shared between similar features.

One benefit of using dense and low-dimensional vectors is computational: the majority of neural network toolkits do not play well with very high-dimensional, sparse vectors. However, this is just a technical obstacle, which can be resolved with some engineering effort.

The main benefit of the dense representations is in generalization power: if we believe some features may provide similar clues, it is worthwhile to provide a representation that is able to capture these similarities. For example, assume we have observed the word *dog* many times during training, but only observed the word *cat* a handful of times, or not at all. If each of the words is associated with its own dimension, occurrences of *dog* will not tell us anything about the occurrences of *cat*. However, in the dense vectors representation the learned vector for *dog* may be similar to the learned vector for *cat*, allowing the model to share statistical strength between the two events. This argument assumes that we saw enough occurrences of the word *cat* such that its vector will be similar to that of *dog*, or otherwise that "good" vectors are somehow given to us. Such "good" word-vectors (also called *pre-trained embeddings*) can be obtained from a large corpus of text through algorithms that make use of the distributional hypothesis. Such algorithms are discussed in more depth in Chapter 10.

In cases where we have relatively few distinct features in the category, and we believe there are no correlations between the different features, we may use the one-hot representation. However, if we believe there are going to be correlations between the different features in the group (for example, for part-of-speech tags, we may believe that the different verb inflections VB and VBZ may behave similarly as far as our task is concerned) it may be worthwhile to let the network figure out the correlations and gain some statistical strength by sharing the parameters. It may be the case that under some circumstances, when the feature space is relatively small and the training data is plentiful, or when we do not wish to share statistical information between distinct words, there are gains to be made from using the one-hot representations. However, this is still an open research question, and there is no strong evidence to either side. The majority of work (pioneered by Chen and Manning [2014], Collobert and Weston [2008], Collobert et al. [2011]) advocate the use of dense, trainable embedding vectors for all features. For work using neural network architecture with sparse vector encodings, see Johnson and Zhang [2015].

8.2   COMBINING DENSE VECTORS

Each feature corresponds to a dense vector, and the different vectors need to be combined somehow. The prominent options are concatenation, summation (or averaging), and combinations of the two.

8.2.1   WINDOW-BASED FEATURES

Consider the case of encoding a window of size k words to each side of a focus word at position i. Assume $k = 2$; we need to encode the words at positions $i-2$, $i-1$, $i+1$ and $i+2$. Assume the window items are the words a, b, c, and d, and let a,b,c and d be the corresponding word vectors. If we do not care about the relative positions of the words within the window, we will encode the window as a sum: $a + b + c + d$. If we do care about the relative positions, we rather use concatenation: $[a;b;c;d]$. Here, even though a word will have the same vector regardless of its position within the window, the word's position is reflected by its position within the concatenation.[2]

We may not care much about the order, but would want to consider words further away from the context word less than words that are closer to it. This can be encoded as a weighted sum, i.e., $\frac{1}{2}a + b + c + \frac{1}{2}d$.

These encodings can be mixed and matched. Assume we care if the feature occurs before or after the focus word, but do not care about the distance as long as it is within the window. This can be encoded using a combination of summation and concatenation: $[(a + b); (c + d)]$.

A note on notation   When describing network layers that get concatenated vectors x, y, and z as input, some authors use explicit concatenation ($[x; y; z]W + b$) while others use an affine transformation ($xU + yV + zW + b$). If the weight matrices U, V, W in the affine transformation are different[3] than one another, the two notations are equivalent.

8.2.2   VARIABLE NUMBER OF FEATURES: CONTINUOUS BAG OF WORDS

Feed-forward networks assume a fixed dimensional input. This can easily accommodate the case of a feature-extraction function that extracts a fixed number of features: each feature is represented as a vector, and the vectors are concatenated. This way, each region of the resulting input vector corresponds to a different feature. However, in some cases the number of features is not known in advance (for example, in document classification it is common that each word in the sentence is a feature). We thus need to represent an unbounded number of features using a fixed size vector. One way of achieving this is through a so-called *continuous bag of words* (CBOW) representation [Mikolov et al., 2013b]. The CBOW is very similar to the traditional bag-of-words representation in which we discard order information, and works by either summing or averaging the embedding

---

[2]Alternatively, we could have a separate embedding for each word/position pair, i.e., a^1 and a^{-2} will represent the word a when it appears in relative positions $+1$ and -2, respectively. Following this approach, we could then use a sum and still be sensitive to position information: $a^{-2} + b^{-1} + c^{+1} + d^{+2}$. This approach will not share information between instances of words when they appear in different positions, and may be harder to use with externally trained word vectors.

[3]The matrices should be *different* in the sense that a change to one will not be reflected in the others. It is OK for the matrices to happen to share the same values, of course.

vectors of the corresponding features:[4]

$$\text{CBOW}(f_1, \ldots, f_k) = \frac{1}{k} \sum_{i=1}^{k} v(f_i).$$ (8.1)

A simple variation on the CBOW representation is weighted CBOW, in which different vectors receive different weights:

$$\text{WCBOW}(f_1, \ldots, f_k) = \frac{1}{\sum_{i=1}^{k} a_i} \sum_{i=1}^{k} a_i v(f_i).$$ (8.2)

Here, each feature f_i has an associated weight a_i, indicating the relative importance of the feature. For example, in a document classification task, a feature f_i may correspond to a word in the document, and the associated weight a_i could be the word's TF-IDF score.

8.3 RELATION BETWEEN ONE-HOT AND DENSE VECTORS

Representing features as dense vectors is an integral part of the neural network framework, and, consequentially, the differences between using sparse and dense feature representations are subtler than they may appear at first. In fact, using sparse, one-hot vectors as input when training a neural network amounts to dedicating the first layer of the network to learning a dense embedding vector for each feature based on the training data.

When using dense vectors, each categorical feature value f_i is mapped to a dense, d-dimensional vector $v(f_i)$. This mapping is performed through the use of an *embedding layer* or a *lookup layer*. Consider a vocabulary of $|V|$ words, each embedded as a d dimensional vector. The collection of vectors can then be thought of as a $|V| \times d$ embedding matrix $\boldsymbol{E}$ in which each row corresponds to an embedded feature. Let $\boldsymbol{f_i}$ be the one-hot representation of feature f_i, that is, a $|V|$-dimensional vector, which is all zeros except for one index, corresponding to the value of the ith feature, in which the value is 1. The multiplication $\boldsymbol{f_i} \boldsymbol{E}$ will then "select" the corresponding row of $\boldsymbol{E}$. Thus, $v(f_i)$ can be defined in terms of $\boldsymbol{E}$ and $\boldsymbol{f_i}$:

$$v(f_i) = \boldsymbol{f_i} \boldsymbol{E}.$$ (8.3)

And, similarly,

$$\text{CBOW}(f_1, \ldots, f_k) = \sum_{i=1}^{k} (\boldsymbol{f_i} \boldsymbol{E}) = \left(\sum_{i=1}^{k} \boldsymbol{f_i} \right) \boldsymbol{E}.$$ (8.4)

---

[4]Note that if the $v(f_i)$s were one-hot vectors rather than dense feature representations, the CBOW (Equation (8.1)) and WCBOW (Equation (8.2)) would reduce to the traditional (weighted) bag-of-words representations, which is in turn equivalent to a sparse feature-vector representation in which each binary indicator feature corresponds to a unique "word."

The input to the network is then considered to be a collection of one-hot vectors. While this is elegant and well-defined mathematically, an efficient implementation typically involves a hash-based data structure mapping features to their corresponding embedding vectors, without going through the one-hot representation.

Consider a network which uses a "traditional" sparse representation for its input vectors, and no embedding layer. Assuming the set of all available features is V and we have k "on" features $f_1, \ldots, f_k$, $f_i \in V$, the network's input is:

$$x = \sum_{i=1}^{k} f_i \qquad x \in \mathbb{N}_+^{|V|} \tag{8.5}$$

and so the first layer (ignoring the nonlinear activation) is:

$$xW + b = \left(\sum_{i=1}^{k} f_i \right) W + b \tag{8.6}$$

$$W \in \mathbb{R}^{|V| \times d}, \quad b \in \mathbb{R}^d.$$

This layer selects rows of W corresponding to the input features in x and sums them, then adding a bias term. This is very similar to an embedding layer that produces a CBOW representation over the features, where the matrix W acts as the embedding matrix. The main difference is the introduction of the bias vector b, and the fact that the embedding layer typically does not undergo a nonlinear activation but rather is passed on directly to the first layer. Another difference is that this scenario forces each feature to receive a separate vector (row in W) while the embedding layer provides more flexibility, allowing for example for the features "next word is dog" and "previous word is dog" to share the same vector. However, these differences are small and subtle. When it comes to multi-layer feed-forward networks, the difference between dense and sparse inputs is smaller than it may seem at first sight.

8.4   ODDS AND ENDS

8.4.1   DISTANCE AND POSITION FEATURES

The linear distance in between two words in a sentence may serve as an informative feature. For example, in an event extraction task[5] we may be given a trigger word and a candidate argument word, and asked to predict if the argument word is indeed an argument of the trigger. Similarly, in a coreference-resolution task (deciding if which of the previously mentioned entities, if at all, a pronoun such as *he* or *she* refers to), we may be given a pair of (pronoun, candidate word) and asked to predict if they co-refer or not. The distance (or relative position) between the trigger

---

[5]The event extraction task involves identification of events from a predefined set of event types. For example, identification of "purchase" events or "terror-attack" events. Each event type can be triggered by various triggering words (commonly verbs), and has several slots (arguments) that needs to be filled (i.e., Who purchased? What was purchased? At what amount?).

and the argument is a strong signal for these prediction tasks. In the "traditional" NLP setup, distances are usually encoded by binning the distances into several groups (i.e., 1, 2, 3, 4, 5–10, 10+) and associating each bin with a one-hot vector. In a neural architecture, where the input vector is not composed of binary indicator features, it may seem natural to allocate a single input entry to the distance feature, where the numeric value of that entry is the distance. However, this approach is not taken in practice. Instead, distance features are encoded similarly to the other feature types: each bin is associated with a d-dimensional vector, and these distance-embedding vectors are then trained as regular parameters in the network [dos Santos et al., 2015, Nguyen and Grishman, 2015, Zeng et al., 2014, Zhu et al., 2015a].

8.4.2 PADDING, UNKNOWN WORDS, AND WORD DROPOUT

Padding   In some cases your feature extractor will look for things that do not exist. For example, when working with parse trees, you may have a feature looking for the left-most dependant of a given word, but the word may not have any dependents to its left. Perhaps you are looking at the word to positions to the right of the current one, but you are at the end of the sequence and two positions to the right is past the end. What should be done in such situations? When using a bag-of-features approach (i.e., summing) you could just leave the feature out of the sum. When using a concatenation, you may provide a zero-vector in the place. These two approaches work fine technically, but could be sub-optimal for your problem domain. Maybe knowing that there is no left-modifier is informative? The suggested solution would be to add a special symbol (*padding symbol*) to your embedding vocabulary, and use the associated padding vector in these cases. Depending on the problem at hand, you may want to use different padding vectors for different situations (i.e., no-left-modifier may be a different vector than no-right-modifier). Such paddings are important for good prediction performance, and are commonly used. Unfortunately, their use is not often reported, or quickly glossed over, in many research papers.

Unknown Words   Another case where a requested feature vector will not be available is for *out-of-vocabulary* (*OOV*) items. You are looking for the word on the left, observe the value variational, but this word was not a part of your training vocabulary, so you don't have an embedding vector for it. This case is different from the padding case, because the item is there, but you just don't know it. The solution is similar, however, reserve a special symbol, UNK, representing an unknown token, for use in such cases. Again, you may or may not want to use different unknown symbols for different vocabularies. In any case, it is advised to *not* share the padding and the unknown vectors, as they reflect two very different conditions.

Word Signatures   Another technique for dealing with unknown words is backing-off from the word forms to *word signatures*. Using the UNK symbol for unknown words is essentially backing-off from all unknown words to the same signature. But, depending on the task one is trying to solve, one may come up with more fine-grained strategies. For example, we may replace unknown words that end with *ing* with an *___ing* symbol, words that end with *ed* with an *___ed* symbol, words that start with *un* with an *un___* symbol, numbers with a *NUM* symbol, and so on. The list of mappings is hand-crafted to reflect informative backing-off patterns. This approach is often used in practice, but rarely reported in deep-learning papers. While there are approaches that allow to automatically learn such backing-off behavior as part of the model training without needing to manually define the backing-off patterns (see discussion on sub-word units in Section 10.5.5), they are in many cases an overkill and hard-coding the patterns is as effective and more computationally efficient.

Word Dropout   Reserving a special embedding vector for unknown words is not enough—if all the features in the training set have their own embedding vectors, the unknown-word condition will not be observed in training: the associated vector will not receive any updates, and the model will not be tuned to handle the unknown condition. This is equivalent to just using a random vector when an unknown word is encountered at test time. The model needs to be exposed to the unknown-word condition during training. A possible solution would be to replace all (or some) of the features with a low frequency in the training with the unknown symbol (i.e., pre-process the data, replacing words with a frequency below a threshold with *unknown*). This solution works, but has the disadvantage of losing some training data—these rare words will not receive any signal. A better solution is the use of *word-dropout*: when extracting features in training, randomly replace words with the unknown symbol. The replacement should be based on the word's frequency: less frequent words will be more likely to be replaced by the unknown symbol than frequent ones. The random replacement should be decided on runtime—a word that was dropped once may or may not be dropped when it is encountered again (say, in different iterations over the training data). There is no established formula for deciding on the word dropout rate. Works in my group use $\frac{\alpha}{\#(w)+\alpha}$, where α is a parameter for controlling the aggressiveness of the dropout [Kiperwasser and Goldberg, 2016b].

Word Dropout as Regularization   Besides better adaptation to unknown words, word dropout may also be beneficial for preventing overfitting and improving robustness by not letting the model rely too much on any single word being present [Iyyer et al., 2015]. When used this way, word dropout should be applied frequently also to frequent words. Indeed, the suggestion of Iyyer et al. [2015] is to drop word instances according to a Bernoulli trial with probability p, regardless of their frequency. When word dropout is a applied as a regularizer, you may not want to replace the dropped words with the unknown symbol in some circumstances. For example, when the feature representation is a bag-of-words over the document and more than a quarter of the words are dropped, replacing the dropped words with the unknown word symbol will create a feature representation that is not likely to occur at test time, where such a large concentration of unknown words is unlikely.

8.4.3   FEATURE COMBINATIONS

Note that the feature extraction stage in the neural network settings deals only with extraction of *core* features. This is in contrast to the traditional linear-model-based NLP systems in which the feature designer had to manually specify not only the core features of interest but also interactions between them (e.g., introducing not only a feature stating "word is X" and a feature stating "tag is Y" but also combined feature stating "word is X and tag is Y" or sometimes even "word is X, tag is Y and previous word is Z"). The combination features are crucial in linear models because they introduce more dimensions to the input, transforming it into a space where the data-points are closer to being linearly separable. On the other hand, the space of possible combinations is very large, and the feature designer has to spend a lot of time coming up with an effective set of feature combinations. One of the promises of the nonlinear neural network models is that one needs to define only the core features. The nonlinearity of the classifier, as defined by the network structure, is expected to take care of finding the indicative feature combinations, alleviating the need for feature combination engineering.

As discussed in Section 3.3, kernel methods [Shawe-Taylor and Cristianini, 2004], and in particular polynomial kernels [Kudo and Matsumoto, 2003], also allow the feature designer to specify only core features, leaving the feature combination aspect to the learning algorithm. In contrast to neural network models, kernels methods are convex, admitting exact solutions to the optimization problem. However, the computational complexity of classification in kernel methods scales linearly with the size of the training data, making them too slow for most practical purposes, and not suitable for training with large datasets. On the other hand, the computational complexity of classification using neural networks scales linearly with the size of the network, regardless of the training data size.[6]

8.4.4   VECTOR SHARING

Consider a case where you have a few features that share the same vocabulary. For example, when assigning a part-of-speech to a given word, we may have a set of features considering the previous word, and a set of features considering the next word. When building the input to the classifier, we will concatenate the vector representation of the previous word to the vector representation of the next word. The classifier will then be able to distinguish the two different indicators, and treat them differently. But should the two features share the same vectors? Should the vector for "dog:previous-word" be the same as the vector of "dog:next-word"? Or should we assign them two distinct vectors? This, again, is mostly an empirical question. If you believe words behave differently when they appear in different positions (e.g., word X behaves like word Y when in the previous position, but X behaves like Z when in the next position) then it may be a good idea to use two different vocabularies and assign a different set of vectors for each feature type. However,

---

[6]Of course, one still needs to go over the entire dataset when training, and sometimes go over the dataset several times. This makes training time scale linearly with the dataset size. However, each example, in either training or test time, is processed in a constant time (for a given network). This is in contrast to a kernel classifier, in which each example is processed in a time that scales linearly with the dataset size.

if you believe the words behave similarly in both locations, then something may be gained by using a shared vocabulary for both feature types.

8.4.5   DIMENSIONALITY

How many dimensions should we allocate for each feature? Unfortunately, there are no theoretical bounds or even established best-practices in this space. Clearly, the dimensionality should grow with the number of the members in the class (you probably want to assign more dimensions to word embeddings than to part-of-speech embeddings) but how much is enough? In current research, the dimensionality of word-embedding vectors range between about 50 to a few hundreds, and, in some extreme cases, thousands. Since the dimensionality of the vectors has a direct effect on memory requirements and processing time, a good rule of thumb would be to experiment with a few different sizes, and choose a good trade-off between speed and task accuracy.

8.4.6   EMBEDDINGS VOCABULARY

What does it mean to associate an embedding vector for *every* word? Clearly, we cannot associate one with all possible values, and need to restrict ourselves to every value from a finite vocabulary. This vocabulary is usually based on the training set, or, if we use pre-trained embeddings, on the training on which the pre-trained embeddings were trained. It is recommended that the vocabulary will also include a designated UNK symbol, associating a special vector to all words that are not in the vocabulary.

8.4.7   NETWORK'S OUTPUT

For multi-class classification problems with k classes, the network's output is a k-dimensional vector in which every dimension represents the strength of a particular output class. That is, the output remains as in the traditional linear models—scalar scores to items in a discrete set. However, as we saw in Chapter 4, there is a $d \times k$ matrix associated with the output layer. The columns of this matrix can be thought of as d dimensional embeddings of the output classes. The vector similarities between the vector representations of the k classes indicate the model's learned similarities between the output classes.

Historical Note   Representing words as dense vectors for input to a neural network was popularized by Bengio et al. [2003] in the context of neural language modeling. It was introduced to NLP tasks in the pioneering work of Collobert, Weston, and colleagues [Collobert and Weston, 2008, Collobert et al., 2011].[7] Using embeddings for representing not only words but arbitrary features was popularized following Chen and Manning [2014].

---

[7]While the work by Bengio, Collobert, Weston, and colleagues popularized the approaches, they were not the first to use them. Earlier authors that use dense continuous-space vectors for representing word inputs to neural networks include Lee et al. [1992] and Forcada and Ñeco [1997]. Similarly, continuous-space language models were used for machine-translation already by Schwenk et al. [2006].

8.5   EXAMPLE: PART-OF-SPEECH TAGGING

The POS-tagging task (Section 7.4) we are given a sentence of n words $w_1, w_2, \ldots, w_n$, and a word position i, and need to predict the tag of w_i. Assuming we tag the words from left to right, we can also look at the previous tag predictions, $\hat{p}_1, \ldots, \hat{p}_{i-1}$. A list of concrete core features is given in Section 7.4, here we discuss encoding them as an input vector. We need a feature function $x = \phi(s, i)$, getting a sentence s comprised of words and previous tagging decisions and an input position i, and returning a feature vector x. We assume a function $suf(w, k)$ that returns the k-letter suffix of word w, and similarly $pref(w, k)$ that returns the prefix.

We begin with the three boolean questions: *word-is-capitalized*, *word-contains-hyphen* and *word-contains-digit*. The most natural way to encode these is to associate each of them with its own dimension, with a value of 1 if the condition holds for word w_i and 0 otherwise.[8] We will put these in a 3-dimensional vector associated with word i, c_i.

Next, we need to encode words, prefixes, suffixes, and part-of-speech tags in various positions in the window. We associate each word w_i with an embedding vector $v_w(w_i) \in \mathbb{R}^{d_w}$. Similarly, we associate each two-letter suffix $suf(w_i, 2)$ with an embedding vector $v_s(suf(w_i, 2))$ and similarly for three-letter suffixes $v_s(suf(w_i, 3))$, $v_s(\cdot) \in \mathbb{R}^{d_s}$. Prefixes get the same treatment, with embeddings $v_p(\cdot) \in \mathbb{R}^{d_p}$. Finally, each POS-tag receives an embedding $v_t(p_i) \in \mathbb{R}^{d_t}$. Each position i can be associated with a vector v_i of the relevant word information (word form, prefixes, suffixes, Boolean features):

$$v_i = [c_i; v_w(w_i); v_s(suf(w_i, 2)); v_s(suf(w_i, 3)); v_p(pref(w_i, 2)); v_p(pref(w_i, 3))]$$

$$v_i \in \mathbb{R}^{3+d_w+2d_s+2d_p}.$$

Our input vector x is then a concatenation of the following vectors:

$$x = \phi(s, i) = [v_{i-2}; v_{i-1}; v_i; v_{i+1}; v_{i+2}; v_t(p_{i-1}); v_t(p_{i-2})]$$

$$x \in \mathbb{R}^{5(3+d_w+2d_s+2d_p)+2d_t}.$$

Discussion   Note that the words in each position share the same embedding vectors—when creating v_i and v_{i-1} we read from the same embedding tables—and that a vector v_i does not "know" its relative position. However, because of the vector concatenation, the vector x "knows" that which relative position each v is associated with because of its relative position within x. This allows us to share some information between the words in the different positions (the vector of the word *dog* will receive updates when the word is at relative position -2 as well as when it is in relative position $+1$), but will also be treated differently by the model when it appears in different relative positions, because it will be multiplied by a different part of the matrix in the first layer of the network.

---

[8]A value of -1 for the negative condition is also a possible choice.

An alternative approach would be to associate each word-and-position pair with its own embedding, i.e., instead of a single table v_w we will have five embedding tables $v_{w_{-2}}, v_{w_{-1}}, v_{w_0}, v_{w_{+1}}, v_{w_{+2}}$, and use appropriate one for each relative word position. This approach will substantially increase the number of parameters in the model (we will need to learn five-times as many embedding vectors), and will not allow sharing between the different words. It will also be somewhat more wasteful in terms of computation, as in the previous approach we could compute the vector v_i for each word in the sentence once, and then re-use them when looking at different positions i, while in the alternative approach the vectors v_i will need to be re-computed for each position i we are looking at. Finally, it will be harder to use pre-trained word vectors, because the pre-trained vectors do not have location information attached to them. However, this alternative approach would allow us to treat each word position completely independently from the others, if we wanted to.[9]

Another point to consider is capitalization. Should the words *Dog* and *dog* receive different embeddings? While capitalization is an important clue for tagging, in our case the capitalization status of word w_i is already encoded in the boolean features c_i. It is thus advisable to lower-case all words in the vocabulary before creating or querying the embedding table.

Finally, the prefix-2 and prefix-3 features are redundant with each other (one contains the other) and similarly for the suffixes. Do we really need both? Can we make them share information? Indeed, we could use letter embeddings instead of suffix embeddings, and replace the two suffix embeddings with a vector composed of the concatenation of the three last letters in the word. In Section 16.2.1, we will see an alternative approach, that uses character-level recurrent neural networks (RNNs) to capture prefix, suffix and various other properties of the word form.

8.6   EXAMPLE: ARC-FACTORED PARSING

In the Arc-Factored parsing task (Section 7.7) we are given a sentence of n words $w_{1:n}$ and their parts-of-speech $p_{1:n}$, and need to predict a parse tree. Here, we are concerned with the features for scoring a single attachment decision between words w_h and w_m, where w_h is the candidate head-word and w_m is the candidate modifier word.

A list of concrete core features was given in Section 7.7, and here we discuss encoding them as an input vector. We define a feature function $x = \phi(h, m, sent)$ receiving a sentence comprised of word and POS-tags, and the positions of a head-word (h) and a modifier-word (m).

First, we need to consider the head word, its POS-tag, and the words and POS-tags in a five-word window around the head word (two words to each side). We associate each word w in our vocabulary with an embedding vector $v_w(w) \in \mathbb{R}^{d_w}$ and similarly each part-of-speech tag p with an embedding vector $v_t(p) \in \mathbb{R}^{d_t}$. We then define the vector representation of a word at position i to be $v_i = [v_w(w_i); v_t(p_i] \in \mathbb{R}^{d_w + d_t}$, the concatenation of the word and POS vector.

[9]Note that, mathematically, even that last benefit is not a real benefit—when used as an input to a neural network, the first layer could potentially *learn* to look only at certain dimensions of the embeddings when they are used at position -1 and at different dimensions when they are used at position $+2$, achieving the same separation as in the alternative approach. Thus, the original approach is just as expressive as the alternative one, at least in theory.

Then, we associate the head word with a vector h representing the word within its context, and associate the modifier word with a similar vector m:

$$h = [v_{h-2}; v_{h-1}; v_h; v_{h+1}; v_{h+2}]$$

$$m = [v_{m-2}; v_{m-1}; v_m; v_{m+1}; v_{m+2}].$$

This takes care of the elements in the first block of features. Note that, like with the part-of-speech tagging features, this encoding cares about the relative position of each of the context words. If we didn't care about the positions, we could have instead represented the head word as $h' = [v_h; (v_{h-2} + v_{h-1} + v_{h+1} + v_{h+2})]$. This sums the context words into a bag-of-words, losing their positional information, yet, concatenates the context and the focus words, retaining the distinction between them.

We now turn to the *distance* and *direction* features. While we could assign the distance a single dimension with the numeric distance value, it is common to bin the distance into k discrete bins (say 1, 2, 3, 4–7, 8–10, 11+), and associate each bin with a d_d-dimensional embedding. The direction is a Boolean feature, and we represent it as its own dimension.[10] We denote the vector containing the binned distance embedding concatenated with the Boolean direction feature as d.

Finally, we need to represent the words and POS-tags between the head and the modifier. Their number is unbounded and varies between different instances, so we cannot use concatenation. Fortunately, we do not care about the relative positions of the intervening items, so we can use a bag-of-words encoding. Concretely, we represent the between-context words as a vector c defined as the average of the words and POS between vectors:

$$c = \sum_{i=h}^{m} v_i.$$

Note that this sum potentially captures also the number of elements between the head and modifier words, making the distance feature potentially redundant.

Our final representation of an attachment decision to be scored, x is then encoded as the concatenation of the various elements:

---

[10]While this encoding of the dimension is very natural, Pei et al. [2015] follow a different approach in their parser. Perhaps motivated by the importance of distance information, they chose to not mark it as an input feature, but instead to use two different scoring functions, one for scoring left-to-right arcs and another for scoring right-to-left arcs. This gives a lot of power to the direction information, while substantially increasing the number of parameters in the model.

$$x = \phi(h, m, sent) = [h; m; c; d],$$

where:

$$v_i = [v_w(w_i); v_t(p_i)]$$

$$h = [v_{h-2}; v_{h-1}; v_h; v_{h+1}; v_{h+2}]$$

$$m = [v_{m-2}; v_{m-1}; v_m; v_{m+1}; v_{m+2}]$$

$$c = \sum_{i=h}^{m} v_i$$

$$d = \text{binned distance embeddings; direction indicator.}$$

Note how we combine positional window-based features with bag-of-word features by simple concatenation. The neural network layers on top of x can then infer transformation and feature combinations between the elements in the different windows, as well as between the different elements in the bag-of-words representation. The process of creating the representation x—the embedding tables for the words, POS-tags and binned distances, as well as the different concatenations and summations, is also part of the neural network. It is reflected in the computation-graph construction, and its parameters are trained jointly with the network.

The features creation part of the network could be even more complex. For example, if we had reasons to believe that the interactions between a word and its POS-tag, and the interactions within a context window, are more important than the interactions across elements of different entities, we could have reflected that in the input encoding by creating further nonlinear transformations in the feature-encoding process, i.e., replacing v_i with $v_i' = g(v_i W^v + b^v)$ and h with $h' = g([v_{h-2}'; v_{h-1}'; v_h'; v_{h+1}'; v_{h+2}']W^h + b^h)$, and setting: $x = [h'; m'; c; d]$.

CHAPTER 9

Language Modeling

9.1 THE LANGUAGE MODELING TASK

Language modeling is the task of assigning a probability to sentences in a language ("what is the probability of seeing the sentence *the lazy dog barked loudly?*"). Besides assigning a probability to each sequence of words, the language models also assigns a probability for the likelihood of a given word (or a sequence of words) to follow a sequence of words ("what is the probability of seeing the word *barked* after the seeing sequence *the lazy dog?*").[1]

Perfect performance at the language modeling task, namely predicting the next word in a sequence with a number of guesses that is the same as or lower than the number of guesses required by a human participant, is an indication of human level intelligence,[2] and is unlikely to be achieved in the near future. Even without achieving human-level performance, language modeling is a crucial components in real-world applications such as machine-translation and automatic speech recognition, where the system produces several translation or transcription hypotheses, which are then scored by a language model. For these reasons, language modeling plays a central role in natural-language processing, AI, and machine-learning research.

Formally, the task of language modeling is to assign a probability to any sequence of words $w_{1:n}$, i.e., to estimate $P(w_{1:n})$. Using the chain-rule of probability, this can be rewritten as:

$$P(w_{1:n}) = P(w_1)P(w_2 \mid w_1)P(w_3 \mid w_{1:2})P(w_4 \mid w_{1:3})\ldots P(w_n \mid w_{1:n-1}). \quad (9.1)$$

That is, a sequence of word-prediction tasks where each word is predicted conditioned on the preceding words. While the task of modeling a single word based on its left context seem more manageable than assigning a probability score to an entire sentence, the last term in the equation

---

[1]Note that the ability to assign a probability for a word following a sequence of words $p(w_{i_1}|w_1, w_2, \ldots, w_{i-1})$ and the ability to assign a probabilities to arbitrary sequences of words $p(w_1, w_2, \ldots, w_k)$ are equivalent, as one can be derived from the other. Assume we can model probabilities of sequences. Then the conditional probability of a word can be expressed as a fraction of two sequences:

$$p(w_i|w_1, w_2, \ldots, w_{i-1}) = \frac{p(w_1, w_2, \ldots, w_{i-1}, w_i)}{p(w_1, w_2, \ldots, w_{i-1})}.$$

Alternatively, if we could model the conditional probability of a word following a sequence of words, we could use the chain rule to express the probability of sequences as a product of conditional probabilities:

$$p(w_1, \ldots, w_k) = p(w_1|<s>) \times p(w_2|<s>, w_1) \times p(w_3|<s>, w_1, w_2) \times \cdots \times p(w_k|<s>, w_1, \ldots, w_{k-1}),$$

where <s> is a special start-of-sequence symbol.

[2]Indeed, any question can be posed as a next-word-guessing task, e.g., *the answer to question X is ___*. Even without such pathological cases, predicting the next word in the text requires knowledge of syntactic and semantic rules of the language, as well as vast amounts of world knowledge.

still requires conditioning on $n - 1$ words, which is as hard as modeling an entire sentence. For this reason, language models make use of the *markov-assumption*, stating that the future is independent of the past given the present. More formally, a kth order markov-assumption assumes that the next word in a sequence depends only on the last k words:

$$P(w_{i+1} \mid w_{1:i}) \approx P(w_{i+1} \mid w_{i-k:i}).$$

Estimating the probability of the sentence then becomes

$$P(w_{1:n}) \approx \prod_{i=1}^{n} P(w_i \mid w_{i-k:i-1}), \tag{9.2}$$

where $w_{-k+1}, \ldots, w_0$ are defined to be special padding symbols.

Our task is then to accurately estimate $P(w_{i+1} \mid w_{i-k:i})$ given large amounts of text.

While the kth order markov assumption is clearly wrong for any k (sentences can have arbitrarily long dependencies, as a simple example consider the strong dependence between the first word of the sentence being *what* and the last one being *?*), it still produces strong language modeling results for relatively small values of k, and was the dominant approach for language modeling for decades. This chapter discusses kth order language models. In Chapter 14 we discuss language modeling techniques that do not make the markov assumption.

9.2   EVALUATING LANGUAGE MODELS: PERPLEXITY

There are several metrics for evaluating language modeling. The application-centric ones evaluate them in the context of performing a higher-level task, for example by measuring the improvement in translation quality when switching the language-modeling component in a translation system from model A to model B.

A more intrinsic evaluation of language models is using *perplexity* over unseen sentences. Perplexity is an information theoretic measurement of how well a probability model predicts a sample. Low perplexity values indicate a better fit. Given a text corpus of n words $w_1, \ldots, w_n$ (n can be in the millions) and a language model function LM assigning a probability to a word based on its history, the perplexity of LM with respect to the corpus is:

$$2^{-\frac{1}{n} \sum_{i=1}^{n} \log_2 \mathrm{LM}(w_i \mid w_{1:i-1})}.$$

Good language models (i.e., reflective of real language usage) will assign high probabilities to the events in the corpus, resulting in lower perplexity values.

The perplexity measure is a good indicator of the quality of a language model.[3] Perplexities are corpus specific—perplexities of two language models are only comparable with respect to the same evaluation corpus.

---

[3]It is important to note, however, that in many cases improvement in perplexity scores do not transfer to improvement in extrinsic, task-quality scores. In that sense, the perplexity measure is good for comparing different language models in terms of their ability to pick-up regularities in sequences, but is not a good measure for assessing progress in language understanding or language-processing tasks.

9.3 TRADITIONAL APPROACHES TO LANGUAGE MODELING

The traditional approach to language models assumes a k-order markov property, and model $P(w_{i+1} = m|w_{1:i}) \approx P(w_{i+1} = m|w_{i-k:i})$. The role of the language model then is to provide good estimates $\hat{p}(w_{i+1} = m|w_{i-k:i})$. The estimates are usually derived from corpus counts. Let $\#(w_{i:j})$ be the count of the sequence of words $w_{i:j}$ in a corpus. The maximum likelihood estimate (MLE) of $\hat{p}(w_{i+1} = m|w_{i-k:i})$ is then:

$$\hat{p}_{\text{MLE}}(w_{i+1} = m|w_{i-k:i}) = \frac{\#(w_{i-k:i+1})}{\#(w_{i-k:i})}.$$

While effective, this baseline approach has a big shortcoming: if the event $w_{i-k:i+1}$ was never observed in the corpus ($\#(w_{i-k:i+1}) = 0$), the probability assigned to it will be 0, and this in turn will result in a 0-probability assignment to the entire corpus because of the multiplicative nature of the sentence probability calculation. A zero probability translates to an infinite perplexity—which is very bad. Zero events are quite common: consider a trigram language model, which only conditions on 2 words, and a vocabulary of 10,000 words (which is rather small). There are $10{,}000^3 = 10^{12}$ possible word triplets—it is clear that many of them won't be observed in training corpora of, say, 10^{10} words. While many of these events don't occur because they do not make sense, many others just did not occur in the corpus.

One way of avoiding zero-probability events is using *smoothing techniques*, ensuring an allocation of a (possibly small) probability mass to every possible event. The simplest example is probably *additive smoothing*, also called *add-α smoothing* [Chen and Goodman, 1999, Goodman, 2001, Lidstone, 1920]. It assumes each event occurred at least α times in addition to its observations in the corpus. The estimate then becomes

$$\hat{p}_{\text{add-}\alpha}(w_{i+1} = m|w_{i-k:i}) = \frac{\#(w_{i-k:i+1}) + \alpha}{\#(w_{i-k:i}) + \alpha|V|},$$

where $|V|$ is the vocabulary size and $0 < \alpha \leq 1$. Many more elaborate smoothing techniques exist.

Another popular family of approaches is using *back-off*: if the $k$gram was not observed, compute an estimate based on a $(k-1)$gram. A representative sample of this family is *Jelinek Mercer interpolated smoothing* [Chen and Goodman, 1999, Jelinek and Mercer, 1980]:

$$\hat{p}_{\text{int}}(w_{i+1} = m|w_{i-k:i}) = \lambda_{w_{i-k:i}} \frac{\#(w_{i-k:i+1})}{\#(w_{i-k:i})} + (1 - \lambda_{w_{i-k:i}})\hat{p}_{\text{int}}(w_{i+1} = m|w_{i-(k-1):i}).$$

For optimal performance, the values $\lambda_{w_{i-k:i}}$ should depend on the content of the conditioning context $w_{i-k:i}$: rare contexts should receive different treatments than frequent ones.

The current state-of-the-art non-neural language modeling technique uses *modified Kneser Ney smoothing* [Chen and Goodman, 1996], which is a variant of the technique proposed by Kneser and Ney [1995]. For details, see Chen and Goodman [1996] and Goodman [2001].

9.3.1 FURTHER READING

Language modeling is a very vast topic, with decades of research. A good, formal overview of the task, as well as motivations behind the perplexity measure can be found in the class notes by Michael Collins.[4] A good overview and empirical evaluation of smoothing techniques can be found in the works of Chen and Goodman [1999] and Goodman [2001]. Another review of traditional language modeling techniques can be found in the background chapters of the Ph.D. thesis of Mikolov [2012]. For a recent advance in non-neural language modeling, see Pelemans et al. [2016].

9.3.2 LIMITATIONS OF TRADITIONAL LANGUAGE MODELS

Language modeling approaches based on smoothed MLE estimates ("traditional") are easy to train, scale to large corpora, and work well in practice. They do, however, have several important shortcomings.

The smoothing techniques are intricate and based on back off to lower-order events. This assumes a fixed backing-up order, that needs to be designed by hand, and makes it hard to add more "creative" conditioning contexts (i.e., if one wants to condition on the k previous words *and* on the genre of the text, should the backoff first discard of the kth previous word, or of the genre variable?). The sequential nature of the backoff also makes it hard to scale toward larger ngrams in order to capture long-range dependencies: in order to capture a dependency between the next word and the word 10 positions in the past, one needs to see a relevant 11-gram in the text. In practice, this very rarely happens, and the model backs off from the long history. It could be that a better option would be to back off from the intervening words, i.e., allow for ngrams with "holes" in them. However, these are tricky to define while retaining a proper generative probabilistic framework.[5]

Scaling to larger ngrams is an inherent problem for MLE-based language models. The nature of natural language and the large number of words in the vocabulary means that statistics for larger ngrams will be sparse. Moreover, scaling to larger ngrams is very expensive in terms of memory requirements. The number of possible ngrams over a vocabulary V is $|V|^n$: increasing the order by one will result in a $|V|$-fold increase to that number. While not all of the theoretical ngrams are valid or will occur in the text, the number of observed events does grow at least multiplicatively when increasing the ngram size by 1. This makes it very taxing to work larger conditioning contexts.

Finally, MLE-based language models suffer from lack of generalization across contexts. Having observed *black car* and *blue car* does not influence our estimates of the event *red car* if we haven't see it before.[6]

---

[4]http://www.cs.columbia.edu/~mcollins/lm-spring2013.pdf
[5]Although see lines of work on factored language models (i.e., A. Bilmes and Kirchhoff [2003]) and on maximum-entropy (log-linear) language models, starting with Rosenfeld [1996], as well as recent work by Pelemans et al. [2016].
[6]Class-based language models [Brown et al., 1992] try to tackle this by clustering the words using distributional algorithms, and conditioning on the induced word-classes instead of or in addition to the words.

9.4   NEURAL LANGUAGE MODELS

Nonlinear neural network models solve some of the shortcomings of traditional language models: they allow conditioning on increasingly large context sizes with only a linear increase in the number of parameters, they alleviate the need for manually designing backoff orders, and they support generalization across different contexts.

A model of the form presented in this chapter was popularized by Bengio et al. [2003].[7]

The input to the neural network is a k gram of words $w_{1:k}$, and the output is a probability distribution over the next word. The k context words $w_{1:k}$ are treated as a word window: each word w is associated with an embedding vector $v(w) \in \mathbb{R}^{d_w}$, and the input vector x a concatenation of the k words:

$$x = [v(w_1); v(w_2); \ldots; v(w_k)].$$

The input x is then fed to an MLP with one or more hidden layers:

$$\hat{y} = P(w_i | w_{1:k}) = LM(w_{1:k}) = \text{softmax}(\boldsymbol{h}\boldsymbol{W^2} + \boldsymbol{b^2})$$

$$\boldsymbol{h} = g(\boldsymbol{x}\boldsymbol{W^1} + \boldsymbol{b^1})$$

$$\boldsymbol{x} = [v(w_1); v(w_2); \ldots; v(w_k)] \qquad (9.3)$$

$$v(w) = \boldsymbol{E}_{[w]}$$

$$w_i \in V \quad \boldsymbol{E} \in \mathbb{R}^{|V| \times d_w} \quad \boldsymbol{W^1} \in \mathbb{R}^{k \cdot d_w \times d_{\text{hid}}} \quad \boldsymbol{b^1} \in \mathbb{R}^{d_{\text{hid}}} \quad \boldsymbol{W^2} \in \mathbb{R}^{d_{\text{hid}} \times |V|} \quad \boldsymbol{b^2} \in \mathbb{R}^{|V|}.$$

V is a finite vocabulary, including the unique symbols UNK for unknown words, <s> for sentence initial padding, and </s> for end-of-sequence marking. The vocabulary size, $|V|$, ranges between 10,000–1,000,000 words, with the common sizes revolving around 70,000.

Training   The training examples are simply word k grams from the corpus, where the identities of the first $k-1$ words are used as features, and the last word is used as the target label for the classification. Conceptually, the model is trained using cross-entropy loss. Working with cross entropy loss works very well, but requires the use of a costly softmax operation which can be prohibitive for very large vocabularies, prompting the use of alternative losses and/or approximations (see below).

Memory and Computational Efficiency   Each of the k input words contributes d_w dimensions to x, and moving from k to $k+1$ words will increase the dimensions of the weight matrix $\boldsymbol{W^1}$ from $k \cdot d_w \times d_{\text{hid}}$ to $(k+1) \cdot d_w \times d_{\text{hid}}$, a small linear increase in the number of parameters, in contrast to a polynomial increase in the case of the traditional, count-based language models. This is possible because the feature combinations are computed in the hidden layer. Increasing the order k will likely require enlarging the dimension of d_{hid} as well, but this is still a very

---

[7]A similar model was presented as early as 1988 by Nakamura and Shikano [1988] in their work on word class prediction with neural networks.

modest increase in the number of parameters compared to the traditional modeling case. Adding additional nonlinear layers to capture more complex interactions is also relatively cheap.

Each of the vocabulary words is associated with one d_w dimensional vector (a row in $\boldsymbol{E}$) and one d_{hid} dimensional vector (a column in $\boldsymbol{W^2}$). Thus, a new vocabulary items will result in a linear increase in the number of parameters, again much better than the traditional case. However, while the input vocabulary (the matrix $\boldsymbol{E}$) requires only lookup operations and can grow without affecting the computation speed, the size of the output vocabulary greatly affects the computation time: the softmax at the output layer requires an expensive matrix-vector multiplication with the matrix $\boldsymbol{W^2} \in \mathbb{R}^{d_{\text{hid}} \times |V|}$, followed by $|V|$ exponentiations. This computation dominates the runtime, and makes language modeling with large vocabulary sizes prohibitive.

Large output spaces   Working with neural probabilistic language models with large output spaces (i.e., efficiently computing the softmax over the vocabulary) can be prohibitive both at training time and at test time. Dealing with large output spaces efficiently is an active research question. Some of the existing solutions are as follows.

Hierarchical softmax [Morin and Bengio, 2005] allows to compute the probability of a single word in $O(\log|V|)$ time rather than $O(|V|)$. This is achieved by structuring the softmax computation as tree traversal, and the probability of each word as the product of branch selection decisions. Assuming one is interested in the probability of a single word (rather than getting the distribution over all words) this approach provides clear benefits in both training and testing time.

Self-normalizing aproaches, such as noise-contrastive estimation (NCE) [Mnih and Teh, 2012, Vaswani et al., 2013] or adding normalizing term to the training objective [Devlin et al., 2014]. The NCE approach improves training time performance by replacing the cross-entropy objective with a collection of binary classification problems, requiring the evaluation of the assigned scores for k random words rather than the entire vocabulary. It also improves test-time prediction by pushing the model toward producing "approximately normalized" exponentiated scores, making the model score for a word a good substitute for its probability. The normalization term approach of Devlin et al. [2014] similarly improves test time efficiency by adding a term to the training objective that encourages the exponentiated model scores to sum to one, making the explicit summation at test time unnecessary (the approach does not improve training time efficiency).

Sampling Approaches approximate the training-time softmax over a smaller subset of the vocabulary [Jean et al., 2015].

A good review and comparison of these and other techniques for dealing with large output vocabularies is available in Chen et al. [2016].

An orthogonal line of work is attempting to sidestep the problem by working at the characters level rather than words level.

Desirable Properties   Putting aside the prohibitive cost of using the large output vocabulary, the model has very appealing properties. It achieves better perplexities than state-of-the-art traditional language models such as Kneser-Ney smoothed models, and can scale to much larger orders than is possible with the traditional models. This is achievable because parameters are associated only with individual words, and not with $k$grams. Moreover, the words in different positions share parameters, making them share statistical strength. The hidden layers of the models are in charge of finding informative word combinations, and can, at least in theory, learn that for some words only sub-parts of the $k$gram are informative: it can learn to back-up to smaller $k$grams if needed, like a traditional language model, and do it in a context-dependent way. It can also learn skip-grams, i.e., that for some combinations it should look at words 1, 2, and 5, skipping words 3 and 4.[8]

Another appealing property of the model, besides the flexibility of the $k$gram orders, is the ability to generalize across contexts. For example, by observing that the words *blue, green, red, black*, etc. appear in similar contexts, the model will be able to assign a reasonable score to the event *green car* even though it never observed this combination in training, because it did observe *blue car* and *red car*.

The combination of these properties—the flexibility of considering only parts of the conditioning context and the ability to generalize to unseen contexts—together with the only linear dependence on the conditioning context size in terms of both memory and computation, make it very easy to increase the size of the conditioning context without suffering much from data sparsity and computation efficiency.

The ease in which the neural language model can incorporate large and flexible conditioning contexts allow for creative definitions of contexts. For example, Devlin et al. [2014] propose a machine translation model in which the probability of the next word is conditioned on the previous k words in the generated translation, as well as on m words in the source language that the given position in the translation is based on. This allows the model to be sensitive to topic-specific jargon and multi-word expressions in the source language, and indeed results in much improved translation scores.

Limitations   Neural language models of the form presented here do have some limitations: predicting the probability of a word in context is much more expensive than using a traditional language model, and working with large vocabulary sizes and training corpora can become prohibitive. However, they do make better use of the data, and can get very competitive perplexities even with relatively small training set sizes.

When applied in the context of a machine-translation system, neural language models do not always improve the translation quality over traditional Kneser-Ney smoothed language models. However, translation quality does improve when the probabilities from a traditional language model and a neural one are interpolated. It seems that the models complement each other: the neural language models generalize better to unseen events, but sometimes this generalization can hurt the performance, and the rigidity of the traditional models is preferred. As an example, consider the opposite of the colors example above: a model is asked to assign a probability to the sentence *red horse*. A traditional model will assign it a very low score, as it likely observed such

---

[8]Such skip-grams were explored also for non-neural language models; see Pelemans et al. [2016] and the references therein.

an event only a few times, if at all. On the other hand, a neural language model may have seen *brown horse*, *black horse*, and *white horse*, and also learned independently that *black*, *white*, *brown*, and *red* can appear in similar contexts. Such a model will assign a much higher probability to the event *red horse*, which is undesired.

9.5   USING LANGUAGE MODELS FOR GENERATION

Language models can also be used for generating sentences. After training a language model on a given collection of text, one can generate ("sample") random sentences from the model according to their probability using the following process: predict a probability distribution over the first word conditioned on the start symbol, and draw a random word according to the predicted distribution. Then, predict a probability distribution over the second word conditioned on the first, and so on, until predicting the end-of-sequence </s> symbol. Already with $k = 3$ this produces very passable text, and the quality improves with higher orders.

When decoding (generating a sentence) from a trained language-model in this way, one can either choose the highest scoring prediction (word) at each step, or sample a random word according to the predicted distribution. Another option is to use *beam search* in order to find a sequence with a globally high probability (following the highest-prediction at each step may result in sub-optimal overall probability, as the process may "trap itself into a corner," leading to prefixes that are followed by low-probability events. This is called the *label-bias* problem, discussed in depth by Andor et al. [2016] and Lafferty et al. [2001].

Sampling from a multinomial distribution   A multinomial distribution over $|V|$ elements associates a probability value $p_i \geq 0$ for each item $0 < i \leq |V|$, such that $\sum_{i=1}^{|V|} p_i = 1$. In order to sample a random item from a multinomial distribution according to its probability, the following algorithm can be used:

1: $i \leftarrow 0$
2: $s \sim U[0, 1]$ ▷ a uniform random number between 0 and 1
3: **while** $s \geq 0$ **do**
4:     $i \leftarrow i + 1$
5:     $s \leftarrow s - p_i$
6: **return** i

This is a naive algorithm, with a computational complexity linear in the vocabulary size $O(|V|)$. This can be prohibitively slow using large vocabularies. For peaked distributions where the values are sorted by decreasing probability, the average time would be much faster. The *alias method* [Kronmal and Peterson, Jr., 1979] is an efficient algorithm for sampling from arbitrary multinomial distributions with large vocabularies, allowing sampling in $O(1)$ after linear time pre-processing.

9.6   BYPRODUCT: WORD REPRESENTATIONS

Language models can be trained on *raw text*: for training a k-order language model one just needs to extract $(k + 1)$grams from running text, and treat the $(k + 1)$th word as the supervision signal. Thus, we can generate practically unlimited training data for them.

Consider the matrix W^2 appearing just before the final softmax. Each column in this matrix is a d_{hid} dimensional vector that is associated with a vocabulary item. During the final score computation, each column in W^2 is multiplied by the context representation h, and this produces the score of the corresponding vocabulary item. Intuitively, this should cause words that are likely to appear in similar contexts to have similar vectors. Following the distributional hypothesis according to which words that appear in similar contexts have similar meanings, words with similar meanings will have similar vectors. A similar argument can be made about the rows of the embedding matrix E. As a byproduct of the language modeling process, we also learn useful word representations in the rows and columns of the matrices E and W^2.

In the next chapter we further explore the topic of learning useful word representations from raw text.

CHAPTER 10 •

Pre-trained
Word Representations

A main component of the neural network approach is the use of embeddings—representing each feature as a vector in a low dimensional space. But where do the vectors come from? This chapter surveys the common approaches.

10.1 RANDOM INITIALIZATION

When enough supervised training data is available, one can just treat the feature embeddings the same as the other model parameters: initialize the embedding vectors to random values, and let the network-training procedure tune them into "good" vectors.

Some care has to be taken in the way the random initialization is performed. The method used by the effective WORD2VEC implementation [Mikolov et al., 2013b,a] is to initialize the word vectors to uniformly sampled random numbers in the range $[-\frac{1}{2d}, \frac{1}{2d}]$ where d is the number of dimensions. Another option is to use *xavier initialization* (see Section 5.2.2) and initialize with uniformly sampled values from $\left[-\frac{\sqrt{6}}{\sqrt{d}}, \frac{\sqrt{6}}{\sqrt{d}}\right]$.

In practice, one will often use the random initialization approach to initialize the embedding vectors of commonly occurring features, such as part-of-speech tags or individual letters, while using some form of supervised or unsupervised pre-training to initialize the potentially rare features, such as features for individual words. The pre-trained vectors can then either be treated as fixed during the network training process, or, more commonly, treated like the randomly initialized vectors and further tuned to the task at hand.

10.2 SUPERVISED TASK-SPECIFIC PRE-TRAINING

If we are interested in task A, for which we only have a limited amount of labeled data (for example, syntactic parsing), but there is an auxiliary task B (say, part-of-speech tagging) for which we have much more labeled data, we may want to pre-train our word vectors so that they perform well as predictors for task B, and then use the trained vectors for training task A. In this way, we can utilize the larger amounts of labeled data we have for task B. When training task A we can either treat the pre-trained vectors as fixed, or tune them further for task A. Another option is to train jointly for both objectives; see Chapter 20 for more details.

10.3   UNSUPERVISED PRE-TRAINING

The common case is that we do not have an auxiliary task with large enough amounts of annotated data (or maybe we want to help bootstrap the auxiliary task training with better vectors). In such cases, we resort to "unsupervised" auxiliary tasks, which can be trained on huge amounts of unannotated text.

The techniques for training the word vectors are essentially those of supervised learning, but instead of supervision for the task that we care about, we instead create practically unlimited number of supervised training instances from raw text, hoping that the tasks that we created will match (or be close enough to) the final task we care about.[1]

The key idea behind the unsupervised approaches is that one would like the embedding vectors of "similar" words to have similar vectors. While word similarity is hard to define and is usually very task-dependent, the current approaches derive from the distributional hypothesis [Harris, 1954], stating that *words are similar if they appear in similar contexts*. The different methods all create supervised training instances in which the goal is to either predict the word from its context, or predict the context from the word.

In the final section of Chapter 9, we saw how language modeling creates word vectors as a byproduct of training. Indeed, language modeling can be treated as an "unsupervised" approach in which a word is predicted based on the context of the k preceding words. Historically, the algorithm of Collobert and Weston [Collobert and Weston, 2008, Collobert et al., 2011] and the WORD2VEC family of algorithms described below [Mikolov et al., 2013b,a] were inspired by this property of language modeling. The WORD2VEC algorithms are designed to perform the same side effects as language modeling, using a more efficient and more flexible framework. The GLOVE algorithm by Pennington et al. [2014] follows a similar objective. These algorithms are also deeply connected to another family of algorithms which evolved in the NLP and IR communities, and that are based on matrix factorization [Levy and Goldberg, 2014]. Word embeddings algorithms are discussed in Section 10.4.

An important benefit of training word embeddings on large amounts of unannotated data is that it provides vector representations for words that do not appear in the supervised training set. Ideally, the representations for these words will be similar to those of related words that do appear in the training set, allowing the model to generalize better on unseen events. It is thus desired that the similarity between word vectors learned by the unsupervised algorithm captures the same aspects of similarity that are useful for performing the intended task of the network.

Arguably, the choice of auxiliary problem (what is being predicted, based on what kind of context) affects the resulting vectors much more than the learning method that is being used to train them. Section 10.5 surveys different choices of auxiliary problems.

Word embeddings derived by unsupervised training algorithms have applications in NLP beyond using them for initializing the word-embeddings layer of neural network model. These are discussed in Chapter 11.

---

[1]The interpretation of creating auxiliary problems from raw text is inspired by Ando and Zhang [2005a,b].

10.3.1 USING PRE-TRAINED EMBEDDINGS

When using pre-trained word embeddings, there are some choices that should be taken. The first choice is about pre-processing: Should the pre-trained word vectors be used as is, or should each vector be normalized to unit length? This is task dependent. For many word embedding algorithms, the norm of the word vector correlates with the word's frequency. Normalizing the words to unit length removes the frequency information. This could either be a desirable unification, or an unfortunate information loss.

The second choice regards fine-tuning the pre-trained vectors for the task. Consider an embedding matrix $E \in \mathbb{R}^{|V| \times d}$ associating words from vocabulary V with d-dimensional vectors. A common approach is to treat E as model parameters, and change it with the rest of the network. While this works well, it has the potential undesirable effect of changing the representations for words that appear in the training data, but not for other words that used to be close to them in the original pre-trained vectors E. This may hurt the generalization properties we aim to get from the pre-training procedure. An alternative is to leave the pre-trained vectors E fixed. This keeps the generalization, but prevents the model from adapting the representations for the given task. A middle ground is to keep E fixed, but use an additional matrix $T \in \mathbb{R}^{d \times d}$. Instead of looking at the rows of E, we look at rows of a transformed matrix $E' = ET$. The transformation matrix T is tuned as part of the network, allowing to fine-tune some aspects of the pre-trained vectors for the task. However, the task-specific adaptations are in the form of linear transformations that apply to all words, not just those seen in training. The downside of this approach is the inability to change the representations of some words but not others (for example, if *hot* and *cold* received very similar vectors, it could be very hard for a linear transformation T to separate them). Another option is to keep E fixed, but use an additional matrix $\Delta \in \mathbb{R}^{|V| \times d}$ and take the embedding matrix to be $E' = E + \Delta$ or $E' = ET + \Delta$. The Δ matrix is initialized to 0 and trained with the network, allowing to learn additive changes to specific words. Adding a strong regularization penalty over Δ will encourage the fine-tuned representations to stay close to the original ones.[2]

10.4 WORD EMBEDDING ALGORITHMS

The neural networks community has a tradition of thinking in terms of *distributed representations* [Hinton et al., 1987]. In contrast to local representations, in which entities are represented as discrete symbols and the interactions between entities are encoded as a set of discrete relations between symbols forming a graph, in distributed representations each entity is instead represented as a vector of value ("a pattern of activations"), and the meaning of the entity and its relation to other entities are captured by the activations in the vector, and the similarities between different vectors. In the context of language processing, it means that words (and sentences) should not be mapped to discrete dimensions but rather mapped to a shared low dimensional space, where

---

[2]Note that all the updates during gradient-based training are additive, and so without regularization, updating E during training and keeping E fixed but updating Δ and looking at $E + \Delta$ will result in the same final embeddings. The approaches only differ when regularization is applied.

each word will be associated with a d-dimensional vector, and the meaning of the word will be captured by its relation to other words and the activation values in its vector.

The natural language processing community has a tradition in thinking in terms of *distributional semantics*, in which a meaning of a word could be derived from its distribution in a corpus, i.e., from the aggregate of the contexts in which it is being used. Words that tend to occur in similar contexts tend to have similar meanings.

These two approaches to representing words—in terms of patterns of activations that are learned in the context of a larger algorithm and in terms of co-occurrence patterns with other words or syntactic structures, give rise to seemingly very different views of word representations, leading to different algorithmic families and lines of thinking.

In Section 10.4.1 we will explore the distributional approach to word representation, and in Section 10.4.2 we'll explore the distributed approaches. Section 10.4.3 will connect the two worlds, and show that for the most part, current state-of-the-art distributed representations of words are using distributional signals to do most of their heavy lifting, and that the two algorithmic families are deeply connected.

10.4.1 DISTRIBUTIONAL HYPOTHESIS AND WORD REPRESENTATIONS

The *Distributional Hypothesis* about language and word meaning states that words that occur in the same contexts tend to have similar meanings [Harris, 1954]. The idea was popularized by Firth [1957] through the saying "you shall know a word by the company it keeps." Intuitively, when people encounter a sentence with an unknown word such as the word *wampimuk* in *Marco saw a hairy little wampinuk crouching behind a tree*, they infer the meaning of the word based on the context in which it occurs. This idea has given rise to the field of *distributional semantics*: a research area interested in quantifying semantic similarities between linguistic items according to their distributional properties in large text corpora. For a discussion of the linguistic and philosophical basis of the distributional hypothesis, see Sahlgren [2008].

Word-context Matrices

In NLP, a long line of research[3] captures the distributional properties of words using word-context matrices, in which each row i represents a word, each column j represents a linguistic context in which words can occur, and a matrix entry $M_{[i,j]}$ quantifies the strength of association between a word and a context in a large corpus. In other words, each word is represented as a sparse vector in high dimensional space, encoding the weighted bag of contexts in which it occurs. Different definitions of contexts and different ways of measuring the association between a word and a context give rise to different word representations. Different distance functions can be used to measure the distances between word vectors, which are taken to represent the semantic distances between the associated words.

---

[3]See the survey of Turney and Pantel [2010] and Baroni and Lenci [2010] for an overview.

More formally, denote by V_W the set of words (the words vocabulary) and by V_C the set of possible contexts. We assume each word and each context are indexed, such that w_i is the ith word in the words vocabulary and c_j is the jth word in the context vocabulary. The matrix $M^f \in \mathbb{R}^{|V_W| \times |V_C|}$ is the word-context matrix, defined as $M^f_{[i,j]} = f(w_i, c_j)$, where f is an association measure of the strength between a word and a context.

Similarity Measures

Once words are represented as vectors, one can compute similarities between words by computing the similarities between the corresponding vectors. A common and effective measure is the *cosine similarity*, measuring the cosine of the angle between the vectors:

$$\text{sim}_{\cos}(\boldsymbol{u}, \boldsymbol{v}) = \frac{\boldsymbol{u} \cdot \boldsymbol{v}}{\|\boldsymbol{u}\|_2 \|\boldsymbol{v}\|_2} = \frac{\sum_i \boldsymbol{u}_{[i]} \cdot \boldsymbol{v}_{[i]}}{\sqrt{\sum_i (\boldsymbol{u}_{[i]})^2} \sqrt{\sum_i (\boldsymbol{v}_{[i]})^2}}. \tag{10.1}$$

Another popular measure is the *generalized Jacaard similarity*, defined as:[4]

$$\text{sim}_{\text{Jacaard}}(\boldsymbol{u}, \boldsymbol{v}) = \frac{\sum_i \min(\boldsymbol{u}_{[i]}, \boldsymbol{v}_{[i]})}{\sum_i \max(\boldsymbol{u}_{[i]}, \boldsymbol{v}_{[i]})}. \tag{10.2}$$

Word-context Weighting and PMI

The function f is usually based on counts from a large corpus. Denote by $\#(w, c)$ the number of times word w occurred in the context c in the corpus D, and let $|D|$ be the corpus size ($|D| = \sum_{w' \in V_W, c' \in V_C} \#(w', c')$). It is intuitive to define $f(w, c)$ to be the count $f(w, c) = \#(w, c)$ or the normalized count $f(w, c) = P(w, c) = \frac{\#(w, c)}{|D|}$. However, this has the undesired effect of assigning high weights to word-context pairs involving very common contexts (for example, consider the context of a word to be the previous word. Then for a word such as *cat* the events *the cat* and *a cat* will receive much higher scores than *cute cat* and *small cat* even though the later are much more informative). To counter this effect, it is better to define f to favor informative contexts for a given word—contexts that co-occur more with the given word than with other words. An effective metric that captures this behavior is the *pointwise mutual information* (*PMI*): an information-theoretic association measure between a pair of discrete outcomes x and y, defined as:

$$\text{PMI}(x, y) = \log \frac{P(x, y)}{P(x)P(y)}. \tag{10.3}$$

In our case, $\text{PMI}(w, c)$ measures the association between a word w and a context c by calculating the log of the ratio between their joint probability (the frequency in which they co-occur together) and their marginal probabilities (the frequencies in which they occur individually). PMI can be estimated empirically by considering the actual number of observations in a corpus:

$$f(w, c) = \text{PMI}(w, c) = \log \frac{\#(w, c) \cdot |D|}{\#(w) \cdot \#(c)}, \tag{10.4}$$

---

[4]When thinking of $\boldsymbol{u}$ and $\boldsymbol{v}$ as sets, the Jacaard similarity is defined as $\frac{|\boldsymbol{u} \cap \boldsymbol{v}|}{|\boldsymbol{u} \cup \boldsymbol{v}|}$.

where $\#(w) = \sum_{c' \in V_C} \#(w, c')$ and $\#(c) = \sum_{w' \in V_W} \#(w', c)$ are the corpus frequencies of w and c respectively. The use of PMI as a measure of association in NLP was introduced by Church and Hanks [1990] and widely adopted for word similarity and distributional semantic tasks [Dagan et al., 1994, Turney, 2001, Turney and Pantel, 2010].

Working with the PMI matrix presents some computational challenges. The rows of M^{PMI} contain many entries of word-context pairs (w, c) that were never observed in the corpus, for which $PMI(w, c) = \log 0 = -\infty$. A common solution is to use the *positive PMI* (PPMI) metric, in which all negative values are replaced by 0:[5]

$$\text{PPMI}(w, c) = \max\left(\text{PMI}\,(w, c)\,, 0\right). \tag{10.5}$$

Systematic comparisons of various weighting schemes for entries in the word-context similarity matrix show that the PMI, and more so the positive-PMI (PPMI) metrics provide the best results for a wide range of word-similarity tasks [Bullinaria and Levy, 2007, Kiela and Clark, 2014].

A deficiency of PMI is that it tends to assign high value to rare events. For example, if two events occur only once, but occur together, they will receive a high PMI value. It is therefore advisable to apply a count threshold before using the PMI metric, or to otherwise discount rare events.

Dimensionality Reduction through Matrix Factorization

A potential obstacle of representing words as the explicit set of contexts in which they occur is that of data sparsity—some entries in the matrix M may be incorrect because we did not observe enough data points. Additionally, the explicit word vectors are of a very high dimensions (depending on the definition of context, the number of possible contexts can be in the hundreds of thousands, or even millions).

Both issues can be alleviated by considering a low-rank representation of the data using a *dimensionality reduction* technique such as the *singular value decomposition* (SVD).

SVD works by *factorizing* the matrix $M \in \mathbb{R}^{|V_W| \times |V_C|}$ into two narrow matrices: a $W \in \mathbb{R}^{|V_W| \times d}$ word matrix and a $C \in \mathbb{R}^{|V_C| \times d}$ context matrix, such that $WC^\top = M' \in \mathbb{R}^{|V_W| \times |V_C|}$ is the best rank-d approximation of M in the sense that no other rank-d matrix has a closer L_2 distance to M than M'.

The low-rank representation M' can be seen as a "smoothed" version of M: based on robust patterns in the data, some of the measurements are "fixed." This has the effect, for example, of adding words to contexts that they were not seen with, if other words in this context seem to

---

[5]When representing words, there is some intuition behind ignoring negative values: humans can easily think of *positive* associations (e.g., "Canada" and "snow") but find it much harder to invent *negative* ones ("Canada" and "desert"). This suggests that the perceived similarity of two words is influenced more by the positive context they share than by the negative context they share. It therefore makes some intuitive sense to discard the negatively associated contexts and mark them as "uninformative" (0) instead. A notable exception would be in the case of syntactic similarity. For example, all verbs share a very strong negative association with being preceded by determiners, and past tense verbs have a very strong negative association to be preceded by "be" verbs and modals.

co-locate with each other. Moreover, the matrix W allows to represent each word as a dense d-dimensional vector instead of a sparse $|V_C|$-dimensional one, where $d \ll |V_C|$ (typical choices are $50 < d < 300$), such that the d-dimensional vectors captures the most important directions of variation in the original matrix. One can then compute similarities based on the dense d-dim vectors instead of the sparse high-dimensional ones.

The mathematics of SVD   The Singular Value Decomposition (SVD) is an algebraic technique by which an $m \times n$ real or complex matrix M is factorized into three matrices:

$$M = UDV,$$

where U is an $m \times m$ real or complex matrix, D is an $m \times n$ real or complex matrix, and V is an $n \times n$ matrix. The matrices U and $V^\top$ are *orthonormal*, meaning that their rows are unit-length and orthogonal to each other. The matrix D is diagonal, where the elements on the diagonal are the singular values of M, in decreasing order.

The factorization is exact. The SVD has many uses, in machine learning and elsewhere. For our purposes, SVD is used for *dimensionality reduction*—finding low-dimensional representations of high-dimensional data that preserve most of the information in the original data.

Consider the multiplication $U \tilde{D} V$ where $\tilde{D}$ is a version of D in which all but the first k elements on the diagonal are replaced by zeros. We can now zero out all but the first k rows of U and columns of V, as they will be zeroed out by the multiplication anyhow. Deleting the rows and columns leaves us with three matrices, $\tilde{U}$ ($m \times k$), $\times D$ ($k \times k$, diagonal) and V ($k \times n$). The product:

$$M' = \tilde{U} \tilde{D} \tilde{V}$$

is a ($m \times n$) matrix of *rank k*.

The matrix M' is the product of thin matrices ($\tilde{U}$ and $\tilde{V}$, with k much smaller than m and n), and can be thought of as a *low rank approximation* of M.

According to the *Eckart-Young theorem* [Eckart and Young, 1936], the matrix M' is *the best rank-k approximation* of M under L_2 loss. That is, M' is the minimizer of:

$$M' = \operatorname*{argmin}_{X \in \mathbb{R}^{m \times n}} \|X - M\|_2 \quad s.t. \; X \text{ is rank-}k.$$

The matrix M' can be thought of as a smoothed version of M, in the sense that it uses only the k most influential directions in the data.

Approximating row distances The low-dimensional rows of $E = \tilde{U} \tilde{D}$ are low-rank approximations of the high-dimensional rows of the original matrix M, in the sense that computing the dot product between rows of E is *equivalent* to computing the dot-product between the rows of the reconstructed matrix M'. That is, $E_{[i]} \cdot E_{[j]} = M'_{[i]} \cdot M'_{[j]}$.

To see why, consider the $m \times m$ matrix $S^E = E E^\top$. An entry $[i, j]$ in this matrix is equal to the dot product between rows i and j in E: $S^E{}_{[i,j]} = E_{[i]} \cdot E_{[j]}$. Similarly for the matrix $S^{M'} = M'M'^\top$.

We will show that $S^E = S^{M'}$. Recall that $\tilde{V}\tilde{V}^\top = I$ because $\tilde{V}$ is orthonormal. Now:

$$S^{M'} = M'M'^\top = (\tilde{U}\tilde{D}\tilde{V})(\tilde{U}\tilde{D}\tilde{V})^\top = (\tilde{U}\tilde{D}\tilde{V})(\tilde{V}^\top\tilde{D}^\top\tilde{U}^\top) =$$

$$= (\tilde{U}\tilde{D})(\tilde{V}\tilde{V}^\top)(\tilde{D}^\top\tilde{U}^\top) = (\tilde{U}\tilde{D})(\tilde{U}\tilde{D})^\top = E E^\top = S^E.$$

We can thus use the rows of E instead of the high-dimensional rows of M' (and instead of the high-dimensional rows of M. Using a similar argument, we can also use the rows of $(\tilde{D}\tilde{V})^\top$ instead of the columns of M').

When using SVD for word similarity, the rows of M correspond to words, the columns to contexts, and the vectors comprising the rows of E are low-dimensional word representations. In practice, it is often better to not use $E = \tilde{U}\tilde{D}$ but instead to use the more "balanced" version $E = \tilde{U}\sqrt{\tilde{D}}$, or even ignoring the singular values $\tilde{D}$ completely and taking $E = \tilde{U}$.

10.4.2 FROM NEURAL LANGUAGE MODELS TO DISTRIBUTED REPRESENTATIONS

In contrast to the so-called *count-based methods* described above, the neural networks community advocates the use of *distributed representations* of word meanings. In a distributed representation, each word is associated with a vector in $\mathbb{R}^d$, where the "meaning" of the word with respect to some task is captured in the different dimensions of the vector, as well as in the dimensions of other words. Unlike the explicit distributional representations in which each dimension corresponds to a specific context the word occurs in, the dimensions in the distributed representation are not interpretable, and specific dimensions do not necessarily correspond to specific concepts. The distributed nature of the representation means that a given aspect of meaning may be captured by (distributed over) a combination of many dimensions, and that a given dimension may contribute to capturing several aspects of meaning.[6]

Consider the language modeling network in Equation (9.3) in Chapter 9. The context of a word is the k gram of words preceding it. Each word is associated with a vector, and their concatenation is encoded into a d_{hid} dimensional vector h using a nonlinear transformation. The vector h is then multiplied by a matrix W^2 in which each column corresponds to a word, and interactions between h and columns in W^2 determine the probabilities of the different words given the context. The columns of W^2 (as well as the rows of the embeddings matrix E) are distributed

---

[6]We note that in many ways the explicit distributional representations is also "distributed": different aspects of the meaning of a word are captured by groups of contexts the word occurs in, and a given context can contribute to different aspects of meaning. Moreover, after performing dimensionality reduction over the word-context matrix, the dimensions are no longer easily interpretable.

representations of words: the training process determines good values to the embeddings such that they produce correct probability estimates for a word in the context of a k gram, capturing the "meaning" of the words in the columns of W^2 associated with them.

Collobert and Weston

The design of the network in Equation (9.3) is driven by the language modeling task, which poses two important requirements: the need to produce a *probability distributions* over words, and the need to condition on contexts that can be combined using the chain-rule of probability to produce sentence-level probability estimates. The need to produce a probability distribution dictates the need to compute an expensive normalization term involving all the words in the output vocabulary, while the need to decompose according to the chain-rule restricts the conditioning context to preceding k grams.

If we only care about the resulting representations, both of the constraints can be relaxed, as was done by Collobert and Weston [2008] in a model which was refined and presented in greater depth by Bengio et al. [2009]. The first change introduced by Collobert and Weston was changing the context of a word from the preceding k gram (the words to its left) to a word-window surrounding it (i.e., computing $P(w_3|w_1w_2\square w_4w_5)$ instead of $P(w_5|w_1w_2w_3w_4\square)$). The generalization to other kinds of fixed-sized contexts $c_{1:k}$ is straightforward.

The second change introduced by Collobert and Weston is to abandon the probabilistic output requirement. Instead of computing a probability distribution over target words given a context, their model only attempts to assign a score to each word, such that the correct word scores above incorrect ones. This removes the need to perform the computationally expensive normalization over the output vocabulary, making the computation time independent of the output vocabulary size. This not only makes the network much faster to train and use, but also makes it scalable to practically unlimited vocabularies (the only cost of increasing the vocabulary is a linear increase in memory usage).

Let w be a target word, $c_{1:k}$ be an ordered list of context items, and $v_w(w)$ and $v_c(c)$ embedding functions mapping word and context indices to d_{emb} dimensional vectors (from now on we assume the word and context vectors have the same number of dimensions). The model of Collobert and Weston computes a score $s(w, c_{1:k})$ of a word-context pair by concatenating the word and the context embeddings into a vector x, which is fed into an MLP with one hidden layer whose single output is the score assigned to the word-context combination:

$$s(w, c_{1:k}) = g(xU) \cdot v$$
$$x = [v_c(c_1); \ldots; v_c(c_k); v_w(w)]$$
(10.6)

$$U \in \mathbb{R}^{(k+1)d_{emb}\times d_h} \quad v \in \mathbb{R}^{d_h}.$$

The network is trained with a margin-based ranking loss to score correct word-context pairs $(w, c_{1:k})$ above incorrect word-context pairs $(w', c_{1:k})$ with a margin of at least 1. The loss

$L(w, c_{1:k})$ for a given word-context pair is given by:

$$L(w, c, w') = max(0, 1 - (s(w, c_{1:k}) - s(w', c_{1:k}))) \tag{10.7}$$

where w' is a random word from the vocabulary. The training procedure repeatedly goes over word-context pairs from the corpus, and for each one samples a random word w', computes the loss $L(w, c, w')$ using w', and updates parameters U, v and the word and context embeddings to minimize the loss.

The use of randomly sampled words to produce *negative examples* of incorrect word-context to drive the optimization is also at the core of the WORD2VEC algorithm, to be described next.

Word2Vec

The widely popular WORD2VEC algorithm was developed by Tomáš Mikolov and colleagues over a series of papers [Mikolov et al., 2013b,a]. Like the algorithm of Collobert and Weston, WORD2VEC also starts with a neural language model and modifies it to produce faster results. textscWord2VEC is not a single algorithm: it is a software package implementing two different context representations (CBOW and Skip-Gram) and two different optimization objectives (Negative-Sampling and Hierarchical Softmax). Here, we focus on the Negative-Sampling objective (NS).

Like Collobert and Weston's algorithm, the NS variant of WORD2VEC works by training the network to distinguish "good" word-context pairs from "bad" ones. However, WORD2VEC replaces the margin-based ranking objective with a probabilistic one. Consider a set D of correct word-context pairs, and a set $\bar{D}$ of incorrect word-context pairs. The goal of the algorithm is to estimate the probability $P(D = 1|w, c)$ that the word-context pair came from the correct set D. This should be high (1) for pairs from D and low (0) for pairs from $\bar{D}$. The probability constraint dictates that $P(D = 1|w, c) = 1 - P(D = 0|w, c)$. The probability function is modeled as a sigmoid over the score $s(w, c)$:

$$P(D = 1|w, c) = \frac{1}{1 + e^{-s(w,c)}}. \tag{10.8}$$

The corpus-wide objective of the algorithm is to maximize the log-likelihood of the data $D \cup \bar{D}$:

$$\mathcal{L}(\Theta; D, \bar{D}) = \sum_{(w,c) \in D} \log P(D = 1|w, c) + \sum_{(w,c) \in \bar{D}} \log P(D = 0|w, c). \tag{10.9}$$

The positive examples D are generated from a corpus. The negative examples $\bar{D}$ can be generated in many ways. In WORD2VEC, they are generated by the following process: for each good pair $(w, c) \in D$, sample k words $w_{1:k}$ and add each of (w_i, c) as a negative example to $\bar{D}$. This results in the negative samples data $\bar{D}$ being k times larger than D. The number of negative samples k is a parameter of the algorithm.

The negative words w can be sampled according to their corpus-based frequency $\frac{\#(w)}{\sum_{w'} \#(w')}$, or, as done in the WORD2VEC implementation, according to a smoothed version in which the counts are raised to the power of $\frac{3}{4}$ before normalizing: $\frac{\#(w)^{0.75}}{\sum_{w'} \#(w')^{0.75}}$. This second version gives more relative weight to less frequent words, and results in better word similarities in practice.

CBOW   Other than changing the objective from margin-based to a probabilistic one, WORD2VEC also considerably simplify the definition of the word-context scoring function, $s(w, c)$. For a multi-word context $c_{1:k}$, the CBOW variant of WORD2VEC defines the context vector c to be a sum of the embedding vectors of the context components: $c = \sum_{i=1}^{k} c_i$. It then defines the score to be simply $s(w, c) = w \cdot c$, resulting in:

$$P(D = 1 | w, c_{1:k}) = \frac{1}{1 + e^{-(w \cdot c_1 + w \cdot c_2 + ... + w \cdot c_k)}}.$$

The CBOW variant loses the order information between the context's elements. In return, it allows the use of variable-length contexts. However, note that for contexts with bound length, the CBOW can still retain the order information by including the relative position as part of the content element itself, i.e., by assigning different embedding vector to context elements in different relative positions.

Skip-Gram   The skip-gram variant of WORD2VEC scoring decouples the dependence between the context elements even further. For a k-elements context $c_{1:k}$, the skip-gram variant assumes that the elements c_i in the context are independent from each other, essentially treating them as k different contexts, i.e., a word-context pair $(w, c_{i:k})$ will be represented in D as k different contexts: $(w, c_1), \ldots, (w, c_k)$. The scoring function $s(w, c)$ is defined as in the CBOW version, but now each context is single embedding vector:

$$P(D = 1 | w, c_i) = \frac{1}{1 + e^{-w \cdot c_i}}$$

$$P(D = 1 | w, c_{1:k}) = \prod_{i=1}^{k} P(D = 1 | w, c_i) = \prod_{1=i}^{k} \frac{1}{1 + e^{-w \cdot c_i}} \qquad (10.10)$$

$$\log P(D = 1 | w, c_{1:k}) = \sum_{i=1}^{k} \log \frac{1}{1 + e^{-w \cdot c_i}}.$$

While introducing strong independence assumptions between the elements of the context, the skip-gram variant is very effective in practice, and very commonly used.

10.4.3 CONNECTING THE WORLDS

Both the distributional "count-based" method and the distributed "neural" ones are based on the distributional hypothesis, attempting capture the similarity between words based on the similarity between the contexts in which they occur. In fact, Levy and Goldberg [2014] show that the ties between the two worlds are deeper than appear at first sight.

The training of WORD2VEC models result in two embedding matrices, $E^W \in \mathbb{R}^{|V_W| \times d_{emb}}$ and $E^C \in \mathbb{R}^{|V_C| \times d_{emb}}$ representing the words and the contexts, respectively. The context embeddings are discarded after training, and the word embeddings are kept. However, imagine keeping the context embedding matrix E^C and consider the product $E^W \times E^{C \top} = M' \in \mathbb{R}^{|V_W| \times |V_C|}$. Viewed this way, WORD2VEC is factorizing an implicit word-context matrix M'. What are the elements of matrix M'? An entry $M'_{[w,c]}$ corresponds to the dot product of the word and context embedding vectors $w \cdot c$. Levy and Goldberg show that for the combination of skip-grams contexts and the negative sampling objective with k negative samples, the global objective is minimized by setting $w \cdot c = M'_{[w,c]} = \mathrm{PMI}(w, c) - \log k$. That is, WORD2VEC is implicitly factorizing a matrix which is closely related to the well-known word-context PMI matrix! Remarkably, it does so without ever explicitly constructing the matrix M'.[7]

The above analysis assumes that the negative samples are sampled according to the corpus frequency of the words $P(w) = \frac{\#(w)}{\sum_{w'} \#(w')}$. Recall that the WORD2VEC implementation samples instead from a modified distribution $P^{0.75}(w) = \frac{\#(w)^{0.75}}{\sum_{w'} \#(w')^{0.75}}$. Under this sampling scheme, the optimal value changes to $\mathrm{PMI}^{0.75}(w, c) - \log k = \log \frac{P(w,c)}{P^{0.75}(w)P(c)} - \log k$. Indeed, using this modified version of PMI when constructing sparse and explicit distributional vectors improves the similarity in that setup as well.

The WORD2VEC algorithms are very effective in practice, and are highly scalable, allowing to train word representations with very large vocabularies over billions of words of text in a matter of hours, with very modest memory requirements. The connection between the SGNS variant of WORD2VEC and word-context matrix-factorization approaches ties the neural methods and the traditional "count-based" ones, suggesting that lessons learned in the study of "distributional" representation can transfer to the "distributed" algorithms, and vice versa, and that in a deep sense the two algorithmic families are equivalent.

10.4.4 OTHER ALGORITHMS

Many variants on the WORD2VEC algorithms exist, none of which convincingly produce qualitatively or quantitatively superior word representations. This sections list a few of the popular ones.

NCE   The noise-contrastive estimation (NCE) approach of Mnih and Kavukcuoglu [2013] is very similar to the SGNS variant of WORD2VEC, but instead of modeling $P(D = 1 \mid w, c_i)$ as in

---

[7]If the optimal assignment was satisfiable, the skip-grams with negative-sampling (SGNS) solution is the same as the SVD over word-context matrix solution. Of course, the low dimensionality d_{emb} of w and c may make it impossible to satisfy $w \cdot c = \mathrm{PMI}(w, c) - \log k$ for all w and c pairs, and the optimization procedure will attempt to find the best achievable solution, while paying a price for each deviation from the optimal assignment. This is where the SGNS and the SVD objectives differ—SVD puts a quadratic penalty on each deviation, while SGNS uses a more complex penalty term.

Equation (10.10), it is modeled as:

$$P(D = 1 \mid w, c_i) = \frac{e^{-\boldsymbol{w}\cdot\boldsymbol{c_i}}}{e^{-\boldsymbol{w}\cdot\boldsymbol{c_i}} + k \times q(w)} \tag{10.11}$$

$$P(D = 0 \mid w, c_i) = \frac{k \times q(w)}{e^{-\boldsymbol{w}\cdot\boldsymbol{c_i}} + k \times q(w)}, \tag{10.12}$$

where $q(w) = \frac{\#(w)}{|D|}$ is the observed unigram frequency of w in the corpus. This algorithm is based on the noise-contrastive estimation probability modeling technique [Gutmann and Hyvärinen, 2010]. According to Levy and Goldberg [2014], this objective is equivalent to factorizing the word-context matrix whose entries are the log conditional probabilities $\log P(w|c) - \log k$.

GloVe   The GLoVe algorithm [Pennington et al., 2014] constructs an explicit word-context matrix, and trains the word and context vectors $\boldsymbol{w}$ and $\boldsymbol{c}$ attempting to satisfy:

$$\boldsymbol{w} \cdot \boldsymbol{c} + \boldsymbol{b}_{[w]} + \boldsymbol{b}_{[c]} = \log \#(w, c) \quad \forall (w, c) \in D, \tag{10.13}$$

where $\boldsymbol{b}_{[w]}$ and $\boldsymbol{b}_{[c]}$ are word-specific and context-specific trained biases. The optimization procedure looks at observed word context pairs while skipping zero count events. In terms of matrix factorization, if we fix $\boldsymbol{b}_{[w]} = \log \#(w)$ and $\boldsymbol{b}_{[c]} = \log \#(c)$ we'll get an objective that is very similar to factorizing the word-context PMI matrix, shifted by $\log(|D|)$. However, in GloVe these parameters are learned and not fixed, giving it another degree of freedom. The optimization objective is weighted least-squares loss, assigning more weight to the correct reconstruction of frequent items. Finally, when using the same word and context vocabularies, the GloVe model suggests representing each word as the sum of its corresponding word and context embedding vectors.

10.5 THE CHOICE OF CONTEXTS

The choice of context by which a word is predicted has a profound effect on the resulting word vectors and the similarities they encode.

In most cases, the contexts of a word are taken to be other words that appear in its surrounding, either in a short window around it, or within the same sentence, paragraph or document. In some cases the text is automatically parsed by a syntactic parser, and the contexts are derived from the syntactic neighborhood induced by the automatic parse trees. Sometimes, the definitions of words and context change to include also parts of words, such as prefixes or suffixes.

10.5.1 WINDOW APPROACH

The most common approach is a sliding window approach, in which auxiliary tasks are created by looking at a sequence of $2m + 1$ words. The middle word is called the *focus word* and the m words to each side are the *contexts*. Then, either a single task is created in which the goal is to predict the focus word based on all of the context words (represented either using CBOW [Mikolov et al.,

2013b] or vector concatenation [Collobert and Weston, 2008]), or $2m$ distinct tasks are created, each pairing the focus word with a different context word. The $2m$ tasks approach, popularized by Mikolov et al. [2013a] is referred to as a *skip-gram* model. Skip-gram-based approaches are shown to be robust and efficient to train [Mikolov et al., 2013a, Pennington et al., 2014], and often produce state of the art results.

Effect of Window Size   The size of the sliding window has a strong effect on the resulting vector similarities. Larger windows tend to produce more topical similarities (i.e., "dog," "bark" and "leash" will be grouped together, as well as "walked," "run" and "walking"), while smaller windows tend to produce more functional and syntactic similarities (i.e., "Poodle," "Pitbull," "Rottweiler," or "walking,""running,""approaching").

Positional Windows   When using the CBOW or skip-gram context representations, all the different context words within the window are treated equally. There is no distinction between context words that are close to the focus words and those that are farther from it, and likewise there is no distinction between context words that appear before the focus words to context words that appear after it. Such information can easily be factored in by using *positional contexts*: indicating for each context word also its relative position to the focus words (i.e., instead of the context word being "the" it becomes "the:+2," indicating the word appears two positions to the right of the focus word). The use of positional context together with smaller windows tend to produce similarities that are more syntactic, with a strong tendency of grouping together words that share a part of speech, as well as being functionally similar in terms of their semantics. Positional vectors were shown by Ling et al. [2015a] to be more effective than window-based vectors when used to initialize networks for part-of-speech tagging and syntactic dependency parsing.

Variants   Many variants on the window approach are possible. One may lemmatize words before learning, apply text normalization, filter too short or too long sentences, or remove capitalization (see, e.g., the pre-processing steps described by dos Santos and Gatti [2014]). One may sub-sample part of the corpus, skipping with some probability the creation of tasks from windows that have too common or too rare focus words. The window size may be dynamic, using a different window size at each turn. One may weigh the different positions in the window differently, focusing more on trying to predict correctly close word-context pairs than further away ones. Each of these choices is a hyperparameter to be manually set before training, and will effect the resulting vectors. Ideally, these will be tuned for the task at hand. Much of the strong performance of the WORD2VEC implementation can be attributed to specifying good default values for these hyperparameters. Some of these hyperparameters (and others) are discussed in detail in Levy et al. [2015].

10.5.2 SENTENCES, PARAGRAPHS, OR DOCUMENTS

Using a skip-gram (or CBOW) approach, one can consider the contexts of a word to be all the other words that appear with it in the same sentence, paragraph, or document. This is equivalent to using very large window sizes, and is expected to result in word vectors that capture topical similarity (words from the same topic, i.e., words that one would expect to appear in the same document, are likely to receive similar vectors).

10.5.3 SYNTACTIC WINDOW

Some work replace the linear context within a sentence with a syntactic one [Bansal et al., 2014, Levy and Goldberg, 2014]. The text is automatically parsed using a dependency parser, and the context of a word is taken to be the words that are in its proximity in the parse tree, together with the syntactic relation by which they are connected. Such approaches produce highly *functional* similarities, grouping together words than can fill the same role in a sentence (e.g., colors, names of schools, verbs of movement). The grouping is also syntactic, grouping together words that share an inflection [Levy and Goldberg, 2014].

The effect of context   The following table, taken from Levy and Goldberg [2014], shows the top-5 most similar words to some seed words, when using bag-of-words windows of size 5 and 2 (BoW5 and BoW2), as well as dependency-based contexts (DEPS), using the same underlying corpora (Wikipedia), and the same embeddings algorithm (WORD2VEC).

Notice how for some words (e.g., *batman*) the induced word similarities are somewhat agnostic to the contexts, while for others there is a clear trend: the larger window contexts result in more topical similarities (*hogwars* is similar to other terms in the Harry Potter universe, *turing* is related to computability, *dancing* is similar to other inflections of the word) while the syntactic-dependency contexts result in more functional similarities (*hogwarts* similar to other fictional or non-fictional schools, *turing* is similar to other scientists, and *dancing* to other gerunds of entrainment activities). The smaller context window is somewhere in between the two.

This re-affirms that context choices strongly affects the resulting word representations, and stresses the need to take the choice of context into consideration when using "unsupervised" word embeddings.

Target Word	BoW5	BoW2	Deps
batman	nightwing aquaman catwoman superman manhunter	superman superboy aquaman catwoman batgirl	superman superboy supergirl catwoman aquaman
hogwarts	dumbledore hallows half-blood malfoy snape	evernight sunnydale garderobe blandings collinwood	sunnydale collinwood calarts greendale millfield
turing	nondeterministic non-deterministic computability deterministic finite-state	non-deterministic finite-state nondeterministic buchi primality	pauling hotelling heting lessing hamming
florida	gainesville fla jacksonville tampa lauderdale	fla alabama gainesville tallahassee texas	texas louisiana georgia california carolina
object-oriented	aspect-oriented smalltalk event-driven prolog domain-specific	aspect-oriented event-driven objective-c dataflow 4gl	event-driven domain-specific rule-based data-driven human-centered
dancing	singing dance dances dancers tap-dancing	singing dance dances breakdancing clowning	singing rapping breakdancing miming busking

10.5.4 MULTILINGUAL

Another option is using multilingual, translation-based contexts [Faruqui and Dyer, 2014, Hermann and Blunsom, 2014]. For example, given a large amount of sentence-aligned parallel text, one can run a bilingual alignment model such as the IBM model 1 or model 2 (i.e., using the GIZA++ software), and then use the produced alignments to derive word contexts. Here, the context of a word instance is the foreign language words that are aligned to it. Such alignments tend to result in synonym words receiving similar vectors. Some authors work instead on the sentence alignment level, without relying on word alignments [Gouws et al., 2015] or train an end-to-end machine-translation neural network and use the resulting word embeddings [Hill et al., 2014]. An appealing method is to mix a monolingual window-based approach with a multilingual approach, creating both kinds of auxiliary tasks. This is likely to produce vectors that are similar to the window-based approach, but reducing the somewhat undesired effect of the window-based approach in which antonyms (e.g., hot and cold, high and low) tend to receive similar vectors [Faruqui and Dyer, 2014]. For further discussion on multilingual word embeddings and a comparison of different methods see Levy et al. [2017].

10.5.5 CHARACTER-BASED AND SUB-WORD REPRESENTATIONS

An interesting line of work attempts to derive the vector representation of a word from the characters that compose it. Such approaches are likely to be particularly useful for tasks which are syntactic in nature, as the character patterns within words are strongly related to their syntactic function. These approaches also have the benefit of producing very small model sizes (only one vector for each character in the alphabet together with a handful of small matrices needs to be stored), and being able to provide an embedding vector for every word that may be encountered. dos Santos and Gatti [2014], dos Santos and Zadrozny [2014], and Kim et al. [2015] model the embedding of a word using a convolutional network (see Chapter 13) over the characters. Ling et al. [2015b] model the embedding of a word using the concatenation of the final states of two RNN (LSTM) encoders (Chapter 14), one reading the characters from left to right, and the other from right to left. Both produce very strong results for part-of-speech tagging. The work of Ballesteros et al. [2015] show that the two-LSTMs encoding of Ling et al. [2015b] is beneficial also for representing words in dependency parsing of morphologically rich languages.

Deriving representations of words from the representations of their characters is motivated by the *unknown words problem*—what do you do when you encounter a word for which you do not have an embedding vector? Working on the level of characters alleviates this problem to a large extent, as the vocabulary of possible characters is much smaller than the vocabulary of possible words. However, working on the character level is very challenging, as the relationship between form (characters) and function (syntax, semantics) in language is quite loose. Restricting oneself to stay on the character level may be an unnecessarily hard constraint. Some researchers propose a middle-ground, in which a word is represented as a combination of a vector for the word itself with vectors of sub-word units that comprise it. The sub-word embeddings then help in sharing information between different words with similar forms, as well as allowing back-off to the sub-word level when the word is not observed. At the same time, the models are not forced to rely solely on form when enough observations of the word are available. Botha and Blunsom [2014] suggest to model the embedding vector of a word as a sum of the word-specific vector if such vector is available, with vectors for the different morphological components that comprise it (the components are derived using Morfessor [Creutz and Lagus, 2007], an unsupervised morphological segmentation method). Gao et al. [2014] suggest using as core features not only the word form itself but also a unique feature (hence a unique embedding vector) for each of the letter-trigrams in the word.

Another middle ground between characters and words is breaking up words into "meaningful units" which are larger than characters and are automatically derived from the corpus. One such approach is to use Byte-Pair Encoding (BPE) [Gage, 1994], which was introduced by Sennrich et al. [2016a] in the context of Machine Translation and proved to be very effective. In the BPE approach, one decides on a vocabulary size (say 10,000), and then looks for 10,000 units that can represent all the words in the corpus vocabulary according to the following algorithm, taken from Sennrich et al. [2016a].

> We initialize the symbol vocabulary with the character vocabulary, and represent each word as a sequence of characters, plus a special end-of-word symbol '·', which allows us to restore the original tokenization after translation. We iteratively count all symbol pairs and replace each occurrence of the most frequent pair (A, B) with a new symbol AB. Each merge operation produces a new symbol which represents a character n-gram. Frequent character n-grams (or whole words) are eventually merged into a single symbol, thus BPE requires no shortlist. The final symbol vocabulary size is equal to the size of the initial vocabulary, plus the number of merge operations—the latter is the only hyperparameter of the algorithm. For efficiency, we do not consider pairs that cross word boundaries. The algorithm can thus be run on the dictionary extracted from a text, with each word being weighted by its frequency.

10.6   DEALING WITH MULTI-WORD UNITS AND WORD INFLECTIONS

Two issues that are still under-explored with respect to word representations have to do with the definition of a word. The unsupervised word embedding algorithms assume words correspond to tokens (consecutive characters without whitespace or punctuation, see the "What is a word?" discussion in Section 6.1). This definition often breaks.

In English, we have many *multi-token units* such as *New York* and *ice cream*, as well as looser cases such as *Boston University* or *Volga River*, that we may want to assign to single vectors.

In many languages other than English, rich morphological inflection systems make forms that relate to the same underlying concept look differently. For example, in many languages adjectives are inflected for number and gender, causing the word *yellow* describing a plural, masculine noun to have a different form from the word *yellow* describing a singular, feminine noun. Even worse, as the inflection system also dictates the forms of the neighboring words (nouns near the singular feminine form of *yellow* are themselves in a singular feminine form), different inflections of the same word often do not end up similar to each other.

While there are no good solutions to either of these problems, they can both be addressed to a reasonable degree by deterministically pre-processing the text such that it better fits the desired definitions of words.

In the multi-token units case, one can derive a list of such multi-token items, and replace them in the text with single entities (i.e., replacing occurrences of New York with New_York. Mikolov et al. [2013a] proposes a PMI-based method for automatically creating such a list, by considering the PMI of a word pair, and merging pairs with PMI scores that pass some predefined thresholds. The process then iteratively repeats to merge pairs + words into triplets, and so on. Then, the embedding algorithm is run over the pre-processed corpus. This coarse but effective heuristic is implemented as part of the WORD2VEC package, allowing to derive embeddings also for some prominent multi-token items.[8]

In the inflections case, one can mitigate the problem to a large extent by pre-processing the corpus by lemmatizing some or all of the words, embedding the lemmas instead of the inflected forms.

A related pre-processing is POS-tagging the corpus, and replacing words with (word,POS) pairs, creating, for example, the two different token types $book_{NOUN}$ and $book_{VERB}$, that will each receive a different embedding vector. For further discussion on the interplay of morphological inflections and word embeddings algorithms see Avraham and Goldberg [2017], Cotterell and Schutze [2015].

10.7   LIMITATIONS OF DISTRIBUTIONAL METHODS

The distributional hypothesis offers an appealing platform for deriving word similarities by representing words according to the contexts in which they occur. It does, however, have some inherent limitations that should be considered when using the derived representations.

Definition of similarity The definition of similarity in distributional approaches is completely operational: words are similar if used in similar contexts. But in practice, there are many facets of similarity. For example, consider the words *dog*, *cat*, and *tiger*. On the one hand, *cat* is more similar to *dog* than to *tiger*, as both are pets. On the other hand, *cat* can be considered more similar to *tiger* than to *dog* as they are both felines. Some facets may be preferred over others in certain use cases, and some may not be attested by the text as strongly as others. The distributional methods provide very little control over the kind of similarities they induce. This could be controlled to some extent by the choice of conditioning contexts (Section 10.5), but it is far from being a complete solution.

Black Sheeps When using texts as the conditioning contexts, many of the more "trivial" properties of the word may not be reflected in the text, and thus not captured in the representation. This happens because of a well-documented bias in people's use of language, stemming from efficiency constraints on communication: people are less likely to mention known information than they are

---

[8]For in-depth discussion of heuristics for finding informative word collocations, see Manning and Schütze [1999, Chapter 5].

to mention novel one. Thus, when people talk of *white sheep*, they will likely refer to them as *sheep*, while for black sheep they are much more likely to retain the color information and say *black sheep*. A model trained on text data only can be greatly misled by this.

Antonyms Words that are the opposite of each other (*good* vs. *bad, buy* vs. *sell, hot* vs *cold*) tend to appear in similar contexts (things that can be hot can also be cold, things that are bought are often sold). As a consequence, models based on the distributional hypothesis tend to judge antonyms as very similar to each other.

Corpus Biases For better or worse, the distributional methods reflect the usage patterns in the corpora on which they are based, and the corpora in turn reflect human biases in the real world (cultural or otherwise). Indeed, Caliskan-Islam et al. [2016] found that distributional word vectors encode "*every linguistic bias documented in psychology that we have looked for*," including racial and gender stereotypes (i.e., European American names are closer to pleasant terms while African American names are closer to unpleasant terms; female names are more associated with family terms than with career terms; it is possible to predict the percentage of women in an occupation according to U.S. census based on the vector representation of the occupation name). Like with the antonyms case, this behavior may or may not be desired, depending on the use case: if our task is to guess the gender of a character, knowing that nurses are stereotypically females while doctors are stereotypically males may be a desired property of the algorithm. In many other cases, however, we would like to ignore such biases. In any case, these tendencies of the induced word similarities should be taken into consideration when using distributional representations. For further discussion, see Caliskan-Islam et al. [2016] and Bolukbasi et al. [2016].

Lack of Context The distributional approaches aggregate the contexts in which a term occurs in a large corpus. The result is a word representation which is *context independent*. In reality, there is no such thing as a context-independent meaning for a word. As argued by Firth [1935], "*the complete meaning of a word is always contextual, and no study of meaning apart from context can be taken seriously*". An obvious manifestation of this is the case of *polysemy*: some words have obvious multiple senses: a *bank* may refer to a financial institution or to the side of a river, a *star* may an abstract shape, a celebrity, an astronomical entity, and so on. Using a single vector for all forms is problematic. In addition to the multiple senses problem, there are also much subtler context-dependent variations in word meaning.

CHAPTER 11

Using Word Embeddings

In Chapter 10 we discussed algorithms for deriving word vectors from large quantities of unannotated text. Such vectors can be very useful as initialization for the word embedding matrices in dedicated neural networks. They also have practical uses on their own, outside the context of neural networks. This chapter discusses some of these uses.

Notation   In this chapter, we assume each word is assigned an integer index, and use symbols such as w or w_i to refer to both a word and its index. $E_{[w]}$ is then the row in E corresponding to word w. We sometimes use $\boldsymbol{w}$, $\boldsymbol{w_i}$ to denote the vectors corresponding to w and w_i.

11.1   OBTAINING WORD VECTORS

Word-embedding vectors are easy to train from a corpus, and efficient implementations of training algorithms are available. Moreover, one can also download pre-trained word vectors that were trained on very large quantities of text (bearing in mind that differences in training regimes and underlying corpora have a strong influence on the resulting representations, and that the available pre-trained representations may not be the best choice for the particular use case).

As the time of this writing, efficient implementations of the WORD2VEC algorithms are available as a stand-alone binary[1] as well as in the GENSIM python package.[2] A modification of the WORD2VEC binary that allows using arbitrary contexts is also available.[3] An efficient implementation of the GloVe model is available as well.[4] Pre-trained word vectors for English can be obtained from Google[5] and Stanford[6] as well as other sources. Pre-trained vectors in languages other than English can be obtain from the Polyglot project.[7]

11.2   WORD SIMILARITY

Given pre-trained word embedding vectors, the major use aside from feeding them into a neural network is to compute the similarity between two words using a similarity function over vectors $sim(\boldsymbol{u}, \boldsymbol{v})$. A common and effective choice for similarity between vectors is the *cosine similarity*,

---

[1]https://code.google.com/archive/p/word2vec/
[2]https://radimrehurek.com/gensim/
[3]https://bitbucket.org/yoavgo/word2vecf
[4]http://nlp.stanford.edu/projects/glove/
[5]https://code.google.com/archive/p/word2vec/
[6]http://nlp.stanford.edu/projects/glove/
[7]http://polyglot.readthedocs.org

corresponding to the cosine of the angle between the vectors:

$$\text{sim}_{\cos}(\boldsymbol{u}, \boldsymbol{v}) = \frac{\boldsymbol{u} \cdot \boldsymbol{v}}{\|\boldsymbol{u}\|_2 \|\boldsymbol{v}\|_2}. \tag{11.1}$$

When the vectors $\boldsymbol{u}$ and $\boldsymbol{v}$ are of unit-length ($\|\boldsymbol{u}\|_2 = \|\boldsymbol{v}\|_2 = 1$) the cosine similarity reduces to a dot-product $\text{sim}_{\cos}(\boldsymbol{u}, \boldsymbol{v}) = \boldsymbol{u} \cdot \boldsymbol{v} = \sum_i \boldsymbol{u}_{[i]} \boldsymbol{v}_{[i]}$. Working with dot-products is very convenient computationally, and it is common to normalize the embeddings matrix such that each row has unit length. From now on, we assume the embeddings matrix $\boldsymbol{E}$ is normalized in this way.

11.3 WORD CLUSTERING

The word vectors can be easily clustered using clustering algorithms such as *KMeans* that are defined over Euclidean spaces. The clusters can then be used as features in learning algorithms that work with discrete features, or in other systems that require discrete symbols such as IR indexing systems.

11.4 FINDING SIMILAR WORDS

With row-normalized embeddings matrix as described above, the cosine similarity between two words w_1 and w_2 is given by:

$$\text{sim}_{\cos}(w_1, w_2) = \boldsymbol{E}_{[w_1]} \cdot \boldsymbol{E}_{[w_2]}. \tag{11.2}$$

We are often interested in the k most similar words to a given word. Let $\boldsymbol{w} = \boldsymbol{E}_{[w]}$ be the vector corresponding to word w. The similarity to all other words can be computed by the matrix-vector multiplication $\boldsymbol{s} = \boldsymbol{E}\boldsymbol{w}$. The result $\boldsymbol{s}$ is a vector of similarities, where $\boldsymbol{s}_{[i]}$ is the similarity of w to the ith word in the vocabulary (the ith row in $\boldsymbol{E}$). The k most similar words can be extracted by finding the indices corresponding to the k highest values in $\boldsymbol{s}$.

In a optimized modern scientific computing library such as numpy,[8] such matrix-vector multiplication is executed in milliseconds for embedding matrices with hundreds of thousands of vectors, allowing rather rapid calculation of similarities.

Word similarities that result from distributional measures can be combined with other forms of similarity. For example, we can define a similarity measure that is based on orthographic similarity (words that share the same letters). By filtering the list of top-k distributional-similar words to contain words that are also orthographically similar to the target word, we can find spelling variants and common typos of the target word.

---

[8]http://www.numpy.org/

11.4.1   SIMILARITY TO A GROUP OF WORDS

We may be interested in finding the most similar word to a *group* of words. This need arises when we have a list of related words, and want to expand it (for example, we have a list of four countries and want to extend it with names of more countries, or we have a list of gene names, and want find names of additional genes). Another use case is when we want to direct the similarity to be to a given sense of a word. By creating a list of words that are related to that sense, we can direct the similarity query toward that sense.

There are many way of defining similarity of an item to a group, here we take the definition to be the average similarity to the items in the group, i.e., given a group of words $w_{1:k}$ we define its similarity to word w as: $\text{sim}(w, w_{1:k}) = \frac{1}{k} \sum_{i=1}^{k} \text{sim}_{\cos}(w, w_i)$.

Thanks to linearity, computing the average cosine similarity from a group of words to all other words can be again done using a single matrix-vector multiplication, this time between the embedding matrix and the average word vector of the words in the group. The vector s in which $s_{[w]} = \text{sim}(w, w_{1:k})$ is computed by:

$$s = E(w_1 + w_2 + \ldots + w_k)/k. \tag{11.3}$$

11.5   ODD-ONE OUT

Consider an odd-one-out question in which we are given a list of words and need to find the one that does not belong. This can be done by computing the similarity between each word to the average word vector of the group, and returning the least similar word.

11.6   SHORT DOCUMENT SIMILARITY

Sometimes we are interested in computing a similarity between two documents. While the best results are likely to be achieved using dedicated models solutions based on pre-trained word embeddings are often very competitive, especially when dealing with short documents as such web queries, newspaper headlines, or tweets. The idea is to represent each document as a bag-of-words, and define the similarity between the documents to be the sum of the pairwise similarities between the words in the documents. Formally, consider two documents $D_1 = w_1^1, w_2^1, \ldots, w_m^1$ and $D_2 = w_1^2, w_2^2, \ldots, w_n^2$, and define the document similarity as:

$$\text{sim}_{\text{doc}}(D_1, D_2) = \sum_{i=1}^{m} \sum_{j=1}^{n} \cos(w_i^1, w_j^2).$$

Using basic linear algebra, it is straightforward to show that for normalized word vectors this similarity function can be computed as the dot product between the continuous-bag-of-words representations of the documents:

$$\text{sim}_{\text{doc}}(D_1, D_2) = \left(\sum_{i=1}^{m} \boldsymbol{w}_i^1\right) \cdot \left(\sum_{j=1}^{n} \boldsymbol{w}_j^2\right).$$

Consider a document collection $D_{1:k}$, and let $\boldsymbol{D}$ be a matrix in which each row i is the continuous bag-of-words representation of document D_i. Then the similarity between a new document $D' = w'_{1:n}$ and each of the documents in the collection can be computed using a single matrix-vector product: $\boldsymbol{s} = \boldsymbol{D} \cdot \left(\sum_{i=1}^{n} \boldsymbol{w}'_i\right)$.

11.7 WORD ANALOGIES

An interesting observation by Mikolov and colleagues [Mikolov et al., 2013a, Mikolov et al., 2013] that greatly contributed to the popularity of word embeddings is that one can perform "algebra" on the word vectors and get meaningful results. For example, for word embeddings trained using Word2Vec, one could take the vector of the word *king*, subtract the word *man*, add the word *woman* and get that the closest vector to the result (when excluding the words king, man, and woman) belongs to the word *queen*. That is, in vector space $\boldsymbol{w}_{\text{king}} - \boldsymbol{w}_{\text{man}} + \boldsymbol{w}_{\text{woman}} \approx \boldsymbol{w}_{\text{queen}}$. Similar results are obtained for various other semantic relations, for example $\boldsymbol{w}_{\text{France}} - \boldsymbol{w}_{\text{Paris}} + \boldsymbol{w}_{\text{London}} \approx \boldsymbol{w}_{\text{England}}$, and the same holds for many other cities and countries.

This has given rise to the *analogy solving* task in which different word embeddings are evaluated on their ability to answer analogy questions of the form *man:woman → king:?* by solving:

$$\text{analogy}(m : w \rightarrow k :?) = \underset{v \in V \setminus \{m,w,k\}}{\text{argmax}} \cos(\boldsymbol{v}, \boldsymbol{k} - \boldsymbol{m} + \boldsymbol{w}). \tag{11.4}$$

Levy and Goldberg [2014] observe that for normalized vectors, solving the maximization in Equation (11.4) is equivalent to solving Equation (11.5), that is, searching for a word that is similar to king, similar to man, and dissimilar to woman:

$$\text{analogy}(m : w \rightarrow k :?) = \underset{v \in V \setminus \{m,w,k\}}{\text{argmax}} \cos(\boldsymbol{v}, \boldsymbol{k}) - \cos(\boldsymbol{v}, \boldsymbol{m}) + \cos(\boldsymbol{v}, \boldsymbol{w}). \tag{11.5}$$

Levy and Goldberg refer to this method as 3CosAdd. The move from arithmetics between words in vector space to arithmetics between word similarities helps to explain to some extent the ability of the word embeddings to "solve" analogies, as well as suggest which kinds of analogies can be recovered by this method. It also highlights a possible deficiency of the 3CosAdd analogy recovery method: because of the additive nature of the objective, one term in the summation may dominate the expression, effectively ignoring the others. As suggested by Levy and Goldberg, this can be alleviated by changing to a multiplicative objective (3CosMul):

$$\text{analogy}(m : w \rightarrow k :?) = \underset{v \in V \setminus \{m,w,k\}}{\text{argmax}} \frac{\cos(\boldsymbol{v}, \boldsymbol{k}) \cos(\boldsymbol{v}, \boldsymbol{w})}{\cos(\boldsymbol{v}, \boldsymbol{m}) + \epsilon}. \tag{11.6}$$

While the analogy-recovery task is somewhat popular for evaluating word embeddings, it is not clear what success on a benchmark of analogy tasks says about the quality of the word embeddings beyond their suitability for solving this specific task.

11.8   RETROFITTING AND PROJECTIONS

More often than not, the resulting similarities do not fully reflect the similarities one has in mind for their application. Often, one can come up with or have access to a representative and relatively large list of word pairs that reflects the desired similarity better than the word embeddings, but has worse coverage. The *retrofitting* method of Faruqui et al. [2015] allows to use such data in order to improve the quality of the word embeddings matrix. Faruqui et al. [2015] show the effectiveness of the approach by using information derived from WordNet and PPDB (Section 6.2.1) to improve pre-trained embedding vectors.

The method assumes pre-trained word embedding matrix E as well as a graph $\mathcal{G}$ that encodes binary word to word similarities—nodes in the graph are words, and words are similar if they are connected by an edge. Note that the graph representation is very general, and a list of word pairs that are considered similar easily fits within the framework. The method works by solving an optimization problems that searches for a new word embeddings matrix $\hat{E}$ whose rows are close both to the corresponding rows in E but also to the rows corresponding to their neighbors in the graph $\mathcal{G}$. Concretely, the optimization objective is:

$$\underset{\hat{E}}{\mathrm{argmin}} \sum_{i=1}^{n} \left(\alpha_i \| \hat{E}_{[w_i]} - E_{[w_i]} \|^2 + \sum_{(w_i, w_j) \in \mathcal{G}} \beta_{ij} \| \hat{E}_{[w_i]} - \hat{E}_{[w_j]} \|^2 \right), \qquad (11.7)$$

where α_i and β_{ij} reflect the importance of a word being similar to itself or to another word. In practice, α_i are typically set uniformly to 1, while β_{ij} is set to the inverse of the degree of w_i in the graph (if a word has many neighbors, it has smaller influence on each of them). The approach works quite well in practice.

A related problem is when one has two embedding matrices: one with a small vocabulary $E^S \in \mathbb{R}^{|V_S| \times d_{\mathrm{emb}}}$ and another one with a large vocabulary $E^L \in \mathbb{R}^{|V_L| \times d_{\mathrm{emb}}}$ that were trained separately, and are hence incompatible. Perhaps the smaller vocabulary matrix was trained using a more expensive algorithm (possibly as part of a larger and more complex network), and the larger one was downloaded from the web. There is some overlap in the vocabularies, and one is interested in using word vectors from the larger matrix E^L for representing words that are not available in the smaller one E^S. One can then bridge the gap between the two embedding spaces using a *linear projection*[9] [Kiros et al., 2015, Mikolov et al., 2013]. The training objective is searching for a good projection matrix $M \in \mathbb{R}^{d_{\mathrm{emb}} \times d_{\mathrm{emb}}}$ that will map rows in E^L such that they are close to

---

[9]Of course, for this to work one needs to assume a linear relation between the two spaces. The linear projection method often works well in practice.

corresponding rows in E^S by solving the following optimization problem:

$$\underset{M}{\operatorname{argmin}} \sum_{w \in V_S \cap V_L} \|E^L_{[w]} \cdot M - E^S_{[w]}\|. \tag{11.8}$$

The learned matrix can then be used to project also the rows of E^L that do not have corresponding rows in E^S. This approach was successfully used by Kiros et al. [2015] to increase the vocabulary size of an LSTM-based sentence encoder (the sentence encoding model of Kiros et al. [2015] is discussed in Section 17.3).

Another cute (if somewhat less robust) application of the projection approach was taken by Mikolov et al. [2013] who learned matrices to project between embedding vectors trained on language A (say English) to embedding vectors trained on language B (say Spanish) based on a seed list of known word-word translation between the languages.

11.9   PRACTICALITIES AND PITFALLS

While off-the-shelf, pre-trained word embeddings can be downloaded and used, it is advised to not just blindly download word embeddings and treat them as a black box. Choices such as the source of the training corpus (but not necessarily its size: larger is not always better, and a smaller but cleaner, or smaller but more domain-focused corpora, are often more effective for a given use case), the contexts that were used for defining the distributional similarities, and many hyper-parameters of the learning can greatly influence the results. In presence of an annotated test set for the similarity task one cares about, it is best to experiment with several setting and choose the setup that works best on a development set. For discussion on the possible hyper-parameters and how they may affect the resulting similarities, see the work of Levy et al. [2015].

When using off-the-shelf embedding vectors, it is better to use the same tokenization and text normalization schemes that were used when deriving the corpus.

Finally, the similarities induced by word vectors are based on distributional signals, and therefore susceptible to all the limitations of distributional similarity methods described in Section 10.7. One should be aware of these limitations when using word vectors.

CHAPTER 12

Case Study: A Feed-forward Architecture for Sentence Meaning Inference

In Section 11.6 we introduced the sum of pairwise word similarities as a strong baseline for the short document similarity task. Given two sentences, the first one with words $w_1^1, \ldots, w_{\ell_1}^1$ and the second one with words $w_1^2, \ldots, w_{\ell_2}^2$, each word is associated with a corresponding pre-trained word vector $\boldsymbol{w}_{1:\ell_1}^1, \boldsymbol{w}_{1:\ell_2}^2$, and the similarity between the documents is given by:

$$\sum_{i=1}^{\ell_1} \sum_{j=1}^{\ell_2} \mathrm{sim}\left(\boldsymbol{w}_i^1, \boldsymbol{w}_j^2\right).$$

While this is a strong baseline, it is also completely unsupervised. Here, we show how a document similarity score can be greatly improved if we have a source of training data. We will follow the network presented by Parikh et al. [2016] for the *Stanford Natural Language Inference* (SNLI) semantic inference task. Other than providing a strong model for the SNLI task, this model also demonstrates how the basic network components described so far can be combined in various layers, resulting in a complex and powerful network that is trained jointly for a task.

12.1 NATURAL LANGUAGE INFERENCE AND THE SNLI DATASET

In the *natural language inference task*, also called *recognizing textual entailment* (RTE), you are given two texts, s_1 and s_2, and need to decide if s_1 entails s_2 (that is, can you infer s_2 from s_1), contradicts it (they cannot both be true), or if the texts are neutral (the second one neither entails nor contradicts the first). Example sentences for the different conditions are given in Table 12.1.

The entailment task was introduced by Dagan and Glickman [2004], and subsequently established through a series of benchmarks known as the PASCAL RTE Challenges [Dagan et al., 2005]. The task is very challenging,[1] and solving it perfectly entails human level understanding of

---

[1]The SNLI dataset described here focuses on descriptions of scenes that appear in images, and is easier than the general and un-restricted RTE task, which may require rather complex inference steps in order to solve. An example of an entailing pair in the un-restricted RTE task is *About two weeks before the trial started, I was in Shapiro's office in Century City* ⇒ *Shapiro worked in Century City.*

Table 12.1: The Natural Language Inference (Textual Entailment) Task. The examples are taken from the development set of the SNLI dataset.

Two men on bicycles competing in a race.	
Entail	People are riding bikes.
Neutral	Men are riding bicycles on the street.
Contradict	A few people are catching fish.
Two doctors perform surgery on patient.	
Entail	Doctors are performing surgery.
Neutral	Two doctors are performing surgery on a man.
Contradict	Two surgeons are having lunch.

language. For in-depth discussion on the task and approaches to its solution that do not involve neural networks, see the book by Dagan, Roth, Sammons, and Zanzotto in this series [Dagan et al., 2013].

SNLI is a large dataset created by Bowman et al. [2015], containing 570k human-written sentence pairs, each pair manually categorized as entailing, contradicting, or neutral. The sentences were created by presenting image captions to annotators, and asking them, without seeing the image, to write a caption that is definitely a true description of the image (entail), a caption that is might be a true description of the image (neutral), and a caption that is a definitely false description of the image (contradict). After collecting 570k sentence pairs this way, 10% of them were further validated by presenting sentence pairs to different annotators and asking them to categorize the pair into entailing, neutral, or contradicting. The validated sentences are then used for the test and validation sets. The examples in Table 12.1 are from the SNLI dataset.

While simpler than the previous RTE challenge datasets, it is also much larger, and still not trivial to solve (in particular for distinguishing the entailing from the neutral events). The SNLI dataset is a popular dataset for assessing meaning inference models. Notice that the task goes beyond mere pairwise word similarity: for example, consider the second sentence in Table 12.1: the neutral sentence is much more similar (in terms of average word similarity) to the original one than the entailed sentence. We need the ability to highlight some similarities, degrade the strength of others, and also to understand which kind of similarities are meaning preserving (i.e., going from *man* to *patient* in the context of a surgery), and which add new information (i.e., going from *patient* to *man*). The network architecture is designed to facilitate this kind of reasoning.

12.2 A TEXTUAL SIMILARITY NETWORK

The network will work in several stages. In the first stage, our goal is to compute pairwise word similarities that are more suitable for the task. The similarity function for two word vectors is defined to be:

$$\text{sim}(\boldsymbol{w_1}, \boldsymbol{w_2}) = \text{MLP}^{\text{transform}}(\boldsymbol{w_1}) \cdot \text{MLP}^{\text{transform}}(\boldsymbol{w_2}) \tag{12.1}$$

$$\text{MLP}^{\text{transform}}(\boldsymbol{x}) \in \mathbb{R}^{d_s} \quad \boldsymbol{w_1}, \boldsymbol{w_2} \in \mathbb{R}^{d_{\text{emb}}}.$$

That is, we first transform each word vector by use of a trained nonlinear transformation, and then take the dot-product of the transformed vectors.

Each word in sentence $\boldsymbol{a}$ can be similar to several words in sentence $\boldsymbol{b}$, and vice versa. For each word w_i^a in sentence $\boldsymbol{a}$ we compute a ℓ_b-dimensional vector of its similarities to words in sentence $\boldsymbol{b}$, normalized via softmax so that all similarities are positive and sum to one. This is called the *alignment vector* for the word:

$$\boldsymbol{\alpha}_i^a = \text{softmax}(\text{sim}(\boldsymbol{w}_i^a, \boldsymbol{w}_1^b), \dots, \text{sim}(\boldsymbol{w}_i^a, \boldsymbol{w}_{\ell_b}^b)). \tag{12.2}$$

We similarly compute an alignment vector for each word in $\boldsymbol{b}$

$$\boldsymbol{\alpha}_i^b = \text{softmax}(\text{sim}(\boldsymbol{w}_1^a, \boldsymbol{w}_i^b), \dots, \text{sim}(\boldsymbol{w}_{\ell_a}^a, \boldsymbol{w}_i^b))$$

$$\boldsymbol{\alpha}_i^a \in \mathbb{N}_+{}^{\ell_b} \quad \boldsymbol{\alpha}_i^b \in \mathbb{N}_+{}^{\ell_a}.$$

For every word w_i^a we compute a vector $\bar{\boldsymbol{w}}_i^b$ composed of a weighted-sum of the words in $\boldsymbol{b}$ that are aligned to w_i^a, and similarly for every word w_j^b:

$$\bar{\boldsymbol{w}}_i^b = \sum_{j=1}^{\ell_b} \boldsymbol{\alpha}_{i\,[j]}^a \boldsymbol{w}_j^b$$

$$\bar{\boldsymbol{w}}_j^a = \sum_{i=1}^{\ell_a} \boldsymbol{\alpha}_{i\,[j]}^b \boldsymbol{w}_i^a. \tag{12.3}$$

A vector $\bar{\boldsymbol{w}}_i^b$ captures the weighted mixture of words in sentence $\boldsymbol{b}$ that are triggered by the ith word in sentence $\boldsymbol{a}$.

Such weighted sum representations of a sequence of vectors, where the weights are computed by a softmax over scores such as the one in Equation (12.2), are often referred to as *an attention mechanism*. The name comes from the fact that the weights reflect how important is each item in the target sequence to the given source item—how much *attention* should be given to each of the items in the target sequence with respect to the source item. We will discuss attention in more details in Chapter 17, when discussing conditioned-generation models.

The similarity between w_i^a and the corresponding triggered mixture $\bar{\boldsymbol{w}}_i^b$ in sentence $\boldsymbol{b}$ is not necessarily relevant for the NLI task. We attempt to transform each such pair into a representation vector v_i^a that focuses on the important information for the task. This is done using another feed-forward network:

$$v_i^a = \text{MLP}^{\text{pair}}([w_i^a; \bar{w}_i^b])$$
$$v_j^b = \text{MLP}^{\text{pair}}([w_j^b; \bar{w}_j^a]).$$

(12.4)

Note that unlike the similarity function in Equation (12.1) that considered each term individually, here the function can handle both terms differently.

Finally, we sum the resulting vectors and pass them into a final MLP classifier for predicting the relation between the two sentences (entail, contradict, or neutral):

$$v^a = \sum_i v_i^a$$

$$v^b = \sum_j v_j^b$$

(12.5)

$$\hat{y} = \text{MLP}^{\text{decide}}([v^a; v^b]).$$

In the work of Parikh et al. [2016], all the MLPs have two hidden layers of size 200, and a ReLU activation function. The entire process is captured in the same computation graph, and the network is trained end-to-end using the cross-entropy loss. The pre-trained word embeddings themselves were *not* changed with the rest of the network, relying on $\text{MLP}^{transform}$ to do the needed adaptation. As of the time of this writing, this architecture is the best performing network on the SNLI dataset.

To summarize the architecture, the *transform* network learns a similarity function for word-level alignment. It transforms each word into a space that preserves important word-level similarities. After the transform network, each word vector is similar to other words that are likely to refer to the same entity or the same event. The goal of this network is to find words that *may* contribute to the entailment. We get alignments in both directions: from each word in *a* to multiple words in *b*, and from each word in *b* to multiple words in *a*. The alignments are soft, and are manifested by weighted group membership instead of by hard decisions, so a word can participate in many pairs of similarities. This network is likely to put *men* and *people* next to each other, *men* and *two* next to each other and *man* and *patient* next to each other, and likewise for inflected forms *perform* and *performing*.

The *pair* network then looks at each aligned pair (word + group) using a weighted-CBOW representation, and extracts information relevant to the pair. Is this pair useful for the entailment prediction task? It also looks at sentence each component of the pair came from, and will likely learn that *patient* and *man* are entailing in one direction and not the other.

Finally, the *decide* network looks at the aggregated data from the word pairs, and comes up with a decision based on all the evidence. We have three stages of reasoning: first one recovers weak local evidence in terms of similarity alignment; the second one looks at weighted multi-word units and also adds directionality; and the third integrates all the local evidence into a global decision.

The details of the network are tuned for this particular task and dataset, and it is not clear if they will generalize to other settings. The idea of this chapter was not to introduce a specific network architecture, but rather to demonstrate that complex architectures can be designed, and that it is sometimes worth the effort to do so. A new component introduced in this chapter that is worth noting is the use of the *soft alignment* weights α_i^a (also sometimes called *attention*), in order to compute a weighted sum of elements $\bar{w}_i^b$ [Equation (12.3)]. We will encounter this idea again when discussing attention-based conditioned generation with RNNs in Chapter 17.

PART III

Specialized Architectures

In the previous chapters, we've discussed supervised learning and feed-forward neural networks, and how they can be applied to language tasks. The feed-forward neural networks are for the most part general-purpose classification architectures—nothing in them is tailored specifically for language data or sequences. Indeed, we mostly structured the language tasks to fit into the MLP framework.

In the following chapters, we will explore some neural architectures that are more specialized for dealing with language data. In particular, we will discuss 1D convolutional-and-pooling architectures (CNNs), and recurrent neural networks (RNNs). CNNs are neural architectures that are specialized at identifying informative ngrams and gappy-ngrams in a sequence of text, regardless of their position, but while taking local ordering patterns into account. RNNs are neural architectures that are designed to capture subtle patterns and regularities in sequences, and that allow modeling non-markovian dependencies looking at "infinite windows" around a focus word, while zooming-in on informative sequential patterns in that window. Finally, we will discuss sequence-generation models and conditioned generation.

Feature Extraction   The CNN and RNN architectures explored in this part of the book are primarily used as *feature extractors*. A CNN or an RNN network are not a standalone component, but rather each such network produces a vector (or a sequence of vectors) that are then fed into further parts of the network that will eventually lead to predictions. The network is trained end-to-end (the predicting part and the convolutional/recurrent architectures are trained jointly) such that the vectors resulting from the convolutional or recurrent part of the network will capture the aspects of the input that are useful for the given prediction task. In the following chapters, we introduce feature extractors that are based on the CNN and the RNN architectures. As the time of this writing, RNN-based feature extractors are more established than CNNs as feature extractors for text-based applications. However, the different architectures have different strengths and weaknesses, and the balance between them may shift in the future. Both are worth knowing, and hybrid approaches are also likely to become popular. Chapters 16 and 17 discuss the integration of RNN-based feature extractors in different NLP prediction and generation architectures. Large parts of the discussion in these chapters are applicable also to convolutional networks.

CNNs and RNNs as Lego Bricks   When learning about the CNN and RNN architectures, it is useful to think about them as "Lego Bricks," that can be mixed and matched to create a desired structure and to achieve a desired behavior.

This Lego-bricks-like mixing-and-matching is facilitated by the computation-graph mechanism and gradient-based optimization. It allows treating network architectures such as MLPs, CNNs and RNNs as components, or blocks, that can be mixed and matched to create larger and larger structures—one just needs to make sure that that input and output dimensions of the different components match—and the computation graph and gradient-based training will take care of the rest.

This allows us to create large and elaborate network structures, with multiple layers of MLPs, CNNs and RNNs feeding into each other, and training the entire network in an end-to-end fashion. Several examples are explored in later chapters, but many others are possible, and different tasks may benefit from different architectures. When learning about a new architecture, don't think "which existing component does it replace?" or "how do I use it to solve a task?" but rather "how can I integrate it into my arsenal of building blocks, and combine it with the other components in order to achieve a desired result?".

CHAPTER 13

Ngram Detectors: Convolutional Neural Networks

Sometimes we are interested in making predictions based on ordered sets of items (e.g., the sequence of words in a sentence, the sequence of sentences in a document, and so on). Consider, for example, predicting the sentiment (positive, negative, or neutral) of sentences such as the following.

- *Part of the charm of Satin Rouge is that it avoids the obvious with humor and lightness.*

- *Still, this flick is fun and host to some truly excellent sequences.*

Some of the sentence words are very informative of the sentiment (*charm, fun, excellent*) other words are less informative (*Still, host, flick, lightness, obvious, avoids*) and to a good approximation, an informative clue is informative regardless of its position in the sentence. We would like to feed all of the sentence words into a learner, and let the training process figure out the important clues. One possible solution is feeding a CBOW representation into a fully connected network such as an MLP. However, a downside of the CBOW approach is that it ignores the ordering information completely, assigning the sentences "*it was not good, it was actually quite bad*" and "*it was not bad, it was actually quite good*" the exact same representation. While the global positions of the indicators "*not good*" and "*not bad*" do not matter for the classification task, the local ordering of the words (that the word "*not*" appears right before the word "*bad*") is very important. Similarly, in the corpus-based example *Montias pumps a lot of energy into his nuanced narative, and surrounds himself with a cast of quirky—but not stereotyped—street characters*, there is a big difference between "not stereotyped" (positive indicator) and "not nuanced" (negative indicator). While the examples above are simple cases of negation, some patterns are not as obvious, e.g., "avoids the obvious" vs. "obvious" or vs. "avoids the charm" in the first example. In short, looking at ngrams is much more informative than looking at a bag-of-words.

A naive approach would suggest embedding word-pairs (bi-grams) or word-triplets (tri-grams) rather than words, and building a CBOW over the embedded ngrams. While such an architecture is indeed quite effective, it will result huge embedding matrices, will not scale for longer ngrams, and will suffer from data sparsity problems as it does not share statistical strength between different ngrams (the embedding of "quite good" and "very good" are completely independent of one another, so if the learner saw only one of them during training, it will not be able to deduce anything about the other based on its component words).

The CNN architecture   This chapter introduces the convolution-and-pooling (also called convolutional neural networks, or CNNs) architecture, which is tailored to this modeling problem. A convolutional neural network is designed to identify indicative local predictors in a large structure, and to combine them to produce a fixed size vector representation of the structure, capturing the local aspects that are most informative for the prediction task at hand. I.e., the convolutional architecture will identify ngrams that are predictive for the task at hand, without the need to pre-specify an embedding vector for each possible ngram. (In Section 13.2, we discuss an alternative method that allows working with unbounded ngram vocabularies while keeping a bounded size embedding matrix). The convolutional architecture also allows to share predictive behavior between ngrams that share similar components, even if the exact ngram was never seen at test time.

The convolutional architecture could be expanded into a hierarchy of convolution layers, each one effectively looking at a longer range of ngrams in the sentence. This also allows the model to be sensitive to some non-contiguous ngrams. This is discussed in Section 13.3.

As discussed in the opening section of this part of the book, the CNN is in essence a feature-extracting architecture. It does not constitute a standalone, useful network on its own, but rather is meant to be integrated into a larger network, and to be trained to work in tandem with it in order to produce an end result. The CNN layer's responsibility is to extract meaningful sub-structures that are useful for the overall prediction task at hand.

History and Terminology   Convolution-and-pooling architectures [LeCun and Bengio, 1995] evolved in the neural networks vision community, where they showed great success as object detectors—recognizing an object from a predefined category ("cat," "bicycles") regardless of its position in the image [Krizhevsky et al., 2012]. When applied to images, the architecture is using 2D (grid) convolutions. When applied to text, we are mainly concerned with 1D (sequence) convolutions. Convolutional networks were introduced to the NLP community in the pioneering work of Collobert et al. [2011] who used them for semantic-role labeling, and later by Kalchbrenner et al. [2014] and Kim [2014] who used them for sentiment and question-type classification.

Because of their origins in the computer-vision community, a lot of the terminology around convolutional neural networks is borrowed from computer vision and signal processing, including terms such as *filter*, *channel*, and *receptive-field* which are often used also in the context of text processing. We will mention these terms when introducing the corresponding concepts.

13.1   BASIC CONVOLUTION + POOLING

The main idea behind a convolution and pooling architecture for language tasks is to apply a non-linear (learned) function over each instantiation of a k-word sliding window over the sentence.[1] This function (also called "filter") transforms a window of k words into a scalar value. Several such filters can be applied, resulting in ℓ dimensional vector (each dimension corresponding to a filter)

---

[1]The window-size, k, is sometimes referred to as the *receptive field* of the convolution.

that captures important properties of the words in the window. Then, a "pooling" operation is used to combine the vectors resulting from the different windows into a single ℓ-dimensional vector, by taking the max or the average value observed in each of the ℓ dimensions over the different windows. The intention is to focus on the most important "features" in the sentence, regardless of their location—each filter extracts a different indicator from the window, and the pooling operation zooms in on the important indicators. The resulting ℓ-dimensional vector is then fed further into a network that is used for prediction. The gradients that are propagated back from the network's loss during the training process are used to tune the parameters of the filter function to highlight the aspects of the data that are important for the task the network is trained for. Intuitively, when the sliding window of size k is run over a sequence, the filter function learns to identify informative $k$grams. Figure 13.2 illustrates an application of a convolution-and-pooling network over a sentence.

13.1.1 1D CONVOLUTIONS OVER TEXT

We begin by focusing on the one-dimensional convolution operation.[2] The next section will focus on pooling.

Consider a sequence of words $w_{1:n} = w_1, \ldots, w_n$, each with their corresponding d_{emb} dimensional word embedding $E_{[w_i]} = w_i$. A 1D convolution of width-k works by moving a sliding-window of size k over the sentence, and applying the same "filter" to each window in the sequence, where a filter is a dot-product with a weight vector u, which is often followed by a nonlinear activation function. Define the operator $\oplus(w_{i:i+k-1})$ to be the concatenation of the vectors $w_i, \ldots, w_{i+k-1}$. The concatenated vector of the ith window is then $x_i = \oplus(w_{i:i+k-1}) = [w_i; w_{i+1}; \ldots; w_{i+k-1}]$, $x_i \in \mathbb{R}^{k \cdot d_{emb}}$.

We then apply the filter to each window-vector, resulting scalar values p_i:

$$p_i = g(x_i \cdot u) \tag{13.1}$$

$$x_i = \oplus(w_{i:i+k-1}) \tag{13.2}$$

$$p_i \in \mathbb{R} \quad x_i \in \mathbb{R}^{k \cdot d_{emb}} \quad u \in \mathbb{R}^{k \cdot d_{emb}},$$

where g is a nonlinear activation.

It is customary to use ℓ different filters, $u_1, \ldots, u_\ell$, which can be arranged into a matrix U, and a bias vector b is often added:

$$p_i = g(x_i \cdot U + b) \tag{13.3}$$

$$p_i \in \mathbb{R}^\ell \quad x_i \in \mathbb{R}^{k \cdot d_{emb}} \quad U \in \mathbb{R}^{k \cdot d_{emb} \times \ell} \quad b \in \mathbb{R}^\ell.$$

Each vector p_i is a collection of ℓ values that represent (or summarize) the ith window. Ideally, each dimension captures a different kind of indicative information.

---

[2]1D here refers to a convolution operating over 1-dimensional inputs such as sequences, as opposed to 2D convolutions which are applied to images.

Narrow vs. Wide Convolutions   How many vectors p_i do we have? For a sentence of length n with a window of size k, there are $n - k + 1$ positions in which to start the sequence, and we get $n - k + 1$ vectors $p_{1:n-k+1}$. This is called a *narrow convolution*. An alternative is to pad the sentence with $k - 1$ padding-words to each side, resulting in $n + k + 1$ vectors $p_{1:n+k+1}$. This is called a *wide convolution* [Kalchbrenner et al., 2014]. We use m to denote the number of resulting vectors.

An Alternative Formulation of Convolutions   In our description of convolutions over a sequence of n items $w_{1:n}$ each item is associated with a d-dimensional vector, and the vector are concatenated into a large $1 \times d \cdot n$ sentence vector. The convolution network with a window of size k and ℓ output values is then based on a $k \cdot d \times \ell$ matrix. This matrix is applied to segments of the $1 \times d \cdot n$ sentence matrix that correspond to k-word windows. Each such multiplication results in ℓ values. Each of these k values can be thought of as the result of a dot product between a $k \cdot d \times 1$ vector (a row in the matrix) and a sentence segment.

Another (equivalent) formulation that is often used in the literature is one in which the n vectors are stacked on top of each other, resulting in an $n \times d$ sentence matrix. The convolution operation is then performed by sliding ℓ different $k \times d$ matrices (called "kernels" or "filters") over the sentence matrix, and performing a *matrix convolution* between each kernel and the corresponding sentence-matrix segment. The matrix convolution operation between two matrices is defined as performing element-wise multiplication of the two matrices, and summing the results. Each of the ℓ sentence-kernel convolution operations produces a single value, for a total of ℓ values. It is easy to convince oneself that the two approaches are indeed equivalent, by observing that each kernel corresponds to a row in the $k \cdot d \times \ell$ matrix, and the convolution with a kernel corresponds to a dot-product with a matrix row.

Figure 13.1 show narrow and wide convolutions in the two notations.

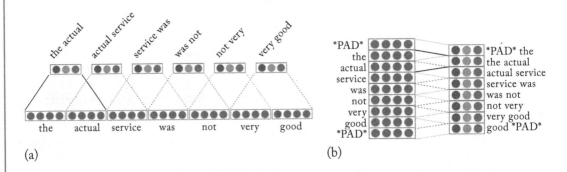

(a)   (b)

Figure 13.1: The inputs and outputs of a narrow and a wide convolution in the vector-concatenation and the vector-stacking notations. (a) A *narrow* convolution with a window of size $k = 2$ and 3-dimensional output ($\ell = 3$), in the vector-concatenation notation. (b) A *wide* convolution with a window of size $k = 2$, a 3-dimensional output ($\ell = 3$), in the vector-stacking notation.

Channels   In computer vision, a picture is represented as a collection of pixels, each representing the color intensity of a particular point. When using an RGB color scheme, each pixel is a combination of three intensity values—one for each of the Red, Green, and Blue components. These are then stored in three different matrices. Each matrix provides a different "view" of the image, and is referred to as a Channel. When applying a convolution to an image in computer vision, it is common to apply a different set of filters to each channel, and then combine the three resulting vectors into a single vector. Taking the different-views-of-the-data metaphor, we can have multiple channels in text processing as well. For example, one channel will be the sequence of words, while another channel is the sequence of corresponding POS tags. Applying the convolution over the words will result in m vectors $p^w_{1:m}$, and applying it over the POS-tags will result in m vectors $p^t_{1:m}$. These two views can then be combined either by summation $p_i = p^w_i + p^t_i$ or by concatenation $p_i = [p^w_i ; p^t_i]$.

To summarize   The main idea behind the convolution layer is to apply the same parameterized function over all k-grams in the sequence. This creates a sequence of m vectors, each representing a particular k-gram in the sequence. The representation is sensitive to the identity and order of the words within a k-gram, but the same representation will be extracted for a k-gram regardless of its position within the sequence.

13.1.2 VECTOR POOLING

Applying the convolution over the text results in m vectors $p_{1:m}$, each $p_i \in \mathbb{R}^\ell$. These vectors are then combined (*pooled*) into a single vector $c \in \mathbb{R}^\ell$ representing the entire sequence. Ideally, the vector c will capture the essence of the important information in the sequence. The nature of the important information that needs to be encoded in the vector c is task dependent. For example, if we are performing sentiment classification, the essence are informative ngrams that indicate sentiment, and if we are performing topic-classification, the essence are informative ngrams that indicate a particular topic.

During training, the vector c is fed into downstream network layers (i.e., an MLP), culminating in an output layer which is used for prediction.[3] The training procedure of the network calculates the loss with respect to the prediction task, and the error gradients are propagated all the way back through the pooling and convolution layers, as well as the embedding layers. The training process tunes the convolution matrix U, the bias vector b, the downstream network, and potentially also the embeddings matrix E such that the vector c resulting from the convolution and pooling process indeed encodes information relevant to the task at hand.[4]

---

[3]The input to the downstream network can be either c itself, or a combination of c and other vectors.

[4]Besides being useful for prediction, a by-product of the training procedure is a set of parameters W, B, and embeddings E that can be used in a convolution and pooling architecture to encode arbitrary length sentences into fixed-size vectors, such that sentences that share the same kind of predictive information will be close to each other.

Max-pooling The most common pooling operation is *max pooling*, taking the maximum value across each dimension.

$$c_{[j]} = \max_{1 < i \leq m} p_{i\,[j]} \qquad \forall j \in [1, \ell], \tag{13.4}$$

$p_{i\,[j]}$ denotes the jth component of p_i. The effect of the max-pooling operation is to get the most salient information across window positions. Ideally, each dimension will "specialize" in a particular sort of predictors, and max operation will pick on the most important predictor of each type.

Figure 13.2 provides an illustration of the convolution and pooling process with a max-pooling operation.

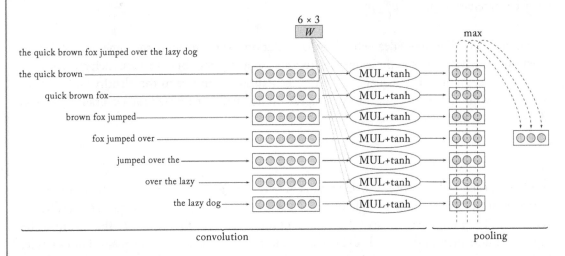

Figure 13.2: 1D convolution+pooling over the sentence "the quick brown fox jumped over the lazy dog." This is a narrow convolution (no padding is added to the sentence) with a window size of 3. Each word is translated to a 2-dim embedding vector (not shown). The embedding vectors are then concatenated, resulting in 6-dim window representations. Each of the seven windows is transfered through a 6×3 filter (linear transformation followed by element-wise tanh), resulting in seven 3-dimensional filtered representations. Then, a max-pooling operation is applied, taking the max over each dimension, resulting in a final 3-dimensional pooled vector.

Average Pooling The second most common pooling type being *average-pooling*—taking the average value of each index instead of the max:

$$c = \frac{1}{m} \sum_{i=1}^{m} p_i. \tag{13.5}$$

One view of average-pooling is that of taking a continuous bag-of-words (CBOW) of the k-gram representations resulting from the convolutions rather than from the sentence words.

K-max Pooling   Another variation, introduced by Kalchbrenner et al. [2014] is *k-max pooling* operation, in which the top k values in each dimension are retained instead of only the best one, while preserving the order in which they appeared in the text.[5] For example, consider the following matrix:

$$\begin{bmatrix} 1 & 2 & 3 \\ 9 & 6 & 5 \\ 2 & 3 & 1 \\ 7 & 8 & 1 \\ 3 & 4 & 1 \end{bmatrix}.$$

A 1-max pooling over the column vectors will result in $[9 \ 8 \ 5]$, while a 2-max pooling will result in the following matrix: $\begin{bmatrix} 9 & 6 & 3 \\ 7 & 8 & 5 \end{bmatrix}$ whose rows will then be concatenated to $[9 \ 6 \ 3 \ 7 \ 8 \ 5]$.

The k-max pooling operation makes it possible to pool the k most active indicators that may be a number of positions apart; it preserves the order of the features, but is insensitive to their specific positions. It can also discern more finely the number of times the feature is highly activated [Kalchbrenner et al., 2014].

Dynamic Pooling   Rather than performing a single pooling operation over the entire sequence, we may want to retain some positional information based on our domain understanding of the prediction problem at hand. To this end, we can split the vectors p_i into r distinct groups, apply the pooling separately on each group, and then concatenate the r resulting ℓ-dimensional vectors $c_1, \ldots, c_r$. The division of the p_is into groups is performed based on domain knowledge. For example, we may conjecture that words appearing early in the sentence are more indicative than words appearing late. We can then split the sequence into r equally sized regions, applying a separate max-pooling to each region. For example, Johnson and Zhang [2015] found that when classifying documents into topics, it is useful to have 20 average-pooling regions, clearly separating the initial sentences (where the topic is usually introduced) from later ones, while for a sentiment classification task a single max-pooling operation over the entire sentence was optimal (suggesting that one or two very strong signals are enough to determine the sentiment, regardless of the position in the sentence).

Similarly, in a relation extraction kind of task we may be given two words and asked to determine the relation between them. We could argue that the words before the first word, the words after the second word, and the words between them provide three different kinds of infor-

---

[5]In this chapter, we use k to denote the window-size of the convolution. The k in k-max pooling is a different, and unrelated, value. We use the letter k for consistency with the literature.

mation [Chen et al., 2015]. We can thus split the p_i vectors accordingly, pooling separately the windows resulting from each group.

13.1.3 VARIATIONS

Rather than a single convolutional layer, several convolutional layers may be applied in parallel. For example, we may have four different convolutional layers, each with a different window size in the range 2–5, capturing k-gram sequences of varying lengths. The result of each convolutional layer will then be pooled, and the resulting vectors concatenated and fed to further processing [Kim, 2014].

The convolutional architecture need not be restricted into the linear ordering of a sentence. For example, Ma et al. [2015] generalize the convolution operation to work over syntactic dependency trees. There, each window is around a node in the syntactic tree, and the pooling is performed over the different nodes. Similarly, Liu et al. [2015] apply a convolutional architecture on top of dependency paths extracted from dependency trees. Le and Zuidema [2015] propose performing max pooling over vectors representing the different derivations leading to the same chart item in a chart parser.

13.2   ALTERNATIVE: FEATURE HASHING

Convolutional networks for text work as very effective feature detectors for consecutive k-grams. However, they require many matrix multiplications, resulting in non-negligible computation. A more time-efficient alternative would be to just use k-gram embeddings directly, and then pool the k-grams using average pooling (resulting in a continuous-bag-of-ngrams representations) or max pooling. A downside of the approach is that it requires allocating a dedicated embedding vector for each possible k-gram, which can be prohibitive in terms of memory as the number of k-grams in the training corpus can be very large.

A solution to the problems is the use of the *feature hashing* technique that originated in linear models [Ganchev and Dredze, 2008, Shi et al., 2009, Weinberger et al., 2009] and recently adopted to neural networks [Joulin et al., 2016]. The idea behind feature hashing is that we don't pre-compute vocabulary-to-index mapping. Instead, we allocate an embedding matrix E with N rows (N should be sufficiently large, but not prohibitive, say in the millions or tens of millions). When a k-gram is seen in training, we assign it to a row in E by applying a *hash function h* that will deterministically map it into a number in the range $[1, N]$, $i = h(\text{k-gram}) \in [1, N]$. We then use the corresponding row $E_{[h(\text{k-gram})]}$ as the embedding vector. Every k-gram will be dynamically assigned a row index this way, without the need to store an explicit kgram-to-index mapping or to dedicate an embedding vector to each k-gram. Some k-grams may share the same embedding vector due to hash collisions (indeed, with the space of possible k-grams being much larger than the number of allocated embedding vectors such collisions are bound to happen), but as most k-grams are not informative for the task the collisions will be smoothed out by the training process. If one wants to be more careful, several distinct hash functions $h_1, \ldots, h_r$ can be used, and each

k-gram represented as the sum of the rows corresponding to its hashes ($\sum_{i=1}^{r} E_{[h_i\,(\text{k-gram})]}$). This way, if an informative k-gram happens to collide with another informative k-gram using one hash, it still likely to have a non-colliding representation from one of the other hashes.

This hashing trick (also called *hash kernel*) works very well in practice, resulting in very efficient bag-of-ngrams models. It is recommended as a go-to baseline before considering more complex approaches or architectures.

13.3 HIERARCHICAL CONVOLUTIONS

The 1D convolution approach described so far can be thought of as an ngram detector. A convolution layer with a window of size k is learning to identify indicative k-grams in the input.

The approach can be extended into a *hierarchy of convolutional layers*, in which a sequence of convolution layers are applied one after the other. Let $\text{CONV}_{\Theta}^{k}(w_{1:n})$ be the result of applying a convolution with window size k and parameters Θ to each k-size window in the sequence $w_{1:n}$:

$$\begin{aligned} p_{1:m} &= \text{CONV}_{U,b}^{k}(w_{1:n}) \\ p_i &= g(\oplus(w_{i:i+k-1}) \cdot U + b) \\ m &= \begin{cases} n - k + 1 & \text{narrow convolution} \\ n + k + 1 & \text{wide convolution.} \end{cases} \end{aligned} \tag{13.6}$$

We can now have a succession of r convolutional layers that feed into each other as follows:

$$\begin{aligned} p_{1:m_1}^{1} &= \text{CONV}_{U^1,b^1}^{k_1}(w_{1:n}) \\ p_{1:m_2}^{2} &= \text{CONV}_{U^2,b^2}^{k_2}(p_{1:m_1}^{1}) \\ &\cdots \\ p_{1:m_r}^{r} &= \text{CONV}_{U^r,b^r}^{k_r}(p_{1:m_{r-1}}^{r-1}). \end{aligned} \tag{13.7}$$

The resulting vectors $p_{1:m_r}^{r}$ capture increasingly larger effective windows ("*receptive-fields*") of the sentence. For r layers with a window of size k, each vector p_i^r will be sensitive to a window of $r(k-1)+1$ words.[6] Moreover, the vector p_i^r can be sensitive to *gappy-ngrams* of $k+r-1$ words, potentially capturing patterns such as "*not __ good*" or "*obvious __ predictable __ plot*" where __ stands for a short sequence of words, as well more specialized patterns where the gaps

---

[6]To see why, consider that the first convolution layer transforms each sequence of k neighboring word-vectors into vectors representing k-grams. Then, the second convolution layer will combine each k consecutive k-gram-vectors into vectors that capture a window of $k + (k-1)$ words, and so on, until the rth convolution will capture $k + (r-1)(k-1) = r(k-1) + 1$ words.

can be further specialized (i.e., "a sequence of words that do not contain *not*" or "a sequence of words that are adverb-like").[7] Figure 13.3 shows a two-layer hierarchical convolution with $k = 2$.

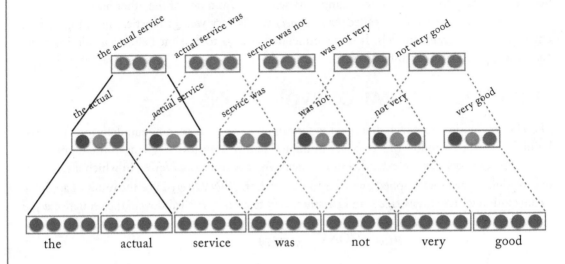

Figure 13.3: Two-layer hierarchical convolution with k=2.

Strides, Dilation and Pooling   So far, the convolution operation is applied to each k-word window in the sequence, i.e., windows starting at indices $1, 2, 3, \ldots$. This is said to have a *stride* of size 1. Larger strides are also possible, i.e., with a stride of size 2 the convolution operation will be applied to windows starting at indices $1, 3, 5, \ldots$. More generally, we define $\text{CONV}^{k,s}$ as:

$$\boldsymbol{p_{1:m}} = \text{CONV}^{k,s}_{U,b}(\boldsymbol{w_{1:n}})$$

$$\boldsymbol{p_i} = g(\oplus(\boldsymbol{w}_{1+(i-1)s:(s+k)i}) \cdot \boldsymbol{U} + \boldsymbol{b}),$$

$$(13.8)$$

where s is the stride size. The result will be a shorter output sequence from the convolutional layer.

In a *dilated convolution architecture* [Strubell et al., 2017, Yu and Koltun, 2016] the hierarchy of convolution layers each has a stride size of $k - 1$ (i.e., $\text{CONV}^{k,k-1}$). This allows an exponential growth in the effective window size as a function of the number of layers. Figure 13.4 shows convolution layers with different stride lengths. Figure 13.5 shows a dilated convolution architecture.

An alternative to the dilation approach is to keep the stride-size fixed at 1, but shorten the sequence length between each layer by applying local pooling, i.e, consecutive k'-gram of vectors

---

[7]To see why, consider a sequence of two convolution layer each with a window of size 2 over the sequence *funny and appealing*. The first convolution layer will encode *funny and* and *and appealing* as vectors, and may choose to retain the equivalent of "*funny* ___" and "___ *appealing*" in the resulting vectors. The second convolution layer can then combine these into "*funny* ___ *appealing*," "*funny* ___" or "___ *appealing*."

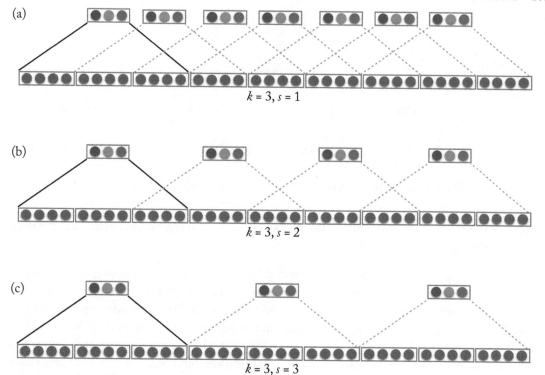

Figure 13.4: Strides. (a–c) Convolution layer with k=3 and stride sizes 1, 2, 3.

can be converted into a single vector using max pooling or averaged pooling. Even if we pool just every two neighboring vectors, each convolutional-and-pooling layer in the hierarchy will halve the length of the sequence. Similar to the dilation approach, we again gain an exponential decrease in sequence length as a function of the number of layers.

Parameter Tying and Skip-connections   Another variation that can be applied to the hierarchical convolution architecture is performing *parameter-tying*, using the same set of parameters U, b in all the parameter layers. This results in more parameter sharing, as well as allowing to use an unbounded number of convolution layers (as all the convolution layers share the same parameters, the number of convolution layers need not be set in advance), which in turn allows to reduce arbitrary length sequences into a single vector by using a sequence of narrow convolutions, each resulting in a shorter sequence of vectors.

When using deep architectures, *skip-connections* are sometimes useful: these work by feeding into the ith layer not only the vectors resulting from the $i − 1$th layer, but also vectors from

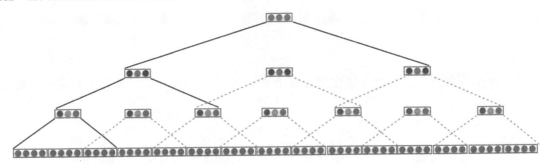

Figure 13.5: Three-layer dilated hierarchical convolution with $k=3$.

previous layers which are combined to the vectors of the $i-1$th layer using either concatenation, averaging, or summation.

Further Reading   The use of hierarchical and dilated convolution and pooling architectures is very common in the computer-vision community, where various deep architectures—comprising of arrangements of many convolutions and pooling layers with different strides—have been proposed, resulting in very strong image classification and object recognition results [He et al., 2016, Krizhevsky et al., 2012, Simonyan and Zisserman, 2015]. The use of such deep architectures for NLP is still more preliminary. Zhang et al. [2015] provide initial experiments with text classification with hierarchical convolutions over characters, and Conneau et al. [2016] provide further results, this time with very deep convolutional networks. The work of Strubell et al. [2017] provides a good overview of hierarchical and dilated architectures for a sequence labeling task. Kalchbrenner et al. [2016] use dilated convolutions as encoders in an encoder-decoder architecture (Section 17.2) for machine translation. The hierarchy of convolutions with local pooling approach is used by Xiao and Cho [2016], who apply it to a sequence of character in a document-classification task, and then feed the resulting vectors into a recurrent neural network. We return to this example in Section 16.2.2, after discussing recurrent-neural-networks.

CHAPTER 14

Recurrent Neural Networks: Modeling Sequences and Stacks

When dealing with language data, it is very common to work with sequences, such as words (sequences of letters), sentences (sequences of words), and documents. We saw how feed-forward networks can accommodate arbitrary feature functions over sequences through the use of vector concatenation and vector addition (CBOW). In particular, the CBOW representations allows to encode arbitrary length sequences as fixed sized vectors. However, the CBOW representation is quite limited, and forces one to disregard the order of features. The convolutional networks also allow encoding a sequence into a fixed size vector. While representations derived from convolutional networks are an improvement over the CBOW representation as they offer some sensitivity to word order, their order sensitivity is restricted to mostly local patterns, and disregards the order of patterns that are far apart in the sequence.[1]

Recurrent neural networks (RNNs) [Elman, 1990] allow representing arbitrarily sized sequential inputs in fixed-size vectors, while paying attention to the structured properties of the inputs. RNNs, particularly ones with gated architectures such as the LSTM and the GRU, are very powerful at capturing statistical regularities in sequential inputs. They are arguably the strongest contribution of deep-learning to the statistical natural-language processing tool-set.

This chapter describes RNNs as an abstraction: an interface for translating a sequence of inputs into a fixed sized output, that can then be plugged as components in larger networks. Various architectures that use RNNs as a component are discussed. In the next chapter, we deal with concrete instantiations of the RNN abstraction, and describe the Elman RNN (also called Simple RNN), the Long-short-term Memory (LSTM), and the Gated Recurrent Unit (GRU). Then, in Chapter 16 we consider examples of modeling NLP problems using with RNNs.

In Chapter 9, we discussed language modeling and the Markov assumption. RNNs allow for language models that do not make the Markov assumption, and condition the next word on the entire sentence history (all the words preceding it). This ability opens the way to *conditioned generation models*, where a language model that is used as a generator is conditioned on some other signal, such as a sentence in another language. Such models are described in more depth in Chapter 17.

---

[1]However, as discussed in Section 13.3, hierarchical and dilated convolutional architectures do have the potential of capturing relatively long-range dependencies within a sequence.

14.1   THE RNN ABSTRACTION

We use $x_{i:j}$ to denote the sequence of vectors $x_i, \ldots, x_j$. On a high-level, the RNN is a function that takes as input an arbitrary length ordered sequence of n d_{in}-dimensional vectors $x_{1:n} = x_1, x_2, \ldots, x_n, (x_i \in \mathbb{R}^{d_{in}})$ and returns as output a single d_{out} dimensional vector $y_n \in \mathbb{R}^{d_{out}}$:

$$y_n = \text{RNN}(x_{1:n}) \tag{14.1}$$

$$x_i \in \mathbb{R}^{d_{in}} \quad y_n \in \mathbb{R}^{d_{out}}.$$

This implicitly defines an output vector y_i for each prefix $x_{1:i}$ of the sequence $x_{1:n}$. We denote by $\text{RNN}^\star$ the function returning this sequence:

$$y_{1:n} = \text{RNN}^\star(x_{1:n})$$
$$y_i = \text{RNN}(x_{1:i}) \tag{14.2}$$

$$x_i \in \mathbb{R}^{d_{in}} \quad y_i \in \mathbb{R}^{d_{out}}.$$

The output vector y_n is then used for further prediction. For example, a model for predicting the conditional probability of an event e given the sequence $x_{1:n}$ can be defined as $p(e = j|x_{1:n}) = \text{softmax}(\text{RNN}(x_{1:n}) \cdot W + b)_{[j]}$, the jth element in the output vector resulting from the softmax operation over a linear transformation of the RNN encoding $y_n = \text{RNN}(x_{1:n})$. The RNN function provides a framework for conditioning on the entire history $x_1, \ldots, x_i$ without resorting to the Markov assumption which is traditionally used for modeling sequences, described in Chapter 9. Indeed, RNN-based language models result in very good perplexity scores when compared to ngram-based models.

Looking in a bit more detail, the RNN is defined recursively, by means of a function R taking as input a state vector s_{i-1} and an input vector x_i and returning a new state vector s_i. The state vector s_i is then mapped to an output vector y_i using a simple deterministic function $O(\cdot)$.[2] The base of the recursion is an initial state vector, s_0, which is also an input to the RNN. For brevity, we often omit the initial vector s_0, or assume it is the zero vector.

When constructing an RNN, much like when constructing a feed-forward network, one has to specify the dimension of the inputs x_i as well as the dimensions of the outputs y_i. The dimensions of the states s_i are a function of the output dimension.[3]

---

[2] Using the O function is somewhat non-standard, and is introduced in order to unify the different RNN models to to be presented in the next chapter. For the Simple RNN (Elman RNN) and the GRU architectures, O is the identity mapping, and for the LSTM architecture O selects a fixed subset of the state.

[3] While RNN architectures in which the state dimension is independent of the output dimension are possible, the current popular architectures, including the Simple RNN, the LSTM, and the GRU do not follow this flexibility.

$$\text{RNN}^{\star}(x_{1:n}; s_0) = y_{1:n}$$

$$y_i = O(s_i) \qquad (14.3)$$

$$s_i = R(s_{i-1}, x_i)$$

$$x_i \in \mathbb{R}^{d_{in}}, \quad y_i \in \mathbb{R}^{d_{out}}, \quad s_i \in \mathbb{R}^{f(d_{out})}.$$

The functions R and O are the same across the sequence positions, but the RNN keeps track of the states of computation through the state vector s_i that is kept and being passed across invocations of R.

Graphically, the RNN has been traditionally presented as in Figure 14.1.

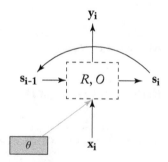

Figure 14.1: Graphical representation of an RNN (recursive).

This presentation follows the recursive definition, and is correct for arbitrarily long sequences. However, for a finite sized input sequence (and all input sequences we deal with are finite) one can *unroll* the recursion, resulting in the structure in Figure 14.2.

While not usually shown in the visualization, we include here the parameters θ in order to highlight the fact that the same parameters are shared across all time steps. Different instantiations of R and O will result in different network structures, and will exhibit different properties in terms of their running times and their ability to be trained effectively using gradient-based methods. However, they all adhere to the same abstract interface. We will provide details of concrete instantiations of R and O—the Simple RNN, the LSTM, and the GRU—in Chapter 15. Before that, let's consider working with the RNN abstraction.

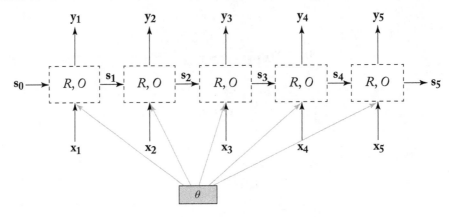

Figure 14.2: Graphical representation of an RNN (unrolled).

First, we note that the value of s_i (and hence y_i) is based on the entire input $x_1, \ldots, x_i$. For example, by expanding the recursion for $i = 4$ we get:

$$s_4 = R(s_3, x_4)$$

$$= R(\overbrace{R(s_2, x_3)}^{s_3}, x_4)$$

$$= R(R(\overbrace{R(s_1, x_2)}^{s_2}, x_3), x_4) \qquad (14.4)$$

$$= R(R(R(\overbrace{R(s_0, x_1)}^{s_1}, x_2), x_3), x_4).$$

Thus, s_n and y_n can be thought of as *encoding* the entire input sequence.[4] Is the encoding useful? This depends on our definition of usefulness. The job of the network training is to set the parameters of R and O such that the state conveys useful information for the task we are tying to solve.

14.2 RNN TRAINING

Viewed as in Figure 14.2 it is easy to see that an unrolled RNN is just a very deep neural network (or rather, a very large *computation graph* with somewhat complex nodes), in which the same parameters are shared across many parts of the computation, and additional input is added at various layers. To train an RNN network, then, all we need to do is to create the unrolled computation graph for a given input sequence, add a loss node to the unrolled graph, and then use the backward

---

[4]Note that, unless R is specifically designed against this, it is likely that the later elements of the input sequence have stronger effect on s_n than earlier ones.

(backpropagation) algorithm to compute the gradients with respect to that loss. This procedure is referred to in the RNN literature as *backpropagation through time* (BPTT) [Werbos, 1990].[5]

What is the objective of the training? It is important to understand that the RNN does not do much on its own, but serves as a trainable component in a larger network. The final prediction and loss computation are performed by that larger network, and the error is back-propagated through the RNN. This way, the RNN learns to encode properties of the input sequences that are useful for the further prediction task. The supervision signal is not applied to the RNN directly, but through the larger network.

Some common architectures of integrating the RNN within larger networks are given below.

14.3   COMMON RNN USAGE-PATTERNS

14.3.1   ACCEPTOR

One option is to base the supervision signal only at the final output vector, y_n. Viewed this way, the RNN is trained as an *acceptor*. We observe the final state, and then decide on an outcome.[6] For example, consider training an RNN to read the characters of a word one by one and then use the final state to predict the part-of-speech of that word (this is inspired by Ling et al. [2015b]), an RNN that reads in a sentence and, based on the final state decides if it conveys positive or negative sentiment (this is inspired by Wang et al. [2015b]) or an RNN that reads in a sequence of words and decides whether it is a valid noun-phrase. The loss in such cases is defined in terms of a function of $y_n = O(s_n)$. Typically, the RNN's output vector y_n is fed into a fully connected layer or an MLP, which produce a prediction. The error gradients are then backpropagated through the rest of the sequence (see Figure 14.3).[7] The loss can take any familiar form: cross entropy, hinge, margin, etc.

14.3.2   ENCODER

Similar to the acceptor case, an encoder supervision uses only the final output vector, y_n. However, unlike the acceptor, where a prediction is made solely on the basis of the final vector, here the

---

[5]Variants of the BPTT algorithm include unrolling the RNN only for a fixed number of input symbols at each time: first unroll the RNN for inputs $x_{1:k}$, resulting in $s_{1:k}$. Compute a loss, and backpropagate the error through the network (k steps back). Then, unroll the inputs $x_{k+1:2k}$, this time using s_k as the initial state, and again backpropagate the error for k steps, and so on. This strategy is based on the observations that for the Simple RNN variant, the gradients after k steps tend to vanish (for large enough k), and so omitting them is negligible. This procedure allows training of arbitrarily long sequences. For RNN variants such as the LSTM or the GRU that are designed specifically to mitigate the vanishing gradients problem, this fixed size unrolling is less motivated, yet it is still being used, for example when doing language modeling over a book without breaking it into sentences. A similar variant unrolls the network for the entire sequence in the forward step, but only propagates the gradients back for k steps from each position.

[6]The terminology is borrowed from Finite-State Acceptors. However, the RNN has a potentially infinite number of states, making it necessary to rely on a function other than a lookup table for mapping states to decisions.

[7]This kind of supervision signal may be hard to train for long sequences, especially so with the Simple RNN, because of the vanishing gradients problem. It is also a generally hard learning task, as we do not tell the process on which parts of the input to focus. Yet, it does work very well in many cases.

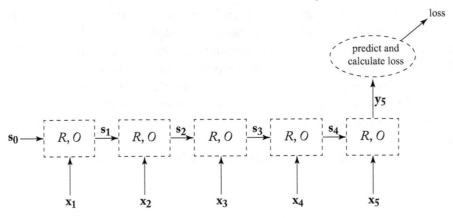

Figure 14.3: Acceptor RNN training graph.

final vector is treated as an encoding of the information in the sequence, and is used as additional information together with other signals. For example, an extractive document summarization system may first run over the document with an RNN, resulting in a vector y_n summarizing the entire document. Then, y_n will be used together with other features in order to select the sentences to be included in the summarization.

14.3.3 TRANSDUCER

Another option is to treat the RNN as a transducer, producing an output $\hat{t}_i$ for each input it reads in. Modeled this way, we can compute a local loss signal $L_{\text{local}}(\hat{t}_i, t_i)$ for each of the outputs $\hat{t}_i$ based on a true label t_i. The loss for unrolled sequence will then be: $L(\hat{t}_{1:n}, t_{1:n}) = \sum_{i=1}^{n} L_{\text{local}}(\hat{t}_i, t_i)$, or using another combination rather than a sum such as an average or a weighted average (see Figure 14.4). One example for such a transducer is a sequence tagger, in which we take $x_{i:n}$ to be feature representations for the n words of a sentence, and t_i as an input for predicting the tag assignment of word i based on words $1:i$. A CCG super-tagger based on such an architecture provides very strong CCG super-tagging results [Xu et al., 2015], although in many cases a transducer based on a bi-directional RNN (biRNN, see Section 14.4 below) is a better fit for such tagging problems.

A very natural use-case of the transduction setup is for language modeling, in which the sequence of words $x_{1:i}$ is used to predict a distribution over the $(i + 1)$th word. RNN-based language models are shown to provide vastly better perplexities than traditional language models [Jozefowicz et al., 2016, Mikolov, 2012, Mikolov et al., 2010, Sundermeyer et al., 2012].

Using RNNs as transducers allows us to relax the Markov assumption that is traditionally taken in language models and HMM taggers, and condition on the entire prediction history.

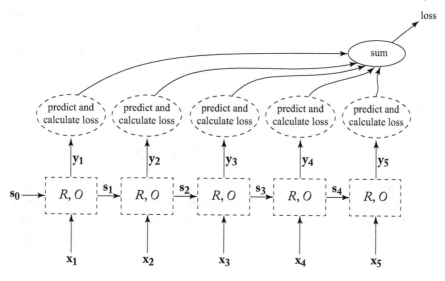

Figure 14.4: Transducer RNN training graph.

Special cases of the RNN transducer is the *RNN generator*, and the related *conditioned-generation* (also called *encoder-decoder*) and the *conditioned-generation with attention* architectures. These will be discussed in Chapter 17.

14.4   BIDIRECTIONAL RNNS (BIRNN)

A useful elaboration of an RNN is a *bidirectional-RNN* (also commonly referred to as biRNN) [Graves, 2008, Schuster and Paliwal, 1997].[8] Consider the task of sequence tagging over a sentence $x_1, \ldots, x_n$. An RNN allows us to compute a function of the ith word x_i based on the past—the words $x_{1:i}$ up to and including it. However, the *following* words $x_{i+1:n}$ may also be useful for prediction, as is evident by the common sliding-window approach in which the focus word is categorized based on a window of k words surrounding it. Much like the RNN relaxes the Markov assumption and allows looking arbitrarily back into the past, the biRNN relaxes the fixed window size assumption, allowing to look arbitrarily far at both the past and the future within the sequence.

Consider an input sequence $x_{1:n}$. The biRNN works by maintaining two separate states, s_i^f and s_i^b for each input position i. The *forward state* s_i^f is based on $x_1, x_2, \ldots, x_i$, while the *backward state* s_i^b is based on $x_n, x_{n-1}, \ldots, x_i$. The forward and backward states are generated by two different RNNs. The first RNN (R^f, O^f) is fed the input sequence $x_{1:n}$ as is, while the second RNN (R^b, O^b) is fed the input sequence in reverse. The state representation s_i is

---

[8]When used with a specific RNN architecture such as an LSTM, the model is called biLSTM.

then composed of both the forward and backward states. The output at position i is based on the concatenation of the two output vectors $y_i = [y_i^f ; y_i^b] = [O^f(s_i^f); O^b(s_i^b)]$, taking into account both the past and the future. In other words, y_i, the biRNN encoding of the ith word in a sequence is the concatenation of two RNNs, one reading the sequence from the beginning, and the other reading it from the end.

We define $\text{biRNN}(x_{1:n}, i)$ to be the output vector corresponding to the ith sequence position:[9]

$$\text{biRNN}(x_{1:n}, i) = y_i = [\text{RNN}^f(x_{1:i}); \text{RNN}^b(x_{n:i})]. \tag{14.6}$$

The vector y_i can then be used directly for prediction, or fed as part of the input to a more complex network. While the two RNNs are run independently of each other, the error gradients at position i will flow both forward and backward through the two RNNs. Feeding the vector y_i through an MLP prior to prediction will further mix the forward and backward signals. Visual representation of the biRNN architecture is given in Figure 14.5.

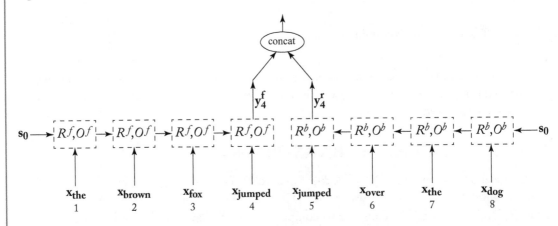

Figure 14.5: Computing the biRNN representation of the word *jumped* in the sentence "the brown fox jumped over the dog."

Note how the vector y_4, corresponding to the word *jumped*, encodes an infinite window around (and including) the focus vector x_{jumped}.

Similarly to the RNN case, we also define $\text{biRNN}^\star(x_{1:n})$ as the sequence of vectors $y_{1:n}$:

$$\text{biRNN}^\star(x_{1:n}) = y_{i:n} = \text{biRNN}(x_{1:n}, 1), \ldots, \text{biRNN}(x_{1:n}, n). \tag{14.7}$$

---

[9]The biRNN vector can either a simple concatenation of the two RNN vectors as in Equation (14.6), or followed by another linear-transformation to reduce its dimension, often back to the dimension of the single RNN input:

$$\text{biRNN}(x_{1:n}, i) = y_i = [\text{RNN}^f(x_{1:i}); \text{RNN}^b(x_{n:i})]W. \tag{14.5}$$

This is variant is often used when stacking several biRNNs on top of each other as discussed in Section 14.5.

The n output vectors $y_{i:n}$ can be efficiently computed in linear time by first running the forward and backward RNNs, and then concatenating the relevant outputs. This architecture is depicted in Figure 14.6.

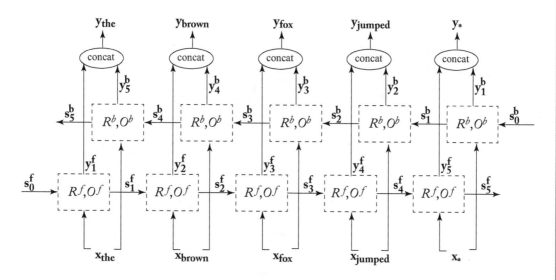

Figure 14.6: Computing the biRNN* for the sentence "the brown fox jumped."

The biRNN is very effective for tagging tasks, in which each input vector corresponds to one output vector. It is also useful as a general-purpose trainable feature-extracting component, that can be used whenever a window around a given word is required. Concrete usage examples are given in Chapter 16.

The use of biRNNs for sequence tagging was introduced to the NLP community by Irsoy and Cardie [2014].

14.5 MULTI-LAYER (STACKED) RNNS

RNNs can be stacked in layers, forming a grid [Hihi and Bengio, 1996]. Consider k RNNs, $RNN_1, \ldots, RNN_k$, where the jth RNN has states $s^j_{1:n}$ and outputs $y^j_{1:n}$. The input for the first RNN are $x_{1:n}$, while the input of the jth RNN ($j \geq 2$) are the outputs of the RNN below it, $y^{j-1}_{1:n}$. The output of the entire formation is the output of the last RNN, $y^k_{1:n}$. Such layered architectures are often called *deep RNNs*. A visual representation of a three-layer RNN is given in Figure 14.7. biRNNs can be stacked in a similar fashion.[10]

---

[10]The term *deep-biRNN* is used in the literature to describe to different architecture: in the first, the biRNN state is a concatenation of two deep RNNs. In the second, the output sequence of on biRNN is fed as input to another. My research group found the second variant to often performs better.

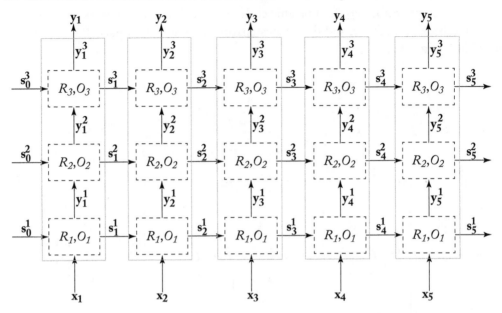

Figure 14.7: A three-layer ("deep") RNN architecture.

While it is not theoretically clear what is the additional power gained by the deeper architecture, it was observed empirically that deep RNNs work better than shallower ones on some tasks. In particular, Sutskever et al. [2014] report that a four-layers deep architecture was crucial in achieving good machine-translation performance in an encoder-decoder framework. Irsoy and Cardie [2014] also report improved results from moving from a one-layer biRNN to an architecture with several layers. Many other works report result using layered RNN architectures, but do not explicitly compare to one-layer RNNs. In the experiment of my research group, using two or more layers indeed often improves over using a single one.

14.6   RNNS FOR REPRESENTING STACKS

Some algorithms in language processing, including those for transition-based parsing [Nivre, 2008], require performing feature extraction over a stack. Instead of being confined to looking at the k top-most elements of the stack, the RNN framework can be used to provide a fixed-sized vector encoding of the entire stack.

The main intuition is that a stack is essentially a sequence, and so the stack state can be represented by taking the stack elements and feeding them in order into an RNN, resulting in a final encoding of the entire stack. In order to do this computation efficiently (without performing an $O(n)$ stack encoding operation each time the stack changes), the RNN state is maintained together with the stack state. If the stack was push-only, this would be trivial: whenever a new element x is pushed into the stack, the corresponding vector x will be used together with the RNN state s_i in order to obtain a new state s_{i+1}. Dealing with pop operation is more challenging, but can be solved by using the persistent-stack data-structure [Goldberg et al., 2013, Okasaki, 1999]. Persistent, or immutable, data-structures keep old versions of themselves intact when modified. The persistent stack construction represents a stack as a pointer to the head of a linked list. An empty stack is the empty list. The push operation appends an element to the list, returning the new head. The pop operation then returns the parent of the head, but keeping the original list intact. From the point of view of someone who held a pointer to the previous head, the stack did not change. A subsequent push operation will add a new child to the same node. Applying this procedure throughout the lifetime of the stack results in a tree, where the root is an empty stack and each path from a node to the root represents an intermediary stack state. Figure 14.8 provides an example of such a tree. The same process can be applied in the computation graph construction, creating an RNN with a tree structure instead of a chain structure. Backpropagating the error from a given node will then affect all the elements that participated in the stack when the node was created, in order. Figure 14.9 shows the computation graph for the stack-RNN corresponding to the last state in Figure 14.8. This modeling approach was proposed independently by Dyer et al. [2015] and Watanabe and Sumita [2015] for transition-based dependency parsing.

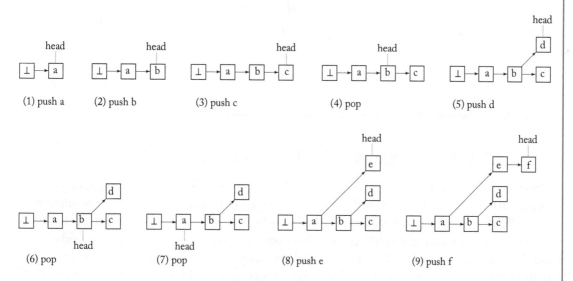

Figure 14.8: An immutable stack construction for the sequence of operations *push a; push b; push c; pop; push d; pop; pop; push e; push f.*

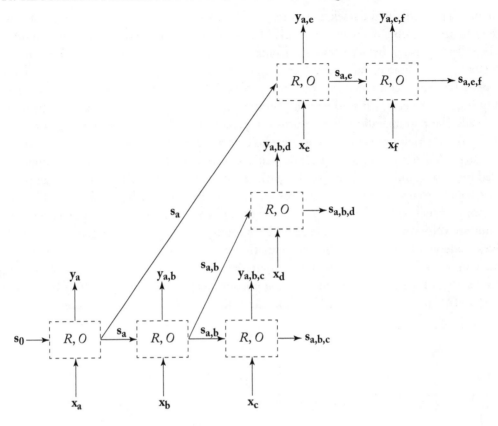

Figure 14.9: The stack-RNN corresponding to the final state in Figure 14.8.

14.7   A NOTE ON READING THE LITERATURE

Unfortunately, it is often the case that inferring the exact model form from reading its description in a research paper can be quite challenging. Many aspects of the models are not yet standardized, and different researchers use the same terms to refer to slightly different things. To list a few examples, the inputs to the RNN can be either one-hot vectors (in which case the embedding matrix is internal to the RNN) or embedded representations; the input sequence can be padded with start-of-sequence and/or end-of-sequence symbols, or not; while the output of an RNN is usually assumed to be a vector which is expected to be fed to additional layers followed by a softmax for prediction (as is the case in the presentation in this tutorial), some papers assume the softmax to be part of the RNN itself; in multi-layer RNN, the "state vector" can be either the output of the top-most layer, or a concatenation of the outputs from all layers; when using the encoder-decoder framework, conditioning on the output of the encoder can be interpreted in various different ways; and so on. On top of that, the LSTM architecture described in the next section has many small variants, which are all referred to under the common name LSTM. Some of these choices are made explicit in the papers, other require careful reading, and others still are not even mentioned, or are hidden behind ambiguous figures or phrasing.

As a reader, be aware of these issues when reading and interpret model descriptions. As a writer, be aware of these issues as well: either fully specify your model in mathematical notation, or refer to a different source in which the model is fully specified, if such a source is available. If using the default implementation from a software package without knowing the details, be explicit of that fact and specify the software package you use. In any case, don't rely solely on figures or natural language text when describing your model, as these are often ambiguous.

CHAPTER 15

Concrete Recurrent Neural Network Architectures

After describing the RNN abstraction, we are now in place to discuss specific instantiations of it. Recall that we are interested in a recursive function $s_i = R(x_i, s_{i-1})$ such that s_i encodes the sequence $x_{1:n}$. We will present several concrete instantiations of the abstract RNN architecture, providing concrete definitions of the functions R and O. These include the *Simple RNN* (S-RNN), the *Long Short-Term Memory* (LSTM) and the *Gated Recurrent Unit* (GRU).

15.1 CBOW AS AN RNN

On particularly simple choice of R is the addition function:

$$s_i = R_{\text{CBOW}}(x_i, s_{i-1}) = s_{i-1} + x_i$$
$$y_i = O_{\text{CBOW}}(s_i) = s_i \tag{15.1}$$

$$s_i, y_i \in \mathbb{R}^{d_s}, \quad x_i \in \mathbb{R}^{d_s}.$$

Following the definition in Equation (15.1), we get the continuous-bag-of-words model: the state resulting from inputs $x_{1:n}$ is the sum of these inputs. While simple, this instantiation of the RNN ignores the sequential nature of the data. The Elman RNN, described next, adds dependence on the sequential ordering of the elements.[1]

15.2 SIMPLE RNN

The simplest RNN formulation that is sensitive to the ordering of elements in the sequence is known as an Elman Network or Simple-RNN (S-RNN). The S-RNN was proposed by Elman [1990] and explored for use in language modeling by Mikolov [2012]. The S-RNN takes the following form:

$$s_i = R_{\text{SRNN}}(x_i, s_{i-1}) = g(s_{i-1}W^s + x_i W^x + b)$$
$$y_i = O_{\text{SRNN}}(s_i) = s_i \tag{15.2}$$

$$s_i, y_i \in \mathbb{R}^{d_s}, \quad x_i \in \mathbb{R}^{d_x}, \quad W^x \in \mathbb{R}^{d_x \times d_s}, \quad W^s \in \mathbb{R}^{d_s \times d_s}, \quad b \in \mathbb{R}^{d_s}.$$

---

[1]The view of the CBOW representation as an RNN is not a common one in the literature. However, we find it to be a good stepping stone into the Elman RNN definition. It is also useful to have the simple CBOW encoder in the same framework as the RNNs as it can also serve the role of an encoder in a conditioned generation network such as those described in Chapter 17.

That is, the state s_{i-1} and the input x_i are each linearly transformed, the results are added (together with a bias term) and then passed through a nonlinear activation function g (commonly tanh or ReLU). The output at position i is the same as the hidden state in that position.[2]

An equivalent way of writing Equation (15.2) is Equation (15.3), both are used in the literature:

$$s_i = R_{\text{SRNN}}(x_i, s_{i-1}) = g([s_{i-1}; x_i]W + b)$$
$$y_i = O_{\text{SRNN}}(s_i) = s_i$$

(15.3)

$$s_i, y_i \in \mathbb{R}^{d_s}, \quad x_i \in \mathbb{R}^{d_x}, \quad W \in \mathbb{R}^{(d_x+d_s)\times d_s}, \quad b \in \mathbb{R}^{d_s}.$$

The S-RNN is only slightly more complex than the CBOW, with the major difference being the nonlinear activation function g. However, this difference is a crucial one, as adding the linear transformation followed by the nonlinearity makes the network sensitive to the order of the inputs. Indeed, the Simple RNN provides strong results for sequence tagging [Xu et al., 2015] as well as language modeling. For comprehensive discussion on using Simple RNNs for language modeling, see the Ph.D. thesis by Mikolov [2012].

15.3 GATED ARCHITECTURES

The S-RNN is hard to train effectively because of the vanishing gradients problem [Pascanu et al., 2012]. Error signals (gradients) in later steps in the sequence diminish quickly in the back-propagation process, and do not reach earlier input signals, making it hard for the S-RNN to capture long-range dependencies. Gating-based architectures, such as the LSTM [Hochreiter and Schmidhuber, 1997] and the GRU [Cho et al., 2014b] are designed to solve this deficiency.

Consider the RNN as a general purpose computing device, where the state s_i represents a finite memory. Each application of the function R reads in an input x_{i+1}, reads in the current memory s_i, operates on them in some way, and writes the result into memory, resulting in a new memory state s_{i+1}. Viewed this way, an apparent problem with the S-RNN architecture is that the memory access is not controlled. At each step of the computation, the entire memory state is read, and the entire memory state is written.

How does one provide more controlled memory access? Consider a binary vector $g \in \{0, 1\}^n$. Such a vector can act as a *gate* for controlling access to n-dimensional vectors, using the hadamard-product operation $x \odot g$:[3] Consider a memory $s \in \mathbb{R}^d$, an input $x \in \mathbb{R}^d$ and a gate $g \in 0, 1^d$. The computation $s' \leftarrow g \odot x + (1 - g) \odot (s)$ "reads" the entries in x that correspond to the 1 values in g, and writes them to the new memory s'. Then, locations that weren't

---

[2]Some authors treat the output at position i as a more complicated function of the state, e.g., a linear transformation, or an MLP. In our presentation, such further transformation of the output are not considered part of the RNN, but as separate computations that are applied to the RNNs output.
[3]The hadamard-product is a fancy name for element-wise multiplication of two vectors: the hadamard product $x = u \odot v$ results in $x_{[i]} = u_{[i]} \cdot v_{[i]}$.

read to are copied from the memory s to the new memory s' through the use of the gate $(1 - g)$. Figure 15.1 shows this process for updating the memory with positions 2 and 5 from the input.

$$
\begin{bmatrix} 8 \\ 11 \\ 3 \\ 7 \\ 5 \\ 15 \end{bmatrix} \leftarrow \begin{bmatrix} 0 \\ 1 \\ 0 \\ 0 \\ 0 \\ 1 \end{bmatrix} \odot \begin{bmatrix} 10 \\ 11 \\ 12 \\ 13 \\ 14 \\ 15 \end{bmatrix} + \begin{bmatrix} 1 \\ 0 \\ 1 \\ 1 \\ 1 \\ 0 \end{bmatrix} \odot \begin{bmatrix} 8 \\ 9 \\ 3 \\ 7 \\ 5 \\ 8 \end{bmatrix}
$$
$$
\quad s' \qquad\qquad g \qquad x \qquad\qquad (1-g) \qquad s
$$

Figure 15.1: Using binary gate vector g to control access to memory s'.

The gating mechanism described above can serve as a building block in our RNN: gate vectors can be used to control access to the memory state s_i. However, we are still missing two important (and related) components: the gates should not be static, but be controlled by the current memory state and the input, and their behavior should be learned. This introduced an obstacle, as learning in our framework entails being differentiable (because of the backpropagation algorithm) and the binary 0-1 values used in the gates are not differentiable.[4]

A solution to the above problem is to approximate the hard gating mechanism with a soft—but differentiable—gating mechanism. To achieve these *differentiable gates*, we replace the requirement that $g \in \{0, 1\}^n$ and allow arbitrary real numbers, $g' \in \mathbb{R}^n$, which are then pass through a sigmoid function $\sigma(g')$. This bounds the value in the range $(0, 1)$, with most values near the borders. When using the gate $\sigma(g') \odot x$, indices in x corresponding to near-one values in $\sigma(g')$ are allowed to pass, while those corresponding to near-zero values are blocked. The gate values can then be conditioned on the input and the current memory, and trained using a gradient-based method to perform a desired behavior.

This controllable gating mechanism is the basis of the LSTM and the GRU architectures, to be defined next: at each time step, differentiable gating mechanisms decide which parts of the inputs will be written to memory, and which parts of memory will be overwritten (forgotten). This rather abstract description will be made concrete in the next sections.

15.3.1 LSTM

The Long Short-Term Memory (LSTM) architecture [Hochreiter and Schmidhuber, 1997] was designed to solve the vanishing gradients problem, and is the first to introduce the gating mechanism. The LSTM architecture explicitly splits the state vector s_i into two halves, where one half

---

[4]It is in principle possible to learn also models with non-differentiable components such as binary gates using reinforcement-learning techniques. However, as the time of this writing such techniques are brittle to train. Reinforcement learning techniques are beyond the scope of this book.

is treated as "memory cells" and the other is working memory. The memory cells are designed to preserve the memory, and also the error gradients, across time, and are controlled through *differentiable gating components*—smooth mathematical functions that simulate logical gates. At each input state, a gate is used to decide how much of the new input should be written to the memory cell, and how much of the current content of the memory cell should be forgotten. Mathematically, the LSTM architecture is defined as:[5]

$$s_j = R_{\text{LSTM}}(s_{j-1}, x_j) = [c_j ; h_j]$$

$$c_j = f \odot c_{j-1} + i \odot z$$

$$h_j = o \odot \tanh(c_j)$$

$$i = \sigma(x_j W^{xi} + h_{j-1} W^{hi})$$

$$f = \sigma(x_j W^{xf} + h_{j-1} W^{hf}) \tag{15.4}$$

$$o = \sigma(x_j W^{xo} + h_{j-1} W^{ho})$$

$$z = \tanh(x_j W^{xz} + h_{j-1} W^{hz})$$

$$y_j = O_{\text{LSTM}}(s_j) = h_j$$

$$s_j \in \mathbb{R}^{2 \cdot d_h}, \; x_i \in \mathbb{R}^{d_x}, \; c_j, h_j, i, f, o, z \in \mathbb{R}^{d_h}, \; W^{xo} \in \mathbb{R}^{d_x \times d_h}, \; W^{ho} \in \mathbb{R}^{d_h \times d_h}.$$

The state at time j is composed of two vectors, c_j and h_j, where c_j is the memory component and h_j is the hidden state component. There are three gates, i, f, and o, controlling for input, forget, and output. The gate values are computed based on linear combinations of the current input x_j and the previous state h_{j-1}, passed through a sigmoid activation function. An update candidate z is computed as a linear combination of x_j and h_{j-1}, passed through a tanh activation function. The memory c_j is then updated: the forget gate controls how much of the previous memory to keep ($f \odot c_{j-1}$), and the input gate controls how much of the proposed update to keep ($i \odot z$). Finally, the value of h_j (which is also the output y_j) is determined based on the content of the memory c_j, passed through a tanh nonlinearity and controlled by the output gate. The gating mechanisms allow for gradients related to the memory part c_j to stay high across very long time ranges.

For further discussion on the LSTM architecture see the Ph.D. thesis by Alex Graves [2008], as well as Chris Olah's description.[6] For an analysis of the behavior of an LSTM when used as a character-level language model, see Karpathy et al. [2015].

---

[5]There are many variants on the LSTM architecture presented here. For example, forget gates were not part of the original proposal in Hochreiter and Schmidhuber [1997], but are shown to be an important part of the architecture. Other variants include peephole connections and gate-tying. For an overview and comprehensive empirical comparison of various LSTM architectures, see Greff et al. [2015].

[6]http://colah.github.io/posts/2015-08-Understanding-LSTMs/

The vanishing gradients problem in Recurrent Neural Networks and its Solution   Intuitively, recurrent neural networks can be thought of as very deep feed-forward networks, with shared parameters across different layers. For the Simple-RNN [Equation (15.3)], the gradients then include repeated multiplication of the matrix W, making it very likely for the values to vanish or explode. The gating mechanism mitigate this problem to a large extent by getting rid of this repeated multiplication of a single matrix.

For further discussion of the exploding and vanishing gradient problem in RNNs, see Section 10.7 in Bengio et al. [2016]. For further explanation of the motivation behind the gating mechanism in the LSTM (and the GRU) and its relation to solving the vanishing gradient problem in recurrent neural networks, see Sections 4.2 and 4.3 in the detailed course notes of Cho [2015].

LSTMs are currently the most successful type of RNN architecture, and they are responsible for many state-of-the-art sequence modeling results. The main competitor of the LSTM-RNN is the GRU, to be discussed next.

Practical Considerations   When training LSTM networks, Jozefowicz et al. [2015] strongly recommend to always initialize the bias term of the forget gate to be close to one.

15.3.2 GRU

The LSTM architecture is very effective, but also quite complicated. The complexity of the system makes it hard to analyze, and also computationally expensive to work with. The gated recurrent unit (GRU) was recently introduced by Cho et al. [2014b] as an alternative to the LSTM. It was subsequently shown by Chung et al. [2014] to perform comparably to the LSTM on several (non textual) datasets.

Like the LSTM, the GRU is also based on a gating mechanism, but with substantially fewer gates and without a separate memory component.

$$
\begin{aligned}
s_j = R_{\text{GRU}}(s_{j-1}, x_j) &= (1 - z) \odot s_{j-1} + z \odot \tilde{s}_j \\
z &= \sigma(x_j W^{xz} + s_{j-1} W^{sz}) \\
r &= \sigma(x_j W^{xr} + s_{j-1} W^{sr}) \\
\tilde{s}_j &= \tanh(x_j W^{xs} + (r \odot s_{j-1}) W^{sg})
\end{aligned}
\tag{15.5}
$$

$$
y_j = O_{\text{GRU}}(s_j) = s_j
$$

$$
s_j, \tilde{s}_j \in \mathbb{R}^{d_s}, \quad x_i \in \mathbb{R}^{d_x}, \quad z, r \in \mathbb{R}^{d_s}, \quad W^{xo} \in \mathbb{R}^{d_x \times d_s}, \quad W^{so} \in \mathbb{R}^{d_s \times d_s}.
$$

One gate (r) is used to control access to the previous state s_{j-1} and compute a proposed update $\tilde{s}_j$. The updated state s_j (which also serves as the output y_j) is then determined based on an interpolation of the previous state s_{j-1} and the proposal $\tilde{s}_j$, where the proportions of the interpolation are controlled using the gate z.[7]

The GRU was shown to be effective in language modeling and machine translation. However, the jury is still out between the GRU, the LSTM and possible alternative RNN architectures, and the subject is actively researched. For an empirical exploration of the GRU and the LSTM architectures, see Jozefowicz et al. [2015].

15.4   OTHER VARIANTS

Improvements to non-gated architectures   The gated architectures of the LSTM and the GRU help in alleviating the vanishing gradients problem of the Simple RNN, and allow these RNNs to capture dependencies that span long time ranges. Some researchers explore simpler architectures than the LSTM and the GRU for achieving similar benefits.

Mikolov et al. [2014] observed that the matrix multiplication $s_{i-1}W^s$ coupled with the nonlinearity g in the update rule R of the Simple RNN causes the state vector s_i to undergo large changes at each time step, prohibiting it from remembering information over long time periods. They propose to split the state vector s_i into a slow changing component c_i ("context units") and a fast changing component h_i.[8] The slow changing component c_i is updated according to a linear interpolation of the input and the previous component: $c_i = (1-\alpha)x_i W^{x1} + \alpha c_{i-1}$, where $\alpha \in (0, 1)$. This update allows c_i to accumulate the previous inputs. The fast changing component h_i is updated similarly to the Simple RNN update rule, but changed to take c_i into account as well:[9] $h_i = \sigma(x_i W^{x2} + h_{i-1} W^h + c_i W^c)$. Finally, the output y_i is the concatenation of the slow and the fast changing parts of the state: $y_i = [c_i; h_i]$. Mikolov et al. demonstrate that this architecture provides competitive perplexities to the much more complex LSTM on language modeling tasks.

The approach of Mikolov et al. can be interpreted as constraining the block of the matrix W^s in the S-RNN corresponding to c_i to be a multiple of the identity matrix (see Mikolov et al. [2014] for the details). Le et al. [2015] propose an even simpler approach: set the activation function of the S-RNN to a ReLU, and initialize the biases b as zeroes and the matrix W^s as the identify matrix. This causes an untrained RNN to copy the previous state to the current state, add the effect of the current input x_i and set the negative values to zero. After setting this initial bias toward state copying, the training procedure allows W^s to change freely. Le et al. demonstrate that this simple modification makes the S-RNN comparable to an LSTM with the same number of parameters on several tasks, including language modeling.

---

[7]The states s are often called h in the GRU literature.

[8]We depart from the notation in Mikolov et al. [2014] and reuse the symbols used in the LSTM description.

[9]The update rule diverges from the S-RNN update rule also by fixing the nonlinearity to be a sigmoid function, and by not using a bias term. However, these changes are not discussed as central to the proposal.

Beyond differential gates   The gating mechanism is an example of adapting concepts from the theory of computation (memory access, logical gates) into differentiable—and hence gradient-trainable—systems. There is considerable research interest in creating neural network architectures to simulate and implement further computational mechanisms, allowing better and more fine grained control. One such example is the work on a *differentiable stack* [Grefenstette et al., 2015] in which a stack structure with push and pop operations is controlled using an end-to-end differentiable network, and the *neural turing machine* [Graves et al., 2014] which allows read and write access to content-addressable memory, again, in a differentiable system. While these efforts are yet to result in robust and general-purpose architectures that can be used in non-toy language processing applications, they are well worth keeping an eye on.

15.5   DROPOUT IN RNNS

Applying dropout to RNNs can be a bit tricky, as dropping different dimensions at different time steps harms the ability of the RNN to carry informative signals across time. This prompted Pham et al. [2013], Zaremba et al. [2014] to suggest applying dropout only on the non-recurrent connection, i.e., only to apply it between layers in deep-RNNs and not between sequence positions.

More recently, following a variational analysis of the RNN architecture, Gal [2015] suggests applying dropout to all the components of the RNN (both recurrent and non-recurrent), but crucially retain the same dropout mask across time steps. That is, the dropout masks are sampled once per sequence, and not once per time step. Figure 15.2 contrasts this form of dropout ("variational RNN") with the architecture proposed by Pham et al. [2013], Zaremba et al. [2014].

The variational RNN dropout method of Gal is the current best-practice for applying dropout in RNNs.

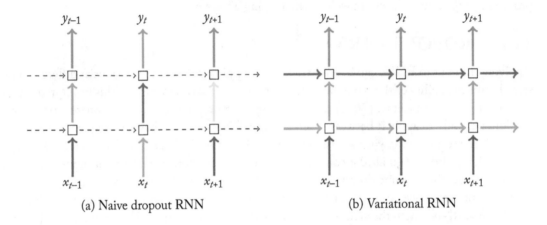

(a) Naive dropout RNN   (b) Variational RNN

Figure 15.2: Gal's proposal for RNN dropout (b), vs. the previous suggestion by Pham et al. [2013], Zaremba et al. [2014] (a). Figure from Gal [2015], used with permission. Each square represents an RNN unit, with horizontal arrows representing time dependence (recurrent connections). Vertical arrows represent the input and output to each RNN unit. Colored connections represent dropped-out inputs, with different colors corresponding to different dropout masks. Dashed lines correspond to standard connections with no dropout. Previous techniques (naive dropout, left) use different masks at different time steps, with no dropout on the recurrent layers. Gal's proposed technique (Variational RNN, right) uses the same dropout mask at each time step, including the recurrent layers.

CHAPTER 16

Modeling
with Recurrent Networks

After enumerating common usage patterns in Chapter 14 and learning the details of concrete RNN architectures in Chapter 15, we now explore the use of RNNs in NLP applications through some concrete examples. While we use the generic term RNN, we usually mean gated architectures such as the LSTM or the GRU. The Simple RNN consistently results in lower accuracies.

16.1 ACCEPTORS

The simplest use of RNNs is as acceptors: read in an input sequence, and produce a binary or multi-class answer at the end. RNNs are very strong sequence learners, and can pick-up on very intricate patterns in the data.

This power is often not needed for many natural language classification tasks: the word-order and sentence structure turn out to not be very important in many cases, and bag-of-words or bag-of-ngrams classifier often works just as well or even better than RNN-acceptors.

This section presents two examples of acceptor usages for language problems. The first is a canonical one: sentiment classification. The approach works well, but less powerful approaches can also prove competitive. The second is a somewhat contrived example: it does not solve any "useful" task on its own, but demonstrates the power of RNNs and the kind of patterns they are capable of learning.

16.1.1 SENTIMENT CLASSIFICATION

Sentence-Level Sentiment Classification

In the sentence-level sentiment classification task, we are given a sentence, often as part of a review, and need to assign it one of two values: POSITIVE or NEGATIVE.[1] This is a somewhat simplistic view of the sentiment detection task—but one which is often used nonetheless. This is also the task that motivated our discussion of convolutional neural networks, in Chapter 13. An example of naturally occurring POSITIVE and NEGATIVE sentences in the movie-reviews domain would be the following:[2]

---

[1] In a more challenging variant, the goal is a three-way classification into POSITIVE, NEGATIVE, and NEUTRAL.
[2] These examples are taken from the *Stanford Sentiment Treebank* [Socher et al., 2013b].

Positive: *It's not life-affirming—it's vulgar and mean, but I liked it.*

Negative: *It's a disappointing that it only manages to be decent instead of dead brilliant.*

Note that the positive example contains some negative phrases (*not life affirming, vulgar, and mean*), while the negative examples contains some positive ones (*dead brilliant*). Correctly predicting the sentiment requires understanding not only the individual phrases but also the context in which they occur, linguistic constructs such as negation, and the overall structure of the sentence. Sentiment classification is a tricky and challenging task, and properly solving it involves handling such issues as sarcasm and metaphor. The definition of sentiment is also not straightforward. For a good overview of the challenges in sentiment classification and its definition, see the comprehensive review by Pang and Lee [2008]. For our current purpose, however, we will ignore the complexities in definition and treat it as a data-driven, binary classification task.

The task is straightforward to model using an RNN-acceptor: after tokenization, the RNN reads in the words of the sentence one at a time. The final RNN state is then fed into an MLP followed by a softmax-layer with two outputs. The network is trained with cross-entropy loss based on the gold sentiment labels. For a finer-grained classification task, where one needs to assign a sentiment on scale of 1–5 or 1–10 (a "star rating"), it is straightforward to change the MLP to produce 5 outputs instead of 2. To summarize the architecture:

$$p(\text{label} = k \mid w_{1:n}) = \hat{y}_{[k]}$$

$$\hat{y} = \text{softmax}(\text{MLP}(\text{RNN}(\boldsymbol{x}_{1:n}))) \tag{16.1}$$

$$\boldsymbol{x}_{1:n} = \boldsymbol{E}_{[w_1]}, \ldots, \boldsymbol{E}_{[w_n]}.$$

The word embeddings matrix $\boldsymbol{E}$ is initialized using pre-trained embeddings learned over a large external corpus using an algorithm such as Word2Vec or GloVe with a relatively wide window.

It is often helpful to extend the model in Equation (16.1) by considering two RNNs, one reading the sentence in its given order and the other one reading it in reverse. The end states of the two RNNs are then concatenated and fed into the MLP for classification:

$$p(\text{label} = k \mid w_{1:n}) = \hat{y}_{[k]}$$

$$\hat{y} = \text{softmax}(\text{MLP}([\text{RNN}^{\text{f}}(\boldsymbol{x}_{1:n}); \text{RNN}^{\text{b}}(\boldsymbol{x}_{n:1})])) \tag{16.2}$$

$$\boldsymbol{x}_{1:n} = \boldsymbol{E}_{[w_1]}, \ldots, \boldsymbol{E}_{[w_n]}.$$

These bidirectional models produce strong results for the task [Li et al., 2015].

For longer sentences, Li et al. [2015] found it useful to use a hierarchical architecture, in which the sentence is split into smaller spans based on punctuation. Then, each span is fed into a forward and a backward RNN as described in Equation (16.2). Sequence of resulting vectors (one for each span) are then fed into an RNN acceptor such as the one in Equation (16.1). Formally, given a sentence $w_{1:n}$ which is split into m spans, $w^1_{1:\ell_1}, \ldots, w^m_{1:\ell_m}$, the architecture is given by:

$$p(\text{label} = k \mid w_{1:n}) = \hat{y}_{[k]}$$
$$\hat{y} = \text{softmax}(\text{MLP}(\text{RNN}(z_{1:m})))$$
$$z_i = [\text{RNN}^f(x^i_{1:\ell_i}); \text{RNN}^b(x^i_{\ell_i:1})] \tag{16.3}$$
$$x^i_{1:\ell_i} = E_{[w^i_1]}, \ldots, E_{[w^i_{\ell_i}]}.$$

Each of the m different spans may convey a different sentiment. The higher-level acceptor reads the summary $z_{1:m}$ produced by the lower level encoders, and decides on the overall sentiment.

Sentiment classification is also used as a test-bed for hierarchical, tree-structured recursive neural networks, as described in Chapter 18.

Document Level Sentiment Classification

The document level sentiment classification is similar to the sentence level one, but the input text is much longer—consisting of multiple sentences—and the supervision signal (sentiment label) is given only at the end, not for the individual sentences. The task is harder than sentence-level classification, as the individual sentences may convey different sentiments than the overall one conveyed by the document.

Tang et al. [2015] found it useful to use a hierarchical architecture for this task, similar to the one used by Li et al. [2015]. [Equation (16.3)]: each sentence s_i is encoded using a gated RNN producing a vector z_i, and the vectors $z_{1:n}$ are then fed into a second gated RNN, producing a vector $h = \text{RNN}(z_{1:n})$ which is then used for prediction: $\hat{y} = \text{softmax}(\text{MLP}(h))$.

The authors experimented also with a variant in which all the intermediate vectors from the document-level RNN are kept, and their average is fed into the MLP ($h_{1:n} = \text{RNN}^*(z_{1:n})$, $\hat{y} = \text{softmax}(\text{MLP}(\frac{1}{n}\sum_{i=1}^n h_i))$. This produced slightly higher results in some cases.

16.1.2 SUBJECT-VERB AGREEMENT GRAMMATICALITY DETECTION

Grammatical English sentences obey the constraint that the head of the subject of a present-tense verb must agree with in on the number inflection (* denote ungrammatical sentences):

(1) a.   The *key is* on the table.
     b.   *The *key are* on the table.
     c.   *The *keys is* on the table.
     d.   The *keys are* on the table.

This relationship is non-trivial to infer from the sequence alone, as the two elements can be separated by arbitrary long sentential material, which may include nouns of the opposite number:

(2)   a.   The *keys* to the cabinet in the corner of the room *are* on the table.
      b.   *The *keys* to the cabinet in the corner of the room *is* on the table.

Given the difficulty in identifying the subject from the linear sequence of the sentence, dependencies such as subject-verb agreement serve as an argument for structured syntactic representations in humans [Everaert et al., 2015]. Indeed, given a correct syntactic parse tree of the sentence, the relation between the verb and its subject becomes trivial to extract:

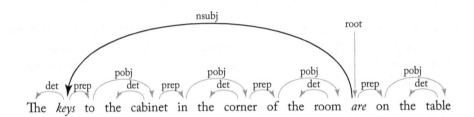

In work with Linzen and Dupoux [Linzen et al., 2016], we set out to find if RNNs, which are sequential learners, can pick up on this rather syntactic regularity, by learning from word sequences alone. We set up several prediction tasks based on naturally occurring text from Wikipedia to test this. One of the tasks was grammaticality detection: the RNN is tasked with reading a sentence, and at the end deciding if it is grammatical or not. In our setup, grammatical sentences were Wikipedia sentences that contain a present-tense verb, while ungrammatical ones are Wikipedia sentences with a present-tense verb in which we picked up one of the present-tense verbs at random and flipped its form from singular to plural or the other way around.[3] Note that a bag-of-words or bag-of-ngrams model is likely to have a very hard time solving this particular problem, as the dependency between the verb and the subject relies on the structure of the sentence which is lost when moving to a bag-of-words representation, and can also span more than any number of words n.

The model was trained as a straightforward acceptor:

$$\hat{y} = \text{softmax}(\text{MLP}(\text{RNN}(E_{[w_1]}, \ldots, E_{[w_n]})))$$

using cross-entropy loss. We had tens of thousands training sentences, and hundreds of thousands test sentences (many of the agreement cases are not hard, and we wanted the test set to contain a substantial amount of hard cases).

This is a hard task, with very indirect supervision: the supervision signal did not include any clue as to where the grammaticality clue is. The RNN had to learn the concept of number (that plural and singular words belong to different groups), the concept of agreement (that the form of the verb should match the form of the subject) and the concept of subjecthood (to identify which

---

[3]Some fine details: we identified verbs using automatically assigned POS-tags. We used a vocabulary of the most frequent 10,000 words in the corpus, and words not in the vocabulary were replaced with their automatically assigned POS tag.

of the nouns preceding the verb determines the verb's form). Identification of the correct subject requires learning to identify syntactic markers of nested structures, in order to be able to skip over distracting nouns in nested clauses. The RNN handled the learning task remarkably well, and managed to solve the vast majority (> 99% accuracy) of the test set cases. When focusing on the really hard cases, in which the verb and its subject were separated by 4 nouns of the opposite number, the RNN still managed to get accuracy of over 80%. Note that if it were to learn a heuristic of predicting the number of the last noun, its accuracy would have been 0% on these cases, and for a heuristic of choosing a random preceding noun the accuracy would have been 20%.

To summarize, this experiment demonstrates the learning power of gated RNNs, and the kinds of subtle patterns and regularities in the data they can pick up on.

16.2 RNNS AS FEATURE EXTRACTORS

A major use case of RNNs is as flexible, trainable feature extractors, that can replace parts of the more traditional feature extraction pipelines when working with sequences. In particular, RNNs are good replacements for window-based extractors.

16.2.1 PART-OF-SPEECH TAGGING

Let's re-consider the part-of-speech tagging problem under the RNN setup.

The skeleton: deep biRNN   POS-tagging is a special case of the sequence tagging task, assigning an output tag to each of the n input words. This makes a biRNN an ideal candidate for the basic structure.

Given a sentence with words $s = w_{1:n}$, we will translate them into input vectors $x_{1:n}$ using a feature function $x_i = \phi(s, i)$. The input vectors will be fed into a deep biRNN, producing output vectors $y_{1:n} = \text{biRNN}^*(x_{1:n})$. Each of the vectors y_i will then be fed into an MLP which will predict one of k possible output tags for the word. Each vector y_i is focused on position i in the sequence, but also has information regarding the entire sequence surrounding that position (an "infinite window"). Through the training procedure, the biRNN will learn to focus on the sequential aspects that are informative for predicting the label for w_i, and encode them in the vector y_i.

From words to inputs with character-level RNNs   How do we map a word w_i to an input vector x_i? One possibility is to use an embedding matrix, which can be either randomly initialized or pre-trained using a technique such as WORD2VEC with positional window contexts. Such mapping will be performed through an embedding matrix E, mapping words to embedding vectors $e_i = E_{[w_i]}$. While this works well, it can also suffer from coverage problems for vocabulary items not seen during training or pre-training. Words are made of characters, and certain suffixes and prefixes, as well as other orthographic cues such as the presence of capitalization, hyphens, or digits can provide strong hints regarding the word's ambiguity class. In Chapters 7 and 8 we discussed integrating such information using designated features. Here, we will replace these manually designed feature extractors with RNNs. Specifically, we will use two character-level RNNs. For a word w made of characters $c_1, \ldots, c_\ell$, we will map each character into a corresponding embedding vector c_i. The word will then be encoded using a forward RNN and reverse RNN over the characters. These RNNs can then either replace the word embedding vector, or, better yet, be concatenated to it:

$$x_i = \phi(s, i) = [E_{[w_i]}; \text{RNN}^f(c_{1:\ell}); \text{RNN}^b(c_{\ell:1})].$$

Note that the forward-running RNN focuses on capturing suffixes, the backward-running RNN focuses on prefixes, and both RNNs can be sensitive to capitalization, hyphens, and even word length.

The final model   The tagging models then becomes:

$$p(t_i = j \mid w_1, \ldots, w_n) = \text{softmax}(\text{MLP}(\text{biRNN}(x_{1:n}, i)))_{[j]}$$

$$x_i = \phi(s, i) = [E_{[w_i]}; \text{RNN}^f(c_{1:\ell}); \text{RNN}^b(c_{\ell:1})].$$

(16.4)

The model is trained using cross-entropy loss. Making use of word dropout (Section 8.4.2) for the word embeddings is beneficial. An illustration of the architecture is given in Figure 16.1.

A similar tagging model is described in the work of Plank et al. [2016], in which it was shown to produce very competitive results for a wide range of languages.

Character-level Convolution and Pooling   In the architecture above, words are mapped to vectors using forward-moving and backward-moving RNNs over the word's characters. An alternative is to represent words using character-level convolution and pooling neural networks (CNN, Chapter 13). Ma and Hovy [2016] demonstrate that using a one-layer convolutional-and-pooling layer with a window-size of $k = 3$ over each word's characters is indeed effective for part-of-speech tagging and named-entity recognition tasks.

Structured models   In the above model, the tagging prediction for word i is performed independently of the other tags. This may work well, but one could also condition the ith tag on the previous model predictions. The conditioning can be either the previous k tags (following a markov assumption), in which case we use tag embeddings $E_{[t]}$, resulting in:

$$p(t_i = j \mid w_1, \ldots, w_n, t_{i-1}, \ldots, t_{i-k}) = \text{softmax}(\text{MLP}([\text{biRNN}(x_{1:n}, i); E_{[t_{i-1}]}; \ldots; E_{[t_{i-k}]}]))_{[j]},$$

or on the entire sequence of previous predictions $t_{1:i-1}$, in which case an RNN is used for encoding the tag sequence:

$$p(t_i = j \mid w_1, \ldots, w_n, t_{1:i-1}) = \text{softmax}(\text{MLP}([\text{biRNN}(x_{1:n}, i); \text{RNN}^t(t_{1:i-1})]))_{[j]}.$$

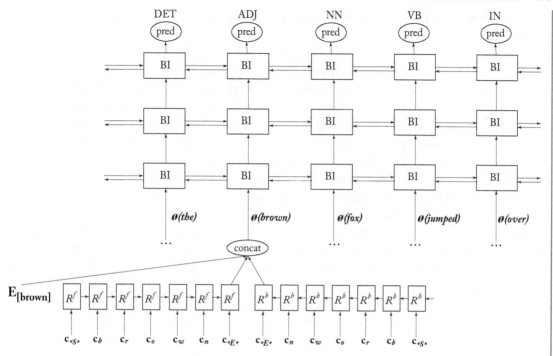

Figure 16.1: Illustration of the RNN tagging architecture. Each word w_i is converted into a vector $\phi(w_i)$ which is a concatenation of an embedding vector and the end states of forward- and backward-moving character level RNNs. The word vectors are then fed into a deep biRNN. The output of each of the outer layer biRNN states is then fed into a predicting network (MLP followed by softmax) resulting in a tag prediction. Note that each tagging prediction can conditions on the entire input sentence.

In both cases, the model can be run in greedy mode, predicting the tags t_i in sequence, or using dynamic programming search (in the markov case) or beam-search (in both cases) to find a high-scoring tagging sequence. Such a model was used for CCG-supertagging (assigning each word one of a large number of tags encoding a rich syntactic structure) by Vaswani et al. [2016]. Structured prediction training for such models is discussed in Chapter 19.

16.2.2 RNN–CNN DOCUMENT CLASSIFICATION

In the sentiment classification examples in Section 16.1.1, we had embedding vectors feeding into a forward-moving RNN and a backward-moving RNN, followed by a classification layer [Equation (16.2)]. In the tagger example in Section 16.2.1, we saw that the word embeddings can be supplemented (or replaced) with character-level models such as RNNs or CNNs over the characters, in order to improve the model's coverage and help it deal with unseen words, inflections, and typos.

The same approach can be effective also for document classification: instead of feeding word-embeddings into the two RNNs, we feed vectors that result either from character-level RNNs over each word, or from a convolutional-and-pooling layer applied over each word.

Another alternative is to apply a hierarchical convolution-and-pooling network (Section 13.3) on the characters, in order to get a shorter sequence of vectors that represent units that are beyond characters but are not necessarily words (the captured information may capture either more or less than a single word), and then feed the resulting sequence of vectors into the two RNNs and the classification layer. Such an approach is explored by Xiao and Cho [2016] on several document classification tasks. More specifically, their hierarchical architecture includes a series of convolutional and pooling layers. At each layer, a convolution with window size k is applied to the sequence of input vectors, and then max-pooling is applied between each two neighboring resulting vectors, halving the sequence length. After several such layers (with window sizes varying between 5 and 3 as a function of the layer, i.e., widths of 5, 5, 3), the resulting vectors are fed into forward-running and backward-running GRU RNNs, which are then fed into a classification component (a fully connected layer followed by softmax). They also apply dropout between the last convolutional layer and the RNNs, and between the RNN and the classification component. This approach is effective for several document classification tasks.

16.2.3   ARC-FACTORED DEPENDENCY PARSING

We revisit the arc-factored dependency-parsing task from Section 7.7. Recall that we are given a sentence *sent* with words $w_{1:n}$ and corresponding POS-tags $t_{1:n}$, and need to assign, for each word pair (w_i, w_j) a score indicating the strength assigned to word w_i being the head of word w_j. In Section 8.6 we derived an intricate feature function for the task, based on windows surrounding the head and modifier words, the words between the head and modifier words, and their POS tags. This intricate feature function can be replaced by a concatenation of two biRNN vectors, corresponding to the head and the modifier words.

Specifically, given words and POS-tags $w_{1:n}$ and $t_{1:n}$ with the corresponding embedding vectors $\boldsymbol{w}_{1:n}$ and $\boldsymbol{t}_{1:n}$, we create a biRNN encoding $\boldsymbol{v}_i$ for each sentence position by concatenating the word and POS vectors, and feeding them into a deep-biRNN:

$$\boldsymbol{v}_{1:n} = \text{biRNN}^{\star}(\boldsymbol{x}_{1:n})$$

$$\boldsymbol{x}_i = [\boldsymbol{w}_i ; \boldsymbol{t}_i].$$

(16.5)

We then score a head-modifier candidate by passing the concatenation of the biRNN vectors through an MLP:

$$\text{ArcScore}(h, m, w_{1:n}, t_{1:n}) = MLP(\phi(h, m, s)) = MLP([\boldsymbol{v}_h ; \boldsymbol{v}_m]).$$

(16.6)

Illustration of the architecture is given in Figure 16.2. Notice that the biRNN vectors v_i encode the words in context, essentially forming an infinite window to each side of the word w_i, which is sensitive to both the POS-tag sequence and the word sequence. Moreover, the concatenation $[v_h; v_m]$ include RNNs running up to each word in each direction, and in particular it covers the sequence of positions between w_h and w_m, and the distance between them. The biRNN is trained as part of the larger network, and learns to focus on the important aspects of the sequence the syntactic parsing task (structured-training of the arc-factored parser is explained in Section 19.4.1).

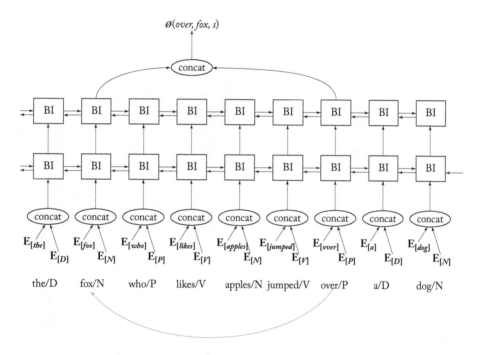

Figure 16.2: Illustration of the arc-factored parser feature extractor for the arc between *fox* and *over*.

Such a feature extractor was used in the work of Kiperwasser and Goldberg [2016b], in which it was shown to produce state-of-the-art parsing results for the arc-factored approach, rivaling the scores of much more complex parsing models. A similar approach was taken also by Zhang et al. [2016], achieving similar results with a different training regime.

In general, whenever one is using words as features in a task that is sensitive to word order or sentence structure, the words can be replaced by their trained biLSTM vectors. Such an approach was taken by Kiperwasser and Goldberg [2016b] and Cross and Huang [2016a,b] in the context of *transition-based* syntactic parsing, with impressive results.

CHAPTER 17

Conditioned Generation

As discussed in Chapter 14, RNNs can act as non-markovian language models, conditioning on the entire history. This ability makes them suitable for use as *generators* (generating natural language sequences) and *conditioned generators*, in which the generated output is conditioned on a complex input. This chapter discusses these architectures.

17.1 RNN GENERATORS

A special case of using the RNN-transducer architecture for language modeling (Section 14.3.3) is *sequence generation*. Any language model can be used for generation, as described in Section 9.5. For the RNN-transducer, generation works by tying the output of the transducer at time i with its input at time $i + 1$: after predicting a distribution over the next output symbols $p(t_i = k|t_{1:i-1})$, a token t_i is chosen and its corresponding embedding vector is fed as the input to the next step. The process stops when generating a special end-of-sequence symbol, often denoted as $</s>$. The process is depicted in Figure 17.1.

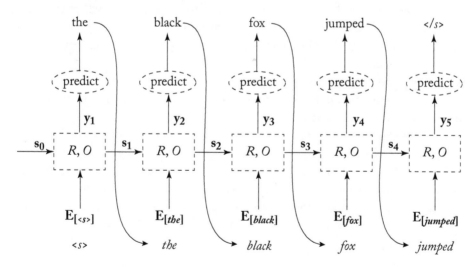

Figure 17.1: Transducer RNN used as a generator.

Similar to the case of generation from an $n$gram language model (Section 9.5), when generating from a trained RNN transducer one can either choose the highest probability item at each step, sample an item according to the model's predicted distribution, or use beam-search for finding a globally high-probability output.

An impressive demonstration of the ability of gated RNN to condition on arbitrarily long histories is through a RNN-based language model that is trained on characters rather than on words. When used as a generator, the trained RNN language model is tasked with generating random sentences character by character, each character conditioning on the previous ones [Sutskever et al., 2011]. Working on the character level forces the model to look further back into the sequence in order to connect letters to words and words to sentences, and to form meaningful patterns. The generated texts not only resemble fluent English, but also show sensitivity to properties that are not captured by $n$gram language models, including line lengths and nested parenthesis balancing. When trained on C source code, the generated sequences adhere to indentation patterns, and the general syntactic constraints the C language. For an interesting demonstration and analysis of the properties of RNN-based character level language models, see Karpathy et al. [2015].

17.1.1 TRAINING GENERATORS

When training the generator, the common approach is to simply train it as a transducer that aims to put a large probability mass on the next token in the observed sequence based on the previously observed tokens (i.e., training as a language model).

More concretely, for every n words sentence $w_1, \ldots, w_n$ in the training corpus, we produce an RNN transducer with $n + 1$ inputs and $n + 1$ corresponding outputs, where the first input is the start-of-sentence symbol, followed by the n words of the sentence. The first expected output is then w_1, the second expected output is w_2, and so on, and the $n + 1$th expected output is the end-of-sentence symbol.

This training approach is often called *teacher-forcing*, as the generator is fed the observed word even if its own prediction put a small probability mass on it, and in test time it would have generated a different word at this state.

While this works, it does not handle well deviations from the gold sequences. Indeed, when applied as a generator, feeding on its own predictions rather than on gold sequences, the generator will be required to assign probabilities given states not observed in training. Searching for a high-probability output sequence using beam-search may also benefit from a dedicated training procedure. As of this writing, coping with these situations is still an open research question, which is beyond the scope of this book. We briefly touch upon this when discussing structured prediction in Chapter 19.3.

17.2 · CONDITIONED GENERATION (ENCODER-DECODER)

While using the RNN as a generator is a cute exercise for demonstrating its strength, the power of the RNN transducer is really revealed when moving to a *conditioned generation* framework.

The generation framework generates the next token t_{j+1} based on the previously generated tokens $\hat{t}_{1:j}$:

$$\hat{t}_{j+1} \sim p(t_{j+1} = k \mid \hat{t}_{1:j}). \tag{17.1}$$

This is modeled in the RNN framework as:

$$p(t_{j+1} = k \mid \hat{t}_{1:j}) = f(\text{RNN}(\hat{t}_{1:j}))$$
$$\hat{t}_j \sim p(t_j \mid \hat{t}_{1:j-1}), \tag{17.2}$$

or, if using the more detailed recursive definition:

$$p(t_{j+1} = k \mid \hat{t}_{1:j}) = f(O(s_{j+1}))$$
$$s_{j+1} = R(\hat{t}_j, s_j) \tag{17.3}$$
$$\hat{t}_j \sim p(t_j \mid \hat{t}_{1:j-1}),$$

where f is a parameterized function that maps the RNN state to a distribution over words, for example $f(x) = \text{softmax}(xW + b)$ or $f(x) = \text{softmax}(\text{MLP}(x))$.

In the conditioned generation framework, the next token is generated based on the previously generated tokens, and an additional conditioning context c.

$$\hat{t}_{j+1} \sim p(t_{j+1} = k \mid \hat{t}_{1:j}, c). \tag{17.4}$$

When using the RNN framework, the context c is represented as a vector c:

$$p(t_{j+1} = k \mid \hat{t}_{1:j}, c) = f(\text{RNN}(v_{1:j}))$$
$$v_i = [\hat{t}_i; c] \tag{17.5}$$
$$\hat{t}_j \sim p(t_j \mid \hat{t}_{1:j-1}, c),$$

or, using the recursive definition:

$$p(t_{j+1} = k \mid \hat{t}_{1:j}, c) = f(O(s_{j+1}))$$
$$s_{j+1} = R(s_j, [\hat{t}_j; c]) \tag{17.6}$$
$$\hat{t}_j \sim p(t_i \mid \hat{t}_{1:j-1}, c).$$

At each stage of the generation process the context vector c is concatenated to the input $\hat{t}_j$, and the concatenation is fed into the RNN, resulting in the next prediction. Figure 17.2 illustrates the architecture.

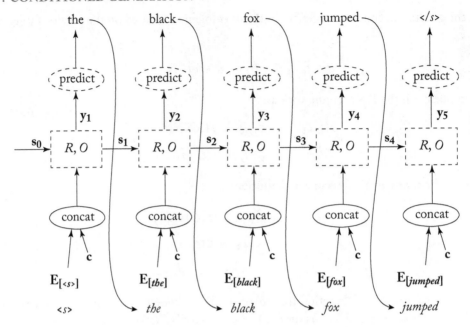

Figure 17.2: Conditioned RNN generator.

What kind of information can be encoded in the context c? Pretty much any data we can put our hands on during training, and that we find useful. For example, if we have a large corpus of news items categorized into different topics, we can treat the topic as a conditioning context. Our language model will then be able to generate texts conditioned on the topic. If we are interested in movie reviews, we can condition the generation on the genre of the movie, the rating of the review, and perhaps the geographic region of the author. We can then control these aspects when generating text. We can also condition on *inferred* properties, that we automatically extract from the text. For example, we can derive heuristics to tell us if a given sentence is written in first person, if it contains a passive-voice construction, and the level of vocabulary used in it. We can then use these aspects as conditioning context for training, and, later, for text generation.

17.2.1 SEQUENCE TO SEQUENCE MODELS

The context c can have many forms. In the previous subsection, we described some fixed-length, set-like examples of conditioning contexts. Another popular approach takes c to be itself a sequence, most commonly a piece of text. This gives rise to the *sequence to sequence* conditioned generation framework, also called the *encoder–decoder* framework [Cho et al., 2014a, Sutskever et al., 2014].

In sequence to sequence conditioned generation, we have a source sequence $x_{1:n}$ (for example reflecting a sentence in French) and we are interested in generating a target output sequence $t_{1:m}$ (for example the translation of the sentence into English). This works by *encoding* the source sentence $x_{1:n}$ into a vector using an encoder function $c = \text{Enc}(x_{1:n})$, commonly an RNN: $c = \text{RNN}^{\text{enc}}(x_{1:n})$. A conditioned generator RNN (*decoder*) is then used to generate the desired output $t_{1:m}$ according to Equation (17.5). The architecture is illustrated in Figure 17.3.

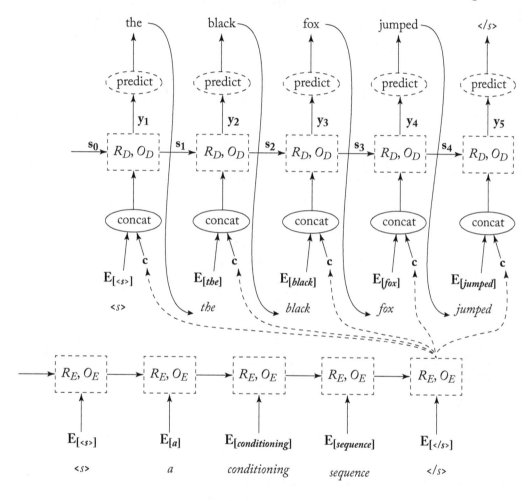

Figure 17.3: Sequence-to-sequence RNN generator.

This setup is useful for mapping sequences of length n to sequences of length m. The encoder summarizes the source sentence as a vector c, and the decoder RNN is then used to predict (using a language modeling objective) the target sequence words conditioned on the previously predicted words as well as the encoded sentence c. The encoder and decoder RNNs are trained jointly. The supervision happens only for the decoder RNN, but the gradients are propagated all the way back to the encoder RNN (see Figure 17.4).

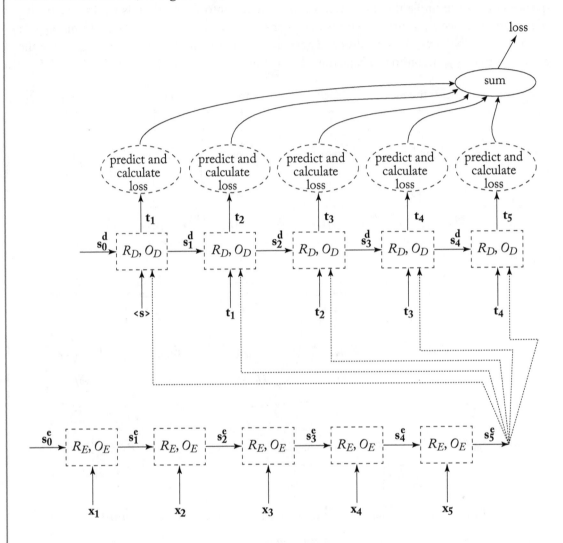

Figure 17.4: Sequence-to-sequence RNN training graph.

17.2.2 APPLICATIONS

The sequence-to-sequence approach is very general, and can potentially fit any case where a mapping from an input sequence to an output sequence is needed. We list some example use cases from the literature.

Machine Translation   The sequence-to-sequence approach was shown to be surprisingly effective for Machine Translation [Sutskever et al., 2014] using deep LSTM RNNs. In order for the technique to work, Sutskever et al. found it effective to input the source sentence in reverse, such that x_n corresponds to the first word of the sentence. In this way, it is easier for the second RNN to establish the relation between the first word of the source sentence to the first word of the target sentence.

   While the success of the sequence-to-sequence approach in French-to-English translation is impressive, it is worth noting that the approach of Sutskever et al. [2014] required eight layers of high-dimensional LSTMs, is very computationally expensive, and is non-trivial to train well. Later in this chapter (Section 17.4) we describe *attention-based architectures*, an elaboration on the sequence-to-sequence architecture that is much more useful for machine translation.

Email Auto-response   Here, the task is to map an email, that can be potentially long, into a short answer such as *Yes, I'll do it, Great, see you on Wednesday* or *It won't work out*. Kannan et al. [2016] describe an implementation of the auto-response feature for the Google Inbox product. The core of the solution is a straightforward sequence to sequence conditioned generation model based on an LSTM encoder that reads in the email, and an LSTM decoder that generates an appropriate response. This component is trained on many email-response pairs. Of course, in order to successfully integrate the response generation component into a product, it needs to be supplemented by additional modules, to schedule the triggering of the response component, to ensure diversity of responses and balance negative and positive responses, maintain user privacy, and so on. For details, see Kannan et al. [2016].

Morphological Inflection   In the morphological inflection task, the input is a base word and a desired inflection request, and the output is an inflected form of the word. For example, for the Finnish word *bruttoarvo* and the desired inflection pos=N,case=IN+ABL,num=PL the desired output is *bruttoarvoista*. While the task has traditionally been approached using hand-crafted lexicons and finite-state transducers, it is also a very good fit for character level sequence-to-sequence conditioned generation models [Faruqui et al., 2016]. Results of the SIGMORPHON 2016 shared task on inflection generation indicate that recurrent neural network approaches outperform all other participating approaches [Cotterell et al., 2016]. The second-place system [Aharoni et al., 2016] used a sequence-to-sequence model with a few enhancements for the task, while the winning system [Kann and Schütze, 2016] used an ensemble of *attentive* sequence-to-sequence models, such as the ones described in Section 17.4.

Other Uses   Mapping a sequence of n items to a sequence of m items is very general, and almost any task can be formulated in an encode-and-generate solution. However, the fact that a task *can* be formulated this way, does not mean that it should be—perhaps better architectures are more suitable for it, or are easier to learn. We now describe several applications that seem to be needlessly hard to learn under the encoder-decoder framework, and for which other, better-suited architectures exist. The fact that the authors managed to get decent accuracies with the encoder-decoder framework attests to the power of the framework.

Filippova et al. [2015] use the architecture for performing *sentence compression by deletion*. In this task, we are given a sentence such as *"Alan Turing, known as the father of computer science, the codebreaker that helped win World War 2, and the man tortured by the state for being gay, is to receive a pardon nearly 60 years after his death"* and are required to produce a shorter ("compressed") version containing the main information in the sentence by deleting words from the original sentence. An example compression would be *"Alan Turing is to receive a pardon."* Filippova et al. [2015] model the problem as a sequence-to-sequence mapping in which the input sequence is the input sentence (possibly coupled with syntactic information derived from an automatically produced parse-tree), and the output is a sequence of KEEP, DELETE, and STOP decisions. The model was trained on a corpus of about 2 million sentence-and-compression pairs extracted automatically from news articles [Filippova and Altun, 2013], producing state-of-the-art results.[1]

Gillick et al. [2016] perform part-of-speech tagging and named-entity recognition by treating it as a sequence-to-sequence problem mapping a sequence of unicode bytes to a sequence of spans predictions of the form S12,L13,PER,S40,L11,LOC indicating a 13-bytes long PERSON entity starting at offset 12, and an 11-bytes long LOCATION entity starting at offset 40.[2]

Vinyals et al. [2014] perform syntactic parsing as a sequence-to-sequence task mapping a sentence to a set of constituency bracketing decisions.

17.2.3   OTHER CONDITIONING CONTEXTS

The conditioned-generation approach is very flexible—the encoder needn't be an RNN. Indeed, the conditioning context vector can be based on a single word, a CBOW encoding, be generated by a convolutional network, or based on some other complex computation.

Furthermore, the conditioning context need not even be text-based. In a dialog setting (in which the RNN is trained to produce responses to messages in a dialog) Li et al. [2016] use as context a trainable embedding vector which is associated with the *user* who wrote the response. The intuition is that different users have different communication styles, based on their age, gender, social role, background knowledge, personality traits and many other latent factors. By conditioning on the user when generating the response, the network can learn to adapt its predictions while still using an underlying language model as a backbone. Moreover, as a side effect of training the generator, the network also learns *user embeddings*, producing similar vectors to users who have similar communication styles. At test time, one can influence the style of the generated response by feeding in a particular user (or average user vector) as a conditioning context.

---

[1]While impressive, the sequence-to-sequence approach is arguably an overkill for this task, in which we map a sequence of n words into a sequence of n decisions, where the ith decision relates directly to the ith word. This is in essence a sequence tagging task, and a biLSTM transducer, such as those described in the previous chapter, could be a better fit. Indeed, the work of Klerke et al. [2016] shows that similar (though a bit lower) accuracies can be obtained using a biRNN transducer trained on *several orders of magnitude* less data.

[2]This is, again, a sequence tagging task which can be performed well using a biLSTM transducer, or a structured biLSTM transducer (biLSTM-CRF), as described in Section 19.4.2.

Departing further away from language, a popular use-case is in *image captioning*: an input image is encoded as a vector (usually using a multi-layer convolutional network[3]) and this vector is used as a conditioning context for an RNN generator that is trained to predict image descriptions [Karpathy and Li, 2015, Mao et al., 2014, Vinyals et al., 2015].

Work by Huang et al. [2016] extend the captioning task to the more elaborate one of *visual story telling*, in which the input is a series of images, and the output is a story describing the progression in the images. Here, the encoder is an RNN that reads in a sequence of image vectors.

17.3 UNSUPERVISED SENTENCE SIMILARITY

It is often desired to have vector representations of sentences such that similar sentences have similar vectors. This problem is somewhat ill defined (what does it mean for sentences to be similar?), and is still an open research question, but some approaches produce reasonable results. Here, we focus on unsupervised approaches, in the sense that they can be trained from un-annotated data. The result of the training is an *encoder* function $\text{ENC}(w_{1:n})$ such that similar sentences are encoded to similar vectors.

Most approaches are based on the sequence-to-sequence framework: an encoder RNN is trained to produced context vectors c that will then be used by an RNN decoder to perform a task. As a consequence, the important information from the sentence with respect to the task must be captured in c. Then, the decoder RNN is thrown away, and the encoder is used to generate sentence representations c, under the premise that similar sentences will have similar vectors. The resulting similarity function across sentences, then, crucially relies on the task of the decoder was trained to perform.

Auto Encoding   The auto-encoding approach is a conditioned generation model in which a sentence is encoded using an RNN, and then the decoder attempts to reconstruct the input sentence. This way, the model is trained to encode the information that is needed to reconstruct the sentence, again, hopefully resulting in similar sentences having similar vectors. The sentence reconstruction objective may not be ideal for general sentence similarity, however, as it is likely to push apart representations of sentences that convey similar meanings but use different words.

Machine Translation   Here, a sequence-to-sequence network is trained to translate sentences from English to another language. Intuitively, the vectors produced by the encoder are useful for translation, and so they encode the essence of the sentence that is needed to translate it properly, resulting in sentences that will be translated similarly to have similar vectors. This method requires a large corpus for the conditioned generation task, such as a parallel corpus used in machine translation.

---

[3]Mapping images to vectors using neural architectures is a well-studied topic with established best practices and many success stories. It also falls outside the scope of this book.

Skip-thoughts   The model of Kiros et al. [2015], assigned the name *skip-thought vectors* by its authors, presents an interesting objective to the sentence similarity problem. The model extend the distributional hypothesis from words to sentences, arguing that sentences are similar if they appear in similar contexts, where a context of a sentence are the sentences surrounding it. The skip-thoughts model is thus a conditioned generation model where an RNN encoder maps a sentence to a vector, and then one decoder is trained to reconstruct the previous sentence based on the encoded representation, and a second decoder is trained to reconstruct the following sentence. The trained skip-thought encoder produces impressive results in practice, mapping sentences such as:

(a) *he ran his hand inside his coat, double-checking that the unopened letter was still there;* and

(b) *he slipped his hand between his coat and his shirt, where the folded copies lay in a brown envelope.*

to similar vectors.

Syntactic Similarity   The work of Vinyals et al. [2014] demonstrate that an encoder-decoder can produce decent results for *phrase-based syntactic parsing*, by encoding the sentence and requiring the decoder to reconstruct a linearized parse tree as a stream of bracketing decisions, i.e., mapping from:

the boy opened the door

to:

(S (NP DT NN) (VP VBD (NP DT NN)))

The encoded sentence representations under such training are likely to capture the syntactic structure of the sentence.

17.4   CONDITIONED GENERATION WITH ATTENTION

In the encoder-decoder networks described in Section 17.2 the input sentence is encoded into a single vector, which is then used as a conditioning context for an RNN-generator. This architectures forces the encoded vector $c = \mathrm{RNN}^{\mathrm{enc}}(x_{1:n})$ to contain all the information required for generation, and requires the generator to be able to extract this information from the fixed-length vector. Given these rather strong requirements, the architecture works surprisingly well. However, in many cases it can be substantially improved by the addition of an *attention mechanism*. The *conditioned generation with attention* architecture [Bahdanau et al., 2014] relaxes the condition that the entire source sentence be encoded as a single vector. Instead, the input sentence is encoded as a sequence of vectors, and the decoder uses a *soft attention mechanism* in order to decide on which parts of the encoding input it should focus. The encoder, decoder, and attention mechanism are all trained jointly in order to play well with each other.

More concretely, the encoder-decoder with attention architecture encodes a length n input sequence $x_{1:n}$ using a biRNN, producing n vectors $c_{1:n}$:

$$c_{1:n} = \text{ENC}(x_{1:n}) = \text{biRNN}^\star(x_{1:n}).$$

The generator (decoder) can then use these vectors as a read-only memory representing the conditioning sentence: at any stage j of the generation process, it chooses which of the vectors $c_{1:n}$ it should attend to, resulting in a focused context vector $c^j = \text{attend}(c_{1:n}, \hat{t}_{1:j})$.

The focused context vector c^j is then used for conditioning the generation at step j:

$$p(t_{j+1} = k \mid \hat{t}_{1:j}, x_{1:n}) = f(O(s_{j+1}))$$
$$s_{j+1} = R(s_j, [\hat{t}_j ; c^j])$$
$$c^j = \text{attend}(c_{1:n}, \hat{t}_{1:j}) \tag{17.7}$$
$$\hat{t}_j \sim p(t_j \mid \hat{t}_{1:j-1}, x_{1:n}).$$

In terms of representation power, this architectures subsumes the previous encoder-decoder architecture: by setting $\text{attend}(c_{1:n}, \hat{t}_{1:j}) = c_n$, we get Equation (17.6).

How does the function $\text{attend}(\cdot, \cdot)$ look like? As you may have guessed by this point, it is a trainable, parameterized function. This text follows the attention mechanism described by Bahdanau et al. [2014], who were the first to introduce attention in the context of sequence to sequence generation.[4] While this particular attention mechanism is popular and works well, many variants are possible. The work of Luong et al. [2015] explores some of them in the context of machine translation.

The implemented attention mechanism is *soft*, meaning that at each stage the decoder sees a weighted average of the vectors $c_{1:n}$, where the weights are chosen by the attention mechanism.

More formally, at stage j the soft attention produces a mixture vector c^j:

$$c^j = \sum_{i=1}^{n} \alpha^j_{[i]} \cdot c_i.$$

$\alpha^j \in \mathbb{R}^n_+$ is the vector of attention weights for stage j, whose elements $\alpha^j_{[i]}$ are all positive and sum to one.

The values $\alpha^j_{[i]}$ are produced in a two stage process: first, unnormalized attention weights $\bar{\alpha}^j_{[i]}$ are produced using a feed-forward network MLP^{att} taking into account the decoder state at time j and each of the vectors c_i:

$$\bar{\alpha}^j = \bar{\alpha}^j_{[1]}, \ldots, \bar{\alpha}^j_{[n]} =$$
$$= \text{MLP}^{\text{att}}([s_j ; c_1]), \ldots, \text{MLP}^{\text{att}}([s_j ; c_n]). \tag{17.8}$$

---

[4]The description of the decoder part of the model differs in some small aspects from that of Bahdanau et al. [2014], and is more similar to that of Luong et al. [2015].

The unnormalized weights $\bar{\alpha}^j$ are then normalized into a probability distribution using the soft-max function:

$$\alpha^j = \text{softmax}(\bar{\alpha}^j_{[1]}, \ldots, \bar{\alpha}^j_{[n]}).$$

In the context of machine translation, one can think of MLP^{att} as computing a *soft alignment* between the current decoder state s_j (capturing the recently produced foreign words) and each of the source sentence components c_i.

The complete attend function is then:

$$\text{attend}(c_{1:n}, \hat{t}_{1:j}) = c^j$$

$$c^j = \sum_{i=1}^{n} \alpha^j_{[i]} \cdot c_i$$

$$\alpha^j = \text{softmax}(\bar{\alpha}^j_{[1]}, \ldots, \bar{\alpha}^j_{[n]})$$ (17.9)

$$\bar{\alpha}^j_{[i]} = \text{MLP}^{\text{att}}([s_j; c_i]),$$

and the entire sequence-to-sequence generation with attention is given by:

$$p(t_{j+1} = k \mid \hat{t}_{1:j}, x_{1:n}) = f(O_{\text{dec}}(s_{j+1}))$$

$$s_{j+1} = R_{\text{dec}}(s_j, [\hat{t}_j; c^j])$$

$$c^j = \sum_{i=1}^{n} \alpha^j_{[i]} \cdot c_i$$

$$c_{1:n} = \text{biRNN}^{\star}_{\text{enc}}(x_{1:n})$$

$$\alpha^j = \text{softmax}(\bar{\alpha}^j_{[1]}, \ldots, \bar{\alpha}^j_{[n]})$$ (17.10)

$$\bar{\alpha}^j_{[i]} = \text{MLP}^{\text{att}}([s_j; c_i])$$

$$\hat{t}_j \sim p(t_j \mid \hat{t}_{1:j-1}, x_{1:n})$$

$$f(z) = \text{softmax}(\text{MLP}^{\text{out}}(z))$$

$$\text{MLP}^{\text{att}}([s_j; c_i]) = v \tanh([s_j; c_i]U + b).$$

A sketch of the architecture is given in Figure 17.5.

Why use the biRNN encoder to translate the conditioning sequence $x_{1:n}$ into the context vectors $c_{1:n}$ instead of letting the attention mechanism look directly at $x_{1:n}$? Couldn't we just use $c^j = \sum_{i=1}^{n} \alpha^j_{[i]} \cdot x_i$ and $\bar{\alpha}^j_{[i]} = \text{MLP}^{\text{att}}([s_j; x_i])$? We could, but we get important benefits from the encoding process. First, the biRNN vectors c_i represent the items x_i *in their sentential context*,

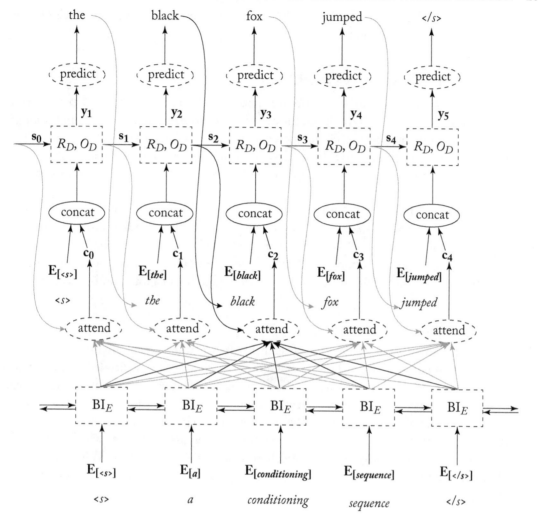

Figure 17.5: Sequence-to-sequence RNN generator with attention.

that is, they represent a window focused around the input item x_i and not the item itself. Second, by having a trainable encoding component that is trained jointly with the decoder, the encoder and decoder evolve together and the network can learn to encode relevant properties of the input that are useful for decoding, and that may not be present at the source sequence $x_{1:n}$ directly. For example, the biRNN encoder may learn to encode the *position* of x_i within the sequence, and the decoder could use this information to access the elements in order, or learn to pay more attention to elements in the beginning of the sequence then to elements at its end.

Attentive conditioned generation models are very powerful, and work very well on many sequence to sequence generation tasks.

17.4.1 COMPUTATIONAL COMPLEXITY

The conditioned generation *without* attention is relatively cheap: the encoding is performed in linear time in the input length ($O(n)$), and the decoding is performed in linear time in the output length ($O(m)$). While generating a distribution over words from a large vocabulary is in itself expensive, this is an orthogonal issue to this analysis, in which we consider the vocabulary scoring as a constant time operation. The overall complexity of the sequence to sequence generation process is then $O(m + n)$.[5]

What is the cost of adding the attention mechanism? The encoding of the input sequence remains an $O(n)$ linear time operation. However, each step of the decoding process now needs to compute c^j. This entails n evaluations of MLP^{att} followed by a normalization step and a summation of n vectors. The complexity of a decoding step grew from a constant time operation to linear in the length of the conditioning sentence ($O(n)$), resulting in a total runtime of $O(m \times n)$.

17.4.2 INTERPRETABILITY

Non-attentive encoder-decoder networks (much like most other neural architectures) are extremely opaque: we do not have a clear understanding on what exactly is encoded in the encoded vector, how this information is exploited in the decoder, and what prompted a particular decoder behavior. An important benefit of the attentive architecture is that it provides a simple way of peeking inside some of the reasoning in the decoder and what it learned. At each stage of the decoding process, one can look at the produced attention weights α^j and see which areas of the source sequence the decoder found relevant when producing the given output. While this is still a weak form of interpretability, it is leaps and bounds beyond the opaqueness of the non-attentive models.

17.5 ATTENTION-BASED MODELS IN NLP

Conditioned-generation with attention is a very powerful architecture. It is the main algorithm driving state-of-the-art machine translation, and provides strong results on many other NLP tasks. This section provides a few examples of its usage.

---

[5]While the output length m is in principle not bounded, in practice the trained decoders do learn to produce outputs with a length distribution similar to lengths in the training dataset, and in the worst case one can always put a hard limit on the length of generated sentences.

17.5.1 MACHINE TRANSLATION

While we initially described machine translation in the context of plain sequence to sequence generation, current state-of-the-art machine translation systems are powered by models that employ attention.

The first results with attentive sequence-to-sequence models for machine translation are due to Bahdanau et al. [2014], who essentially used the architecture described in the previous section as is (using a GRU-flavored RNN), employing beam-search when generating from the decoder at test time. While Luong et al. [2015] explored variations on the attention mechanism leading to some gains, most progress in neural machine translation use the attentive sequence-to-sequence architecture as is (either with LSTMs or GRUs), while changing its inputs.

While we cannot expect to cover neural machine translation in this rather short section, we list some improvements due to Sennrich and colleagues that push the boundaries of the state-of-the-art.

Sub-word Units   In order to deal with vocabularies of highly inflected languages (as well as to restrict the vocabulary size in general), Sennrich et al. [2016a] propose moving to working with sub-word units that are smaller than a token. Their algorithm processes the source and target side texts using an algorithm called BPE in search for prominent subword units (the algorithm itself is described at the end of Section 10.5.5). When run on English, this stage is likely to find units such as er, est, un, low and wid. The source and target sentences are then processed to split words according to the induced segmentation (i.e., converting the widest network into the wid_ _est net_ _work). This processed corpus is then fed into an attentive sequence-to-sequence training. After decoding test sentences, the output is processed once more to un-split the sub-word units back into words. This process reduces the number of unknown tokens, makes it easier to generalize to new vocabulary items, and improves translation quality. Related research effort attempt to work directly on the character level (encoding and decoding characters instead of words), with notable success [Chung et al., 2016].

Incorporating monolingual data   The sequence-to-sequence models are trained on parallel corpora of aligned sentences in the source and target languages. Such corpora exist, but are naturally much smaller than available *monolingual data*, which is essentially infinite. Indeed, the previous generation of statistical machine translation systems[6] train a *translation model* on the parallel data, and a separate *language model* on much larger monolingual data. The sequence-to-sequence architecture does not currently allow such a separation, training the language model (decoder) and translation model (encoder-decoder interaction) jointly.

How can we make use of target-side monolingual data in a sequence-to-sequence framework? Sennrich et al. [2016b] propose the following training protocol: when attempting to translate from source to target, first train a translation model from target to source, and use it to

---

[6]For an overview, see the book of Koehn [2010] as well as the book on syntax-based machine translation in this series [Williams et al., 2016].

translate a large monolingual corpus of target sentences. Then, add the resulting (target,source) pairs to the parallel corpus as (source,target) examples. Train a source to target MT system on the combined corpus. Note that while the system now trains on automatically produced examples, all of the target side sentences it sees are original, so the language modeling component is never trained on automatically produced text. While somewhat of a hack, this training protocol brings substantial improvements in translation quality. Further research will likely yield cleaner solutions for integrating monolingual data.

Linguistic Annotations   Finally, Sennrich and Haddow [2016] show that the attentive sequence-to-sequence architecture can learn better translation model if its input is supplemented with linguistic annotations. That is, given a source sentence $w_1, \ldots, w_n$, rather than creating the input vectors $x_{1:n}$ by simply assigning an embedding vector to each word ($x_i = E_{[w_i]}$), the sentence is run through a linguistic annotation pipeline that includes part-of-speech tagging, syntactic dependency parsing and lemmatization. Each word is then supplemented with an encoding vector of its part of speech tag (p_i), it's dependency label with respect to its head (r_i), its lemma (l_i), and morphological features (m_i). The input vectors $x_{1:n}$ is then defined as concatenation of these features: $x_i = [w_i; p_i; r_i; l_i; m_i]$. These additional features consistently improve translation quality, indicating that linguistic information is helpful even in the presence of powerful models than can in theory learn the linguistic concepts on their own. Similarly, Aharoni and Goldberg [2017] show that by training the decoder in a German to English translation system to produce linearized syntactic trees instead of a sequence of words, the resulting translations exhibit more consistent reordering behavior, and better translation quality. These works barely scratch the surface with respect to integrating linguistic information. Further research may come up with additional linguistic cues that could be integrated, or improved ways of integrating the linguistic information.

Open issues   As of the time of this writing, major open issues in neural machine translation include scaling up the size of the output vocabulary (or removing the dependence on it by moving to character-based outputs), training while taking the beam-search decoding into account, and speeding up training and decoding. Another topic that becomes popular is the move to models that make use of syntactic information. That said, the field is moving extremely fast, and this paragraph may not be relevant by the time the book gets to press.

17.5.2 MORPHOLOGICAL INFLECTION

The morphological inflection task discussed above in the context of sequence to sequence models also work better when used with an attentive sequence-to-sequence architecture, as evident by the architecture of the winning system in the SIGMORPHON shared task on morphological reinflection [Cotterell et al., 2016]. The winning system [Kann and Schütze, 2016] essentially use an off-the-shelf attentive sequence to sequence model. The input to the shared task is a word form and a desired inflection, given as a list of target part-of-speech tags and morphological features, e.g., NOUN Gender=Male Number=Plural, and the desired output as an inflected form. This is translated to a sequence to sequence model by creating an input sequence that is the list of inflection information, followed by the list of characters of the input word. The desired output is then the list of characters in the target word.

17.5.3 SYNTACTIC PARSING

While more suitable architectures exist, the work of Vinyals et al. [2014] show that attentive sequence to sequence models can produce competitive syntactic parsing results, by reading in a sentence (a word at a time) and outputting a sequence of bracketing decisions. This may not seem like an ideal architecture for parsing—indeed, one can get superior results with better tailored architectures, as evident by the work of Cross and Huang [2016a]. However, considering the generality of the architecture, the system works surprisingly well, and produces impressive parsing results. In order to get fully competitive results, some extra steps must be taken: the architecture needs a lot of training data. It is trained on parse-trees produced by running two treebank-trained parsers on a large text corpus, and selecting trees on which the two parsers agree (high-confidence parses). In addition, for the final parser, an ensemble (Section 5.2.3) of several attention networks is used.

PART IV

Additional Topics

CHAPTER 18

Modeling Trees with Recursive Neural Networks

The RNN is very useful for modeling sequences. In language processing, it is often natural and desirable to work with tree structures. The trees can be syntactic trees, discourse trees, or even trees representing the sentiment expressed by various parts of a sentence [Socher et al., 2013b]. We may want to predict values based on specific tree nodes, predict values based on the root nodes, or assign a quality score to a complete tree or part of a tree. In other cases, we may not care about the tree structure directly but rather reason about spans in the sentence. In such cases, the tree is merely used as a backbone structure which helps guide the encoding process of the sequence into a fixed size vector.

The *recursive neural network* abstraction (RecNN) [Pollack, 1990], popularized in NLP by Richard Socher and colleagues [Socher, 2014, Socher et al., 2010, 2011, 2013a] is a generalization of the RNN from sequences to (binary) trees.[1]

Much like the RNN encodes each sentence prefix as a state vector, the RecNN encodes each tree-node as a state vector in $\mathbb{R}^d$. We can then use these state vectors either to predict values of the corresponding nodes, assign quality values to each node, or as a semantic representation of the spans rooted at the nodes.

The main intuition behind the recursive neural networks is that each subtree is represented as a d-dimensional vector, and the representation of a node p with children c_1 and c_2 is a function of the representation of the nodes: $vec(p) = f(vec(c_1), vec(c_2))$, where f is a composition function taking two d-dimensional vectors and returning a single d-dimensional vector. Much like the RNN state s_i is used to encode the entire sequence $x_{1:i}$, the RecNN state associated with a tree node p encodes the entire subtree rooted at p. See Figure 18.1 for an illustration.

18.1 FORMAL DEFINITION

Consider a binary parse tree $\mathcal{T}$ over an n-word sentence. As a reminder, an ordered, unlabeled tree over a string $x_1, \ldots, x_n$ can be represented as a unique set of triplets (i, k, j), s.t. $i \leq k \leq j$. Each such triplet indicates that a node spanning words $x_{i:j}$ is parent of the nodes spanning $x_{i:k}$ and $x_{k+1:j}$. Triplets of the form (i, i, i) correspond to terminal symbols at the tree leaves (the words x_i). Moving from the unlabeled case to the labeled one, we can represent a tree as a set of

---

[1]While presented in terms of binary parse trees, the concepts easily transfer to general recursively defined data structures, with the major technical challenge is the definition of an effective form for R, the combination function.

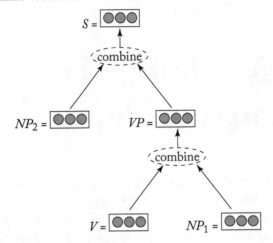

Figure 18.1: Illustration of a recursive neural network. The representations of V and NP$_1$ are combined to form the representation of VP. The representations of VP and NP$_2$ are then combined to form the representation of S.

6-tuples $(A \rightarrow B, C, i, k, j)$, whereas i, k, and j indicate the spans as before, and A, B, and C are the node labels of of the nodes spanning $x_{i:j}$, $x_{i:k}$, and $x_{k+1:j}$, respectively. Here, leaf nodes have the form $(A \rightarrow A, A, i, i, i)$, where A is a pre-terminal symbol. We refer to such tuples as *production rules*. For an example, consider the syntactic tree for the sentence "the boy saw her duck."

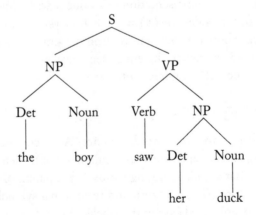

Its corresponding unlabeled and labeled representations are as shown in Table 18.1.

Table 18.1: Unlabeled and labeled representations

Unlabeled	Labeled	Corresponding Span	
(1,1,1)	(Det, Det, Det, 1, 1, 1)	$x_{1:1}$	the
(2,2,2)	(Nound, Noun, Noun, 2, 2, 2)	$x_{2:2}$	boy
(3,3,3)	(Verb, Verb, Verb, 3, 3, 3)	$x_{3:3}$	saw
(4, 4, 4)	(Det, Det, Det, 4, 4, 4)	$x_{4:4}$	her
(5, 5, 5)	(Noun, Noun, Noun, 5, 5, 5)	$x_{5:5}$	duck
(4, 4, 5)	(NP, Det, Noun, 4, 4, 5)	$x_{4:5}$	her duck
(3, 3, 5)	(VP, Verb, NP, 3, 3, 5)	$x_{3:5}$	saw her duck
(1, 1, 2)	(NP, Det, Nound, 1, 1, 2)	$x_{1:2}$	the boy
(1, 2, 5)	(S, NP, VP, 1 2, 5)	$x_{1:5}$	the boy saw her duck

The set of production rules above can be uniquely converted to a set of tree nodes $q_{i:j}^A$ (indicating a node with symbol A over the span $x_{i:j}$) by simply ignoring the elements (B, C, k) in each production rule. We are now in position to define the recursive neural network.

A recursive neural network (RecNN) is a function that takes as input a parse tree over an n-word sentence $x_1, \ldots, x_n$. Each of the sentence's words is represented as a d-dimensional vector $\boldsymbol{x}_i$, and the tree is represented as a set $\mathcal{T}$ of production rules $(A \to B, C, i, j, k)$. Denote the nodes of $\mathcal{T}$ by $q_{i:j}^A$. The RecNN returns as output a corresponding set of *inside state vectors* $\boldsymbol{s}_{i:j}^A$, where each inside state vector $\boldsymbol{s}_{i:j}^A \in \mathbb{R}^d$ represents the corresponding tree node $q_{i:j}^A$, and encodes the entire structure rooted at that node. Like the sequence RNN, the tree-shaped RecNN is defined recursively using a function R, where the inside vector of a given node is defined as a function of the inside vectors of its direct children.[2] Formally:

$$\text{RecNN}(x_1, \ldots, x_n, \mathcal{T}) = \{\boldsymbol{s}_{i:j}^A \in \mathbb{R}^d \mid q_{i:j}^A \in \mathcal{T}\}$$

$$\boldsymbol{s}_{i:i}^A = v(x_i) \tag{18.1}$$

$$\boldsymbol{s}_{i:j}^A = R(A, B, C, \boldsymbol{s}_{i:k}^B, \boldsymbol{s}_{k+1:j}^C) \qquad q_{i:k}^B \in \mathcal{T}, \ q_{k+1:j}^C \in \mathcal{T}.$$

The function R usually takes the form of a simple linear transformation, which may or may not be followed by a nonlinear activation function g:

$$R(A, B, C, \boldsymbol{s}_{i:k}^B, \boldsymbol{s}_{k+1:j}^C) = g([\boldsymbol{s}_{i:k}^B; \boldsymbol{s}_{k+1:j}^C]W). \tag{18.2}$$

---

[2]Le and Zuidema [2014] extend the RecNN definition such that each node has, in addition to its inside state vector, also an *outside state vector* representing the entire structure around the subtree rooted at that node. Their formulation is based on the recursive computation of the classic inside-outside algorithm, and can be thought of as the biRNN counterpart of the tree RecNN. For details, see Le and Zuidema [2014].

This formulation of R ignores the tree labels, using the same matrix $W \in \mathbb{R}^{2d \times d}$ for all combinations. This may be a useful formulation in case the node labels do not exist (e.g., when the tree does not represent a syntactic structure with clearly defined labels) or when they are unreliable. However, if the labels are available, it is generally useful to include them in the composition function. One approach would be to introduce *label embeddings* $v(A)$ mapping each non-terminal symbol to a d_{nt} dimensional vector, and change R to include the embedded symbols in the combination function:

$$R(A, B, C, s^B_{i:k}, s^C_{k+1:j}) = g([s^B_{i:k}; s^C_{k+1:j}; v(A); v(B)]W) \qquad (18.3)$$

(here, $W \in \mathbb{R}^{2d+2d_{nt} \times d}$). Such approach is taken by Qian et al. [2015]. An alternative approach, due to Socher et al. [2013a] is to untie the weights according to the non-terminals, using a different composition matrix for each B, C pair of symbols:[3]

$$R(A, B, C, s^B_{i:k}, s^C_{k+1:j}) = g([s^B_{i:k}; s^C_{k+1:j}]W^{BC}). \qquad (18.4)$$

This formulation is useful when the number of non-terminal symbols (or the number of possible symbol combinations) is relatively small, as is usually the case with phrase-structure parse trees. A similar model was also used by Hashimoto et al. [2013] to encode subtrees in semantic-relation classification task.

18.2   EXTENSIONS AND VARIATIONS

As all of the definitions of R above suffer from the vanishing gradients problem of the Simple RNN, several authors sought to replace it with functions inspired by the LSTM gated architecture, resulting in Tree-shaped LSTMs [Tai et al., 2015, Zhu et al., 2015b]. The question of optimal tree representation is still very much an open research question, and the vast space of possible combination functions R is yet to be explored. Other proposed variants on tree-structured RNNs includes a *recursive matrix-vector model* [Socher et al., 2012] and *recursive neural tensor network* [Socher et al., 2013b]. In the first variant, each word is represented as a combination of a vector and a matrix, where the vector defines the word's static semantic content as before, while the matrix acts as a learned "operator" for the word, allowing more subtle semantic compositions than the addition and weighted averaging implied by the concatenation followed by linear transformation function. In the second variant, words are associated with vectors as usual, but the composition function becomes more expressive by basing it on tensor instead of matrix operations.

In our own work [Kiperwasser and Goldberg, 2016a], we propose a tree encoder that is not restricted to binary trees but instead can work with arbitrary branching trees. The encoding is based on RNNs (specifically LSTMs), where each subtree encoding is recursively defined as the merging of two RNN states, one running over the encodings of the left subtrees (from left to

---

[3]While not explored in the literature, a trivial extension would condition the transformation matrix also on A.

right) and ending in the root node, and the other running over the encodings of the right subtrees (from right to left), and ending in the root node.

18.3 TRAINING RECURSIVE NEURAL NETWORKS

The training procedure for a recursive neural network follows the same recipe as training other forms of networks: define a loss, spell out the computation graph, compute gradients using back-propagation,[4] and train the parameters using SGD.

With regard to the loss function, similar to the sequence RNN one can associate a loss either with the root of the tree, with any given node, or with a set of nodes, in which case the individual node's losses are combined, usually by summation. The loss function is based on the labeled training data which associates a label or other quantity with different tree nodes.

Additionally, one can treat the RecNN as an Encoder, whereas the inside-vector associated with a node is taken to be an encoding of the tree rooted at that node. The encoding can potentially be sensitive to arbitrary properties of the structure. The vector is then passed as input to another network.

For further discussion on recursive neural networks and their use in natural language tasks, refer to the Ph.D. thesis of Socher [2014].

18.4 A SIMPLE ALTERNATIVE–LINEARIZED TREES

The RecNN abstraction provides a flexible mechanism for encoding trees as vectors, using a recursive, compositional approach. The RecNN encodes not only the given tree, but also all of its subtrees. If this recursiveness of the encoding is not needed, and all we need is a vector representation of an entire tree, that is sensitive to the tree structure, simpler alternatives may work well. In particular, linearizing trees into linear sequence that is then fed into a gated RNN acceptor (or a biRNN encoder) has proven to be very effective in several works [Choe and Charniak, 2016, Luong et al., 2016, Vinyals et al., 2014]. Concretely, the tree for the sentence *the boy saw her duck*, presented above, will be translated into the linear string:

(S (NP (Det the Det) (Noun boy Noun) NP) (VP (Verb saw Verb) (NP (Det her Det) (Noun duck Noun) NP) VP) S)

which will then be fed into a gated RNN such as an LSTM. The final state of the RNN can then be used as the vector representation of the tree. Alternatively, the tree structure can be scored by training an RNN language model over such linearized parse-trees, and taking the language-model probability of the linearized parse tree to stand for its quality.

---

[4]Before the introduction of the computation graph abstraction, the specific backpropagation procedure for computing the gradients in a RecNN as defined above was referred to as the back-propagation through structure (BPTS) algorithm [Goller and Küchler, 1996].

18.5 OUTLOOK

The concept of recursive, tree-structured networks is powerful, intriguing, and seems very suited for dealing with the recursive nature of language. However, as of the end of 2016, it is safe to say that they don't yet show any real and consistent benefits over simpler architectures. Indeed, in many cases sequence-level models such as RNNs capture the desired regularities just as well. Either we have not yet found the killer-application for tree-structured networks, or we have not yet found the correct architecture or training regimes. Some comparison and analysis of the use of tree-structured vs. sequence-structured networks for language tasks can be found in the work of Li et al. [2015]. As it stands, the use of tree-structured networks for processing language data is still an open research area. Finding the killer-app for such networks, providing better training regimes, or showing that tree-like architectures are not needed are all exciting research directions.

CHAPTER 19

Structured Output Prediction

Many problems in NLP involve structured outputs: cases where the desired output is not a class label or distribution over class labels, but a structured object such as a sequence, a tree, or a graph. Canonical examples are sequence tagging (e.g., part-of-speech tagging) sequence segmentation (chunking, NER), syntactic parsing, and machine translation. In this chapter, we discuss the application of neural network models for structured tasks.

19.1 SEARCH-BASED STRUCTURED PREDICTION

The common approach to structured data prediction is search based. For in-depth discussion of search-based structure prediction in pre-deep-learning NLP, see the book by Smith [2011]. The techniques can easily be adapted to use a neural network. In the neural networks literature, such models were discussed under the framework of *energy-based learning* [LeCun et al., 2006, Section 7]. They are presented here using setup and terminology familiar to the NLP community.

Search-based structured prediction is formulated as a search problem over possible structures:

$$\text{predict}(x) = \underset{y \in \mathcal{Y}(x)}{\text{argmax}}\, \text{score}_{\text{global}}(x, y), \tag{19.1}$$

where x is an input structure, y is an output over x (in a typical example x is a sentence and y is a tag-assignment or a parse-tree over the sentence), $\mathcal{Y}(x)$ is the set of all valid structures over x, and we are looking for an output y that will maximize the score of the x, y pair.

19.1.1 STRUCTURED PREDICTION WITH LINEAR MODELS

In the rich literature on structure prediction with linear and log-linear models, the scoring function is modeled as a linear function:

$$\text{score}_{\text{global}}(x, y) = \boldsymbol{w} \cdot \Phi(x, y), \tag{19.2}$$

where Φ is a feature extraction function and $\boldsymbol{w}$ is a weight vector.

In order to make the search for the optimal y tractable, the structure y is decomposed into parts, and the feature function is defined in terms of the parts, where $\phi(p)$ is a part-local feature extraction function:

$$\Phi(x, y) = \sum_{p \in \text{parts}(x, y)} \phi(p). \tag{19.3}$$

Each part is scored separately, and the structure score is the sum of the component parts scores:

$$\text{score}_{\text{global}}(x, y) = w \cdot \Phi(x, y) = w \cdot \sum_{p \in y} \phi(p) = \sum_{p \in y} w \cdot \phi(p) = \sum_{p \in y} \text{score}_{\text{local}}(p), \quad (19.4)$$

where $p \in y$ is a shorthand for $p \in \text{parts}(x, y)$. The decomposition of y into parts is such that there exists an inference algorithm that allows for efficient search for the best scoring structure given the scores of the individual parts.

19.1.2 NONLINEAR STRUCTURED PREDICTION

One can now trivially replace the linear scoring function over parts with a neural network:

$$\text{score}_{\text{global}}(x, y) = \sum_{p \in y} \text{score}_{\text{local}}(p) = \sum_{p \in y} \text{NN}(\phi(p)), \quad (19.5)$$

where $\phi(p)$ maps the part p into a d_{in} dimensional vector.

In case of a one hidden-layer feed-forward network:

$$\text{score}_{\text{global}}(x, y) = \sum_{p \in y} \text{MLP}_1(\phi(p)) = \sum_{p \in y} (g(\phi(p)W^1 + b^1))w \quad (19.6)$$

$\phi(p) \in \mathbb{R}^{d_{in}}$, $W^1 \in \mathbb{R}^{d_{in} \times d_1}$, $b^1 \in \mathbb{R}^{d_1}$, $w \in \mathbb{R}^{d_1}$. A common objective in structured prediction is making the gold structure y score higher than any other structure y', leading to the following (generalized perceptron [Collins, 2002]) loss:

$$\max_{y'} \text{score}_{\text{global}}(x, y') - \text{score}_{\text{global}}(x, y). \quad (19.7)$$

The maximization is performed using a dedicated search algorithm, which is often based on dynamic programming or a similar search technique.

In terms of implementation, this means: create a computation graph CG_p for each of the possible parts, and calculate its score. Then, run inference (i.e., search) to find the best scoring structure y' according to the scores of its parts. Connect the output nodes of the computation graphs corresponding to parts in the gold (predicted) structure y (y') into a summing node CG_y (CG'_y). Connect CG_y and CG'_y using a "minus" node, CG_l, and compute the gradients.

As argued in LeCun et al. [2006, Section 5], the generalized perceptron loss may not be a good loss function when training structured prediction neural networks as it does not have a margin, and a margin-based hinge loss is preferred:

$$\max(0, m + \max_{y' \neq y} \text{score}_{\text{global}}(x, y') - \text{score}_{\text{global}}(x, y)). \quad (19.8)$$

It is trivial to modify the implementation above to work with the hinge loss.

Note that in both cases we lose the nice properties of the linear model. In particular, the model is no longer convex. This is to be expected, as even the simplest nonlinear neural network is already non-convex. Nonetheless, we could still use standard neural network optimization techniques to train the structured model.

Training and inference is slower, as we have to evaluate the neural network (and take gradients) once for each part, a total of $|\text{parts}(x, y)|$ times.

Cost Augmented Training   Structured prediction is a vast field, and this book does not attempt to cover it fully. For the most part, the loss functions, regularizers and methods described in, e.g., Smith [2011], are easily transferable to the neural network framework, although losing convexity and many of the associated theoretical guarantees. One technique that is worth mentioning specifically is *cost augmented training*, also called *loss augmented inference*. While it brings modest gains when used in linear structured prediction, my research group found it essential to successfully training neural network-based structured-prediction models using the generalized perceptron or the margin based losses, especially when using strong feature extractors such as RNNs.

The maximization term in Equations (19.7) and (19.8) is looking for a structure y' that receives a high score according to the current model, and is also wrong. Then the loss reflects the difference in scores between y' and the gold structure y. Once the model is sufficiently well trained, the incorrect structure y' and the correct one y are likely to be similar to each other (because the model learned to assign high scores to structures that are reasonably good). Recall that the global score function is in fact composed of a sum of local part scores. Parts that appear in both scoring terms (of y' and of y) will cancel each other out, and will result in gradients of 0 for the associated network parameters. If y and y' are similar to each other, then most parts will overlap and cancel out this way, leading to an overall very small update for the example.

The idea behind cost-augmented training is to change the maximization to find structures y' that score well under the model *and are also relatively wrong* in the sense that they have many incorrect parts. Formally, the hinge objective changes to:

$$\max\left(0, m + \max_{y' \neq y}\left(\text{score}_{\text{global}}(x, y') + \rho\Delta(y, y')\right) - \text{score}_{\text{global}}(x, y)\right), \qquad (19.9)$$

where ρ is a scalar hyperparameter indicating the relative importance of Δ vs. the model score, and $\Delta(y, y')$ is a function counting the number of incorrect parts in y' with respect to y:

$$\Delta(y, y') = |\{p : p \in y', p \notin y\}|. \qquad (19.10)$$

Practically, the new maximization can be implemented by increasing the local score of each incorrect part by ρ before calling the maximization procedure.

The use of cost augmented inference surfaces highly incorrect examples and result in more loss terms that do not cancel out, causing more effective gradient updates.

19.1.3 PROBABILISTIC OBJECTIVE (CRF)

The error-based and margin-based losses above attempt to score the correct structure above incorrect ones, but does not tell anything about the ordering of the structures below the highest scoring one, or the score distances between them.

In contrast, a discriminative probabilistic loss attempts to assign a probability to each possible structure given the input, such that the probability of the correct structure is maximized. The probabilistic losses are concerned with the scores of all possible structures, not just the highest scoring one.

In a probabilistic framework (also known as conditional random fields, or CRF), each of the parts scores is treated as a *clique potential* (see Lafferty et al. [2001], Smith [2011]) and the score of each structure y is defined to be:

$$\text{score}_{\text{CRF}}(x, y) = P(y|x) = \frac{e^{\text{score}_{global}(x,y)}}{\sum_{y' \in \mathcal{Y}(x)} e^{\text{score}_{global}(x,y')}}$$

$$= \frac{\exp(\sum_{p \in y} \text{score}_{\text{local}}(p))}{\sum_{y' \in \mathcal{Y}(x)} \exp(\sum_{p \in y'} \text{score}_{\text{local}}(p))} \tag{19.11}$$

$$= \frac{\exp(\sum_{p \in y} \text{NN}(\phi(p)))}{\sum_{y' \in \mathcal{Y}(x)} \exp(\sum_{p \in y'} \text{NN}(\phi(p)))}.$$

The scoring function defines a conditional distribution $P(y|x)$, and we wish to set the parameters of the network such that corpus conditional log likelihood $\sum_{(x_i,y_i) \in \text{training}} \log P(y_i|x_i)$ is maximized.

The loss for a given training example (x, y) is then:

$$L_{\text{CRF}}(y', y) = -\log \text{score}_{\text{CRF}}(x, y). \tag{19.12}$$

That is, the loss is related to the distance of the probability of the correct structure from 1. The CRF loss can be seen as an extension of the hard-classification cross-entropy loss to the structured case.

Taking the gradient with respect to the loss in Equation (19.12) is as involved as building the associated computation graph. The tricky part is the denominator (the *partition function*) which requires summing over the potentially exponentially many structures in $\mathcal{Y}$. However, for some problems, a dynamic programming algorithm exists for efficiently solving the summation in polynomial time (i.e., the forward-backward viterbi recurrences for sequences and the CKY inside-outside recurrences for tree structures). When such an algorithm exists, it can be adapted to also create a polynomial-size computation graph.

19.1.4 APPROXIMATE SEARCH

Sometimes, efficient search algorithms for the prediction problem are not available. We may not have an efficient way of finding the best scoring structure (solving the maximization) in Equations (19.7), (19.8), or (19.9), or not have an efficient algorithm for computing the partition function (denominator) in Equation (19.11). In such cases, one can resort to *approximate inference* algorithms, such as beam search. When using beam search, the maximization and summation are with respect to the items in the beam. For example, one may use beam search for looking for a structure with an approximately high score, and for the partition function sum over the structures remaining in the beam instead of over the exponentially large $\mathcal{Y}(x)$. A related technique when working with inexact search is *early-update*: instead of computing the loss over complete structures, compute it over partial structures as soon as the gold items falls off the beam. For an analysis of the early update techniques and alternative loss-computation and update strategies when learning under approximate search, see Huang et al. [2012].

19.1.5 RERANKING

When searching over all possible structures is intractable, inefficient, or hard to integrate into a model, another alternative to beam search is the use of *reranking*. In the reranking framework [Charniak and Johnson, 2005, Collins and Koo, 2005] a base model is used to produce a list of the k-best scoring structures. A more complex model is then trained to score the candidates in the k-best list such that the best structure with respect to the gold one is scored highest. As the search is now performed over k items rather than over an exponential space, the complex model can condition on (extract features from) arbitrary aspects of the scored structure. The base model that is used for predicting the k-best structures can be based on a simpler model, with stronger independence assumptions, which can produce reasonable, but not great, results. Reranking methods are natural candidates for structured prediction using neural network models, as they allow the modeler to focus on the feature extraction and network structure, while removing the need to integrate the neural network scoring into a decoder. Indeed, reranking methods are often used for experimenting with neural models that are not straightforward to integrate into a decoder, such as convolutional, recurrent, and recursive networks. Works using the reranking approach include Auli et al. [2013], Le and Zuidema [2014], Schwenk et al. [2006], Socher et al. [2013a], Zhu et al. [2015a], and Choe and Charniak [2016].

19.1.6 SEE ALSO

Beyond the examples in Section 19.4, sequence-level CRFs with neural network clique potentials are discussed in Peng et al. [2009] and Do et al. [2010], where they are applied to sequence labeling of biological data, OCR data, and speech signals, and by Wang and Manning [2013] who apply them on traditional natural language tagging tasks (chunking and NER). Similar sequence tagging architecture is also described in Collobert and Weston [2008], Collobert et al. [2011]. A hinge-based approach was used by Pei et al. [2015] for arc-factored dependency parsing with a manually defined feature extractor, and by Kiperwasser and Goldberg [2016b] using a biLSTM feature extractor. The probabilistic approach was used by Durrett and Klein [2015] for a CRF constituency parser. The approximate beam-based partition function (approximate CRF) was effectively used by Zhou et al. [2015] in a transition-based parser, and later by Andor et al. [2016] for various tasks.

19.2   GREEDY STRUCTURED PREDICTION

In contrast to the search-based structured prediction approaches, there are greedy approaches that decompose the structured problem into a sequence of local prediction problems and training a classifier to perform each local decision well. At test time, the trained classifier is used in a greedy manner. Examples of this approach are left-to-right tagging models [Giménez and Màrquez, 2004] and greedy transition-based parsing [Nivre, 2008].[1] Because they do not assume search, greedy approaches are not restricted in the kind of features that are available to them, and can use rich conditioning structures. This make greedy approaches quite competitive in terms of prediction accuracies for many problems.

However, the greedy approaches are heuristic by definition, and have the potential of suffering from *error-propagation*: prediction errors that are made early in the sequence cannot be fixed, and can propagate into larger errors later on. The problem is especially severe when using a method with a *limited horizon* into the sentence, such as common with window-based feature extractors. Such methods process the sentence tokens in a fixed order, and only see a local window around the prediction point. They have no way of knowing what the future of the sequence hold, and are likely to be misled by the local context into incorrect decisions.

Fortunately, the use of RNNs (and especially biRNNs) mitigate the effect considerably. A feature extractor which is based on a biRNN can essentially see through the end of the input, and be trained to extract useful information from arbitrarily far sequence positions. This ability turn greedy local models that are trained with biRNN extractor into greedy *global* models: each decision can condition on the entire sentence, making the process less susceptible to being "surprised" later on by an unexpected output. As each prediction can become more accurate, the overall accuracy grows considerably.

Indeed, works in syntactic parsing show that greedy prediction models that are trained with global biRNN feature extractors rival the accuracy of search-based methods that combine global search with local feature extractors [Cross and Huang, 2016a, Dyer et al., 2015, Kiperwasser and Goldberg, 2016b, Lewis et al., 2016, Vaswani et al., 2016].

In addition to global feature extractors, the greedy methods can benefit from training techniques that aim to mitigate the error propagation problem by either attempting to take easier predictions before harder ones (the easy-first approach [Goldberg and Elhadad, 2010]) or making training conditions more similar to testing conditions by exposing the training procedure to inputs that result from likely mistakes [Hal Daumé III et al., 2009, Goldberg and Nivre, 2013]. These are effective also for training greedy neural network models, as demonstrated by Ma et al.

---

[1]Transition-based parsers are beyond the scope of this book, but see Kübler et al. [2008], Nivre [2008], and Goldberg and Nivre [2013] for an overview.

[2014] (easy-first tagger) and Ballesteros et al. [2016], Kiperwasser and Goldberg [2016b] (dynamic oracle training for greedy dependency parsing).

19.3 CONDITIONAL GENERATION AS STRUCTURED OUTPUT PREDICTION

Finally, RNN generators, especially in the conditioned generator setup (Chapter 17), can also be seen as an instance of structured-prediction. The series of predictions made by the generator produces a structured output $\hat{t}_{1:n}$. Each individual prediction has an associated score (or probability) $score(\hat{t}_i \mid \hat{t}_{1:i-1})$ and we are interested in output sequence with maximal score (or maximal probability), i.e., such that $\sum_{i=1}^{n} score(\hat{t}_i | \hat{t}_{1:i-1})$ is maximized. Unfortunately, the non-markovian nature of the RNN means that the scoring function *cannot* be decomposed into factors that allow for exact search using standard dynamic programming techniques, and approximate search must be used.

One popular approximate technique is using *greedy prediction*, taking the highest scoring item at each stage. While this approach is often effective, it is obviously non-optimal. Indeed, using beam search as an approximate search often works far better than the greedy approach.

At this stage, it is important to consider how conditioned generators are *trained*. As described in Section 17.1.1, generators are trained using a *teacher-forcing* technique: they are trained using a probabilistic objective that attempts to assign high probability mass to gold observed sequences. Given a gold sequence $t_{1:n}$, at each stage i the model is trained to assign a high probability mass to the gold event $\hat{t}_i = t_i$ conditioned on the gold history $t_{1:i-1}$.

There are two shortcomings with this approach: first, it is based on the *gold history* $t_{1:i-1}$ while in practice the generator will be tasked with assigning scores based on its *predicted history* $\hat{t}_{1:i-1}$. Second, it is a locally normalized model: the model assigns a probability distribution over each event, and thus susceptible to the *label bias* problem,[2] which can hurt the quality of solutions returned by beam search. Both of these problems were tackled in the NLP and machine-learning communities, but are not yet fully explored in the RNN generation setting.

The first problem can be mitigated using training protocols such SEARN [Hal Daumé III et al., 2009], DAGGER [Ross and Bagnell, 2010, Ross et al., 2011], and exploration-training with dynamic oracles [Goldberg and Nivre, 2013]. Application of these techniques in the context of RNN generators is proposed by Bengio et al. [2015] under the term *scheduled sampling*.

The second problem can be treated by discarding of the locally normalized objective and moving to global, sequence-level objectives that are more suitable for beam decoding. Such objectives include the beam approximations of the structured hinge loss [Equation (19.8)] and the CRF loss [Equation (19.11)] discussed in Section 19.1.4 above. Wiseman and Rush [2016] discuss global sequence-level scoring objectives for RNN generators.

---

[2]For a discussion of the label bias problem, see Section 3 of Andor et al. [2016] and the references therein.

19.4   EXAMPLES

19.4.1   SEARCH-BASED STRUCTURED PREDICTION: FIRST-ORDER DEPENDENCY PARSING

Consider the dependency-parsing task, described in Section 7.7. The input is an n-words sentence $s = w_1, \ldots, w_n$, and we are interested in finding a *dependency parse tree y* over the sentence (Figure 7.1). A dependency parse tree is a rooted directed tree over the words in the sentence. Every word in the tree is assigned a single parent (its *head*), that can be either another word in the sentence or special ROOT element. The parent word is called a *head* and its daughter words are called *modifiers*.

Dependency parsing fits nicely in the search-based structured prediction framework described in Section 19.1. Specifically, Equation (19.5) states that we should assign scores to trees by decomposing them into parts and scoring each part individually. The parsing literature describes many possible factorizations [Koo and Collins, 2010, Zhang and McDonald, 2012], here we focus on the simplest one, due to McDonald et al. [2005]: the *arc-factored* decomposition. Each part will be an arc in the tree (i.e., pair of head word w_h and modifier word w_m). Each arc (w_h, w_m) will be scored individually based on a local scoring function that will asses the quality of the attachment. After assigning a score to each of the possible n^2 arcs, we can run an *inference alogorithm* such as the *Eisner algorithm* [Eisner and Satta, 1999, Kübler et al., 2008, McDonald et al., 2005] to find the valid projective tree[3] whose sum of arc scores is maximal.

Equation (19.5) then becomes:

$$\text{score}_{\text{global}}(x, y) = \sum_{(w_h, w_m) \in y} \text{score}_{\text{local}}(w_h, w_m) = \sum_{(w_h, w_m) \in y} \text{NN}(\phi(h, m, s)), \qquad (19.13)$$

where $\phi(h, m, s)$ is a feature function translating the sentence indices h and m into real-valued vectors. We discussed feature extractors for the parsing task in Sections 7.7 and 8.6 (using manually designed features) and in Section 16.2.3 (using a biRNN feature extractor). Here, assume the feature extractor is given and focus on the training procedure.

Once we decide on a particular form for the NN component (say an MLP, $\text{NN}(x) = (\tanh(xU + b)) \cdot v$), we can easily compute the score $a_{[h,m]}$ of each possible arch (assuming the index of ROOT is 0):

$$a_{[h,m]} = (\tanh(\phi(h, m, s))U + b) \cdot v \qquad \forall h \in 0, \ldots, n \qquad (19.14)$$
$$\forall m \in 1, \ldots, n.$$

---

[3]Parsing people talk about *projective* and *non-projective* trees. Projective trees pose additional constraints on the form of the tree: that it can be drawn over a linearization of the words in the sentence in their original order, without crossing arcs. While the distinction is an important one in the parsing world, it is beyond the scope of this book. For more details, see Kübler et al. [2008] and Nivre [2008].

We then run the Eisner algorithm, resulting in a predicted tree y' with maximal score:

$$y' = \max_{y \in \mathcal{y}} \sum_{(h,m) \in y} a_{[h,m]} = \text{Eisner}(n, \boldsymbol{a}).$$

If we were to use cost-augmented inference, we would have used instead the scores $\bar{a}$:

$$\bar{a}_{[h,m]} = a_{[h,m]} + \begin{cases} 0 & \text{if } (h,m) \in y \\ \rho & \text{otherwise.} \end{cases}$$

Once we have the predicted tree y' and gold tree y, we can create a computation graph for the structured hinge loss of the trees, according to:

$$\max(0, 1 + \underbrace{\sum_{(h',m') \in y'} \tanh(\phi(h',m',s))\boldsymbol{U} + \boldsymbol{b}) \cdot \boldsymbol{v}}_{\max_{y' \neq y} \text{score}_{\text{global}}(s,y')} - \underbrace{\sum_{(h,m) \in y} \tanh(\phi(h,m,s))\boldsymbol{U} + \boldsymbol{b}) \cdot \boldsymbol{v})}_{\text{score}_{\text{global}}(s,y)}.$$

$$(19.15)$$

We then compute the gradients with respect to the loss using backprop, update the parameters accordingly, and move to the next tree in the training set.

This parsing approach is described in Pei et al. [2015] (using the manually designed feature function from Section 8.6) and Kiperwasser and Goldberg [2016b] (using the biRNN feature extractor from Section 16.2.3).

19.4.2 NEURAL-CRF FOR NAMED ENTITY RECOGNITION

Independent Classification   Consider the named entity recognition task described in Section 7.5. It is a sequence segmentation task which is often modeled as *sequence tagging*: each word in the sentence is assigned one of K BIO-tags described in Table 7.1, and the tagging decisions are then deterministically translated into spans. In Section 7.5 we treated NER as a word-in-context classification problem, assuming each tagging decision for each word is performed independently of the others.

Under the independent classification framework, we are given a sentence $s = w_1, \ldots, w_n$, and use a feature function $\phi(i, s)$ to create a feature vector representing the word w_i in the context of the sentence. Then, a classifier such as an MLP is used to predict a score (or a probability) to each tag:

$$\hat{\boldsymbol{t}}_i = \text{softmax}(\text{MLP}(\phi(i,s))) \qquad \forall i \in 1, \ldots, n; \qquad (19.16)$$

here, $\hat{\boldsymbol{t}}_i$ is a vector of predicted tag scores, and $\hat{\boldsymbol{t}}_{i\,[k]}$ is the score of tagging word i with tag k. The predicted tagging $\hat{y}_1, \ldots, \hat{y}_n$ for the sentence is then obtained by independently choosing the highest scoring tag for each sentence position:

$$\hat{y}_i = \underset{k}{\text{argmax}}\, \hat{\boldsymbol{t}}_{i\,[k]} \qquad \forall i \in 1, \ldots, n, \qquad (19.17)$$

and the score of the assignment $\hat{y} = \hat{y}_1, \ldots, \hat{y}_n$ is:

$$\text{score}(s, \hat{y}) = \sum_{i=1}^{n} t_{i\,[\hat{y}_i]}. \tag{19.18}$$

Structured Tagging by Coupling Tag-Pair Decisions   The independent classification approach may work reasonably well in many cases, but is sub-optimal because neighboring decisions influence each other. Consider a sequence such as *Paris Hilton*: the first word can be either a location or a person, and the second word can be either an organization or a person, but if we chose one of them to be a person, the second one should be tagged person with certainty. We would like to have the different tagging decisions influence each other, and have this reflected in the score. A common way to do this is by introducing tag-tag factors: compatibility scores for pairs of neighboring tags. Intuitively, a pair such as B-PER I-PER should receive a high score, while a pair B-PER I-ORG should receive a very low, or even negative score. For a tagset of K possible tags, we introduce a scoring matrix $A \in R^{K \times K}$ in which $A_{[g,h]}$ is the compatibility score of the tag sequence g h.

The scoring function for a tagging assignment is updated to take the tagging factors into account:

$$\text{score}(s, \hat{y}) = \sum_{i=1}^{n} t_{i\,[\hat{y}_i]} + \sum_{i=1}^{n+1} A_{[\hat{y}_{i-1}, \hat{y}_i]}, \tag{19.19}$$

where the tags at locations 0 and $n + 1$ are special *START* and *END* symbols. Given tagging scores for individual words $t_{1:n}$ and the values in A, one can find the sequence $\hat{y}$ maximizing Equation (19.19) using the Viterbi dynamic-programming algorithm.

As we do not need the tag scores in each position to be positive and sum to one, we remove the softmax when computing the scores t_i:

$$\hat{t}_i = \text{MLP}(\phi(i, s)) \qquad \forall i \in 1, \ldots, n. \tag{19.20}$$

The tagging scores t_i are determined by a neural network according to Equation (19.20), and the matrix A can be considered as additional model parameters. We can now proceed to train a structured model using the structured hinge-loss [Equation (19.8)] or the cost-augmented structured hinge loss [Equation (19.9)].

Instead, we will follow Lample et al. [2016] and use the probabilistic CRF objective.

Structured CRF Training   Under the CRF objective, our goal is to assign a probability to each possible tag sequence $y = y_1, \ldots, y_n$ over a sentence s. This is modeled by taking a softmax over all the possible taggings:

$$\text{score}_{\text{CRF}}(s, y) = P(y \mid s) = \frac{e^{\text{score}(s,y)}}{\sum_{y' \in \mathcal{Y}(s)} e^{\text{score}(s,y')}}$$

$$= \frac{\exp(\sum_{i=1}^{n} t_{i\,[y_i]} + \sum_{i=1}^{n} A_{[y_i,y_{i+1}]})}{\sum_{y' \in \mathcal{Y}(s)} \exp(\sum_{i=1}^{n} t_{i\,[y_i']} + \sum_{i=1}^{n} A_{[y_i',y_{i+1}']})}. \tag{19.21}$$

The denominator is the same for all possible taggings y, so finding the best sequence (without its probability) amounts to finding the sequence that maximizes score(s, y), and can be done using Viterbi as above.

The loss is then defined as the negative log likelihood of the correct structure y:

$$-\log P(y|s) = -\left(\sum_{i=1}^{n+1} t_{i\,[y_i]} + \sum_{i=1}^{n+1} A_{[y_{i-1},y_i]}\right) + \log \sum_{y' \in \mathcal{Y}(s)} \exp\left(\sum_{i=1}^{n+1} t_{i\,[y_i']} + \sum_{i=1}^{n+1} A_{[y_{i-1}',y_i']}\right)$$

$$= \underbrace{-\left(\sum_{i=1}^{n+1} t_{i\,[y_i]} + \sum_{i=1}^{n+1} A_{[y_{i-1},y_i]}\right)}_{\text{score of gold}} + \underbrace{\bigoplus_{y' \in \mathcal{Y}(s)} \left(\sum_{i=1}^{n+1} t_{i\,[y_i']} + \sum_{i=1}^{n+1} A_{[y_{i-1}',y_i']}\right)}_{\text{using dynamic program}}, \tag{19.22}$$

where $\bigoplus$ denotes addition in log-space (logadd) and $\bigoplus(a, b, c, d) = \log(e^a + e^b + e^c + e^d)$. The first term can be easily constructed as a computation graph, but the second is a bit less trivial to construct, as it requires summing over the n^k different sequences in $\mathcal{Y}(s)$. Fortunately, it can be solved using a variant of the Viterbi algorithm[4] which we describe below.

Properties of Log-addition   The log-add operation performs addition in log-space. It has the following properties that we use in constructing the dynamic program. They are trivial to prove with basic mathematic manipulation, and the reader is encouraged to do so.

$$\bigoplus(a, b) = \bigoplus(b, a) \qquad \textbf{Commutativity} \tag{19.23}$$

$$\bigoplus(a, \bigoplus(b, c)) = \bigoplus(a, b, c) \qquad \textbf{Associativity} \tag{19.24}$$

$$\bigoplus(a + c, b + c) = \bigoplus(a + b) + c \qquad \textbf{Distributivity} \tag{19.25}$$

---

[4]This algorithm is known as the *forward* algorithm, which is different than the algorithm for computing the *forward* pass in the computation graph.

Denote by $\mathcal{Y}(s, r, k)$ the set of sequences of length r that end with symbol k. The set of all possible sequences over $|s|$ is then $\mathcal{Y}(s) = \mathcal{Y}(s, n + 1, {}^*\text{END}^*)$. Further denote by $\mathcal{Y}(s, r, \ell, k)$ the sequences of length r where the last symbol is k and the second to last symbol is ℓ. Let $\Gamma[r, k] = \bigoplus_{y' \in \mathcal{Y}(s,r,k)} \sum_{i=1}^{r} (t_{i\,[y'_i]} + A_{[y'_{i-1}, y'_i]})$. Our goal is computing $\Gamma[n + 1, {}^*\text{END}^*]$. As a shorthand, define $f(i, y'_{i-1}, y'_i) = t_{i\,[y'_i]} + A_{[y'_{i-1}, y'_i]}$. We now get:

$$\Gamma[r, k] = \bigoplus_{y' \in \mathcal{Y}(s,r,k)} \sum_{i=1}^{r} f(i, y'_{i-1}, y'_i)$$

$$\Gamma[r + 1, k] = \bigoplus_{\ell} \bigoplus_{y' \in \mathcal{Y}(s,r+1,\ell,k)} \left(\sum_{i=1}^{r+1} f(i, y'_{i-1}, y'_i) \right)$$

$$= \bigoplus_{\ell} \bigoplus_{y' \in \mathcal{Y}(s,r+1,\ell,k)} \left(\sum_{i=1}^{r} (f(i, y'_{i-1}, y'_i)) + f(r + 1, y'_{r-1} = \ell, y'_r = k) \right)$$

$$= \bigoplus_{\ell} \left(\bigoplus_{y' \in \mathcal{Y}(s,r+1,\ell,k)} \left(\sum_{i=1}^{r} f(i, y'_{i-1}, y'_i) \right) + f(r + 1, y'_{r-1} = \ell, y'_r = k) \right)$$

$$= \bigoplus_{\ell} \left(\Gamma[r, \ell] + f(r + 1, y'_{r-1} = \ell, y'_r = k) \right)$$

$$= \bigoplus_{\ell} \left(\Gamma[r, \ell] + t_{r+1\,[k]} + A_{[\ell,k]} \right).$$

We obtained the recurrence:

$$\Gamma[r + 1, k] = \bigoplus_{\ell} \left(\Gamma[r, l] + t_{r+1\,[k]} + A_{[\ell,k]} \right) \qquad (19.26)$$

which we can use to construct the computation graph for computing the denominator, $\Gamma[n + 1, {}^*\text{END}^*]$.[5] After building the computation graph, we can compute the gradients using back-propagation.

19.4.3 APPROXIMATE NER-CRF WITH BEAM-SEARCH

In the previous section, we transformed the NER prediction into a structured task by coupling the output tags at positions i and $i - 1$ using a score matrix A assigning a score to each consecutive tag pair. This is akin to using a first-order markov assumption in which the tag in position i is independent of the tags at positions $< i - 1$ given the tag at $i - 1$. This independence assumption allowed us to decompose the sequence scoring and derive efficient algorithms for finding the highest scoring sequence as well as the sum over all possible tag sequences.

---

[5]Observe that this recursion is the same as the one for the best-path Viterbi algorithm, with $\bigoplus$ replaced with a max.

We may want to relax this markov independence assumption and instead condition the tag y_i at all previous tags $y_{1:i-1}$. This can be incorporated into the tagging model by adding an additional RNN over the tag history. We now score a tag sequence $y = y_1, \ldots, y_n$ as:

$$\text{score}(s, \hat{y}) = \sum_{i=1}^{n+1} f([\phi(s, i); \text{RNN}(\hat{y}_{1:i})]), \tag{19.27}$$

where f is a parametric function such as a linear transformation or an MLP, and ϕ is a feature function mapping the word as position i in the sentence s to a vector.[6] In words, we compute the local score of tagging position i with tag k by considering features of sentence position i, as well as an RNN encoding of the tag sequence y_1, y_2, y_{i-1}, k. We then compute the global score as a sum of local scores.

Unfortunately, the RNN component ties the different local scores over all previous tagging decisions, preventing us from using efficient dynamic programming algorithms for finding the exact best tagging sequence or the sum of all possible tag sequences under the model. Instead, we must resort to approximation such as *beam search*. Using a beam of size r, we can develop r different tag sequences $\hat{y}^1, \ldots, \hat{y}^r$.[7] The approximate best tag sequence is then the highest scoring of the r beam sequences:

$$\underset{i \in 1, \ldots, r}{\text{argmax}} \, \text{score}(s, \hat{y}^i).$$

For training, we can use the approximate CRF objective:

$$\text{score}_{\text{ApproxCRF}}(s, y) = \tilde{P}(y|s) = \frac{e^{\text{score}(s, y)}}{\sum_{y' \in \tilde{y}(s, r)} e^{\text{score}(s, y')}} \tag{19.28}$$

$$L_{\text{CRF}}(y', y) = -\log \tilde{P}(y|s)$$

$$= -\text{score}(s, y) + \log \sum_{y' \in \tilde{y}(s, r)} e^{\text{score}(s, y')} \tag{19.29}$$

$$\tilde{\mathcal{Y}}(s, r) = \{y^1, \ldots, y^r\} \cup \{y\}.$$

Instead of normalizing by summing over the entire set of sequences $\mathcal{Y}(s)$, we sum over $\tilde{\mathcal{Y}}(s, r)$: the union of the gold sequence and the r beam sequences. r is a small number, making the summation is trivial. As r approaches n^K we approach the true CRF objective.

---

[6] The feature function ϕ can be based on a word window or a biLSTM, similar to the feature functions for POS-tagging in Sections 8.5 and 16.2.1.

[7] The beam search algorithm works in stages. After obtaining r possible tag sequences of length i ($\hat{y}^1_{1:i}, \ldots, \hat{y}^r_{1:i}$) corresponding to the first i words of the sentence, we extend each sequence with all possible tags, score each of the resulting $r \times K$ sequences, and retain the top scoring r sequences. The process continues until we have r tag sequences over the entire sentence.

CHAPTER 20

Cascaded, Multi-task and Semi-supervised Learning

When processing natural language, it is often the case that we have several tasks that feed into each other. For example, the syntactic parser we discussed in Sections 7.7, 16.2.3, and 19.4.1 takes as input parts of speech tags, that are in themselves automatically predicted by a statistical model. Feeding the predictions of one model as the input of another, when the two models are independent, is called a *pipeline* system. An alternative approach is *model cascading*. In model cascading, rather than feeding the *predictions* of model A (the tagger) into model B (the parser), we instead feed into the parser the *intermediate representations* that are informative for predicting the tags. That is, rather than committing to a particular tagging decision, we pass on the tagging uncertainty to the parser. Model cascading is very easy to implement in deep learning system, by simply passing the vector before the argmax, or even one of the hidden vectors.

A related technique is *multi-task learning* [Caruana, 1997], in which we have several related predictions tasks (that may or may not feed into each other). We would like to leverage the information in one of the tasks in order to improve the accuracy on the other tasks. In deep learning, the idea is to have different networks for the different tasks, but let the networks *share* some of their structure and parameters. This way, a common predictive core (the shared structure) is influenced by all the tasks, and training data for one task may help improve the predictions of the other ones.

A cascading approach lends itself naturally to the multi-task learning framework: instead of just passing in the intermediate output of the tagger to the parser, we can instead plug in the sub-graph of the computation graph that is responsible for the intermediate tagging representation as input to the parser's computation graph, and backpropagate the parser's error all the way back to the (now shared) base of the tagging component.

Another related and similar case is that of *semi-supervised learning*, in which we have supervised training data for task A, and what to use annotated or unannotated data for other tasks in order to improve the performance on task A.

This chapter deals with these three techniques.

20.1 MODEL CASCADING

In model-cascading, large networks are built by composing them out of smaller component networks. For example, in Section 16.2.1 we describe an RNN-based neural network for predicting the part of speech of a word based on its sentential context and the characters that compose it. In a pipeline approach, we would use this network for predicting parts of speech, and then feed the predictions as input features to a neural network that does syntactic chunking or parsing.

Instead, we could think of the hidden layers of this network as an encoding that captures the relevant information for predicting the part of speech. In a cascading approach, we take the hidden layers of this network and connect them (and not the part of speech prediction themselves) as the inputs for the syntactic network. We now have a larger network that takes as input sequences of words and characters, and outputs a syntactic structure.

As a concrete example, consider the tagging and parsing networks described in Sections 16.2.1 and 16.2.3. The tagging network [Equation (16.4)], reproduced here, predicts the tag of the ith word according to:

$$t_i = \underset{j}{\mathrm{argmax}}\, \mathrm{softmax}(\mathrm{MLP}(\mathrm{biRNN}(x_{1:n}, i)))_{[j]}$$

$$x_i = \phi(s, i) = [E_{[w_i]}; \mathrm{RNN}^f(c_{1:\ell}); \mathrm{RNN}^b(c_{\ell:1})] \tag{20.1}$$

while the parsing network [Equation (16.6)] assigns arc-scores according to:

$$\textsc{ArcScore}(h, m, w_{1:n}, t_{1:n}) = MLP(\phi(h, m, s)) = MLP([v_h; v_m])$$

$$v_{1:n} = \mathrm{biRNN}^\star(x_{1:n}) \tag{20.2}$$

$$x_i = [w_i; t_i].$$

The important thing to note here is that the parser takes as input words $w_{1:n}$ *and tags* $t_{1:n}$, and then converts the words and tags into embedding vectors, and concatenates them to form its corresponding input representations $x_{1:n}$.

In the cascading approach, we'll feed the tagger's pre-prediction state directly into the parser, in one joint network. Concretely, denote by z_i the tagger's pre-prediction for word i: $z_i = \mathrm{MLP}(\mathrm{biRNN}(x_{1:n}, i))$. We can now use z_i as the input representation of the ith word in the parser, resulting in:

$$\textsc{ArcScore}(h, m, w_{1:n}) = MLP_{\mathrm{parser}}(\phi(h, m, s)) = MLP_{\mathrm{parser}}([v_h; v_m])$$

$$v_{1:n} = \mathrm{biRNN}^\star_{\mathrm{parser}}(z_{1:n})$$

$$z_i = \mathrm{MLP}_{\mathrm{tagger}}(\mathrm{biRNN}_{\mathrm{tagger}}(x_{1:n}, i)) \tag{20.3}$$

$$x_i = \phi_{\mathrm{tagger}}(s, i) = \left[E_{[w_i]}; \mathrm{RNN}^f_{\mathrm{tagger}}(c_{1:\ell}); \mathrm{RNN}^b_{\mathrm{tagger}}(c_{\ell:1})\right].$$

The computation graph abstraction allows us to easily propagate the error gradients from the syntactic task loss all the way back to the characters.[1]

Figure 20.1 presents a sketch of the entire network.

---

[1]Depending on the situation, we may or may not want to backpropagate the error all the way back.

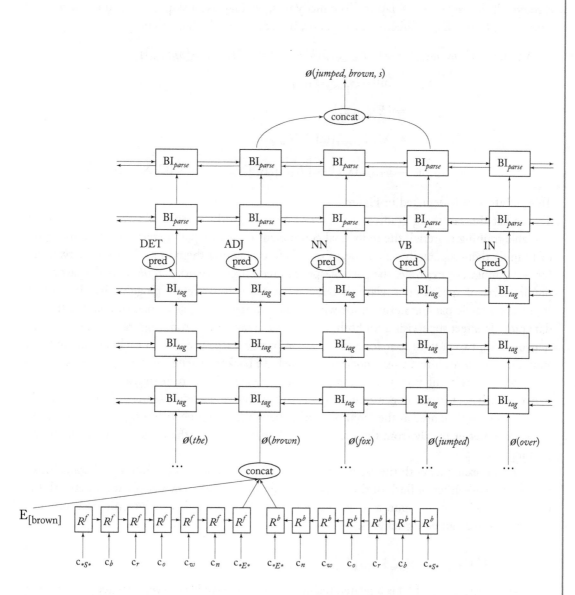

Figure 20.1: Tagging-parsing cascade network [Equation (20.3)].

While the parser has access to the word identities, they may be diluted by the time they pass through all the tagger RNN layers. To remedy this, we may use a skip-connection, and pass the word embeddings $E_{[w_i]}$ directly to the parser, in addition to the tagger's output:

$$\textsc{ArcScore}(h, m, w_{1:n}) = MLP_{\text{parser}}(\phi(h, m, s)) = MLP_{\text{parser}}([v_h; v_m])$$
$$v_{1:n} = \text{biRNN}^{\star}_{\text{parser}}(z_{1:n})$$
$$z_i = [E_{[w_i]}; z'_i] \tag{20.4}$$
$$z'_i = MLP_{\text{tagger}}(\text{biRNN}_{\text{tagger}}(x_{1:n}, i))$$
$$x_i = \phi_{\text{tagger}}(s, i) = \left[E_{[w_i]}; \text{RNN}^f_{\text{tagger}}(c_{1:\ell}); \text{RNN}^b_{\text{tagger}}(c_{\ell:1})\right].$$

This architecture is depicted in Figure 20.2.

To combat the vanishing gradient problem of deep networks, as well as to make better use of available training material, the individual component network's parameters can be bootstrapped by training them separately on a relevant task, before plugging them in to the larger network for further tuning. For example, the part-of-speech predicting network can be trained to accurately predict parts-of-speech on a relatively large annotated corpus, before plugging its hidden layer into the syntactic parsing network for which less training data is available. In case the training data provide direct supervision for both tasks, we can make use of it during training by creating a network with two outputs, one for each task, computing a separate loss for each output, and then summing the losses into a single node from which we backpropagate the error gradients.

Model cascading is very common when using convolutional, recursive, and recurrent neural networks, where, for example, a recurrent network is used to encode a sentence into a fixed sized vector, which is then used as the input of another network. The supervision signal of the recurrent network comes primarily from the upper network that consumes the recurrent network's output as it inputs.

In our example, both the tagger and the parser were based on a biRNN backbone. This is not necessary—either or both of the networks could just as well be a feed-forward network that gets a word-window as input, a convolutional network, or any other architecture that produces vectors and that can pass gradients.

20.2   MULTI-TASK LEARNING

Multi-task learning (MTL) is a related technique, in which we have several related tasks that we assume are correlated, in the sense that learning to solve one is likely to provide "intuitions" about solving the other. For example, consider the *syntactic chunking* task (see *Linguistic Annotation* frame in Section 6.2.2), in which we annotate a sentence with chunk boundaries, producing output such as:

[NP the boy] [PP with] [NP the black shirt] [VP opened] [NP the door] [PP with] [NP a key]

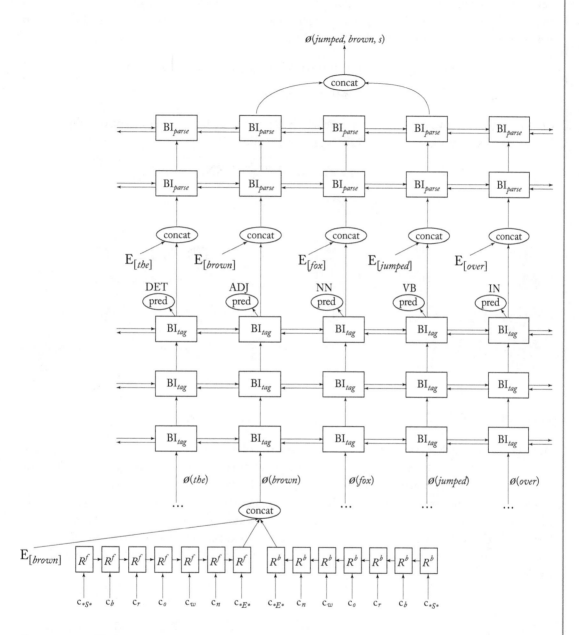

Figure 20.2: Tagging-parsing cascade with skip-connections for the word embeddings [Equation (20.4)].

Like named-entity recognition, chunking is a sequence-segmentation task, and can be reduced to a tagging task using the BIO encoding scheme (see Section 7.5). A network for chunking then may be modeled as a deep biRNN, followed by an MLP for individual tag predictions:

$$p(\text{chunkTag}_i = j) = \text{softmax}(\text{MLP}_{\text{chunk}}(\text{biRNN}_{\text{chunk}}(\boldsymbol{x}_{1:n}, i)))_{[j]}$$

$$\boldsymbol{x}_i = \phi(s, i) = \boldsymbol{E}^{\text{cnk}}_{[w_i]}$$

(20.5)

(for brevity, we removed the character-level RNNs from the input, but they can be trivially added.) Note that this is very similar to a POS-tagging network:

$$p(\text{posTag}_i = j) = \text{softmax}(\text{MLP}_{\text{tag}}(\text{biRNN}_{\text{tag}}(\boldsymbol{x}_{1:n}, i)))_{[j]}$$

$$\boldsymbol{x}_i = \phi(s, i) = \boldsymbol{E}^{\text{tag}}_{[w_i]}.$$

(20.6)

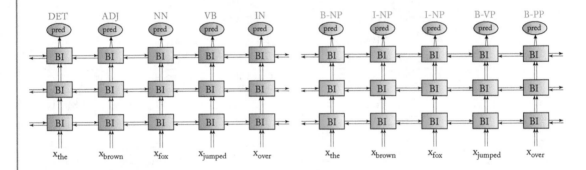

Figure 20.3: Left: POS tagging network. Right: Chunk tagging network.

Both networks are depicted in Figure 20.3. Different colors indicate different sets of parameters.

The syntactic chunking task is synergistic with part-of-speech tagging. Information for predicting chunk boundaries, or the part-of-speech of a word, rely on some shared underlying syntactic representation. Instead of training a separate network for each task, we can create a single network with several outputs. The common approach would be to share the biRNN parameters, but have a dedicated MLP predictor for each task (or have also a shared MLP, in which only the final matrix and bias terms are specialized for a task). This will result in the following, shared network:

$$p(\text{chunkTag}_i = j) = \text{softmax}(\text{MLP}_{\text{chunk}}(\text{biRNN}_{\text{shared}}(\boldsymbol{x}_{1:n}, i)))_{[j]}$$

$$p(\text{posTag}_i = j) = \text{softmax}(\text{MLP}_{\text{tag}}(\text{biRNN}_{\text{shared}}(\boldsymbol{x}_{1:n}, i)))_{[j]}$$

$$\boldsymbol{x}_i = \phi(s, i) = \boldsymbol{E}^{\text{shared}}_{[w_i]}.$$

(20.7)

The two networks use the same deep biRNN and embedding layers, but separate final output predictors. This is depicted in Figure 20.4.

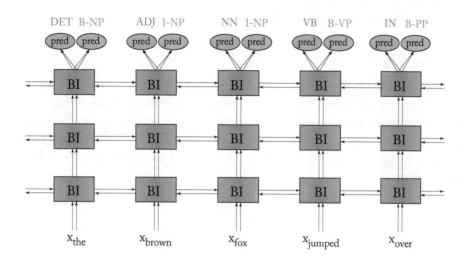

Figure 20.4: A joint POS-tagging and Chunking network. The biRNN parameters are shared, and the biRNN component is specialized for both tasks. The final predictors are separate.

Most of the parameters of the network are shared between the different tasks. Useful information learned from one task can then help to disambiguate other tasks.

20.2.1 TRAINING IN A MULTI-TASK SETUP

The computation graph abstraction makes it very easy to construct such networks and compute the gradients for them, by computing a separate loss for each available supervision signals, and then summing the losses into a single loss that is used for computing the gradients. In case we have several corpora, each with different kind of supervision signal (e.g., we have one corpus for POS and another for chunking), the preferred training protocol would be to choose a corpus at random, pass the example through the relevant part of the computation graph, compute the loss, backpropagate the error, and update the parameters. Then, on the next step, again choose a corpus at random and so on. In practice, this is often achieved by shuffling all the available training examples and going through them in order. The important part is that we potentially compute the gradients with respect to a different loss (and using a different sub-network) for each training example.

In some cases, we may have several tasks, but care more about one of them. That is, we have one or more main tasks, and a few other supporting task which we believe can help the main task, but whose predictions we do not care about. In such cases, we may want to scale the loss of the supporting task to be smaller than the loss of the main tasks. Another option is to first pre-train a network on the supporting tasks, and then take the shared components of this network and continue training it only on the main task.

20.2.2   SELECTIVE SHARING

Going back to the POS-tagging and Chunking example, we could argue that while the tasks share information, the POS-tagging task is in fact somewhat more *low level* than the chunking task: the information needed for performing chunking is more refined than that needed for POS-tagging. In such cases, we may prefer to not share the entire deep biRNN between the two tasks, but rather have the lower layer of the biRNN be shared, and the upper layers be dedicated to the chunking task (Figure 20.5).

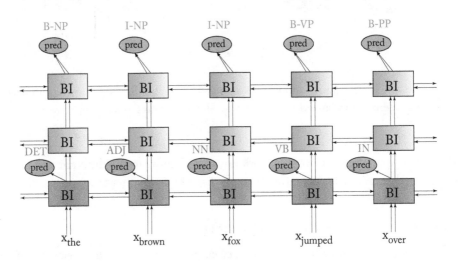

Figure 20.5: A *selectively shared* POS-tagging and Chunking network. The lower layer of the biRNN is shared between the two tasks, but the upper layers are dedicated to chunking.

The lower layer in the biRNN is shared between the two tasks. It is primarily supervised by the POS task, but also receives gradients from the chunking supervision. The upper layers of the network are dedicated to the chunking task—but are trained to work well with the representation of the lower layers.

This selective sharing suggestion follows the work of Søgaard and Goldberg [2016]. A similar approach, using feed-forward rather than recurrent networks, is taken by Zhang and Weiss [2016] under the name *stack propagation*.

The selectively shared MTL network in Figure 20.5 is very similar in spirit to the cascaded setup in discussed in the previous section (Figure 20.1). Indeed, it is often hard to properly draw the boundary between the two frameworks.

Input-output Inversion   Another view of multi-task and cascaded learning is one of input-output inversion. Instead of thinking of some signal (say POS-tags) as *inputs* to a higher level task (say parsing), we can think of them as *outputs* of intermediate layers in the network for the higher level tasks. That is, instead of using the parts-of-speech tags as inputs, they are used instead as a supervision signal to intermediate layers of the network.

20.2.3 WORD-EMBEDDINGS PRE-TRAINING AS MULTI-TASK LEARNING

The chunking and POS-tagging tasks (and indeed, many others) are also synergistic with the *language modeling* task. Information for predicting the chunk boundary are the part-of-speech tag of a word is intimately connected with the ability to predict the identity of the next word, or the previous one: the tasks share a common syntactic-semantic backbone.

Viewed this way, the use of pre-trained word vectors for initializing the embedding layer of a task-specific network is an instance of MTL, with language modeling as a supporting task. The word embedding algorithms are trained with an distributional objective that is a generalization of language modeling, and the word embedding layer of the embedding algorithms is then *shared* with the other task.

The kind of supervision for the pre-training algorithm (i.e., the choice of contexts) should be matched to the task the specialized network is trying to solve. Closer tasks results in larger benefits from MTL.

20.2.4 MULTI-TASK LEARNING IN CONDITIONED GENERATION

MTL can be seamlessly integrated into the conditioned generation framework discussed in Chapter 17. This is done by having a *shared encoder* feeding into different decoders, each attempting to perform a different task. This will force the encoder to encode information that is relevant to each of the tasks. Not only can this information then be shared by the different decoders, it also will potentially allow for training different decoders on different training data, enlarging the overall number of examples available for training. We discuss a concrete example in Section 20.4.4.

20.2.5 MULTI-TASK LEARNING AS REGULARIZATION

Another view of multi-task learning is one of a *regularizer*. The supervision from the supporting tasks prevent the network from overfitting on the main task, by forcing the shared representation to be more general, and useful for prediction beyond the training instances of the main task. Viewed this way, and when the supporting tasks are meant to be used as regularizers, one should not perform the MTL in a sequence where the supporting tasks are tuned first followed by adapting the representation to the main task (as suggested in Section 20.2.1). Rather, all tasks should be learned in parallel.

20.2.6 CAVEATS

While the prospect of MTL is very appealing, some caveats are in order. MTL often does not work well. For example, if the tasks are not closely related, you may not see gains from MTL, and most tasks are indeed not related. Choosing the related tasks for performing MTL can be more of an art than a science.

Even if the tasks are related, but the shared network doesn't have the capacity to support all the tasks, the performance of all of them can degrade. When taking the regularization view, this means that the regularization is too strong, and prevents the model from fitting the individual tasks. In such cases, it is better to increase the model capacity (i.e., increase the number of dimensions in the shared components of the network). If an MTL network with k tasks needs a k-fold increase in capacity (or close to it) in order to support all tasks, it means that there is likely no sharing of predictive structure at all between the tasks, and one should forgo the MTL idea.

When the tasks are very closely related, such as the POS tagging and chunking tasks, the benefits from MTL could be very small. This is especially true when the networks are trained on a single dataset in which each sentence is annotated for both POS-tag and Chunk label. The chunking network can learn the representation it needs without the help of the intermediate POS supervision. We do start to see the benefits of MTL when the POS-training data and the chunking data are *disjoint* (but share sizable portions of the vocabulary), or when the POS-tag data is a *superset* of the Chunk data. In this situation, the MTL allows to effectively enlarge the amount of supervision for the chunking task by training on data with related labels for the POS-tagging task. This lets the Chunk part of the network leverage on and influence the shared representation that was learned based on the POS annotations on the additional data.

20.3 SEMI-SUPERVISED LEARNING

A related framework to both multi-task and cascaded learning is *semi-supervised* learning, in which we have a small amount of training data for a task we care about, and additional training data for other tasks. The other tasks can be either supervised, or unsupervised (i.e., where the supervision can be generated from unannotated corpora, such as in language modeling, word embeddings, or sentence encodings, as discussed in Section 9.6, Chapters 10 and 17.3).

We would like to use the supervision for the additional tasks (or to invent suitable additional tasks) in order to improve the prediction accuracy on the main task. This is a very common scenario, which is an active and important research area: we never have enough supervision for the tasks we care about.

For an overview of *non-neural networks* semi-supervised learning methods in NLP, see the book of Søgaard [2013] in this series.

Within the deep-learning framework, semi-supervised learning can be performed, much like MTL, by learning a representation based on the additional tasks, that can then be used as supplement input or as initialization to the main task. Concretely, one can pre-train word embeddings or sentence representations on unannotated data, and use these to initialize or feed into a POS-tagger, parser or a document summarization system.

In a sense, we have been doing semi-supervised learning ever since we introduced distributional representations pre-trained word embeddings in Chapter 10. Sometimes, problems lend themselves to more specialized solutions, as we explore in Section 20.4.3. The similarities and connections to multi-task learning are also clear: we are using supervision data from one task to improve performance on another. The main difference seem to be in how the different tasks are integrated into the final model, and in the source of the annotated data for the different tasks, but the border between the approaches is rather blurry. In general, it is probably best not to debate about the boundaries of cascaded learning, multi-task learning and semi-supervised learning, but rather see them as a set of complimentary and overlapping techniques.

Other approaches to semi-supervised learning include various regimes in which one or more models are trained on the small labeled data, and are then used to assign labels to large amounts of unlabeled data. The automatically annotated data (possibly following some quality filtering stage based on agreement between the models are other confidence measures) is then used to train a new model, or provide additional features to an existing on. These approaches can be grouped under the collective term *self-training*. Other methods specify constraints on the solution, that should help guide the model (i.e., specifying that some words can only be tagged with certain tags, or that each sentence must contain at least one word tagged as X). Such methods are not (yet) specialized for neural networks, and are beyond the scope of this book. For an overview, see the book by Søgaard [2013].

20.4 EXAMPLES

We now describe a few examples in which we MTL was shown to be effective.

20.4.1 GAZE-PREDICTION AND SENTENCE COMPRESSION

In the sentence compression by deletion task, we are given a sentence such as *"Alan Turing, known as the father of computer science, the codebreaker that helped win World War II, and the man tortured by the state for being gay, is to receive a pardon nearly 60 years after his death"* and are required to produce a shorter ("compressed") version containing the main information in the sentence by deleting words from the original sentence. An example compression would be *"Alan Turing is to receive a pardon."* This can be modeled as a deep biRNN followed by an MLP in which the inputs to the biRNN are the words of the sentence, and the outputs of the MLPs are KEEP or DELETE decisions for each word.

In work with Klerke et al. [2016], we showed that the performance on the sentence deletion by compression task can be improved by using two additional sequence prediction tasks: CCG supertagging and Gaze prediction. The two tasks are added in a selective-sharing architecture, as individual MLPs that feed from the lower layer of the biRNN.

The CCG supertagging task assigns each work with a *CCG supertag*, which is a complex syntactic tag such as (S[dcl]\NP)/PP, indicating its syntactic role with respect to the rest of the sentence.[2]

The Gaze prediction task is a cognitive task that relates to the way people read written language. When reading, our eyes move across the page, fixating on some words, skipping others, and often jumping back to previous words. It is widely believed that eye movement when reading reflects on the sentence processing mechanisms in the brain, which in turn reflects on the sentence structure. Eye-trackers are machines that can accurately track eye-movement while reading, and some eye-tracked corpora are available in which sentences are paired with exact eye-movement measurements of several human subjects. In the gaze-prediction task, the network was trained to predict aspects of the eye-movement behavior on the text (how long of a fixation each word would receive, or which words will trigger back movements). The intuition being that parts of the sentence which are less important are more likely to be skipped or glossed over, and parts that are more important are likely to be fixated more upon when processing the sentence.

The compression data, the syntactic CCG tagging data, and the eye-movement data were completely disjoint from each other, but we observed clear improvements to the compression accuracy when including the additional tasks as supervision.

20.4.2 ARC LABELING AND SYNTACTIC PARSING

Throughout the book, we described an architecture for arc-standard dependency parsing. In particular, in Section 16.2.3 we described biRNN based features, and in Section 19.4.1 a structured prediction learning framework. The parser we described was an *unlabeld parser*—the model assigned a score to each possible head-modifier pair, and the final prediction by the parser was a collection of arcs, representing the best tree over the sentence. However, the scoring function, and the resulting arcs, only took into consideration *which* words are syntactically connected to each other, and not the *nature of the relation* between the words.

Recall from Section 6.2.2 that a dependency parse-tree usually contains also the relation information, in term of a dependency label on each arc, i.e., the *det, prep, pobj, nsubj, etc.* label annotations in Figure 20.6.

Given an unlabeled parsing, the arc-labels can be assigned using an architecture in which a biRNN is used to read the words of the sentence, and then, for arc (h, m) in the tree, concatenate the corresponding biRNN encodings and feed them into an MLP for predicting the arc's label.

Rather than training a separate network for the label prediction, we can treat Unlabeled Parsing and Arc-Labeling as related tasks in a multi-task setting. We then have a single biRNN for the arc-labeler and the parser, and use the encoded biRNN states as inputs both to the arc-scorer and to the arc-labeler. In training, the arc-labeler will only see gold arcs (because we do not

---

[2]CCG and CCG supertags are beyond the scope of this book. A good pointer to start learning about CCG in NLP is the Ph.D. thesis of Julia Hockenmaier [Hockenmaier, 2003]. The concept of supertagging is introduced by Joshi and Srinivas [1994].

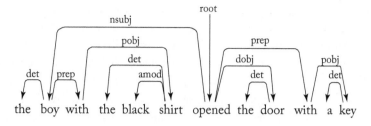

Figure 20.6: Labeled dependency tree.

have label information for the other, hypothetical arcs), while the arc-scorer will see all possible arcs.

Indeed, in the work of Kiperwasser and Goldberg [2016b] we observe that the tasks are indeed closely related. Training the joint network for performing both unlabeled arc-scoring and arc-labeling, using the same shared biRNN encoder, not only results in accurate arc labeling, but also *substantially improves the accuracy of the unlabeled parse trees*.

20.4.3 PREPOSITION SENSE DISAMBIGUATION AND PREPOSITION TRANSLATION PREDICTION

Consider the preposition-sense disambiguation task discussed in Section 7.6. To recall, this is a word-in-context problem, in which we need to assign each preposition with one of K possible *sense labels* (MANNER, PURPOSE, LOCATION, DURATION, etc.). Annotated corpora for the task exist [Litkowski and Hargraves, 2007, Schneider et al., 2016], but are small.

In Section 7.6, we discussed a rich set of core features that can be used for training a preposition-sense disambiguator. Let's denote the feature extractor taking a preposition instance and returning an encoding of these features as a vector as $\phi_{sup}(s, i)$, where s is the input sentence (including words, part-of-speech tags, lemmas, and syntactic parse-tree information), and i is the index of the preposition within the sentence. The feature extractor ϕ_{sup} based on features similar to those in features in Section 7.6, without the WordNet-based features but with pre-trained word-embeddings, is a strong one. Feeding it into an MLP for prediction performs reasonably well (albeit still disappointingly low, below 80% accuracy), and attempts to replace or to supplement it with a biRNN-based feature extractor does not improve the accuracies.

Here, we show how the accuracy of the sense prediction can be improved further using a *semi-supervised* approach, which is based on learning a useful representation from large amounts of unannotated data, that we transform into related and useful prediction tasks.

Specifically, we will be using tasks derived from *sentence-aligned multilingual data*. These are pairs of English sentences and their translation into other languages.[3] When translating from

---

[3]Such resources are readily available from, e.g., proceedings of the European Union (the Europarl corpus, [Koehn, 2005]), or can be mined from the web [Uszkoreit et al., 2010]. These are the resources that drive statistical machine translation.

English to a different language, a preposition can be translated into one of several possible alternatives. The choice of the foreign preposition will be based on the English preposition sense, as reflected by the sentential context in which it appears. While prepositions are ambiguous in all languages, the ambiguity patterns differ across languages. Thus, predicting the foreign preposition into which a given English preposition will be translated based on the English sentential context is a good auxiliary task for preposition sense disambiguation. This is the approach taken by Gonen and Goldberg [2016]. We provide here a high-level overview. For details, refer to the original paper.

Training data is created based on a multilingual sentence-aligned parallel corpus. The corpus is word-aligned using a word-alignment algorithm [Dyer et al., 2013], and tuples of ⟨sentence, preposition-position, foreign-language, foreign-prepositions⟩ are extracted as training examples. Given such a tuple $\langle s = w_{1:n}, i, L, f \rangle$, the prediction task is to predict the translation of the preposition w_i in the context of the sentence s. The possible outputs are taken from a set of language specific options p_L, and the correct output is f.

The hope is that a representation of the context of w_i that is good at predicting the foreign preposition f will also be helpful for predicting the preposition sense. We model the task as an *encoder* $\text{Enc}(s, i)$ that encodes the sentential context of w_i into a vector, and a predictor, which attempts to predict the right preposition. The encoder is very similar to a biRNN, but does not include the preposition itself in order to force the network to pay more attention to the context, while the predictor is a language specific MLP.

$$p(\text{foreign} = f | s, i, L) = \text{softmax}(\text{MLP}^L_{\text{foreign}}(\text{Enc}(s, i)))_{[f]}$$

$$\text{Enc}(s, i) = [\text{RNN}^f(w_{1:i-1}); \text{RNN}^b(w_{n:i+1})]. \tag{20.8}$$

The encoder is shared across the different languages. After training the network on several million ⟨English sentence, foreign-preposition⟩ pairs, we are left with a pre-trained context-encoder that can then be used in the preposition-sense disambiguation network by concatenating it to the supervised feature representation. Our semi-supervised disambiguator is then:

$$p(\text{sense} = j | s, i) = \text{softmax}(\text{MLP}_{\text{sup}}([\phi_{\text{sup}}(s, i); \text{Enc}(s, i)]))_{[j]}, \tag{20.9}$$

where Enc is the pre-trained encoder that is further trained by the sense prediction network, and ϕ_{sup} is the supervised feature extractor. The approach substantially and consistently improve the accuracy of the sense prediction by about 1–2 accuracy points, depending on details of the setup.[4]

---

[4]While an increase of 1–2 accuracy points may not seem very impressive, it is unfortunately in the upper range of what one could realistically expect in semi-supervised scenarios in which the baseline supervised system is already relatively strong, using current semi-supervision techniques. Improvements over weaker baselines are larger.

20.4.4   CONDITIONED GENERATION: MULTILINGUAL MACHINE TRANSLATION, PARSING, AND IMAGE CAPTIONING

MTL can also be easily performed in an encoder-decoder framework. The work of Luong et al. [2016] demonstrated this in the context of machine translation. Their translation system follows the sequence-to-sequence architecture (Section 17.2.1), without attention. While better translation systems exist (notably systems that make use of attention), the focus of the work was to show that improvements from the multi-task setup are possible.

Luong et al explore different setups of multi-task learning under this system. In the first setup (one-to-many), the Encoder component (encoding English sentences into vectors) is shared, and is used with two different decoders: one decoder is generating German translations, and the other decoder is generating linearized parse-trees for the English sentences (i.e., the predicted sequence for *the boy opened the door* should be (S (NP DT NN) (VP VBD (NP DT NN)))). The system is trained on a parallel corpus of ⟨English,German⟩ translation pairs, and on gold parse trees from the Penn Treebank [Marcus et al., 1993]. The translation data and the parsing data are disjoint. Through the multi-task setting, the shared encoder learns to produce vectors that are informative for both tasks. The multi-task encoder-decoder network is effective: the network that is trained for both tasks (one encoder, two decoders) works better than the individual networks consisting of a single encode-decoder pair. This setup likely works because encoding basic elements of the syntactic structure of a sentence are informative for selecting the word order and syntactic structures in the resulting translation, and vice versa. The translation and parsing tasks are indeed synergistic.

In the second setup (many-to-one), there is a single decoder, but several different encoders. The tasks here are machine translation (German to English translation) and image captioning (Image to English description). The decoder is tasked at producing English sentences. One encoder is encoding German sentences, while the other is encoding images. Like before, the datasets for the translation and for the image captioning are disjoint. Again, with some tuning of parameters, training the joint system improves over the individual ones, though the gains are somewhat smaller. Here, there is no real connection between the task of encoding German sentences (which express elaborate predications and complicated syntactic structures) and encoding image contents (which encodes the main components of simple scenes). The benefit seem to be from the fact that both tasks provide supervision for the language-modeling part of the decoder network, allowing it to produce better sounding English sentences. Additionally, the improvement may stem from a regularization effect, in which one (encoder,decoder) pair prevents the other pair from overfitting to its training data.

Despite the rather low baseline, the results of Luong et al. [2016] are encouraging, suggesting there are gains to be had from multi-task learning in the conditional generation framework, when suitable synergistic tasks are chosen.

20.5   OUTLOOK

Cascaded, multi-task, and semi-supervised learning are exciting techniques. The neural networks framework, driven by gradients-based training over a computation graph, provide many seamless opportunities for using these techniques. In many cases, such approaches bring real and consistent gains in accuracy. Unfortunately, as of the time of this writing, the gains are often relatively modest compared to the baseline performance, especially when the baselines are high. This should not discourage you from using the techniques, as the gains often times are real. It should also encourage you to actively work on improving and refining the techniques, so that we see could expect to see greater gains in the future.

CHAPTER 21

Conclusion

21.1 WHAT HAVE WE SEEN?

The introduction of neural networks methods has been transformative for NLP. It prompted a move from linear-models with heavy feature engineering (and in particular the engineering of backoff and combination features) to multi-layer perceptrons that learn the feature combinations (as discussed in the first part of the book); to architectures like convolutional neural networks that can identify generalizable ngrams and gappy-ngrams (as discussed in Chapter 13); to architectures like RNNs and bidirectional RNNs (Chapters 14–16) that can identify subtle patterns and regularities in sequences of arbitrary lengths; and to recursive neural networks (Chapter 18) that can represent trees. They also brought about methods for encoding words as vectors based on distributional similarity, which can be effective for semi-supervised learning (Chapters 10–11); and methods for non-markovian language modeling, which in turn pave the way to flexible conditioned language generation models (Chapter 17), and revolutionized machine translation. The neural methods also present many opportunities for multi-task learning (Chapter 20). Moreover, established pre-neural structured-prediction techniques can be readily adapted to incorporate neural network based feature extractors and predictors (Chapter 19).

21.2 THE CHALLENGES AHEAD

All in all, the field is progressing very quickly, and it is hard to predict what the future will hold. One thing is clear though, at least in my view—with all their impressive advantages, neural networks are not a silver bullet for natural-language understanding and generation. While they provide many improvements over the previous generation of statistical NLP techniques, the core challenges remain: language is discrete and ambiguous, we do not have a good understanding of how it works, and it is not likely that a neural network will learn all the subtleties on its own without careful human guidance. The challenges mentioned in the introduction are ever-present also with the neural techniques, and familiarity with the linguistic concepts and resources presented in Chapter 6 is still as important as ever for designing good language processing systems. The actual performance on many natural language tasks, even low-level and seemingly simple ones such as pronominal coreference resolution [Clark and Manning, 2016, Wiseman et al., 2016] or coordination boundary disambiguation [Ficler and Goldberg, 2016] is still very far from being perfect. Designing learning systems to target such low-level language understanding tasks is as important a research challenge as it was before the introduction of neural NLP methods.

Another important challenge is the opaqueness of the learned representations, and the lack of rigorous theory behind the architectures and the learning algorithms. Research into the interpretability of neural network representations, as well as into better understanding of the learning capacity and training dynamics of various architectures, is crucially needed in order to progress even further.

As of the time of this writing, neural networks are in essence still supervised learning methods, and require relatively large amounts of labeled training data. While the use of pre-trained word-embeddings provides a convenient platform for semi-supervised learning, we are still in very preliminary stages of effectively utilizing unlabeled data and reducing the reliance on annotated examples. Remember that humans can often generalize from a handful of examples, while neural networks usually require at least hundreds of labeled examples in order to perform well, even in the most simple language tasks. Finding effective ways of leveraging small amounts of labeled data together with large amounts of un-annotated data, as well as generalizing across domains, will likely result in another transformation of the field.

Finally, an aspect which was only very briefly glossed over in this book is that language is not an isolated phenomena. When people learn, perceive, and produce language, they do it with a reference to the real world, and language utterances are more often than not grounded in real world entities or experiences. Learning language in a grounded setting, either coupled with some other modality such as images, videos, or robot movement control, or as part of an agent that interacts with the world in order to achieve concrete goals, is another promising research frontier.

Bibliography

Martín Abadi, Ashish Agarwal, Paul Barham, Eugene Brevdo, Zhifeng Chen, Craig Citro, Greg S. Corrado, Andy Davis, Jeffrey Dean, Matthieu Devin, et al. TensorFlow: Large-scale machine learning on heterogeneous systems, 2015. http://tensorflow.org/

Heike Adel, Ngoc Thang Vu, and Tanja Schultz. Combination of recurrent neural networks and factored language models for code-switching language modeling. In *Proc. of the 51st Annual Meeting of the Association for Computational Linguistics—(Volume 2: Short Papers)*, pages 206–211, Sofia, Bulgaria, August 2013.

Roee Aharoni, Yoav Goldberg, and Yonatan Belinkov. *Proc. of the 14th SIGMORPHON Workshop on Computational Research in Phonetics, Phonology, and Morphology*, chapter improving sequence to sequence learning for morphological inflection generation: The BIU-MIT systems for the SIGMORPHON 2016 shared task for morphological reinflection, pages 41–48. Association for Computational Linguistics, 2016. http://aclweb.org/anthology/W16-2007 DOI: 10.18653/v1/W16-2007.

Roee Aharoni and Yoav Goldberg. Towards string-to-tree neural machine translation. *Proc. of ACL*, 2017.

M. A. Aizerman, E. A. Braverman, and L. Rozonoer. Theoretical foundations of the potential function method in pattern recognition learning. In *Automation and Remote Control*, number 25 in Automation and Remote Control, pages 821–837, 1964.

Erin L. Allwein, Robert E. Schapire, and Yoram Singer. Reducing multiclass to binary: A unifying approach for margin classifiers. *Journal of Machine Learning Research*, 1:113–141, 2000.

Rie Ando and Tong Zhang. A high-performance semi-supervised learning method for text chunking. In *Proc. of the 43rd Annual Meeting of the Association for Computational Linguistics (ACL'05)*, pages 1–9, Ann Arbor, Michigan, June 2005a. DOI: 10.3115/1219840.1219841.

Rie Kubota Ando and Tong Zhang. A framework for learning predictive structures from multiple tasks and unlabeled data. *The Journal of Machine Learning Research*, 6:1817–1853, 2005b.

Daniel Andor, Chris Alberti, David Weiss, Aliaksei Severyn, Alessandro Presta, Kuzman Ganchev, Slav Petrov, and Michael Collins. Globally normalized transition-based neural networks. In *Proc. of the 54th Annual Meeting of the Association for Computational Linguistics—(Volume 1: Long Papers)*, pages 2442–2452, 2016. http://aclweb.org/anthology/P16-1231 DOI: 10.18653/v1/P16-1231.

Michael Auli and Jianfeng Gao. Decoder integration and expected BLEU training for recurrent neural network language models. In *Proc. of the 52nd Annual Meeting of the Association for Computational Linguistics—(Volume 2: Short Papers)*, pages 136–142, Baltimore, Maryland, June 2014. DOI: 10.3115/v1/p14-2023.

Michael Auli, Michel Galley, Chris Quirk, and Geoffrey Zweig. Joint language and translation modeling with recurrent neural networks. In *Proc. of the 2013 Conference on Empirical Methods in Natural Language Processing*, pages 1044–1054, Seattle, Washington. Association for Computational Linguistics, October 2013.

Oded Avraham and Yoav Goldberg. The interplay of semantics and morphology in word embeddings. *EACL*, 2017.

Dzmitry Bahdanau, Kyunghyun Cho, and Yoshua Bengio. Neural machine translation by jointly learning to align and translate. *arXiv:1409.0473 [cs, stat]*, September 2014.

Miguel Ballesteros, Chris Dyer, and Noah A. Smith. Improved transition-based parsing by modeling characters instead of words with LSTMs. In *Proc. of the 2015 Conference on Empirical Methods in Natural Language Processing*, pages 349–359, Lisbon, Portugal. Association for Computational Linguistics, September 2015. DOI: 10.18653/v1/d15-1041.

Miguel Ballesteros, Yoav Goldberg, Chris Dyer, and Noah A. Smith. Training with exploration improves a greedy stack-LSTM parser, EMNLP 2016. *arXiv:1603.03793 [cs]*, March 2016. DOI: 10.18653/v1/d16-1211.

Mohit Bansal, Kevin Gimpel, and Karen Livescu. Tailoring continuous word representations for dependency parsing. In *Proc. of the 52nd Annual Meeting of the Association for Computational Linguistics—(Volume 2: Short Papers)*, pages 809–815, Baltimore, Maryland, June 2014. DOI: 10.3115/v1/p14-2131.

Marco Baroni and Alessandro Lenci. Distributional memory: A general framework for corpus-based semantics. *Computational Linguistics*, 36(4):673–721, 2010. DOI: 10.1162/coli_a_00016.

Atilim Gunes Baydin, Barak A. Pearlmutter, Alexey Andreyevich Radul, and Jeffrey Mark Siskind. Automatic differentiation in machine learning: A survey. *arXiv:1502.05767 [cs]*, February 2015.

Emily M. Bender. *Linguistic Fundamentals for Natural Language Processing: 100 Essentials from Morphology and Syntax*. Synthesis Lectures on Human Language Technologies. Morgan & Claypool Publishers, 2013.

Samy Bengio, Oriol Vinyals, Navdeep Jaitly, and Noam Shazeer. Scheduled sampling for sequence prediction with recurrent neural networks. *CoRR*, abs/1506.03099, 2015. http://arxiv.org/abs/1506.03099

Yoshua Bengio. Practical recommendations for gradient-based training of deep architectures. *arXiv:1206.5533 [cs]*, June 2012. DOI: 10.1007/978-3-642-35289-8_26.

Yoshua Bengio, Réjean Ducharme, Pascal Vincent, and Christian Janvin. A neural probabilistic language model. *Journal of Machine Learning Research*, 3:1137–1155, March 2003. ISSN 1532-4435. DOI: 10.1007/10985687_6.

Yoshua Bengio, Jérôme Louradour, Ronan Collobert, and Jason Weston. Curriculum learning. In *Proc. of the 26th Annual International Conference on Machine Learning*, pages 41–48. ACM, 2009. DOI: 10.1145/1553374.1553380.

Yoshua Bengio, Ian J. Goodfellow, and Aaron Courville. *Deep Learning*. MIT Press, 2016.

James Bergstra, Olivier Breuleux, Frédéric Bastien, Pascal Lamblin, Razvan Pascanu, Guillaume Desjardins, Joseph Turian, David Warde-Farley, and Yoshua Bengio. Theano: a CPU and GPU math expression compiler. In *Proc. of the Python for Scientific Computing Conference (SciPy)*, June 2010.

Jeff A. Bilmes and Katrin Kirchhoff. Factored language models and generalized parallel backoff. In *Companion Volume of the Proc. of HLT-NAACL—Short Papers*, 2003. DOI: 10.3115/1073483.1073485.

Zsolt Bitvai and Trevor Cohn. Non-linear text regression with a deep convolutional neural network. In *Proc. of the 53rd Annual Meeting of the Association for Computational Linguistics and the 7th International Joint Conference on Natural Language Processing—(Volume 2: Short Papers)*, pages 180–185, Beijing, China, July 2015. DOI: 10.3115/v1/p15-2030.

Tolga Bolukbasi, Kai-Wei Chang, James Y. Zou, Venkatesh Saligrama, and Adam Tauman Kalai. Quantifying and reducing stereotypes in word embeddings. *CoRR*, abs/1606.06121, 2016. http://arxiv.org/abs/1606.06121

Bernhard E. Boser, Isabelle M. Guyon, and Vladimir N. Vapnik. A training algorithm for optimal margin classifiers. In *Proc. of the 5th Annual ACM Workshop on Computational Learning Theory*, pages 144–152. ACM Press, 1992. DOI: 10.1145/130385.130401.

Jan A. Botha and Phil Blunsom. Compositional morphology for word representations and language modelling. In *Proc. of the 31st International Conference on Machine Learning (ICML)*, Beijing, China, June 2014.

Léon Bottou. Stochastic gradient descent tricks. In *Neural Networks: Tricks of the Trade*, pages 421–436. Springer, 2012. DOI: 10.1007/978-3-642-35289-8_25.

R. Samuel Bowman, Gabor Angeli, Christopher Potts, and D. Christopher Manning. A large annotated corpus for learning natural language inference. In *Proc. of the 2015 Conference on Empirical Methods in Natural Language Processing*, pages 632–642. Association for Computational Linguistics, 2015. http://aclweb.org/anthology/D15-1075 DOI: 10.18653/v1/D15-1075.

Peter Brown, Peter deSouza, Robert Mercer, T. Watson, Vincent Della Pietra, and Jenifer Lai. Class-based n-gram models of natural language. *Computational Linguistics*, 18(4), December 1992. http://aclweb.org/anthology/J92-4003

John A. Bullinaria and Joseph P. Levy. Extracting semantic representations from word co-occurrence statistics: A computational study. *Behavior Research Methods*, 39(3):510–526, 2007. DOI: 10.3758/bf03193020.

A. Caliskan-Islam, J. J. Bryson, and A. Narayanan. Semantics derived automatically from language corpora necessarily contain human biases. *CoRR*, abs/1608.07187, 2016.

Rich Caruana. Multitask learning. *Machine Learning*, 28:41–75, 1997. DOI: 10.1007/978-1-4615-5529-2_5.

Eugene Charniak and Mark Johnson. Coarse-to-fine n-best parsing and MaxEnt discriminative reranking. In *Proc. of the 43rd Annual Meeting of the Association for Computational Linguistics (ACL'05)*, pages 173–180, Ann Arbor, Michigan, June 2005. DOI: 10.3115/1219840.1219862.

Danqi Chen and Christopher Manning. A fast and accurate dependency parser using neural networks. In *Proc. of the 2014 Conference on Empirical Methods in Natural Language Processing (EMNLP)*, pages 740–750, Doha, Qatar. Association for Computational Linguistics, October 2014. DOI: 10.3115/v1/d14-1082.

Stanley F. Chen and Joshua Goodman. An empirical study of smoothing techniques for language modeling. In *34th Annual Meeting of the Association for Computational Linguistics*, 1996. http://aclweb.org/anthology/P96-1041 DOI: 10.1006/csla.1999.0128.

Stanley F. Chen and Joshua Goodman. An empirical study of smoothing techniques for language modeling. *Computer Speech and Language*, 13(4):359–394, 1999. DOI: 10.1006/c-sla.1999.0128.

Wenlin Chen, David Grangier, and Michael Auli. Strategies for training large vocabulary neural language models. In *Proc. of the 54th Annual Meeting of the Association for Computational Linguistics—(Volume 1: Long Papers)*, pages 1975–1985, 2016. http://aclweb.org/anthology/P16-1186 DOI: 10.18653/v1/P16-1186.

Yubo Chen, Liheng Xu, Kang Liu, Daojian Zeng, and Jun Zhao. Event extraction via dynamic multi-pooling convolutional neural networks. In *Proc. of the 53rd Annual Meeting of the Association for Computational Linguistics and the 7th International Joint Conference on Natural Language Processing—(Volume 1: Long Papers)*, pages 167–176, Beijing, China, July 2015. DOI: 10.3115/v1/p15-1017.

Kyunghyun Cho. Natural language understanding with distributed representation. *arXiv:1511.07916 [cs, stat]*, November 2015.

Kyunghyun Cho, Bart van Merrienboer, Dzmitry Bahdanau, and Yoshua Bengio. On the properties of neural machine translation: Encoder-decoder approaches. In *Proc. of SSST-8, 8th Workshop on Syntax, Semantics and Structure in Statistical Translation*, pages 103–111, Doha, Qatar. Association for Computational Linguistics, October 2014a. DOI: 10.3115/v1/w14-4012.

Kyunghyun Cho, Bart van Merrienboer, Caglar Gulcehre, Dzmitry Bahdanau, Fethi Bougares, Holger Schwenk, and Yoshua Bengio. Learning phrase representations using RNN encoder-decoder for statistical machine translation. In *Proc. of the 2014 Conference on Empirical Methods in Natural Language Processing (EMNLP)*, pages 1724–1734, Doha, Qatar. Association for Computational Linguistics, October 2014b. DOI: 10.3115/v1/d14-1179.

Do Kook Choe and Eugene Charniak. Parsing as language modeling. In *Proc. of the Conference on Empirical Methods in Natural Language Processing*, pages 2331–2336, Austin, Texas. Association for Computational Linguistics, November 2016. https://aclweb.org/anthology/D16-1257 DOI: 10.18653/v1/d16-1257.

Grzegorz Chrupala. Normalizing tweets with edit scripts and recurrent neural embeddings. In *Proc. of the 52nd Annual Meeting of the Association for Computational Linguistics—(Volume 2: Short Papers)*, pages 680–686, Baltimore, Maryland, June 2014. DOI: 10.3115/v1/p14-2111.

Junyoung Chung, Caglar Gulcehre, KyungHyun Cho, and Yoshua Bengio. Empirical evaluation of gated recurrent neural networks on sequence modeling. *arXiv:1412.3555 [cs]*, December 2014.

Junyoung Chung, Kyunghyun Cho, and Yoshua Bengio. A character-level decoder without explicit segmentation for neural machine translation. In *Proc. of the 54th Annual Meeting of the Association for Computational Linguistics—(Volume 1: Long Papers)*, pages 1693–1703, 2016. http://aclweb.org/anthology/P16-1160 DOI: 10.18653/v1/P16-1160.

Kenneth Ward Church and Patrick Hanks. Word association norms, mutual information, and lexicography. *Computational Linguistics*, 16(1):22–29, 1990. DOI: 10.3115/981623.981633.

Kevin Clark and Christopher D. Manning. Improving coreference resolution by learning entity-level distributed representations. In *Association for Computational Linguistics (ACL)*, 2016. /u/apache/htdocs/static/pubs/clark2016improving.pdf DOI: 10.18653/v1/p16-1061.

Michael Collins. Discriminative training methods for hidden Markov models: Theory and experiments with perceptron algorithms. In *Proc. of the Conference on Empirical Methods in Natural Language Processing*, pages 1–8. Association for Computational Linguistics, July 2002. DOI: 10.3115/1118693.1118694.

Michael Collins and Terry Koo.   Discriminative reranking for natural language parsing.   *Computational Linguistics*, 31(1):25–70, March 2005.   ISSN 0891-2017. DOI:
10.1162/0891201053630273.

Ronan Collobert and Jason Weston. A unified architecture for natural language processing: Deep
neural networks with multitask learning. In *Proc. of the 25th International Conference on Machine
Learning*, pages 160–167. ACM, 2008. DOI: 10.1145/1390156.1390177.

Ronan Collobert, Jason Weston, Léon Bottou, Michael Karlen, Koray Kavukcuoglu, and Pavel
Kuksa. Natural language processing (almost) from scratch. *The Journal of Machine Learning
Research*, 12:2493–2537, 2011.

Alexis Conneau, Holger Schwenk, Loïc Barrault, and Yann LeCun. Very deep convolutional
networks for natural language processing. *CoRR*, abs/1606.01781, 2016. http://arxiv.org/
abs/1606.01781

Ryan Cotterell and Hinrich Schutze. Morphological word embeddings. *NAACL*, 2015.

Ryan Cotterell, Christo Kirov, John Sylak-Glassman, David Yarowsky, Jason Eisner, and Mans
Hulden. *Proc. of the 14th SIGMORPHON Workshop on Computational Research in Phonetics,
Phonology, and Morphology*, chapter The SIGMORPHON 2016 Shared Task—Morphological
Reinflection, pages 10–22. Association for Computational Linguistics, 2016. http://aclweb
.org/anthology/W16-2002 DOI: 10.18653/v1/W16-2002.

Koby Crammer and Yoram Singer. On the algorithmic implementation of multiclass kernel-
based vector machines. *The Journal of Machine Learning Research*, 2:265–292, 2002.

Mathias Creutz and Krista Lagus. Unsupervised models for morpheme segmentation and morphology learning. *ACM Transactions of Speech and Language Processing*, 4(1):3:1–3:34, February
2007. ISSN 1550-4875. DOI: 10.1145/1187415.1187418.

James Cross and Liang Huang. Incremental parsing with minimal features using bi-directional
LSTM. In *Proc. of the 54th Annual Meeting of the Association for Computational Linguistics—
(Volume 2: Short Papers)*, pages 32–37, 2016a. http://aclweb.org/anthology/P16-2006 DOI:
10.18653/v1/P16-2006.

James Cross and Liang Huang. Span-based constituency parsing with a structure-label system and dynamic oracles. In *Proc. of the 2016 Conference on Empirical Methods in Natural Language Processing (EMNLP)*. Association for Computational Linguistics, 2016b. DOI:
10.18653/v1/d16-1001.

G. Cybenko. Approximation by superpositions of a sigmoidal function. *Mathematics of Control, Signals and Systems*, 2(4):303–314, December 1989. ISSN 0932-4194, 1435-568X. DOI:
10.1007/BF02551274.

Ido Dagan and Oren Glickman. Probabilistic textual entailment: Generic applied modeling of language variability. In *PASCAL Workshop on Learning Methods for Text Understanding and Mining*, 2004.

Ido Dagan, Fernando Pereira, and Lillian Lee. Similarity-based estimation of word cooccurrence probabilities. In *ACL*, 1994. DOI: 10.3115/981732.981770.

Ido Dagan, Oren Glickman, and Bernardo Magnini. The PASCAL recognising textual entailment challenge. In *Machine Learning Challenges, Evaluating Predictive Uncertainty, Visual Object Classification and Recognizing Textual Entailment, First PASCAL Machine Learning Challenges Workshop, MLCW*, pages 177–190, Southampton, UK, April 11–13, 2005. (revised selected papers). DOI: 10.1007/11736790_9.

Ido Dagan, Dan Roth, Mark Sammons, and Fabio Massimo Zanzotto. *Recognizing Textual Entailment: Models and Applications*. Synthesis Lectures on Human Language Technologies. Morgan & Claypool Publishers, 2013. DOI: 10.2200/s00509ed1v01y201305hlt023.

G. E. Dahl, T. N. Sainath, and G. E. Hinton. Improving deep neural networks for LVCSR using rectified linear units and dropout. In *2013 IEEE International Conference on Acoustics, Speech and Signal Processing (ICASSP)*, pages 8609–8613, May 2013. DOI: 10.1109/I-CASSP.2013.6639346.

Hal Daumé III, John Langford, and Daniel Marcu. Search-based structured prediction. *Machine Learning Journal (MLJ)*, 2009. DOI: 10.1007/s10994-009-5106-x.

Hal Daumé III. *A Course In Machine Learning*. Self Published, 2015.

Yann N. Dauphin, Razvan Pascanu, Caglar Gulcehre, Kyunghyun Cho, Surya Ganguli, and Yoshua Bengio. Identifying and attacking the saddle point problem in high-dimensional non-convex optimization. In Z. Ghahramani, M. Welling, C. Cortes, N. D. Lawrence, and K. Q. Weinberger, Eds., *Advances in Neural Information Processing Systems* 27, pages 2933–2941. Curran Associates, Inc., 2014.

Adrià de Gispert, Gonzalo Iglesias, and Bill Byrne. Fast and accurate preordering for SMT using neural networks. In *Proc. of the 2015 Conference of the North American Chapter of the Association for Computational Linguistics: Human Language Technologies*, pages 1012–1017, Denver, Colorado, 2015. DOI: 10.3115/v1/n15-1105.

Jacob Devlin, Rabih Zbib, Zhongqiang Huang, Thomas Lamar, Richard Schwartz, and John Makhoul. Fast and robust neural network joint models for statistical machine translation. In *Proc. of the 52nd Annual Meeting of the Association for Computational Linguistics—(Volume 1: Long Papers)*, pages 1370–1380, Baltimore, Maryland, June 2014. DOI: 10.3115/v1/p14-1129.

Trinh Do, Thierry Arti, and others. Neural conditional random fields. In *International Conference on Artificial Intelligence and Statistics*, pages 177–184, 2010.

Pedro Domingos. *The Master Algorithm*. Basic Books, 2015.

Li Dong, Furu Wei, Chuanqi Tan, Duyu Tang, Ming Zhou, and Ke Xu. Adaptive recursive neural network for target-dependent twitter sentiment classification. In *Proc. of the 52nd Annual Meeting of the Association for Computational Linguistics—(Volume 2: Short Papers)*, pages 49–54, Baltimore, Maryland, June 2014. DOI: 10.3115/v1/p14-2009.

Li Dong, Furu Wei, Ming Zhou, and Ke Xu. Question answering over freebase with multi-column convolutional neural networks. In *Proc. of the 53rd Annual Meeting of the Association for Computational Linguistics and the 7th International Joint Conference on Natural Language Processing—(Volume 1: Long Papers)*, pages 260–269, Beijing, China, July 2015. DOI: 10.3115/v1/p15-1026.

Cicero dos Santos and Maira Gatti. Deep convolutional neural networks for sentiment analysis of short texts. In *Proc. of COLING, the 25th International Conference on Computational Linguistics: Technical Papers*, pages 69–78, Dublin City University, Dublin, Ireland. Association for Computational Linguistics, August 2014.

Cicero dos Santos and Bianca Zadrozny. Learning character-level representations for part-of-speech tagging. In *Proc. of the 31st International Conference on Machine Learning (ICML)*, pages 1818–1826, 2014.

Cicero dos Santos, Bing Xiang, and Bowen Zhou. Classifying relations by ranking with convolutional neural networks. In *Proc. of the 53rd Annual Meeting of the Association for Computational Linguistics and the 7th International Joint Conference on Natural Language Processing—(Volume 1: Long Papers)*, pages 626–634, Beijing, China, July 2015. DOI: 10.3115/v1/p15-1061.

John Duchi, Elad Hazan, and Yoram Singer. Adaptive subgradient methods for online learning and stochastic optimization. *The Journal of Machine Learning Research*, 12:2121–2159, 2011.

Kevin Duh, Graham Neubig, Katsuhito Sudoh, and Hajime Tsukada. Adaptation data selection using neural language models: experiments in machine translation. In *Proc. of the 51st Annual Meeting of the Association for Computational Linguistics—(Volume 2: Short Papers)*, pages 678–683, Sofia, Bulgaria, August 2013.

Greg Durrett and Dan Klein. Neural CRF parsing. In *Proc. of the 53rd Annual Meeting of the Association for Computational Linguistics and the 7th International Joint Conference on Natural Language Processing—(Volume 1: Long Papers)*, pages 302–312, Beijing, China, July 2015. DOI: 10.3115/v1/p15-1030.

Chris Dyer, Victor Chahuneau, and A. Noah Smith. A simple, fast, and effective reparameterization of IBM model 2. In *Proc. of the 2013 Conference of the North American Chapter of the Association for Computational Linguistics: Human Language Technologies*, pages 644–648, 2013. http://aclweb.org/anthology/N13-1073

Chris Dyer, Miguel Ballesteros, Wang Ling, Austin Matthews, and Noah A. Smith. Transition-based dependency parsing with stack long short-term memory. In *Proc. of the 53rd Annual Meeting of the Association for Computational Linguistics and the 7th International Joint Conference on Natural Language Processing—(Volume 1: Long Papers)*, pages 334–343, Beijing, China, July 2015. DOI: 10.3115/v1/p15-1033.

C. Eckart and G. Young. The approximation of one matrix by another of lower rank. *Psychometrika*, 1:211–218, 1936. DOI: 10.1007/bf02288367.

Jason Eisner and Giorgio Satta. Efficient parsing for bilexical context-free grammars and head automaton grammars. In *Proc. of the 37th Annual Meeting of the Association for Computational Linguistics*, 1999. http://aclweb.org/anthology/P99-1059 DOI: 10.3115/1034678.1034748.

Jeffrey L. Elman. Finding structure in time. *Cognitive Science*, 14(2):179–211, March 1990. ISSN 1551-6709. DOI: 10.1207/s15516709cog1402_1.

Martin B. H. Everaert, Marinus A. C. Huybregts, Noam Chomsky, Robert C. Berwick, and Johan J. Bolhuis. Structures, not strings: Linguistics as part of the cognitive sciences. *Trends in Cognitive Sciences*, 19(12):729–743, 2015. DOI: 10.1016/j.tics.2015.09.008.

Manaal Faruqui and Chris Dyer. Improving vector space word representations using multilingual correlation. In *Proc. of the 14th Conference of the European Chapter of the Association for Computational Linguistics*, pages 462–471, Gothenburg, Sweden, April 2014. DOI: 10.3115/v1/e14-1049.

Manaal Faruqui, Jesse Dodge, Kumar Sujay Jauhar, Chris Dyer, Eduard Hovy, and A. Noah Smith. Retrofitting word vectors to semantic lexicons. In *Proc. of the 2015 Conference of the North American Chapter of the Association for Computational Linguistics: Human Language Technologies*, pages 1606–1615, 2015. http://aclweb.org/anthology/N15-1184 DOI: 10.3115/v1/N15-1184.

Manaal Faruqui, Yulia Tsvetkov, Graham Neubig, and Chris Dyer. Morphological inflection generation using character sequence to sequence learning. In *Proc. of the 2016 Conference of the North American Chapter of the Association for Computational Linguistics: Human Language Technologies*, pages 634–643, 2016. http://aclweb.org/anthology/N16-1077 DOI: 10.18653/v1/N16-1077.

Christiane Fellbaum. *WordNet: An Electronic Lexical Database*. Bradford Books, 1998.

Jessica Ficler and Yoav Goldberg. A neural network for coordination boundary prediction. In *Proc. of the 2016 Conference on Empirical Methods in Natural Language Processing*, pages 23–32, Austin, Texas. Association for Computational Linguistics, November 2016. https://aclweb .org/anthology/D16-1003 DOI: 10.18653/v1/d16-1003.

Katja Filippova and Yasemin Altun. Overcoming the lack of parallel data in sentence compression. In *Proc. of the 2013 Conference on Empirical Methods in Natural Language Processing*, pages 1481–1491. Association for Computational Linguistics, 2013. http://aclweb.org/ant hology/D13-1155

Katja Filippova, Enrique Alfonseca, Carlos A. Colmenares, Lukasz Kaiser, and Oriol Vinyals. Sentence compression by deletion with LSTMs. In *Proc. of the 2015 Conference on Empirical Methods in Natural Language Processing*, pages 360–368, Lisbon, Portugal. Association for Computational Linguistics, September 2015. DOI: 10.18653/v1/d15-1042.

Charles J. Fillmore, Josef Ruppenhofer, and Collin F. Baker. FrameNet and representing the link between semantic and syntactic relations. *Language and Linguistics Monographs Series B*, pages 19–62, Institute of Linguistics, Academia Sinica, Taipei, 2004.

John R. Firth. A synopsis of linguistic theory 1930–1955. In *Studies in Linguistic Analysis*, Special volume of the Philological Society, pages 1–32. Firth, John Rupert, Haas William, Halliday, Michael A. K., Oxford, Blackwell Ed., 1957.

John R. Firth. The technique of semantics. *Transactions of the Philological Society*, 34(1):36–73, 1935. ISSN 1467-968X. DOI: 10.1111/j.1467-968X.1935.tb01254.x.

Mikel L. Forcada and Ramón P. Ñeco. Recursive hetero-associative memories for translation. In *Biological and Artificial Computation: From Neuroscience to Technology*, pages 453–462. Springer, 1997. DOI: 10.1007/bfb0032504.

Philip Gage. A new algorithm for data compression. *C Users Journal*, 12(2):23–38, February 1994. ISSN 0898-9788. http://dl.acm.org/citation.cfm?id=177910.177914

Yarin Gal. A theoretically grounded application of dropout in recurrent neural networks. *CoRR*, abs/1512.05287, December 2015.

Kuzman Ganchev and Mark Dredze. *Proc. of the ACL-08: HLT Workshop on Mobile Language Processing*, chapter Small Statistical Models by Random Feature Mixing, pages 19–20. Association for Computational Linguistics, 2008. http://aclweb.org/anthology/W08-0804

Juri Ganitkevitch, Benjamin Van Durme, and Chris Callison-Burch. PPDB: The paraphrase database. In *Proc. of the 2013 Conference of the North American Chapter of the Association for Computational Linguistics: Human Language Technologies*, pages 758–764, 2013. http://aclw eb.org/anthology/N13-1092

Jianfeng Gao, Patrick Pantel, Michael Gamon, Xiaodong He, and Li Deng. Modeling interestingness with deep neural networks. In *Proc. of the Conference on Empirical Methods in Natural Language Processing (EMNLP)*, pages 2–13, Doha, Qatar. Association for Computational Linguistics, October 2014. DOI: 10.3115/v1/d14-1002.

Dan Gillick, Cliff Brunk, Oriol Vinyals, and Amarnag Subramanya. Multilingual language processing from bytes. In *Proc. of the Conference of the North American Chapter of the Association for Computational Linguistics: Human Language Technologies*, pages 1296–1306, 2016. http://aclweb.org/anthology/N16-1155 DOI: 10.18653/v1/N16-1155.

Jesús Giménez and Lluis Màrquez. SVMTool: A general POS tagger generator based on support vector machines. In *Proc. of the 4th LREC*, Lisbon, Portugal, 2004.

Xavier Glorot and Yoshua Bengio. Understanding the difficulty of training deep feedforward neural networks. In *International Conference on Artificial Intelligence and Statistics*, pages 249–256, 2010.

Xavier Glorot, Antoine Bordes, and Yoshua Bengio. Deep sparse rectifier neural networks. In *International Conference on Artificial Intelligence and Statistics*, pages 315–323, 2011.

Yoav Goldberg. A primer on neural network models for natural language processing. *Journal of Artificial Intelligence Research*, 57:345–420, 2016.

Yoav Goldberg and Michael Elhadad. An efficient algorithm for easy-first non-directional dependency parsing. In *Human Language Technologies: The Annual Conference of the North American Chapter of the Association for Computational Linguistics*, pages 742–750, Los Angeles, California, June 2010.

Yoav Goldberg and Joakim Nivre. Training deterministic parsers with non-deterministic oracles. *Transactions of the Association for Computational Linguistics*, 1(0):403–414, October 2013. ISSN 2307-387X.

Yoav Goldberg, Kai Zhao, and Liang Huang. Efficient implementation of beam-search incremental parsers. In *Proc. of the 51st Annual Meeting of the Association for Computational Linguistics—(Volume 2: Short Papers)*, pages 628–633, Sofia, Bulgaria, August 2013.

Christoph Goller and Andreas Küchler. Learning task-dependent distributed representations by backpropagation through structure. In *In Proc. of the ICNN-96*, pages 347–352. IEEE, 1996.

Hila Gonen and Yoav Goldberg. Semi supervised preposition-sense disambiguation using multilingual data. In *Proc. of COLING, the 26th International Conference on Computational Linguistics: Technical Papers*, pages 2718–2729, Osaka, Japan, December 2016. The COLING 2016 Organizing Committee. http://aclweb.org/anthology/C16-1256

Joshua Goodman. A bit of progress in language modeling. *CoRR*, cs.CL/0108005, 2001. http://arxiv.org/abs/cs.CL/0108005 DOI: 10.1006/csla.2001.0174.

Stephan Gouws, Yoshua Bengio, and Greg Corrado. BilBOWA: Fast bilingual distributed representations without word alignments. In *Proc. of the 32nd International Conference on Machine Learning*, pages 748–756, 2015.

A. Graves. *Supervised Sequence Labelling with Recurrent Neural Networks*. Ph.D. thesis, Technische Universität München, 2008. DOI: 10.1007/978-3-642-24797-2.

Alex Graves, Greg Wayne, and Ivo Danihelka. Neural turing machines. *CoRR*, abs/1410.5401, 2014. http://arxiv.org/abs/1410.5401

Edward Grefenstette, Karl Moritz Hermann, Mustafa Suleyman, and Phil Blunsom. Learning to transduce with unbounded memory. In C. Cortes, N. D. Lawrence, D. D. Lee, M. Sugiyama, and R. Garnett, Eds., *Advances in Neural Information Processing Systems 28*, pages 1828–1836. Curran Associates, Inc., 2015. http://papers.nips.cc/paper/5648-learning-to-transduce-with-unbounded-memory.pdf

Klaus Greff, Rupesh Kumar Srivastava, Jan Koutník, Bas R. Steunebrink, and Jürgen Schmidhuber. LSTM: A search space odyssey. *arXiv:1503.04069 [cs]*, March 2015. DOI: 10.1109/tnnls.2016.2582924.

Michael Gutmann and Aapo Hyvärinen. Noise-contrastive estimation: A new estimation principle for unnormalized statistical models. In *International Conference on Artificial Intelligence and Statistics*, pages 297–304, 2010.

Zellig Harris. Distributional structure. *Word*, 10(23):146–162, 1954. DOI: 10.1080/00437956.1954.11659520.

Kazuma Hashimoto, Makoto Miwa, Yoshimasa Tsuruoka, and Takashi Chikayama. Simple customization of recursive neural networks for semantic relation classification. In *Proc. of the Conference on Empirical Methods in Natural Language Processing*, pages 1372–1376, Seattle, Washington. Association for Computational Linguistics, October 2013.

Kaiming He, Xiangyu Zhang, Shaoqing Ren, and Jian Sun. Delving deep into rectifiers: Surpassing human-level performance on ImageNet classification. *arXiv:1502.01852 [cs]*, February 2015. DOI: 10.1109/iccv.2015.123.

Kaiming He, Xiangyu Zhang, Shaoqing Ren, and Jian Sun. Deep residual learning for image recognition. In *The IEEE Conference on Computer Vision and Pattern Recognition (CVPR)*, June 2016. DOI: 10.1109/cvpr.2016.90.

Matthew Henderson, Blaise Thomson, and Steve Young. Deep neural network approach for the dialog state tracking challenge. In *Proc. of the SIGDIAL Conference*, pages 467–471, Metz, France. Association for Computational Linguistics, August 2013.

Karl Moritz Hermann and Phil Blunsom. The role of syntax in vector space models of compositional semantics. In *Proc. of the 51st Annual Meeting of the Association for Computational Linguistics—(Volume 1: Long Papers)*, pages 894–904, Sofia, Bulgaria, August 2013.

Karl Moritz Hermann and Phil Blunsom. Multilingual models for compositional distributed semantics. In *Proc. of the 52nd Annual Meeting of the Association for Computational Linguistics—(Volume 1: Long Papers)*, pages 58–68, Baltimore, Maryland, June 2014. DOI: 10.3115/v1/p14-1006.

Salah El Hihi and Yoshua Bengio. Hierarchical recurrent neural networks for long-term dependencies. In D. S. Touretzky, M. C. Mozer, and M. E. Hasselmo, Eds., *Advances in Neural Information Processing Systems 8*, pages 493–499. MIT Press, 1996.

Felix Hill, Kyunghyun Cho, Sebastien Jean, Coline Devin, and Yoshua Bengio. Embedding word similarity with neural machine translation. *arXiv:1412.6448 [cs]*, December 2014.

Geoffrey E. Hinton, J. L. McClelland, and D. E. Rumelhart. Distributed representations. In D. E. Rumelhart, J. L. McClelland, et al., Eds., *Parallel Distributed Processing: Volume 1: Foundations*, pages 77–109. MIT Press, Cambridge, 1987.

Geoffrey E. Hinton, Nitish Srivastava, Alex Krizhevsky, Ilya Sutskever, and Ruslan R. Salakhutdinov. Improving neural networks by preventing co-adaptation of feature detectors. *arXiv:1207.0580 [cs]*, July 2012.

Sepp Hochreiter and Jürgen Schmidhuber. Long short-term memory. *Neural Computation*, 9(8): 1735–1780, 1997. DOI: 10.1162/neco.1997.9.8.1735.

Julia Hockenmaier. *Data and Models for Statistical Parsing with Combinatory Categorial Grammar*. Ph.D. thesis, University of Edinburgh, 2003. DOI: 10.3115/1073083.1073139.

Kurt Hornik, Maxwell Stinchcombe, and Halbert White. Multilayer feedforward networks are universal approximators. *Neural Networks*, 2(5):359–366, 1989. ISSN 0893-6080. DOI: 10.1016/0893-6080(89)90020-8.

Dirk Hovy, Stephen Tratz, and Eduard Hovy. What's in a preposition? dimensions of sense disambiguation for an interesting word class. In *Coling Posters*, pages 454–462, Beijing, China, August 2010. Coling 2010 Organizing Committee. http://www.aclweb.org/anthology/C 10-2052

(Kenneth) Ting-Hao Huang, Francis Ferraro, Nasrin Mostafazadeh, Ishan Misra, Aishwarya Agrawal, Jacob Devlin, Ross Girshick, Xiaodong He, Pushmeet Kohli, Dhruv Batra, Lawrence C. Zitnick, Devi Parikh, Lucy Vanderwende, Michel Galley, and Margaret Mitchell. Visual storytelling. In *Proc. of the 2016 Conference of the North American Chapter of the Association for Computational Linguistics: Human Language Technologies*, pages 1233–1239, 2016. http://aclweb.org/anthology/N16-1147 DOI: 10.18653/v1/N16-1147.

Liang Huang, Suphan Fayong, and Yang Guo. Structured perceptron with inexact search. In *Proc. of the Conference of the North American Chapter of the Association for Computational Linguistics: Human Language Technologies*, pages 142–151, 2012. http://aclweb.org/anthology/N12-1015

Sergey Ioffe and Christian Szegedy. Batch normalization: Accelerating deep network training by reducing internal covariate shift. *arXiv:1502.03167 [cs]*, February 2015.

Ozan Irsoy and Claire Cardie. Opinion mining with deep recurrent neural networks. In *Proc. of the 2014 Conference on Empirical Methods in Natural Language Processing (EMNLP)*, pages 720–728, Doha, Qatar. Association for Computational Linguistics, October 2014. DOI: 10.3115/v1/d14-1080.

Mohit Iyyer, Jordan Boyd-Graber, Leonardo Claudino, Richard Socher, and Hal Daumé III. A neural network for factoid question answering over paragraphs. In *Proc. of the Conference on Empirical Methods in Natural Language Processing (EMNLP)*, pages 633–644, Doha, Qatar. Association for Computational Linguistics, October 2014a. DOI: 10.3115/v1/d14-1070.

Mohit Iyyer, Peter Enns, Jordan Boyd-Graber, and Philip Resnik. Political ideology detection using recursive neural networks. In *Proc. of the 52nd Annual Meeting of the Association for Computational Linguistics—(Volume 1: Long Papers)*, pages 1113–1122, Baltimore, Maryland, June 2014b. DOI: 10.3115/v1/p14-1105.

Mohit Iyyer, Varun Manjunatha, Jordan Boyd-Graber, and Hal Daumé III. Deep unordered composition rivals syntactic methods for text classification. In *Proc. of the 53rd Annual Meeting of the Association for Computational Linguistics and the 7th International Joint Conference on Natural Language Processing—(Volume 1: Long Papers)*, pages 1681–1691, Beijing, China, July 2015. DOI: 10.3115/v1/p15-1162.

Sébastien Jean, Kyunghyun Cho, Roland Memisevic, and Yoshua Bengio. On using very large target vocabulary for neural machine translation. In *Proc. of the 53rd Annual Meeting of the Association for Computational Linguistics and the 7th International Joint Conference on Natural Language Processing—(Volume 1: Long Papers)*, pages 1–10, 2015. http://aclweb.org/anthology/P15-1001 DOI: 10.3115/v1/P15-1001.

Frederick Jelinek and Robert Mercer. Interpolated estimation of Markov source parameters from sparse data. In *Workshop on Pattern Recognition in Practice*, 1980.

Rie Johnson and Tong Zhang. Effective use of word order for text categorization with convolutional neural networks. In *Proc. of the 2015 Conference of the North American Chapter of the Association for Computational Linguistics: Human Language Technologies*, pages 103–112, Denver, Colorado, 2015. DOI: 10.3115/v1/n15-1011.

Aravind K. Joshi and Bangalore Srinivas. Disambiguation of super parts of speech (or supertags): Allnost parsing. In *COLING Volume 1: The 15th International Conference on Computational Linguistics*, 1994. http://aclweb.org/anthology/C94-1024 DOI: 10.3115/991886.991912.

Armand Joulin, Edouard Grave, Piotr Bojanowski, and Tomas Mikolov. Bag of tricks for efficient text classification. *CoRR*, abs/1607.01759, 2016. http://arxiv.org/abs/1607.01759

Rafal Jozefowicz, Wojciech Zaremba, and Ilya Sutskever. An empirical exploration of recurrent network architectures. In *Proc. of the 32nd International Conference on Machine Learning (ICML-15)*, pages 2342–2350, 2015.

Rafal Jozefowicz, Oriol Vinyals, Mike Schuster, Noam Shazeer, and Yonghui Wu. Exploring the limits of language modeling. *arXiv:1602.02410 [cs]*, February 2016.

Daniel Jurafsky and James H. Martin. *Speech and Language Processing*, 2nd ed. Prentice Hall, 2008.

Nal Kalchbrenner, Edward Grefenstette, and Phil Blunsom. A convolutional neural network for modelling sentences. In *Proc. of the 52nd Annual Meeting of the Association for Computational Linguistics—(Volume 1: Long Papers)*, pages 655–665, Baltimore, Maryland, June 2014. DOI: 10.3115/v1/p14-1062.

Nal Kalchbrenner, Lasse Espeholt, Karen Simonyan, Aäron van den Oord, Alex Graves, and Koray Kavukcuoglu. Neural machine translation in linear time. *CoRR*, abs/1610.10099, 2016. http://arxiv.org/abs/1610.10099

Katharina Kann and Hinrich Schütze. *Proc. of the 14th SIGMORPHON Workshop on Computational Research in Phonetics, Phonology, and Morphology*, chapter MED: The LMU System for the SIGMORPHON 2016 Shared Task on Morphological Reinflection, pages 62–70. Association for Computational Linguistics, 2016. http://aclweb.org/anthology/W16-2010 DOI: 10.18653/v1/W16-2010.

Anjuli Kannan, Karol Kurach, Sujith Ravi, Tobias Kaufmann, Andrew Tomkins, Balint Miklos, Greg Corrado, Laszlo Lukacs, Marina Ganea, Peter Young, and Vivek Ramavajjala. Smart reply: Automated response suggestion for email. In *Proc. of the ACM SIGKDD Conference on Knowledge Discovery and Data Mining (KDD)*, 2016. https://arxiv.org/pdf/1606.04870.pdf DOI: 10.1145/2939672.2939801.

Andrej Karpathy and Fei-Fei Li. Deep visual-semantic alignments for generating image descriptions. In *IEEE Conference on Computer Vision and Pattern Recognition, CVPR*, pages 3128–3137, Boston, MA, June 7–12, 2015. DOI: 10.1109/cvpr.2015.7298932.

Andrej Karpathy, Justin Johnson, and Fei-Fei Li. Visualizing and understanding recurrent networks. *arXiv:1506.02078 [cs]*, June 2015.

Douwe Kiela and Stephen Clark. A systematic study of semantic vector space model parameters. In *Workshop on Continuous Vector Space Models and their Compositionality*, 2014. DOI: 10.3115/v1/w14-1503.

Yoon Kim. Convolutional neural networks for sentence classification. In *Proc. of the Conference on Empirical Methods in Natural Language Processing (EMNLP)*, pages 1746–1751, Doha, Qatar. Association for Computational Linguistics, October 2014. DOI: 10.3115/v1/d14-1181.

Yoon Kim, Yacine Jernite, David Sontag, and Alexander M. Rush. Character-aware neural language models. *arXiv:1508.06615 [cs, stat]*, August 2015.

Diederik Kingma and Jimmy Ba. ADAM: A method for stochastic optimization. *arXiv:1412.6980 [cs]*, December 2014.

Eliyahu Kiperwasser and Yoav Goldberg. Easy-first dependency parsing with hierarchical tree LSTMs. *Transactions of the Association of Computational Linguistics—(Volume 4, Issue 1)*, pages 445–461, 2016a. http://aclweb.org/anthology/Q16-1032

Eliyahu Kiperwasser and Yoav Goldberg. Simple and accurate dependency parsing using bidirectional LSTM feature representations. *Transactions of the Association of Computational Linguistics—(Volume 4, Issue 1)*, pages 313–327, 2016b. http://aclweb.org/anthology/Q16-1023

Karin Kipper, Hoa T. Dang, and Martha Palmer. Class-based construction of a verb lexicon. In *AAAI/IAAI*, pages 691–696, 2000.

Ryan Kiros, Yukun Zhu, Ruslan R Salakhutdinov, Richard Zemel, Raquel Urtasun, Antonio Torralba, and Sanja Fidler. Skip-thought vectors. In C. Cortes, N. D. Lawrence, D. D. Lee, M. Sugiyama, and R. Garnett, Eds., *Advances in Neural Information Processing Systems 28*, pages 3294–3302. Curran Associates, Inc., 2015. http://papers.nips.cc/paper/5950-skip-thought-vectors.pdf

Sigrid Klerke, Yoav Goldberg, and Anders Søgaard. Improving sentence compression by learning to predict gaze. In *Proc. of the Conference of the North American Chapter of the Association for Computational Linguistics: Human Language Technologies*, pages 1528–1533, 2016. http://aclweb.org/anthology/N16-1179 DOI: 10.18653/v1/N16-1179.

Reinhard Kneser and Hermann Ney. Improved backing-off for m-gram language modeling. In *Acoustics, Speech, and Signal Processing, ICASSP-95, International Conference on*, volume 1, pages 181–184, May 1995. DOI: 10.1109/ICASSP.1995.479394.

Philipp Koehn. Europarl: A parallel corpus for statistical machine translation. In *Proc. of MT Summit*, volume 5, pages 79–86, 2005.

Philipp Koehn. *Statistical Machine Translation*. Cambridge University Press, 2010. DOI: 10.1017/cbo9780511815829.

Terry Koo and Michael Collins. Efficient third-order dependency parsers. In *Proc. of the 48th Annual Meeting of the Association for Computational Linguistics*, pages 1–11, 2010. http://ac lweb.org/anthology/P10-1001

Moshe Koppel, Jonathan Schler, and Shlomo Argamon. Computational methods in authorship attribution. *Journal of the American Society for information Science and Technology*, 60(1):9–26, 2009. DOI: 10.1002/asi.20961.

Alex Krizhevsky, Ilya Sutskever, and Geoffrey E. Hinton. ImageNet classification with deep convolutional neural networks. In F. Pereira, C. J. C. Burges, L. Bottou, and K. Q. Weinberger, Eds., *Advances in Neural Information Processing Systems 25*, pages 1097–1105. Curran Associates, Inc., 2012. DOI: 10.1007/978-3-319-46654-5_20.

R. A. Kronmal and A. V. Peterson, Jr. On the alias method for generating random variables from a discrete distribution. *The American Statistician*, 33:214–218, 1979. DOI: 10.2307/2683739.

Sandra Kübler, Ryan McDonald, and Joakim Nivre. *Dependency Parsing*. Synthesis Lectures on Human Language Technologies. Morgan & Claypool Publishers, 2008. DOI: 10.2200/s00169ed1v01y200901hlt002.

Taku Kudo and Yuji Matsumoto. Fast methods for Kernel-based text analysis. In *Proc. of the 41st Annual Meeting on Association for Computational Linguistics—(Volume 1)*, pages 24–31, Stroudsburg, PA, 2003. DOI: 10.3115/1075096.1075100.

John Lafferty, Andrew McCallum, and Fernando CN Pereira. Conditional random fields: Probabilistic models for segmenting and labeling sequence data. In *Proc. of ICML*, 2001.

Guillaume Lample, Miguel Ballesteros, Sandeep Subramanian, Kazuya Kawakami, and Chris Dyer. Neural architectures for named entity recognition. In *Proc. of the Conference of the North American Chapter of the Association for Computational Linguistics: Human Language Technologies*, pages 260–270, 2016. http://aclweb.org/anthology/N16-1030 DOI: 10.18653/v1/N16-1030.

Phong Le and Willem Zuidema. The inside-outside recursive neural network model for dependency parsing. In *Proc. of the Conference on Empirical Methods in Natural Language Processing (EMNLP)*, pages 729–739, Doha, Qatar. Association for Computational Linguistics, October 2014. DOI: 10.3115/v1/d14-1081.

Phong Le and Willem Zuidema. The forest convolutional network: Compositional distributional semantics with a neural chart and without binarization. In *Proc. of the Conference on Empirical Methods in Natural Language Processing*, pages 1155–1164, Lisbon, Portugal. Association for Computational Linguistics, September 2015. DOI: 10.18653/v1/d15-1137.

Quoc V. Le, Navdeep Jaitly, and Geoffrey E. Hinton. A simple way to initialize recurrent networks of rectified linear units. *arXiv:1504.00941 [cs]*, April 2015.

Yann LeCun and Yoshua Bengio. Convolutional networks for images, speech, and time-series. In M. A. Arbib, Ed., *The Handbook of Brain Theory and Neural Networks*. MIT Press, 1995.

Yann LeCun, Leon Bottou, G. Orr, and K. Muller. Efficient BackProp. In G. Orr and Muller K, Eds., *Neural Networks: Tricks of the Trade*. Springer, 1998a. DOI: 10.1007/3-540-49430-8_2.

Yann LeCun, Leon Bottou, Yoshua Bengio, and Patrick Haffner. Gradient based learning applied to pattern recognition. *Proc. of the IEEE*, 86(11):2278–2324, November 1998b.

Yann LeCun and F. Huang. Loss functions for discriminative training of energy-based models. In *Proc. of AISTATS*, 2005.

Yann LeCun, Sumit Chopra, Raia Hadsell, M. Ranzato, and F. Huang. A tutorial on energy-based learning. *Predicting Structured Data*, 1:0, 2006.

Geunbae Lee, Margot Flowers, and Michael G. Dyer. Learning distributed representations of conceptual knowledge and their application to script-based story processing. In *Connectionist Natural Language Processing*, pages 215–247. Springer, 1992. DOI: 10.1007/978-94-011-2624-3_11.

Moshe Leshno, Vladimir Ya. Lin, Allan Pinkus, and Shimon Schocken. Multilayer feedforward networks with a nonpolynomial activation function can approximate any function. *Neural Networks*, 6(6):861–867, 1993. ISSN 0893-6080. http://www.sciencedirect.com/science/article/pii/S0893608005801315 DOI: 10.1016/S0893-6080(05)80131-5.

Omer Levy and Yoav Goldberg. Dependency-based word embeddings. In *Proc. of the 52nd Annual Meeting of the Association for Computational Linguistics—(Volume 2: Short Papers)*, pages 302–308, Baltimore, Maryland, June 2014. DOI: 10.3115/v1/p14-2050.

Omer Levy and Yoav Goldberg. Linguistic regularities in sparse and explicit word representations. In *Proc. of the 18th Conference on Computational Natural Language Learning*, pages 171–180.

Association for Computational Linguistics, 2014. http://aclweb.org/anthology/W14-1618 DOI: 10.3115/v1/W14-1618.

Omer Levy and Yoav Goldberg. Neural word embedding as implicit matrix factorization. In Z. Ghahramani, M. Welling, C. Cortes, N. D. Lawrence, and K. Q. Weinberger, Eds., *Advances in Neural Information Processing Systems 27*, pages 2177–2185. Curran Associates, Inc., 2014.

Omer Levy, Yoav Goldberg, and Ido Dagan. Improving distributional similarity with lessons learned from word embeddings. *Transactions of the Association for Computational Linguistics*, 3 (0):211–225, May 2015. ISSN 2307-387X.

Omer Levy, Anders Søgaard, and Yoav Goldberg. A strong baseline for learning cross-lingual word embeddings from sentence alignments. In *Proc. of the 15th Conference of the European Chapter of the Association for Computational Linguistics*, 2017.

Mike Lewis and Mark Steedman. Improved CCG parsing with semi-supervised supertagging. *Transactions of the Association for Computational Linguistics*, 2(0):327–338, October 2014. ISSN 2307-387X.

Mike Lewis, Kenton Lee, and Luke Zettlemoyer. LSTM CCG parsing. In *Proc. of the Conference of the North American Chapter of the Association for Computational Linguistics: Human Language Technologies*, pages 221–231, 2016. http://aclweb.org/anthology/N16-1026 DOI: 10.18653/v1/N16-1026.

Jiwei Li, Rumeng Li, and Eduard Hovy. Recursive deep models for discourse parsing. In *Proc. of the Conference on Empirical Methods in Natural Language Processing (EMNLP)*, pages 2061–2069, Doha, Qatar. Association for Computational Linguistics, October 2014. DOI: 10.3115/v1/d14-1220.

Jiwei Li, Thang Luong, Dan Jurafsky, and Eduard Hovy. When are tree structures necessary for deep learning of representations? In *Proc. of the Conference on Empirical Methods in Natural Language Processing*, pages 2304–2314. Association for Computational Linguistics, 2015. http://aclweb.org/anthology/D15-1278 DOI: 10.18653/v1/D15-1278.

Jiwei Li, Michel Galley, Chris Brockett, Georgios Spithourakis, Jianfeng Gao, and Bill Dolan. A persona-based neural conversation model. In *Proc. of the 54th Annual Meeting of the Association for Computational Linguistics—(Volume 1: Long Papers)*, pages 994–1003, 2016. http://aclweb.org/anthology/P16-1094 DOI: 10.18653/v1/P16-1094.

G. J. Lidstone. Note on the general case of the Bayes-Laplace formula for inductive or a posteriori probabilities. *Transactions of the Faculty of Actuaries*, 8:182–192, 1920.

Wang Ling, Chris Dyer, Alan W. Black, and Isabel Trancoso. Two/too simple adaptations of Word2Vec for syntax problems. In *Proc. of the Conference of the North American Chapter of the Association for Computational Linguistics: Human Language Technologies*, pages 1299–1304, Denver, Colorado, 2015a. DOI: 10.3115/v1/n15-1142.

Wang Ling, Chris Dyer, Alan W. Black, Isabel Trancoso, Ramon Fermandez, Silvio Amir, Luis Marujo, and Tiago Luis. Finding function in form: Compositional character models for open vocabulary word representation. In *Proc. of the Conference on Empirical Methods in Natural Language Processing*, pages 1520–1530, Lisbon, Portugal. Association for Computational Linguistics, September 2015b. DOI: 10.18653/v1/d15-1176.

Tal Linzen, Emmanuel Dupoux, and Yoav Goldberg. Assessing the ability of LSTMs to learn syntax-sensitive dependencies. *Transactions of the Association for Computational Linguistics*, 4: 521–535, 2016. ISSN 2307-387X. https://www.transacl.org/ojs/index.php/tacl/article/view/972

Ken Litkowski and Orin Hargraves. The preposition project. In *Proc. of the 2nd ACL-SIGSEM Workshop on the Linguistic Dimensions of Prepositions and Their Use in Computational Linguistics Formalisms and Applications*, pages 171–179, 2005.

Ken Litkowski and Orin Hargraves. SemEval-2007 task 06: Word-sense disambiguation of prepositions. In *Proc. of the 4th International Workshop on Semantic Evaluations*, pages 24–29, 2007. DOI: 10.3115/1621474.1621479.

Yang Liu, Furu Wei, Sujian Li, Heng Ji, Ming Zhou, and Houfeng Wang. A dependency-based neural network for relation classification. In *Proc. of the 53rd Annual Meeting of the Association for Computational Linguistics and the 7th International Joint Conference on Natural Language Processing—(Volume 2: Short Papers)*, pages 285–290, Beijing, China, July 2015. DOI: 10.3115/v1/p15-2047.

Minh-Thang Luong, Hieu Pham, and Christopher D. Manning. Effective approaches to attention-based neural machine translation. *arXiv:1508.04025 [cs]*, August 2015.

Minh-Thang Luong, Quoc V. Le, Ilya Sutskever, Oriol Vinyals, and Lukasz Kaiser. Multi-task sequence to sequence learning. In *Proc. of ICLR*, 2016.

Ji Ma, Yue Zhang, and Jingbo Zhu. Tagging the web: Building a robust web tagger with neural network. In *Proc. of the 52nd Annual Meeting of the Association for Computational Linguistics—(Volume 1: Long Papers)*, pages 144–154, Baltimore, Maryland, June 2014. DOI: 10.3115/v1/p14-1014.

Mingbo Ma, Liang Huang, Bowen Zhou, and Bing Xiang. Dependency-based convolutional neural networks for sentence embedding. In *Proc. of the 53rd Annual Meeting of the Associ-*

ation for Computational Linguistics and the 7th International Joint Conference on Natural Language Processing—(Volume 2: Short Papers), pages 174–179, Beijing, China, July 2015. DOI: 10.3115/v1/p15-2029.

Xuezhe Ma and Eduard Hovy. End-to-end sequence labeling via bi-directional LSTM-CNNs-CRF. In *Proc. of the 54th Annual Meeting of the Association for Computational Linguistics—(Volume 1: Long Papers)*, pages 1064–1074, Berlin, Germany, August 2016. http://www.aclweb.org/anthology/P16-1101 DOI: 10.18653/v1/p16-1101.

Christopher Manning and Hinrich Schütze. *Foundations of Statistical Natural Language Processing*. MIT Press, 1999.

Christopher Manning, Prabhakar Raghavan, and Hinrich Schütze. *Introduction to Information Retrieval*. Cambridge University Press, 2008. DOI: 10.1017/cbo9780511809071.

Junhua Mao, Wei Xu, Yi Yang, Jiang Wang, and Alan L. Yuille. Explain images with multimodal recurrent neural networks. *CoRR*, abs/1410.1090, 2014. http://arxiv.org/abs/1410.1090

Ryan McDonald, Koby Crammer, and Fernando Pereira. Online large-margin training of dependency parsers. In *Proc. of the 43rd Annual Meeting of the Association for Computational Linguistics (ACL'05)*, pages 91–98, 2005. http://aclweb.org/anthology/P05-1012 DOI: 10.3115/1219840.1219852.

Ryan McDonald, Joakim Nivre, Yvonne Quirmbach-Brundage, Yoav Goldberg, Dipanjan Das, Kuzman Ganchev, Keith B. Hall, Slav Petrov, Hao Zhang, Oscar Täckström, Claudia Bedini, Núria Bertomeu Castelló, and Jungmee Lee. Universal dependency annotation for multilingual parsing. In *ACL (2)*, pages 92–97, 2013.

Tomáš Mikolov. *Statistical language models based on neural networks*. Ph.D. thesis, Brno University of Technology, 2012.

Tomáš Mikolov. Martin Karafiát, Lukas Burget, Jan Cernocky, and Sanjeev Khudanpur. Recurrent neural network based language model. In *INTERSPEECH, 11th Annual Conference of the International Speech Communication Association*, pages 1045–1048, Makuhari, Chiba, Japan, September 26–30, 2010.

Tomáš Mikolov, Stefan Kombrink, Lukáš Burget, Jan Honza Černocky, and Sanjeev Khudanpur. Extensions of recurrent neural network language model. In *Acoustics, Speech and Signal Processing (ICASSP), IEEE International Conference on*, pages 5528–5531, 2011. DOI: 10.1109/icassp.2011.5947611.

Tomáš Mikolov. Kai Chen, Greg Corrado, and Jeffrey Dean. Efficient estimation of word representations in vector space. *arXiv:1301.3781 [cs]*, January 2013.

Tomáš Mikolov, Quoc V. Le, and Ilya Sutskever. Exploiting similarities among languages for machine translation. *CoRR*, abs/1309.4168, 2013. http://arxiv.org/abs/1309.4168

Tomáš Mikolov, Ilya Sutskever, Kai Chen, Greg S Corrado, and Jeff Dean. Distributed representations of words and phrases and their compositionality. In C. J. C. Burges, L. Bottou, M. Welling, Z. Ghahramani, and K. Q. Weinberger, Eds., *Advances in Neural Information Processing Systems 26*, pages 3111–3119. Curran Associates, Inc., 2013.

Tomáš Mikolov, Wen-tau Yih, and Geoffrey Zweig. Linguistic regularities in continuous space word representations. In *Proc. of the Conference of the North American Chapter of the Association for Computational Linguistics: Human Language Technologies*, pages 746–751, 2013. http://aclweb.org/anthology/N13-1090

Tomáš Mikolov, Armand Joulin, Sumit Chopra, Michael Mathieu, and Marc'Aurelio Ranzato. Learning longer memory in recurrent neural networks. *arXiv:1412.7753 [cs]*, December 2014.

Scott Miller, Jethran Guinness, and Alex Zamanian. Name tagging with word clusters and discriminative training. In *Proc. of the Human Language Technology Conference of the North American Chapter of the Association for Computational Linguistics: HLT-NAACL*, 2004. http://aclweb.org/anthology/N04-1043

Andriy Mnih and Koray Kavukcuoglu. Learning word embeddings efficiently with noise-contrastive estimation. In C. J. C. Burges, L. Bottou, M. Welling, Z. Ghahramani, and K. Q. Weinberger, Eds., *Advances in Neural Information Processing Systems 26*, pages 2265–2273. Curran Associates, Inc., 2013.

Andriy Mnih and Yee Whye Teh. A fast and simple algorithm for training neural probabilistic language models. In John Langford and Joelle Pineau, Eds., *Proc. of the 29th International Conference on Machine Learning (ICML-12)*, pages 1751–1758, New York, NY, July 2012. Omnipress.

Mehryar Mohri, Afshin Rostamizadeh, and Ameet Talwalkar. *Foundations of Machine Learning*. MIT Press, 2012.

Frederic Morin and Yoshua Bengio. Hierarchical probabilistic neural network language model. In Robert G. Cowell and Zoubin Ghahramani, Eds., *Proc. of the 10th International Workshop on Artificial Intelligence and Statistics*, pages 246–252, 2005. http://www.iro.umontreal.ca/~lisa/pointeurs/hierarchical-nnlm-aistats05.pdf

Nikola Mrkšić, Diarmuid Ó Séaghdha, Blaise Thomson, Milica Gasic, Pei-Hao Su, David Vandyke, Tsung-Hsien Wen, and Steve Young. Multi-domain dialog state tracking using recurrent neural networks. In *Proc. of the 53rd Annual Meeting of the Association for Computational Linguistics and the 7th International Joint Conference on Natural Language Processing— (Volume 2: Short Papers)*, pages 794–799, Beijing, China. Association for Computational Linguistics, July 2015. DOI: 10.3115/v1/p15-2130.

Masami Nakamura and Kiyohiro Shikano. A study of English word category prediction based on neural networks. *The Journal of the Acoustical Society of America*, 84(S1):S60–S61, 1988. DOI: 10.1121/1.2026400.

R. Neidinger. Introduction to automatic differentiation and MATLAB object-oriented programming. *SIAM Review*, 52(3):545–563, January 2010. ISSN 0036-1445. DOI: 10.1137/080743627.

Y. Nesterov. A method of solving a convex programming problem with convergence rate O (1/k2). In *Soviet Mathematics Doklady*, 27:372–376, 1983.

Y. Nesterov. *Introductory Lectures on Convex Optimization*. Kluwer Academic Publishers, 2004. DOI: 10.1007/978-1-4419-8853-9.

Graham Neubig, Chris Dyer, Yoav Goldberg, Austin Matthews, Waleed Ammar, Antonios Anastasopoulos, Miguel Ballesteros, David Chiang, Daniel Clothiaux, Trevor Cohn, Kevin Duh, Manaal Faruqui, Cynthia Gan, Dan Garrette, Yangfeng Ji, Lingpeng Kong, Adhiguna Kuncoro, Gaurav Kumar, Chaitanya Malaviya, Paul Michel, Yusuke Oda, Matthew Richardson, Naomi Saphra, Swabha Swayamdipta, and Pengcheng Yin. DyNet: The dynamic neural network toolkit. *CoRR*, abs/1701.03980, 2017. http://arxiv.org/abs/1701.03980

Thien Huu Nguyen and Ralph Grishman. Event detection and domain adaptation with convolutional neural networks. In *Proc. of the 53rd Annual Meeting of the Association for Computational Linguistics and the 7th International Joint Conference on Natural Language Processing— (Volume 2: Short Papers)*, pages 365–371, Beijing, China, July 2015. DOI: 10.3115/v1/p15-2060.

Joakim Nivre. Algorithms for deterministic incremental dependency parsing. *Computational Linguistics*, 34(4):513–553, December 2008. ISSN 0891-2017, 1530-9312. DOI: 10.1162/coli.07-056-R1-07-027.

Joakim Nivre, Željko Agić, Maria Jesus Aranzabe, Masayuki Asahara, Aitziber Atutxa, Miguel Ballesteros, John Bauer, Kepa Bengoetxea, Riyaz Ahmad Bhat, Cristina Bosco, Sam Bowman, Giuseppe G. A. Celano, Miriam Connor, Marie-Catherine de Marneffe, Arantza Diaz de Ilarraza, Kaja Dobrovoljc, Timothy Dozat, Tomaž Erjavec, Richárd Farkas, Jennifer Foster, Daniel Galbraith, Filip Ginter, Iakes Goenaga, Koldo Gojenola, Yoav Goldberg, Berta Gonzales, Bruno Guillaume, Jan Hajič, Dag Haug, Radu Ion, Elena Irimia, Anders Johannsen, Hiroshi Kanayama, Jenna Kanerva, Simon Krek, Veronika Laippala, Alessandro Lenci, Nikola

Ljubešić, Teresa Lynn, Christopher Manning, Cătălina Mărănduc, David Mareček, Héctor Martínez Alonso, Jan Mašek, Yuji Matsumoto, Ryan McDonald, Anna Missilä, Verginica Mititelu, Yusuke Miyao, Simonetta Montemagni, Shunsuke Mori, Hanna Nurmi, Petya Osenova, Lilja Øvrelid, Elena Pascual, Marco Passarotti, Cenel-Augusto Perez, Slav Petrov, Jussi Piitulainen, Barbara Plank, Martin Popel, Prokopis Prokopidis, Sampo Pyysalo, Loganathan Ramasamy, Rudolf Rosa, Shadi Saleh, Sebastian Schuster, Wolfgang Seeker, Mojgan Seraji, Natalia Silveira, Maria Simi, Radu Simionescu, Katalin Simkó, Kiril Simov, Aaron Smith, Jan Štěpánek, Alane Suhr, Zsolt Szántó, Takaaki Tanaka, Reut Tsarfaty, Sumire Uematsu, Larraitz Uria, Viktor Varga, Veronika Vincze, Zdeněk Žabokrtský, Daniel Zeman, and Hanzhi Zhu. Universal dependencies 1.2, 2015. http://hdl.handle.net/11234/1-1548 LINDAT/CLARIN digital library at Institute of Formal and Applied Linguistics, Charles University in Prague.

Chris Okasaki. *Purely Functional Data Structures*. Cambridge University Press, Cambridge, UK, June 1999. DOI: 10.1017/cbo9780511530104.

Mitchell P. Marcus, Beatrice Santorini, and Mary Ann Marcinkiewicz. Building a large annotated corpus of English: The Penn Treebank. *Computational Linguistics*, 19(2), June 1993, Special Issue on Using Large Corpora: II, 1993. http://aclweb.org/anthology/J93-2004

Martha Palmer, Daniel Gildea, and Nianwen Xue. *Semantic Role Labeling*. Synthesis Lectures on Human Language Technologies. Morgan & Claypool Publishers, 2010. DOI: 10.1093/oxfordhb/9780199573691.013.023.

Bo Pang and Lillian Lee. Opinion mining and sentiment analysis. *Foundation and Trends in Information Retrieval*, 2:1–135, 2008. DOI: 10.1561/1500000011.

Ankur P. Parikh, Oscar Täckström, Dipanjan Das, and Jakob Uszkoreit. A decomposable attention model for natural language inference. In *Proc. of EMNLP*, 2016. DOI: 10.18653/v1/d16-1244.

Razvan Pascanu, Tomas Mikolov, and Yoshua Bengio. On the difficulty of training recurrent neural networks. *arXiv:1211.5063 [cs]*, November 2012.

Ellie Pavlick, Pushpendre Rastogi, Juri Ganitkevitch, Benjamin Van Durme, and Chris Callison-Burch. PPDB 2.0: Better paraphrase ranking, fine-grained entailment relations, word embeddings, and style classification. In *Proc. of the 53rd Annual Meeting of the Association for Computational Linguistics and the 7th International Joint Conference on Natural Language Processing— (Volume 2: Short Papers)*, pages 425–430. Association for Computational Linguistics, 2015. http://aclweb.org/anthology/P15-2070 DOI: 10.3115/v1/P15-2070.

Wenzhe Pei, Tao Ge, and Baobao Chang. An effective neural network model for graph-based dependency parsing. In *Proc. of the 53rd Annual Meeting of the Association for Computational Lin-

guistics and the 7th International Joint Conference on Natural Language Processing—(Volume 1: Long Papers), pages 313–322, Beijing, China, July 2015. DOI: 10.3115/v1/p15-1031.

Joris Pelemans, Noam Shazeer, and Ciprian Chelba.   Sparse non-negative matrix language modeling. *Transactions of the Association of Computational Linguistics*, 4(1):329–342, 2016. http://aclweb.org/anthology/Q16-1024

Jian Peng, Liefeng Bo, and Jinbo Xu. Conditional neural fields. In Y. Bengio, D. Schuurmans, J. D. Lafferty, C. K. I. Williams, and A. Culotta, Eds., *Advances in Neural Information Processing Systems 22*, pages 1419–1427. Curran Associates, Inc., 2009.

Jeffrey Pennington, Richard Socher, and Christopher Manning. GloVe: global vectors for word representation. In *Proc. of the Conference on Empirical Methods in Natural Language Processing (EMNLP)*, pages 1532–1543, Doha, Qatar. Association for Computational Linguistics, October 2014. DOI: 10.3115/v1/d14-1162.

Vu Pham, Christopher Kermorvant, and Jérôme Louradour. Dropout improves recurrent neural networks for handwriting recognition. *CoRR*, abs/1312.4569, 2013. http://arxiv.org/abs/1312.4569 DOI: 10.1109/icfhr.2014.55.

Barbara Plank, Anders Søgaard, and Yoav Goldberg. Multilingual part-of-speech tagging with bidirectional long short-term memory models and auxiliary loss. In *Proc. of the 54th Annual Meeting of the Association for Computational Linguistics—(Volume 2: Short Papers)*, pages 412–418. Association for Computational Linguistics, 2016. http://aclweb.org/anthology/P16-2067 DOI: 10.18653/v1/P16-2067.

Jordan B. Pollack. Recursive distributed representations. *Artificial Intelligence*, 46:77–105, 1990. DOI: 10.1016/0004-3702(90)90005-k.

B. T. Polyak. Some methods of speeding up the convergence of iteration methods. *USSR Computational Mathematics and Mathematical Physics*, 4(5):1–17, 1964. ISSN 0041-5553. DOI: 10.1016/0041-5553(64)90137-5.

Qiao Qian, Bo Tian, Minlie Huang, Yang Liu, Xuan Zhu, and Xiaoyan Zhu. Learning tag embeddings and tag-specific composition functions in recursive neural network. In *Proc. of the 53rd Annual Meeting of the Association for Computational Linguistics and the 7th International Joint Conference on Natural Language Processing—(Volume 1: Long Papers)*, pages 1365–1374, Beijing, China, July 2015. DOI: 10.3115/v1/p15-1132.

Lev Ratinov and Dan Roth. *Proc. of the 13th Conference on Computational Natural Language Learning (CoNLL-2009)*, chapter Design Challenges and Misconceptions in Named Entity Recognition, pages 147–155. Association for Computational Linguistics, 2009. http://aclweb.org/anthology/W09-1119

Ronald Rosenfeld. A maximum entropy approach to adaptive statistical language modeling. *Computer, Speech and Language*, 10:187–228, 1996. Longe version: Carnegie Mellon Technical Report CMU-CS-94-138. DOI: 10.1006/csla.1996.0011.

Stéphane Ross and J. Andrew Bagnell. Efficient reductions for imitation learning. In *Proc. of the 13th International Conference on Artificial Intelligence and Statistics*, pages 661–668, 2010.

Stéphane Ross, Geoffrey J. Gordon, and J. Andrew Bagnell. A reduction of imitation learning and structured prediction to no-regret online learning. In *Proc. of the 14th International Conference on Artificial Intelligence and Statistics*, pages 627–635, 2011.

David E. Rumelhart, Geoffrey E. Hinton, and Ronald J. Williams. Learning representations by back-propagating errors. *Nature*, 323(6088):533–536, October 1986. DOI: 10.1038/323533a0.

Ivan A. Sag, Thomas Wasow, and Emily M. Bender. *Syntactic Theory*, 2nd ed., CSLI Lecture Note 152, 2003.

Magnus Sahlgren. The distributional hypothesis. *Italian Journal of Linguistics*, 20(1):33–54, 2008.

Nathan Schneider, Vivek Srikumar, Jena D. Hwang, and Martha Palmer. A hierarchy with, of, and for preposition supersenses. In *Proc. of the 9th Linguistic Annotation Workshop*, pages 112–123, 2015. DOI: 10.3115/v1/w15-1612.

Nathan Schneider, Jena D. Hwang, Vivek Srikumar, Meredith Green, Abhijit Suresh, Kathryn Conger, Tim O'Gorman, and Martha Palmer. A corpus of preposition supersenses. In *Proc. of the 10th Linguistic Annotation Workshop*, 2016. DOI: 10.18653/v1/w16-1712.

Bernhard Schölkopf. The kernel trick for distances. In T. K. Leen, T. G. Dietterich, and V. Tresp, Eds., *Advances in Neural Information Processing Systems 13*, pages 301–307. MIT Press, 2001. http://papers.nips.cc/paper/1862-the-kernel-trick-for-distances.pdf

M. Schuster and Kuldip K. Paliwal. Bidirectional recurrent neural networks. *IEEE Transactions on Signal Processing*, 45(11):2673–2681, November 1997. ISSN 1053-587X. DOI: 10.1109/78.650093.

Holger Schwenk, Daniel Dchelotte, and Jean-Luc Gauvain. Continuous space language models for statistical machine translation. In *Proc. of the COLING/ACL on Main Conference Poster Sessions*, pages 723–730. Association for Computational Linguistics, 2006. DOI: 10.3115/1273073.1273166.

Rico Sennrich and Barry Haddow. *Proc. of the 1st Conference on Machine Translation: Volume 1, Research Papers*, chapter Linguistic Input Features Improve Neural Machine Translation, pages 83–91. Association for Computational Linguistics, 2016. http://aclweb.org/anthology/W16-2209 DOI: 10.18653/v1/W16-2209.

Rico Sennrich, Barry Haddow, and Alexandra Birch. Neural machine translation of rare words with subword units. In *Proc. of the 54th Annual Meeting of the Association for Computational Linguistics—(Volume 1: Long Papers)*, pages 1715–1725, 2016a. http://aclweb.org/antholo gy/P16-1162 DOI: 10.18653/v1/P16-1162.

Rico Sennrich, Barry Haddow, and Alexandra Birch. Improving neural machine translation models with monolingual data. In *Proc. of the 54th Annual Meeting of the Association for Computational Linguistics—(Volume 1: Long Papers)*, pages 86–96. Association for Computational Linguistics, 2016b. http://aclweb.org/anthology/P16-1009 DOI: 10.18653/v1/P16-1009.

Shai Shalev-Shwartz and Shai Ben-David. *Understanding Machine Learning: From Theory to Algorithms*. Cambridge University Press, 2014. DOI: 10.1017/cbo9781107298019.

John Shawe-Taylor and Nello Cristianini. *Kernel Methods for Pattern Analysis*. Cambridge University Press, Cambridge, UK, June 2004. DOI: 10.4018/9781599040424.ch001.

Q. Shi, J. Petterson, G. Dror, J. Langford, A. J. Smola, A. Strehl, and V. Vishwanathan. Hash kernels. In *Artificial Intelligence and Statistics AISTATS'09*, Florida, April 2009.

Karen Simonyan and Andrew Zisserman. Very deep convolutional networks for large-scale image recognition. In *ICLR*, 2015.

Noah A. Smith. *Linguistic Structure Prediction*. Synthesis Lectures on Human Language Technologies. Morgan & Claypool, May 2011. DOI: 10.2200/s00361ed1v01y201105hlt013.

Richard Socher. *Recursive Deep Learning For Natural Language Processing and Computer Vision*. Ph.D. thesis, Stanford University, August 2014.

Richard Socher, Christopher Manning, and Andrew Ng. Learning continuous phrase representations and syntactic parsing with recursive neural networks. In *Proc. of the Deep Learning and Unsupervised Feature Learning Workshop of {NIPS}*, pages 1–9, 2010.

Richard Socher, Cliff Chiung-Yu Lin, Andrew Y. Ng, and Christopher D. Manning. Parsing natural scenes and natural language with recursive neural networks. In Lise Getoor and Tobias Scheffer, Eds., *Proc. of the 28th International Conference on Machine Learning, ICML*, pages 129–136, Bellevue, Washington, June 28–July 2, Omnipress, 2011.

Richard Socher, Brody Huval, Christopher D. Manning, and Andrew Y. Ng. Semantic compositionality through recursive matrix-vector spaces. In *Proc. of the Joint Conference on Empirical Methods in Natural Language Processing and Computational Natural Language Learning*, pages 1201–1211, Jeju Island, Korea. Association for Computational Linguistics, July 2012.

Richard Socher, John Bauer, Christopher D. Manning, and Andrew Y. Ng. Parsing with compositional vector grammars. In *Proc. of the 51st Annual Meeting of the Association for Computational Linguistics—(Volume 1: Long Papers)*, pages 455–465, Sofia, Bulgaria, August 2013a.

Richard Socher, Alex Perelygin, Jean Wu, Jason Chuang, Christopher D. Manning, Andrew Ng, and Christopher Potts. Recursive deep models for semantic compositionality over a sentiment treebank. In *Proc. of the 2013 Conference on Empirical Methods in Natural Language Processing*, pages 1631–1642, Seattle, Washington. Association for Computational Linguistics, October 2013b.

Anders Søgaard. *Semi-Supervised Learning and Domain Adaptation in Natural Language Processing*. Synthesis Lectures on Human Language Technologies. Morgan & Claypool Publishers, 2013. DOI: 10.2200/s00497ed1v01y201304hlt021.

Anders Søgaard and Yoav Goldberg. Deep multi-task learning with low level tasks supervised at lower layers. In *Proc. of the 54th Annual Meeting of the Association for Computational Linguistics—(Volume 2: Short Papers)*, pages 231–235, 2016. http://aclweb.org/anthology/P 16-2038 DOI: 10.18653/v1/P16-2038.

Alessandro Sordoni, Michel Galley, Michael Auli, Chris Brockett, Yangfeng Ji, Margaret Mitchell, Jian-Yun Nie, Jianfeng Gao, and Bill Dolan. A neural network approach to context-sensitive generation of conversational responses. In *Proc. of the Conference of the North American Chapter of the Association for Computational Linguistics: Human Language Technologies*, pages 196–205, Denver, Colorado, 2015. DOI: 10.3115/v1/n15-1020.

Vivek Srikumar and Dan Roth. An inventory of preposition relations. *arXiv:1305.5785*, 2013a.

Nitish Srivastava, Geoffrey Hinton, Alex Krizhevsky, Ilya Sutskever, and Ruslan Salakhutdinov. Dropout: A simple way to prevent neural networks from overfitting. *Journal of Machine Learning Research*, 15:1929–1958, 2014. http://jmlr.org/papers/v15/srivastava14a.html

E. Strubell, P. Verga, D. Belanger, and A. McCallum. Fast and accurate sequence labeling with iterated dilated convolutions. *ArXiv e-prints*, February 2017.

Martin Sundermeyer, Ralf Schlüter, and Hermann Ney. LSTM neural networks for language modeling. In *INTERSPEECH*, 2012.

Martin Sundermeyer, Tamer Alkhouli, Joern Wuebker, and Hermann Ney. Translation modeling with bidirectional recurrent neural networks. In *Proc. of the Conference on Empirical Methods in Natural Language Processing (EMNLP)*, pages 14–25, Doha, Qatar. Association for Computational Linguistics, October 2014. DOI: 10.3115/v1/d14-1003.

Ilya Sutskever, James Martens, and Geoffrey E. Hinton. Generating text with recurrent neural networks. In *Proc. of the 28th International Conference on Machine Learning (ICML-11)*, pages 1017–1024, 2011. DOI: 10.1109/icnn.1993.298658.

Ilya Sutskever, James Martens, George Dahl, and Geoffrey Hinton. On the importance of initialization and momentum in deep learning. In *Proc. of the 30th International Conference on Machine Learning (ICML-13)*, pages 1139–1147, 2013.

Ilya Sutskever, Oriol Vinyals, and Quoc V. V Le. Sequence to sequence learning with neural networks. In Z. Ghahramani, M. Welling, C. Cortes, N. D. Lawrence, and K. Q. Weinberger, Eds., *Advances in Neural Information Processing Systems 27*, pages 3104–3112. Curran Associates, Inc., 2014.

Kai Sheng Tai, Richard Socher, and Christopher D. Manning. Improved semantic representations from tree-structured long short-term memory networks. In *Proc. of the 53rd Annual Meeting of the Association for Computational Linguistics and the 7th International Joint Conference on Natural Language Processing—(Volume 1: Long Papers)*, pages 1556–1566, Beijing, China, July 2015. DOI: 10.3115/v1/p15-1150.

Akihiro Tamura, Taro Watanabe, and Eiichiro Sumita. Recurrent neural networks for word alignment model. In *Proc. of the 52nd Annual Meeting of the Association for Computational Linguistics—(Volume 1: Long Papers)*, pages 1470–1480, Baltimore, Maryland, June 2014. DOI: 10.3115/v1/p14-1138.

Duyu Tang, Bing Qin, and Ting Liu. Document modeling with gated recurrent neural network for sentiment classification. In *Proc. of the Conference on Empirical Methods in Natural Language Processing*, pages 1422–1432. Association for Computational Linguistics, 2015. http://aclweb.org/anthology/D15-1167 DOI: 10.18653/v1/D15-1167.

Matus Telgarsky. Benefits of depth in neural networks. *arXiv:1602.04485 [cs, stat]*, February 2016.

Robert Tibshirani. Regression shrinkage and selection via the lasso. *Journal of the Royal Statistical Society, Series B*, 58:267–288, 1994. DOI: 10.1111/j.1467-9868.2011.00771.x.

T. Tieleman and G. Hinton. Lecture 6.5—RmsProp: Divide the gradient by a running average of its recent magnitude. *COURSERA: Neural Networks for Machine Learning*, 2012.

Joseph Turian, Lev-Arie Ratinov, and Yoshua Bengio. Word representations: A simple and general method for semi-supervised learning. In *Proc. of the 48th Annual Meeting of the Association for Computational Linguistics*, pages 384–394, 2010. http://aclweb.org/anthology/P10-1040

Peter D. Turney. Mining the web for synonyms: PMI-IR vs. LSA on TOEFL. In *ECML*, 2001. DOI: 10.1007/3-540-44795-4_42.

Peter D. Turney and Patrick Pantel. From frequency to meaning: Vector space models of semantics. *Journal of Artificial Intelligence Research*, 37(1):141–188, 2010.

Jakob Uszkoreit, Jay Ponte, Ashok Popat, and Moshe Dubiner. Large scale parallel document mining for machine translation. In *Proc. of the 23rd International Conference on Computational Linguistics (Coling 2010)*, pages 1101–1109, Organizing Committee, 2010. http://aclweb.org/anthology/C10-1124

Tim Van de Cruys. A neural network approach to selectional preference acquisition. In *Proc. of the Conference on Empirical Methods in Natural Language Processing (EMNLP)*, pages 26–35, Doha, Qatar. Association for Computational Linguistics, October 2014. DOI: 10.3115/v1/d14-1004.

Ashish Vaswani, Yinggong Zhao, Victoria Fossum, and David Chiang. Decoding with large-scale neural language models improves translation. In *Proc. of the Conference on Empirical Methods in Natural Language Processing*, pages 1387–1392, Seattle, Washington. Association for Computational Linguistics, October 2013.

Ashish Vaswani, Yinggong Zhao, Victoria Fossum, and David Chiang. Decoding with large-scale neural language models improves translation. In *Proc. of the Conference on Empirical Methods in Natural Language Processing*, pages 1387–1392. Association for Computational Linguistics, 2013. http://aclweb.org/anthology/D13-1140

Ashish Vaswani, Yonatan Bisk, Kenji Sagae, and Ryan Musa. Supertagging with LSTMs. In *Proc. of the Conference of the North American Chapter of the Association for Computational Linguistics: Human Language Technologies*, pages 232–237. Association for Computational Linguistics, 2016. http://aclweb.org/anthology/N16-1027 DOI: 10.18653/v1/N16-1027.

Oriol Vinyals, Lukasz Kaiser, Terry Koo, Slav Petrov, Ilya Sutskever, and Geoffrey Hinton. Grammar as a foreign language. *arXiv:1412.7449 [cs, stat]*, December 2014.

Oriol Vinyals, Alexander Toshev, Samy Bengio, and Dumitru Erhan. Show and tell: A neural image caption generator. In *IEEE Conference on Computer Vision and Pattern Recognition, CVPR*, pages 3156–3164, Boston, MA, June 7–12, 2015. DOI: 10.1109/cvpr.2015.7298935.

Stefan Wager, Sida Wang, and Percy S Liang. Dropout training as adaptive regularization. In C. J. C. Burges, L. Bottou, M. Welling, Z. Ghahramani, and K. Q. Weinberger, Eds., *Advances in Neural Information Processing Systems 26*, pages 351–359. Curran Associates, Inc., 2013.

Mengqiu Wang and Christopher D. Manning. Effect of non-linear deep architecture in sequence labeling. In *IJCNLP*, pages 1285–1291, 2013.

Peng Wang, Jiaming Xu, Bo Xu, Chenglin Liu, Heng Zhang, Fangyuan Wang, and Hongwei Hao. Semantic clustering and convolutional neural network for short text categorization. In *Proc. of the 53rd Annual Meeting of the Association for Computational Linguistics and the 7th International Joint Conference on Natural Language Processing—(Volume 2: Short Papers)*, pages 352–357, Beijing, China, July 2015a. DOI: 10.3115/v1/p15-2058.

Xin Wang, Yuanchao Liu, Chengjie Sun, Baoxun Wang, and Xiaolong Wang. Predicting polarities of tweets by composing word embeddings with long short-term memory. In *Proc. of the 53rd Annual Meeting of the Association for Computational Linguistics and the 7th International*

Joint Conference on Natural Language Processing—(Volume 1: Long Papers), pages 1343–1353, Beijing, China, July 2015b. DOI: 10.3115/v1/p15-1130.

Taro Watanabe and Eiichiro Sumita. Transition-based neural constituent parsing. In *Proc. of the 53rd Annual Meeting of the Association for Computational Linguistics and the 7th International Joint Conference on Natural Language Processing—(Volume 1: Long Papers)*, pages 1169–1179, Beijing, China, July 2015. DOI: 10.3115/v1/p15-1113.

K. Weinberger, A. Dasgupta, J. Attenberg, J. Langford, and A. J. Smola. Feature hashing for large scale multitask learning. In *International Conference on Machine Learning*, 2009. DOI: 10.1145/1553374.1553516.

David Weiss, Chris Alberti, Michael Collins, and Slav Petrov. Structured training for neural network transition-based parsing. In *Proc. of the 53rd Annual Meeting of the Association for Computational Linguistics and the 7th International Joint Conference on Natural Language Processing—(Volume 1: Long Papers)*, pages 323–333, Beijing, China, July 2015. DOI: 10.3115/v1/p15-1032.

P. J. Werbos. Backpropagation through time: What it does and how to do it. *Proc. of the IEEE*, 78(10):1550–1560, 1990. ISSN 0018-9219. DOI: 10.1109/5.58337.

Jason Weston, Antoine Bordes, Oksana Yakhnenko, and Nicolas Usunier. Connecting language and knowledge bases with embedding models for relation extraction. In *Proc. of the Conference on Empirical Methods in Natural Language Processing*, pages 1366–1371, Seattle, Washington. Association for Computational Linguistics, October 2013.

Philip Williams, Rico Sennrich, Matt Post, and Philipp Koehn. *Syntax-based Statistical Machine Translation*. Synthesis Lectures on Human Language Technologies. Morgan & Claypool Publishers, 2016. DOI: 10.2200/s00716ed1v04y201604hlt033.

Sam Wiseman and Alexander M. Rush. Sequence-to-sequence learning as beam-search optimization. In *Proc. of the Conference on Empirical Methods in Natural Language Processing (EMNLP)*. Association for Computational Linguistics, 2016. DOI: 10.18653/v1/d16-1137.

Sam Wiseman, M. Alexander Rush, and M. Stuart Shieber. Learning global features for coreference resolution. In *Proc. of the Conference of the North American Chapter of the Association for Computational Linguistics: Human Language Technologies*, pages 994–1004, 2016. http://aclweb.org/anthology/N16-1114 DOI: 10.18653/v1/N16-1114.

Yijun Xiao and Kyunghyun Cho. Efficient character-level document classification by combining convolution and recurrent layers. *CoRR*, abs/1602.00367, 2016. http://arxiv.org/abs/1602.00367

Wenduan Xu, Michael Auli, and Stephen Clark. CCG supertagging with a recurrent neural network. In *Proc. of the 53rd Annual Meeting of the Association for Computational Linguistics and the 7th International Joint Conference on Natural Language Processing—(Volume 2: Short Papers)*, pages 250–255, Beijing, China, July 2015. DOI: 10.3115/v1/p15-2041.

Wenpeng Yin and Hinrich Schütze. Convolutional neural network for paraphrase identification. In *Proc. of the Conference of the North American Chapter of the Association for Computational Linguistics: Human Language Technologies*, pages 901–911, Denver, Colorado, 2015. DOI: 10.3115/v1/n15-1091.

Fisher Yu and Vladlen Koltun. Multi-scale context aggregation by dilated convolutions. In *ICLR*, 2016.

Wojciech Zaremba, Ilya Sutskever, and Oriol Vinyals. Recurrent neural network regularization. *arXiv:1409.2329 [cs]*, September 2014.

Matthew D. Zeiler. ADADELTA: An adaptive learning rate method. *arXiv:1212.5701 [cs]*, December 2012.

Daojian Zeng, Kang Liu, Siwei Lai, Guangyou Zhou, and Jun Zhao. Relation classification via convolutional deep neural network. In *Proc. of COLING, the 25th International Conference on Computational Linguistics: Technical Papers*, pages 2335–2344, Dublin, Ireland, Dublin City University and Association for Computational Linguistics, August 2014.

Hao Zhang and Ryan McDonald. Generalized higher-order dependency parsing with cube pruning. In *Proc. of the Joint Conference on Empirical Methods in Natural Language Processing and Computational Natural Language Learning*, pages 320–331. Association for Computational Linguistics, 2012. http://aclweb.org/anthology/D12-1030

Tong Zhang. Statistical behavior and consistency of classification methods based on convex risk minimization. *The Annals of Statistics*, 32:56–85, 2004. DOI: 10.1214/aos/1079120130.

Xiang Zhang, Junbo Zhao, and Yann LeCun. Character-level convolutional networks for text classification. In C. Cortes, N. D. Lawrence, D. D. Lee, M. Sugiyama, and R. Garnett, Eds., *Advances in Neural Information Processing Systems 28*, pages 649–657. Curran Associates, Inc., 2015. http://papers.nips.cc/paper/5782-character-level-convolutional-networks-for-text-classification.pdf

Xingxing Zhang, Jianpeng Cheng, and Mirella Lapata. Dependency parsing as head selection. *CoRR*, abs/1606.01280, 2016. http://arxiv.org/abs/1606.01280

Yuan Zhang and David Weiss. Stack-propagation: Improved representation learning for syntax. In *Proc. of the 54th Annual Meeting of the Association for Computational Linguistics—(Volume 1: Long Papers)*, pages 1557–1566, 2016. http://aclweb.org/anthology/P16-1147 DOI: 10.18653/v1/P16-1147.

Hao Zhou, Yue Zhang, Shujian Huang, and Jiajun Chen. A neural probabilistic structured-prediction model for transition-based dependency parsing. In *Proc. of the 53rd Annual Meeting of the Association for Computational Linguistics and the 7th International Joint Conference on Natural Language Processing—(Volume 1: Long Papers)*, pages 1213–1222, Beijing, China, July 2015. DOI: 10.3115/v1/p15-1117.

Chenxi Zhu, Xipeng Qiu, Xinchi Chen, and Xuanjing Huang. A re-ranking model for dependency parser with recursive convolutional neural network. In *Proc. of the 53rd Annual Meeting of the Association for Computational Linguistics and the 7th International Joint Conference on Natural Language Processing—(Volume 1: Long Papers)*, pages 1159–1168, Beijing, China, July 2015a. DOI: 10.3115/v1/p15-1112.

Xiaodan Zhu, Parinaz Sobhani, and Hongyu Guo. Long short-term memory over tree structures. March 2015b.

Hui Zou and Trevor Hastie. Regularization and variable selection via the elastic net. *Journal of the Royal Statistical Society, Series B*, 67:301–320, 2005. DOI: 10.1111/j.1467-9868.2005.00503.x.

Author's Biography

YOAV GOLDBERG

Yoav Goldberg has been working in natural language processing for over a decade. He is a Senior Lecturer at the Computer Science Department at Bar-Ilan University, Israel. Prior to that, he was a researcher at Google Research, New York. He received his Ph.D. in Computer Science and Natural Language Processing from Ben Gurion University (2011). He regularly reviews for NLP and machine learning venues, and serves at the editorial board of *Computational Linguistics*. He published over 50 research papers and received best paper and outstanding paper awards at major natural language processing conferences. His research interests include machine learning for natural language, structured prediction, syntactic parsing, processing of morphologically rich languages, and, in the past two years, neural network models with a focus on recurrent neural networks.

CPSIA information can be obtained
at www.ICGtesting.com
Printed in the USA
FFHW012316150919
54956033-60673FF

27576302

9 781627 052986

9 781627 052986